In this wide-ranging collection of essays, Theda Sk[...] respected author of the award-winning 1979 book *States and Social Revolutions*, updates her arguments about social revolutions. How are we to understand recent revolutionary upheavals in Iran, Nicaragua, and other countries across the globe? Why have social revolutions happened in some countries, but not in others that seem similar in many ways? Skocpol shows how she and other scholars have used ideas about states and societies to identify the particular types of regimes that are susceptible to the growth of revolutionary movements and vulnerable to actual transfers of state power to revolutionary challengers. At this point, Skocpol argues, comparative social scientists have a good grasp on the causes and dynamics of social revolutionary transformations across modern world history, from early modern social revolutions in agrarian-bureaucratic monarchies, through more recent revolutions in certain countries emerging from direct colonial rule, and in dictatorial regimes focused on one-man patrimonial control.

This collection is also of interest for theoretical and methodological reasons. Skocpol engages in thoughtful dialogue with critics of her structural and state-centered approach to the analysis of revolutions. She suggests how culture and ideology can properly be incorporated into historical and comparative studies. And she vigorously defends the value of an institutionalist, comparative, and historical approach against recent theoretical and methodological challenges from Marxists, rational choice theorists, and culturally oriented interpreters of particular revolutions. Readers will be intrigued by Skocpol's spirited responses to Michael Burawoy, Michael Hechter, and William Sewell, Jr. These critics have advocated turns away from comparative and historical analysis in the social sciences. But Skocpol maintains that this is no time to abandon an approach that has, over the past fifteen years, cumulatively generated so much valid knowledge about the causes and processes of social revolutions, as well as other large-scale transformations in the modern world.

*Social revolutions
in the modern world*

CAMBRIDGE STUDIES IN COMPARATIVE POLITICS

General Editor
PETER LANGE Duke University

Associate Editors
ELLEN COMISSO University of California, San Diego
PETER HALL Harvard University
JOEL MIGDAL University of Washington
HELEN MILNER Columbia University
SIDNEY TARROW Cornell University
RONALD ROGOWSKI University of California, Los Angeles

This series publishes comparative research that seeks to explain important, cross-national domestic political phenomena. Based on a broad conception of comparative politics, it hopes to promote critical dialogue among different approaches. While encouraging contributions from diverse theoretical perspectives, the series will particularly emphasize work on domestic institutions and work that examines the relative roles of historical structures and constraints, of individual or organizational choice, and of strategic interaction in explaining political actions and outcomes. This focus includes an interest in the mechanisms through which historical factors impinge on contemporary political choices and outcomes.

Works on all parts of the world are welcomed, and priority will be given to studies that cross traditional area boundaries and that treat the United States in comparative perspective. Many of the books in the series are expected to be comparative, drawing on material from more than one national case, but studies devoted to single countries will also be considered, especially those that pose their problem and analysis in such a way that they make a direct contribution to comparative analysis and theory.

OTHER BOOKS IN THE SERIES

Allan Kornberg and Harold D. Clarke *Citizens and Community: Political Support in a Representative Democracy*
David D. Laitin *Language Repertories and State Construction in Africa*
Catherine Boone *Merchant Capital and the Roots of State Power in Senegal, 1930–1985*
Ellen Immergut *Health Politics: Interests and Institutions in Western Europe*
Sven Steinmo, Kathleen Thelan, and Frank Longstreth, eds. *Structuring Politics: Historical Institutionalism in Comparative Analysis*
Thomas Janoski and Alexander M. Hicks, eds. *The Comparative Political Economy of the Welfare State*
Paul Pierson *Dismantling the Welfare State: Reagan, Thatcher and the Politics of Retrenchment*
Sidney Tarrow *Power in Movement: Social Protest, Reform, and Revolution*
Joel S. Migdal, Atul Kohli, and Vivienne Shue *State Power and Social Forces: Domination and Transformation in the Third World*
Roberto Franzosi *The Puzzle of Strikes: Class and State Strategies in Postwar Italy*

Social revolutions
in the modern world

THEDA SKOCPOL
Harvard University

CAMBRIDGE
UNIVERSITY PRESS

Published by the Press Syndicate of the University of Cambridge
The Pitt Building, Trumpington Street, Cambridge CB2 1RP
40 West 20th Street, New York, NY 10011-4211, USA
10 Stamford Road, Oakleigh, Melbourne 3166, Australia

First published 1994

Printed in the United States of America

Library of Congress Cataloging-in-Publication Data
Skocpol, Theda.
Social revolutions in the modern world / Theda Skocpol.
p.   cm. – (Cambridge studies in comparative politics)
Includes bibliographical references and index.
ISBN 0-521-40088-0 (hc). – ISBN 0-521-40938-1 (pbk.)
1. Social history – Modern, 1500–   2. Economic history.
3. Revolutions.   I. Title. II. Series.
HN16.S54   1994
303.6′4 – dc20   94-3

A catalog record for this book is available from the British Library.

ISBN 0-521-40088-0 hardback
ISBN 0-521-40938-1 paperback

For Bill and Michael Skocpol

Contents

Acknowledgments

Chapter 1 is reprinted by permission from *Politics and Society* (Fall 1973): 1–35.

Chapter 2 is reprinted by permission from Theda Skocpol, "Wallerstein's World Capitalist System: A Theoretical and Historical Critique," *American Journal of Sociology* 82, no. 5 (1977): 1075–1090. © 1977 The University of Chicago.

Chapter 3 originally appeared in *Comparative Studies in Society and History* 22, no. 2 (April 1980): 174–197. © 1980 Cambridge University Press.

Chapter 4 is reprinted by permission from *The Uses of Controversy in Sociology*, edited by Lewis A. Coser and Otto N. Larsen. Copyright © 1976 by The Free Press, a division of Macmillan, Inc.

Chapter 5 is reprinted by permission from *Berkeley Journal of Sociology* 22 (1977–78): 100–113.

Chapter 6 originally appeared in *Comparative Studies in Society and History* 18, no. 2 (April 1976): 175–210. © 1976 Cambridge University Press.

Chapter 7 is reprinted by permission from William H. Sewell, Jr., "Ideologies and Social Revolutions: Reflections on the French Case," *The Journal of Modern History* 57, no. 1 (1985): 57–85. © 1985 The University of Chicago.

Chapter 8 is reprinted by permission from Theda Skocpol, "Cultural Idioms and Political Ideologies in the Revolutionary Reconstruction of State Power: A Rejoinder to Sewell," *The Journal of Modern History* 57, no. 1 (1985): 86–96. © 1985 The University of Chicago.

Chapter 9 is reprinted by permission from Theda Skocpol, "What Makes Peasants Revolutionary?" from *Power and Protest in the Countryside*, edited by Robert P. Weller and Scott E. Guggenheim, pp. 157–194. © 1982 Duke University Press, Durham, N.C.

Chapter 10 originally appeared in *Theory and Society* 11 (1982): 265–283. © 1982 by Theda Skocpol.

Chapter 11 is reprinted by permission from *Politics and Society* 17, no. 4 (December 1989): 489–507.

Chapter 12 is reprinted by permission from Theda Skocpol, "Social Revolutions and Mass Military Mobilization," *World Politics* 40, no. 2 (1988): 147–168. © 1982 The Johns Hopkins University Press.

INTRODUCTION

Explaining social revolutions:
First and further thoughts

States and Social Revolutions: A Comparative Analysis of France, Russia, and China appeared in 1979 – the same year that two new revolutionary upheavals occurred in Iran and Nicaragua. The fall of the Somoza dictatorship in Nicaragua and the crumbling of the modernizing autocracy of the Shah of Iran were events that signaled the continuing relevance – and shifting patterns – of social revolutions in the contemporary world. These episodes drew attention to new explanatory dilemmas about revolutions in Third World dictatorships, even as scholars began to grapple with the intellectual challenges my book posed to previously prevalent theories of revolution.

Many years later, much has changed, both in the realm of scholarship and in the "real world" of states and societies. Central ideas from *States and Social Revolutions* have been embraced, refuted, reworked, and extended by scholars seeking to understand Iran, Nicaragua, and other revolutions of the mid-twentieth century. New sorts of revolutionary transformations have continued to rock the world – most recently, toppling many of the regimes of the "Second World" in the former Soviet Union and Eastern Europe.

Inevitably, scholarly works in the social sciences start to become outdated the moment they are published. This situation is really more fortunate than regrettable, because scholarship is a collective endeavor, and it grows by debate and critical reflection. Once a scholar finishes an article or a book, it becomes whatever others choose to make of it – not only in reviews, but especially through further work that tackles the challenges to understanding and explanation continually thrown up by an ever-changing world. New challenges are bound to be taken up by younger scholars; they may also be taken up by older ones. Even the author of an "established" argument that is challenged by new happenings in the world may find in them – as well as in comments and criticisms from other scholars – occasions to do some further thinking. The publication of this collection of essays on "Revolutions in the Modern World" gives me an opportunity to present just such further thinking, to reflect upon, extend, and (here and there even) revise the arguments put forward years ago in

States and Social Revolutions, taking into account what has happened in scholarly debates and world politics since 1979.

In the concluding essay of this volume, I offer some reflections on major methodological and theoretical tendencies in the recent social-scientific literature about social revolutions and ways of studying them. I shall comment on recent revolutions, and on a variety of scholarly discussions that *States and Social Revolutions* has helped to stimulate. Is comparative and historical analysis a valid way to develop explanations of revolutions? Can social revolutions in recent times be analyzed in terms analogous to those I used to make sense of the French, Russian, and Chinese revolutions? Is the historical, institutionalist, and state-centered approach to explaining revolutions that I advocated in 1979 giving way to a revival of Marxist theorizing, or to the elaboration of formal rational-choice models, or to a radically new departure toward narrative history and cultural interpretation of particular revolutions?

Before we arrive at such reflections in the Conclusion, the body of this volume assembles in one place a selection of essays I have written over the years. The essays are republished in exactly the form that they appeared in various journals and edited books. Some of these essays were written around the time of the publication of *States and Social Revolutions;* they represent explorations of important methodological, theoretical, and comparative-historical arguments synthesized in that book. Reading these pieces is not a substitute for reading the 1979 book, yet they offer some of the relevant intellectual background on which I have drawn since the 1970s. Some of these pieces make points in what may be, for certain readers, a more accessible form than in the earlier book.

Other essays in this collection present true extensions and reworkings of the arguments put forward in 1979. I offer arguments about Iran and other mid-twentieth-century social revolutions that were outside the purview of *States and Social Revolutions.* I look at peasant mobilization by guerrilla movements, a topic that was examined only tangentially in the 1979 study. Additional articles reprinted here represent my thoughts about theoretical and broadly comparative questions about modern social revolutions. These are my contributions to the ongoing scholarly debates that I shall review in the Conclusion.

This introduction is meant to orient readers to the collection as a whole. To begin, it may be helpful to turn back to *States and Social Revolutions* itself, briefly summarizing its central arguments about history, methodology, and theory. After that, I can situate the various "occasional" essays that either accompanied that book or followed it. This overview will give readers a sense of what to look for in each part of this collection.

STATES AND SOCIAL REVOLUTIONS

States and Social Revolutions compared three great transformations of the past: the French Revolution of the late 1700s, the Russian Revolution of 1917 through the 1930s, and the Chinese Revolution of 1911 through the 1960s. All of these were instances of "social revolutions," defined as rapid, basic transformations of a society's state and class structures, accompanied and in part accomplished through popular revolts from below. In all three cases, I argued that autocratic and partially bureaucratized monarchies in predominately agrarian societies were transformed through state breakdowns, elite conflicts, and popular revolts into more centralized, bureaucratic and mass-incorporating national states. Juxtaposing Bourbon France, Romanov Russia, and late Imperial/Manchu China to other agrarian bureaucracies in comparable domestic and international circumstances, I identified a combination of structural conditions conducive to social revolutions.

These old regimes were all subject to geopolitical pressures from competitor states on the international scene. Their institutional structures (especially in France and China) provided leverage to dominant classes, making it possible for those classes to resist efforts by monarchs and their staffs to mobilize resources to meet international competition. Administrative and military breakdowns of the old-regime states were one major condition for the occurrence of social revolution. Such breakdowns occurred in France and China when monarchs and dominant class groups clashed politically over the attempts of monarchs to carry through administrative and fiscal reforms; in Russia, state breakdown occurred directly under the overwhelming impact of defeat in World War I. Yet administrative-military breakdowns alone were not enough to cause social revolutions. Local socioeconomic and political conditions affecting peasants and landlords also mattered. Peasant communities in France, Russia, and China enjoyed (or gained over the course of the revolutionary struggle) a considerable degree of solidarity and autonomy from direct supervision by landlords or their agents, which enabled peasants to revolt against landlords following the breakdown of central administrative and military controls. In France, Russia, and China alike, conjunctures of administrative-military breakdown and peasant-based revolts unleashed further elite and popular conflicts that would lead to revolutionary changes in states and social structures. In contrast, sufficient conditions for social revolution did not occur together in mid-seventeenth-century England, Prussia or Germany in the 1880s, Japan in the 1860s, or Russia in 1905. In these instances, societal political crises happened, but possible social revolutions were defeated, or else political (but not social) revolutions transpired.

Beyond using comparisons among six agrarian-bureaucratic monarchies to develop my analysis of the causes of social revolutions, *States and Social Revolutions* also explored at length the political conflicts and outcomes of the French, Russian, and Chinese revolutions. Here I stressed comparisons and contrasts among the three revolutions, focusing on various institutional legacies from their respective old regimes, the particular nature of revolutionary outbreaks and struggles in each instance, and the varying socioeconomic and geopolitical circumstances in which these revolutions played themselves out.

Revolutionary conflicts gave rise to three distinctive postrevolutionary regimes: a nationalist and militarist bureaucratic state coexisting with capitalist private property in France; a Stalinist, urban-based version of communism, totalitarian and devoted to state-directed heavy industrialization in Russia; and a Maoist, peasant-mobilizing version of communism devoted to promoting dual strategies of economic development in China.

States and Social Revolutions was unusual for its full elaboration of a comparative-historical analysis of *both* the causes and the outcomes of the revolutions it studied. Most theories or historical analyses of revolutions prior to it (and, to tell the truth, most studies of revolutions since 1979 as well) have rested content with accounting only for the causes and conflicts of revolutions, stopping short of an exploration of similar and varying *outcomes,* however these may be defined. For my study of the French, Russian, and Chinese revolutions, however, it was crucial to examine full trajectories of revolutionary transformation, because one of the most controversial as well as analytically fruitful aspects of my book was its insistence that these three revolutions had much in common. Taking sharp issue with those who had previously posited incompatibilities of cause and outcome between a "bourgeois" French Revolution and "socialist" revolutions in Russia and China, I maintained that differences among these three revolutions were variations on shared themes of state breakdown and reconstitution along lines that were neither liberal nor democratic-socialist.

Of course, *States and Social Revolutions* was not only a comparative-historical exploration of events in the past; it was a work with important social-scientific ambitions as well. Methodologically, I argued that the greatest progress in understanding the causes, processes, and outcomes of modern revolutions would come not from single case studies by theorists or historians, and not from large-scale statistical studies using simplified "variables" to predict "political violence" in dozens of countries. In contrast to such approaches, I advocated the use of analytical, historically grounded comparisons of a few cases at a time. I advocated the study of "social revolutions" as complex objects of explanation, including in my definition of the phenomenon to be explained the breakdown of old regimes, processes of conflict among elites and between dominant and subordinate classes, *and* the reconstitution of new regimes that embodied fundamental political, social, and ideological changes. I maintained that scholars should discipline their theoretical imaginations by comparing cases of social revolutionary transformation to "negative" cases, instances where full social revolutions did not happen. This would ensure, I suggested, the refinement or development of historically grounded theoretical hypotheses that would truly illuminate the conditions under which actual social revolutions occurred, versus those in which they did not occur – even in countries and regimes that had many similarities to those that experienced social revolutions.

In addition to its methodological message, *States and Social Revolutions* put forward a new "theoretical frame of reference" meant to inspire and provoke students of all modern revolutions. To be sure, this 1979 book did *not* offer any "general theory," or any universal model – and this point is worth emphasizing, because some scholars (e.g., Arjomand 1986) have dismissed the book as if it unsuccessfully did just that. In the conclusion to *States and Social Revolutions* (Skocpol 1979: 288), I argued that "one cannot mechanically extend the specific causal arguments that have been developed for France, Russia, and China into a 'general theory of revolutions' applicable to all other modern social revolutions." Whereas the French, Russian, and Chinese revolutions had occurred in large-scale agrarian monarchies, I pointed out that other modern social revolutions, including the Mexican, Cuban, and Vietnamese, had occurred (as of 1978) in "small, formerly colonial countries situated in highly vulnerable and dependent positions within the world capitalist economy and international states system" (Skocpol 1979: 288). I argued that the specific concatenations of causes leading to revolutions, as well as those influencing their outcomes, would vary in relation to changing international and world-historical contexts, and also in relation to the particular forms of state power and state-society relationships that characterize different types of states and societies. Social revolutions in former colonial states or in Third World dictatorships would not occur in the same way as revolutions in agrarian-bureaucratic monarchies. "Other revolutions," I concluded (1979: 290), "require analyses in their own right, through comparisons of broadly similar cases among themselves and contrasts of countries that have experienced social revolutions to similarly situated countries that have not undergone social-revolutionary transformations."

Yet *States and Social Revolutions* certainly offered *theoretical principles* meant to guide such further comparative-historical analyses of sets of social revolutions. In explicit argument with the major families of theories of revolution that were prominent in the social sciences prior to 1979, I stressed the value of three basic analytical strategies. Most basically, I argued that *state organizations* – and especially the administrative and coercive organizations that make up the core of all imperial and national states – should be placed at the very center of all attempts to define and explain social revolutions. Social revolutions, I stressed, could not happen without a breakdown of the administrative and coercive powers of an old regime; and their transformations were accompanied and in large part accomplished through conflicts over the reconstitution of coercive and administrative state organizations. By now, a decade and a half after the publication of *States and Social Revolutions,* such a focus on the breakdown and reconstitution of states is pretty much taken for granted by all scholars who study revolutions (although some resist taking a truly organizational approach to the state). But this was not at all the case among theorists of revolution prior to 1979 (Huntington 1968 and Tilly 1978 were partial exceptions). The predominant theories back then – social-psychological, functionalist, and Marxist – tended to treat states and other political organizations as reducible to mass states of mind or to "underlying" socioeconomic processes. It was the most important accomplishment of *States and Social Revolutions,* I believe, to have successfully hit scholars over the head with "the obvious" – the centrality of state power and coercive organizations in all revolutions.

Along with the emphasis on the state, a second principle of analysis that I stressed in *States and Social Revolutions* was widely praised by reviewers of the book (e.g., Billings 1980; Collins 1981; Coser 1979; Goldfrank 1980; Goldstone 1980; Himmelstein and Kimmel 1981; Lowenthal 1981; McNeill 1980; and Monas 1980). Beyond an examination of state–society relations within each domestic context, I argued, a focus on international and world-historical contexts is crucial to the development of valid explanations of the outbreak, conflicts, and outcomes of social revolutions. All states have grown up in given geopolitical and world-economic contexts. Competition among states (including, but not limited to, warfare) has often contributed to the political crises and administrative-military breakdowns that launched social revolutions. Conflicts during revolutionary interregna have involved international tensions and connections, and revolutionary state-builders have often found it necessary or advantageous to go to war with "counterrevolutionary" foreign powers. International economic pressures and opportunities influence the options of state authorities in both old and emerging new regimes. The phase of world history within which revolutions occur matters as well, in part because ideological models of "revolution" and "counterrevolution," based on understandings of earlier revolutionary upheavals, have been available to proponents and opponents of revolution, especially since the time of the French Revolution. I traced geopolitical, world-economic, and (to a lesser extent) transnational cultural influences on all three great revolutions analyzed in *States and Social Revolutions;* and I asserted in that book's conclusion that the relevance of transnational influences was even more obvious when it came to analyzing the causes, processes, and outcomes of mid-twentieth century social revolutions in smaller, dependent nations.

The third principle of analysis put forward in *States and Social Revolutions* was much less readily accepted by reviewers and scholars doing subsequent work on revolutions. Indeed, my arguments in favor of a "structural" and "nonvoluntarist" approach to revolutions have, from 1979 to now, been a source of unending scholarly controversy. I criticized pre-1979 theorists of historical social revolutions for inappropriately imposing reified collective wills on revolutionary origins and outcomes. Willful individuals and acting groups may well abound in revolutions, I maintained, but no single group, or organization, or individual creates a revolutionary crisis, or shapes revolutionary outcomes, through purposive action. It will not do, I asserted, to explain revolutions simply by propositions referring to mass social psychologies, or by propositions referring to class interests or actions, or by propositions referring to the ideological outlooks and derivative actions of vanguard revolutionary leaderships. These were the principal ways scholars went about trying to characterize and explain revolutions prior to 1979. In place of such voluntarist, or "purposive," approaches, I advocated instead a "structural" approach, explicated as follows (Skocpol 1979: 18):

To explain social revolutions, one must find problematic, first, the emergence (not "making" [i.e., by an ideological vanguard]) of a revolutionary situation within an old regime. Then, one must be able to identify the objectively conditioned and complex intermeshing of the various actions of the diversely situated groups – an intermeshing that shapes the revolutionary process and gives rise to the new regime. One can begin to make sense of such complexity only by focusing simultaneously upon the institutionally determined situations and relations of groups within society and upon the interrelations of societies within world-historically developing international structures. To take such an impersonal and nonsubjective viewpoint – one that emphasizes patterns of relationships among groups and societies – is to work from what may in some generic sense be called a structural perspective on sociocultural reality. Such a perspective is essential for the analysis of social revolutions.

The use of this "structural perspective" in my comparative analysis of the French, Russian, and Chinese revolutions prompted me to take analytical and explanatory steps that were truly jarring to many other students of these revolutions. The great heroes and villains of other accounts – the bourgeoisie and the proletariat, the Jacobins, Bolsheviks, and Maoists – found themselves in my accounts downplayed or thoroughly "situated" in institutional and conflictual circumstances. Encompassing cultures and ideologies – such as the Enlightenment, Marxism-Leninism, or Confucianism – that bore so much explanatory weight for other scholars, became much less important for me. I treated revolutionary leaderships not as the master planners of revolutionary crises or outcomes, but as "marginal elites" who found themselves, whether they liked it or not, "building" amid state breakdowns and fierce conflicts new "state organizations" that were more centralized and bureaucratic than old regimes. The leaderships that won out in violent conflicts were not those with the most coherent or innovative ideologies; they were those that most successfully used popular political mobilizations for state-building purposes: to create militias, committees of surveillance, armies, and bureaucracies. My structuralism thoroughly deromanticized – and to some degree devillainized – revolutions. Perhaps in part for this reason, that structuralism was the most disturbing part of my theoretical advocacy for a very wide range of scholars, people otherwise holding many different views and values about revolutions (for examples of complaints in early reviews of the 1979 book, see Bendix 1980; Dunn 1982; Himmelstein and Kimmel 1981; Kiernan 1980; and Lowenthal 1981).

The rise of rational-choice and culturalist tendencies in the social sciences since 1979 has ensured that critics continue to come forward to take issue with the structuralism of *States and Social Revolutions*. While disagreeing sharply with each other, both rational-choice and culturalist scholars believe that they have more voluntarist approaches than I do to explaining social revolutions. It remains to be seen, however, whether the kind of structuralism I advocated in

1979 needs to be abandoned, modified, or supplemented to achieve theoretical advances in our explanations of revolutions, past and present.

INTELLECTUAL GROUNDWORK AND FURTHER ARGUMENTS

Scholars who write big, synthetic books vary greatly among themselves in their proclivity to also write articles. Some "put it all" in the book, saying little or nothing in articles either before or after the comprehensive book. I happen to be an avid article writer as well as an author of the occasional fat book. I use articles to work out crucial parts of the intellectual groundwork en route to a book. And I use articles after the fact to tie up loose ends, or to address new intellectual puzzles that arise as the ideas of the book meet with additional real-world happenings. Occasionally, I also respond to what I take to be important and thoughtful criticisms from other scholars. For one or another of these purposes, the various articles of mine collected in this volume were written and published between the mid-1970s and the late 1980s. Let me say a bit about those assembled into each part of the book.

Doing macroscopic social science

The three articles brought together in Part I were written as I worked out the theoretical and methodological underpinnings of my comparative-historical analysis of the French, Russian, and Chinese revolutions. I sought to define my distinctive approach to macropolitical analysis and comparative history in relation to the ideas of influential older scholars. The 1970s were an intellectually exciting time in the macroscopic social sciences. Grand comparative-historical books by scholars such as Perry Anderson (1974), Reinhard Bendix (1978), Samuel P. Huntington (1968), Barrington Moore, Jr. (1966), Charles Tilly (1975; and Tilly, Tilly, Tilly 1975), and Immanuel Wallerstein (1974) riveted the attention of graduate students and young professors. Modernization theorists of the 1950s and early 1960s tended to posit one evolutionary path toward the modern world, focusing on industrialization, urbanization, and Western-style values as the motors that would carry "traditional" societies into "modernity." In contrast, the comparative-historical scholarship of the late 1960s and 1970s stressed *alternative* routes to the modern world, grounded in varying cultures (e.g., Bendix 1978), class structures and alliances (e.g., Moore 1966), and political regimes (e.g., Huntington 1968). What is more, some scholars – above all Immanuel Wallerstein (1974) – questioned the primacy of national states as units of analysis and theorizing. Wallerstein argued that historically oriented social science should focus on analyzing the emergence, development, and (he assumed eventual) demise of the "capitalist world system" as a whole.

"A Critical Review . . ." shows how I came to understand the strengths and weaknesses of *Social Origins of Dictatorship and Democracy: Lord and Peas-*

ant in the Making of the Modern World by Barrington Moore, Jr. (1966). Moore was the teacher (along with Seymour Martin Lipset) who had the greatest intellectual impact on me during my years as a graduate student at Harvard University in the early 1970s. Moore's *Social Origins* asked why England, France, and the United States developed into liberal democratic polities, while Germany and Japan became authoritarian and fascist, and Russia and China developed into communist dictatorships, To explain these political variations, Moore used Marxist ideas about class interests and relationships; yet he jettisoned the traditional Marxist emphasis on the industrial bourgeoisie and proletariat as the key political protagonists in modernizing societies. Instead, Moore argued that different political routes to the modern world in his sets of nations could be explained in terms of the timing and forms of commercial agriculture, class relationships between peasants and landlords, and the kinds of alliances that landed upper classes made with commercial and industrial bourgeoisies.

My essay on *Social Origins* was both appreciative and critical. I applauded Moore's commitment to analytical comparative history, his appreciation of a variety of political patterns among historically developing nations, and his reorientation of Marxist class analysis toward the agrarian sector. At the same time, I faulted Moore for deriving political outcomes from class relations and interests alone. I argued that to understand differences between liberal and authoritarian lines of political development, and to make sense of revolutions from above and below, the institutional variations among monarchical states had to be taken into account. In particular, I drew ideas from Weberian traditions of historical political sociology, arguing for the explanatory relevance of bureaucratization, degrees of state centralization, and patterns of institutionalized political relationships between dominant classes and monarchs and their staffs. All of these ways of analyzing state structures and state-dominant class relationships became central to the arguments I made in *States and Social Revolutions*. In essence, I used a close intellectual confrontation with Moore's *Social Origins* as a way to work out the similar, yet distinctive, approach to comparative-historical political analysis that I would use in my own studies of revolutions (and beyond).

At the close of my essay on *Social Origins,* I chided Barrington Moore for neglecting the ways in which his various instances of national political development were actually interconnected, not independent of one another. World-historical timing and sequences affected political options for developing nations, I argued; and so did the interdependencies of countries within transnational economic networks and geopolitical systems of military competition or domination among nations. Ironically, my critique of *Social Origins* was published just as another "big book" came along that seemed to meet the need for a world-historical and transnational reorientation of ways of understanding economic and political development. Especially among young scholars, much excitement was aroused by the 1974 publication of Immanuel Wallerstein's *The Modern*

World-System: Capitalist Agriculture and the Origins of the European World-Economy in the Sixteenth Century.

Because I was asked to contribute to a review symposium on Wallerstein's ambitious book, I took the occasion to articulate another appreciative critique (which can usefully be read along with my critique of Moore). Wallerstein's insistence on a world-historical approach to development was to be welcomed, I argued, but not his economic reductionism or his teleological treatment of the whole world as a single seamless "system." Class structures and conflicts, I insisted, could not be reduced to the positions of nations or regions in international trade. Even more clearly, I advocated the analysis of states as administrative and military organizations embedded in international geopolitical systems of military competition. Methodologically, I rejected Immanuel Wallerstein's call for a focus solely on the "world capitalist system" as a single "unit of analysis" in historical sociology. Comparative-historical studies of regions or of imperial and national states, seen as embedded in world-historical and international contexts, still struck me as the best strategy for developing better explanations of patterns of economic and political development in the modern world.

"The Uses of Comparative History in Macrosocial Inquiry," coauthored with Margaret Somers, is one of the few methodological pieces I have ever written (see also the conclusion to Skocpol 1984). In general, I prefer to *do* historical social science, rather than writing methodological or theoretical prescriptions for others to follow. All the same, writing "The Uses of Comparative History" allowed me to situate the methodological approach of *States and Social Revolutions* in relation to other comparative-historical approaches, such as those used in Reinhard Bendix's *Kings or Peoples* (1978) and Jeffery Paige's *Agrarian Revolution* (1975). Somers and I argued that there are three major types of comparative-historical scholarship in the social sciences. Some scholars, such as Paige, use comparisons to provide parallel demonstrations of the applicability of one grand theoretical model. Others, like Bendix, use comparisons to develop contrasts among cases, suggesting the ways in which each is distinctive, and revealing the limits of apparently "general" theories or concepts. Finally, scholars such as Barrington Moore (1966) use comparative history for analytical purposes, to develop or test causal hypotheses about the similarities and differences of the cases included in a study. As this methodological essay explained, my work on the causes and outcomes of social revolutions primarily employed the third, "macroanalytic" approach, juxtaposing periods in the histories of France, Russia, China, England, Germany, and Japan in order to explore the validity of previous hypotheses about the causes of revolutions – and to generate new causal analogies and hypotheses as well.

Making sense of the great revolutions

Part II of this collection features articles that succinctly present theoretical and historical arguments that appeared, stated differently, in *States and Social*

Revolutions. The selection "France, Russia, China" hardly needs any discussion, for its self-evident purpose is to give a short overview of my comparative analysis of the causes and outcomes of the three great social revolutions. The other two selections, however, deserve brief comment.

"Explaining Revolutions," nicely sums up the theoretical and methodological conclusions I had drawn by 1976 from my broad explorations in classical theory and comparative social science. The most-up-to-date social scientific theories of that time about "political violence" or "collective action" would not at all suffice, I argued, to characterize and explain the historical and cross-national incidence (and nonincidence) of social revolutions in the modern world. Finding fault with social-psychological theories, with Parsonsian structural-functional theories, with classical Marxian class-conflict theories, and even with Charles Tilly's (1978) coalitional and polity-centered approach, I called for "an historically grounded, social-structural style of explanation" of revolutions. Social scientists should not fear to study complex and multifaceted phenomena such as social revolutions, I maintained, even if there were only a relatively small number of actual instances in history – and certainly too few for the use of statistical techniques requiring a large number of independent cases. The causes and outcomes of social revolutions could be studied in a rigorous way without resorting to grand theories of generalized phenomena, and without reliance on statistical studies. The alternative to the standard social-scientific approach was not, I insisted, merely to resort to narratives of single historical cases in isolation from one another. Instead, comparative-historical analysis could be used to explore and generate valid causal hypotheses about social revolutions (and other, comparably complex macrohistorical phenomena). This essay is as close as there is to a theoretical and methodological manifesto for the approach used in *States and Social Revolution*.

Ellen Kay Trimberger and I collaborated to write "Revolutions and the World-Historical Development of Capitalism." By the time we prepared this short piece, I developed my comparative-historical analysis of social revolutions "from below" in France, Russia, and China, while Kay had published an important book (Trimberger 1978) on political "revolutions from above" in Meiji Japan and Attaturk's Turkey. Her work on the relationships of state bureaucrats and landed classes strongly influenced my thinking, as I worked out the arguments of *States and Social Revolutions*. Our joint essay, reprinted here, does not adequately reflect all of the ways in which we shared ideas and influenced one another. But this essay did give the two of us a chance to sum up, very straightforwardly, how our joint arguments about revolutions from above and below forced a modification, or repudiation, of classical Marxist arguments about modes of production and class conflicts in revolutions. In particular, we highlighted the difference it makes to recognize that landed class relations have been central to revolutionary transformations in agrarian-bureaucratic states. Social revolutions have not occurred in advanced-industrial capitalist societies, as Marx expected. Trimberger and I also underlined the fundamental explanatory reorientations involved in considering states not simply as agents of class interests, but as administrative and military organizations and geopolitical actors with goals and capacities that may be partially at odds with dominant class interests.

A *dialogue about culture and ideology in revolutions*

The final two parts of this volume present essays that go well beyond the arguments of my 1979 book. New intellectual issues, and additional social revolutions beyond the French, Russian, and Chinese cases take center stage from now on. Readers may be surprised to see that Part III includes an article not authored by me. There have, of course, been many thoughtful critiques of *States and Social Revolutions,* yet I would not go so far as actually to reprint them in a collection of my own essays. In one instance, though, there occurred a true *debate* – between the the culturally oriented social historian of France William Sewell, Jr., and me – that seemed significant enough to deserve full reproduction. Many people have seen this "Sewell–Skocpol" debate as a useful articulation of two different approaches to the study of culture and ideology in revolutions.

The original impetus for the debate was an "author meets the critics" panel, convened to discuss *States and Social Revolutions* at the 1981 Annual Meeting of the American Historical Association; afterward, Sewell and I accepted an invitation from the *Journal of Modern History* to produce a complementary set of essays. Sewell revised and extended the remarks he had prepared for the AHA panel, and I took his critique as an occasion to reflect on issues about culture and ideology in revolutions. As I readily acknowledged, I gave short shrift to such issues in *States and Social Revolutions,* where I was preoccupied with reworking class analysis in relation to a state-centered understanding of social revolutions. I did not do a comparable job of analyzing the relationship of state breakdowns and revolutionary state-building to ideas and movements aimed at "remaking the world" in all of its social and moral dimensions (for a discussion of such movements, see Walzer 1980).

Much of the colloquy between Sewell and myself has to do with how to understand the role of Enlightenment ideas in the French Revolution. Working with anthropological ideas about systems of meaning and belief, Sewell sees culture as "constitutive of social order." He analyzes the processes and outcomes of the French Revolution in terms of the sudden rise to hegemony – starting on August 4, 1789 – of a system of Enlightenment ideas and moral ideals. Sewell offers an "anonymous" and "impersonal" – and very holistic – approach to analyzing cultural systems in social revolutions, and calls for the application of this approach to other instances besides France. The implication of his argument is that in each social revolution we will find a new system of culture suddenly replacing an old one.

Somewhat ironically, given my reputation as a nonvoluntarist "structuralist," I advocate a more actor-centered and action-oriented approach than the one put forward by Sewell. Multiple "cultural idioms," I argue, always coexist in societies and in revolutionary situations. Variously situated groups draw upon and combine these idioms to define situations and make morally charged arguments about changes they would like to see happen (or prevent happening). Ideologies are forged – and constantly reworked – by groups engaged in political conflicts over state-building and social change. No one cultural system will ever give us "the key" to the processes and outcomes of revolutionary conflicts. We will make analytical progress, I argue, only if we examine cultural and ideological influences in the context of concrete political struggles.

My rejoinder to Sewell concludes with a few thoughts about what might be found in truly *comparative*-historical studies about the place and activities of ideological movements in social revolutions. I suggest that the political conflicts and organizations of some social revolutions – including the French, Russian, and Iranian – have allowed considerable space for the activities of literate intellectual or clerical elites devoted to "remaking the world" ideologically. Such ideological leaderships have sought to mobilize popular followers through speeches in legislatures, electoral campaigns, sermons, and the activities of political parties. But in other social revolutions, such as the Mexican, the struggles have largely involved the clash of armies in the countryside. In such cases, there may have been less of a role for appeals to transformative and transcendent sets of ideas, such as the Enlightenment, or the Marxist theory of history, or a militant reading of Shi'a Islam. In short, I suggest that a truly comparative-historical analysis of the role of cultural idioms and ideological movements in revolution would encourage us to discover and explain variations across modern social revolutions, as well as similarities.

From classical to contemporary social revolutions

Part IV of this collection features the most important attempts I have made to analyze recent social revolutions that have occurred in patterns apparently quite different from those that characterized the classic revolutions in France, Russia, and China. Some of the essays in this part also suggest analytical integrations between my earlier arguments about social revolutions in agrarian-bureaucratic monarchies and arguments (by me and others) about more guerrilla-led revolutions and revolutions in contemporary Third World dictatorships. All too often, critics of my approach to revolutions are unaware of the essays collected in this part of the book – essays that represent important extensions and additions to what I had to say in 1979. These essays offer further comparative-historical studies that are sensitive to the changing types of regimes, societies, and international situations within which social revolutions have occurred over the course of modern world history.

In "What Makes Peasants Revolutionary?" I offered a critical perspective on the literature about peasants and revolution that was so fashionable in the social sciences during the 1970s, and I took steps toward developing an integrated explanation of the alternative kinds of peasant participation that have figured in the full range of modern social revolutions. With the sole exception of the Iranian Revolution, all modern social revolutions from the French Revolution onward have involved *either* widespread, autonomous revolutions by peasant villages (as in France, Russia, Mexico, and Bolivia) *or* the mobilization of peasants by professional revolutionaries operating as armed guerrilla movements in the countryside (as in China, Vietnam, Cuba, and the revolutions against Portuguese colonialism in Africa). Especially in the immediate wake of the Vietnamese Revolution and the war between the United States and North Vietnam, social scientists in the West became preoccupied with the issue of which types of peasants were most likely to become "revolutionary" – an issue that most scholars wrote about without taking into account the alternative routes (just mentioned) by which peasants could become involved in revolutionary transformations. In addition to debating "which peasants" were "most revolutionary," scholars also focused on whether (and how) capitalist or Western "imperialist" expansion into the Third World would affect peasantries, perhaps propelling them to support nationalist or communist revolutionary movements. In this essay, I closely examined the – often mutually contradictory – arguments of Eric Wolf (1969), Jeffery Paige (1975), James Scott (1976), Samuel Popkin (1979), and Joel Migdal (1974).

Taking bits and pieces from each of these writers, and adding my own state-centered insights, I concluded that no single kind of peasantry or rural social structure is inherently revolution-prone. Various kinds of peasants can become crucial actors in social revolutions – particularly when rural dwellers are mobilized by revolutionary guerrillas, whose leaders come from outside the peasantry. Even more than the economic effects of world capitalism, moreover, international geopolitical and domestic political conditions must be investigated to discover whether revolutionary leaderships will arise and turn toward rural guerrilla warfare – as did, for example, the Vietnamese Communists, when they were faced with the challenge of fending off French and Japanese colonial rulers, and then fighting against U.S. military intervention.

If and when revolutionary leaderships oriented to peasant mobilization for guerrilla warfare do arise, then we must analyze the conditions under which such leaderships can (or cannot) set up sustained "exchanges" with peasant groups, offering local "collective goods" such as military protection or development projects, in return for peasant participation in nationwide armed movements aimed at seizing state power. The conditions that matter are as likely to be political and military conditions affecting states and organized leadership groups, as they are to be features of peasant social structures or grievances as such. Echoing Barrington Moore's dictum (1966: 457) that "before looking at the peasant, it is necessary to look at the whole society," I concluded that the "forms of revolt open to peasants, as well as the political results conceivably achievable by peasant protests, have been powerfully shaped by the stakes of political struggles, domestic and intersocietal, going on within the ranks of dominant strata." To decide "What Makes Peasants Revolutionary," we must analyze states in relation to international contexts and dominant social groups, as well as the local situations of peasantries themselves.

"Rentier State and Shi'a Islam" took up the case of the Iranian Revolution of 1979, the instance that raises the most questions about the analytical perspective I developed in *States and Social Revolutions*. This article was written right after my book won the 1980 American Sociological Association Award for a Distinguished Contribution to Scholarship. The winner of that award is invited to deliver something called "the Sorokin Lecture" – named after Pitirim Sorokin, himself an earlier student of revolutions. Given that the Shah of Iran had just fallen from power in the face of a massive alliance that had soon given way to a dictatorship led by Shi'a Islamic clerics, I felt it incumbent upon me to say something about "the Iranian case" – a revolution that was just as surprising to me as to other so-called experts in the social sciences. So I spent much of 1980 studying modern Iranian history and thinking about how to use, or adapt, my state-centered approach to cope with this special instance of social revolution. What should I say about a massive old-regime state whose bureaucracies and armies crumbled *without* first facing defeat in war or strong military competition from abroad? Even more pressing, what should I say about a revolution that apparently was "made" – quite deliberately – by urban social movements, in the absence of either peasant revolts or a rural guerrilla movement? What role did Shi'a religious culture, and militant Shi'a ideology, play in the overthrow of the Shah and the forging of a mass-based clerical dictatorship?

Working out my views on the Iranian Revolution convinced me that this social revolution, like others, occurred through a conjuncture of state weakness and popular revolts rooted in relatively autonomous communities. A close look at the revenue sources and internal structures of the Shah's regime offered insights about why that regime came into profound political crisis after international markets for oil shifted in the 1970s. What is more, the patrimonial nature of the Pahlavi dictatorship accounted for why Iran's armies and bureaucracies were incapable of staging a military coup, and were instead likely to break apart once the Shah left the scene.

As for the massive urban popular demonstrations that brought about the Shah's departure, my inquiries revealed that cultural and social structural developments in Iran after the 1960s encouraged the growth of relatively solidary urban communities of bazaar merchants and artisans. These communities became linked to Shi'a Islamic clerics who enjoyed considerable "space" to raise revenues, organize congregants, and spread ideas critical to the Shah's rule. I argued that the content of Shi'a ideas contributed to the willingness of urban demonstrators to risk repression and martyrdom in the ever-escalating demonstrations and strikes that finally prompted the Shah (with U.S. encouragement) to depart from Iran. But I did not offer a purely or primarily culturalist explanation (contrary to what is argued by Nichols 1986: 182–83). I argued that changing religious institutional arrangements and state–society ties had to be specified in order to understand why Iran's preexisting Shi'a Islamic culture could prove conducive to social revolution in the later 1970s, but not earlier. I used an institutional, organizational, and conflict-centered approach to analyze the role of culture and ideology in the genesis of the Iranian Revolution – putting into practice the kind of approach I advocated in my debate with William Sewell (the debate reprinted in Part III of this volume).

The "Rentier State" essay also discussed the "outcomes" of the Iranian Revolution, as they were taking shape through the summer of 1981. Here I feel certain that my state-centered perspective proved its worth, even in a predictive sense. At the point when my essay went to press, many other scholars were predicting the imminent demise of the radical Shi'a clerics who had violently shoved aside other anti-Shah forces and erected a dictatorship dedicated to institutionalizing what I called an "Islamic Republic of Virtue." Working with a mixture of wishful thinking and assumptions from modernization or Marxist theories, many other analysts were predicting that the clerics would soon fall from power, because their methods and ideas were not suited to rule under modern, urban conditions. But my state-centered framework led me to believe that the key to success in revolutionary state-building is the capacity of a morally confident leadership to create coercive organizations and mobilize popular support through militias, committees of surveillance, and the like. These tasks were exactly the ones that the militant Shiite preachers and imams of Iran were best suited to carry out. These clerics enjoyed direct access to urban followers through patronage networks centered in the mosques and bazaars. Their religious beliefs gave them, and some of their followers, a sense of moral certainty in the face of the overwhelming stresses occasioned by domestic conflicts and an emerging war with Iraq. Even in the summer of 1981, when assassinations were weakening the ranks of the Islamic Republican party, I felt relatively sure that a popularly rooted clerical dictatorship would be institutionalized and would persist for many years as the Iranian revolutionary "outcome." I was right.

"Explaining Revolutions in the Contemporary Third World" is a synthetic essay coauthored by Jeff Goodwin and me. This piece drew on the ideas I developed in the previous two articles; even more, it drew on Goodwin's (1988) doctoral dissertation about revolutionary movements in Central America and Southeast Asia. (The comparative research design for this dissertation, now a forthcoming book, will be discussed in the Conclusion.) Goodwin and I examined mid-twentieth-century social revolutions in certain former colonies and independent Third World dictatorships. We argued that socioeconomic conditions as such cannot explain where revolutionary movements have gained strong followings, even less can such conditions tell us where would-be movements have actually succeeded in overthrowing challenged regimes. Most other scholars, we argued, have given too much explanatory weight to rural social structures or to international forces working for or against revolutions.

Goodwin and I focused instead on the types of political regimes and state–society relations that are susceptible to social revolution. Politically exclusionary authoritarian regimes in the Third World have been the ones most likely to generate broad, cross-class political support for revolutionary movements (all of which, except in Iran, have been led by armed guerrillas). But many such revolutionary movements – even ones with broad social support – fail actually to seize state power. Here is where additional features of "regime vulnerability" become crucial. We argued that directly ruled colonies, such as Vietnam, are more vulnerable to guerrilla victories than are indirectly ruled ones, such as Malaysia and the Philippines. This is because indirectly ruled colonies have influential domestic elites and upper classes that have a stake in the continuation of (some version of existing) governing institutions after the foreign colonial power withdraws. In accord with the findings of other scholars (including Dix 1984; Farhi 1990; Foran 1992; Goldstone 1986; and Wickham-Crowley 1992), Goodwin and I also argued that neopatrimonial dictatorships – such as the governments of Fulgencio Batista's Cuba, Anastasio Debayle Somoza's Nicaragua, and the Mohammad Reza Pahlavi's Iran – have proved much more susceptible to revolutionary overthrow than corporate military dictatorships, such as that of El Salvador. Neopatrimonial dictatorships tend to alienate upper-class groups as well as others in the society. They also feature the use of "divide and rule" manipulations within bureaucratic and military organizations, rendering them brittle and subject to sudden disorganization if the personalistic ruler dies or is forced to step down. Military coups are unlikely to follow after neopatrimonial rule in such regimes (unless certain kinds of military institutions exist: see Snyder 1992). Instead, neopatrimonial regimes facing oppositional movements may suddenly collapse and open up a vacuum into which revolutionaries can step. This is exactly what happened in Cuba, Nicaragua, and Iran. But in El Salvador, groups of military officers, sometimes allied with domestic reform politicians, have succeeded one another – and these regimes sustained prolonged warfare against the revolutionary guerrilla forces that have considerable social support, especially in parts of the countryside.

The final essay in Part IV, "Social Revolutions and Mass Military Mobilization," reflects broadly – and soberly – on what social revolutionary transformations have actually accomplished for states and peoples in the modern world (for a related essay, see Skocpol and Kestnbaum 1990). I wrote this essay at the time that millions of Iranians and Iraqis were dying in the war between those nations. Yet the article also builds on a theme that has long been central to my understanding of revolutionary outcomes. Along with Samuel P. Huntington

(1968: 266), I have always held that a "complete revolution involves the creation and institutionalization of a new political order" into which an "explosion" of popular participation in national affairs is channeled. Belying the liberal or democratic hopes of many of their participants, social revolutions have led to stronger – more centralized, bureaucratic, and coercive – national states than the old regimes they replaced.

What do revolutionary states actually *do* with their strengthened, mass-mobilizing institutions? Many scholars have focused on the uses of state power to promote capitalist or socialist forms of economic development. But in fact revolutionized states are rarely very adept at furthering economic development. What they do best is to mobilize popular participation for international warfare. With a few exceptions (that can be explained by special geopolitical circumstances) regimes emerging from revolutions have found it both necessary and advantageous to go to war with "counterrevolutionary" foreign enemies. Because of the ways in which popular participation is mobilized by state-building revolutionary leaderships during the course of domestic political struggles, it proves relatively easy to channel such participation into fervent military activities. Consequently, I argued, the mission that revolutionized regimes perform best is to motivate masses of ordinary people – people who were excluded from politics under the old regime – to die for the glory of their national state. Looking at the matter without romanticism, this has certainly been the chief political accomplishment of such otherwise diverse social revolutions as the French Revolution of the late eighteenth century, and the Vietnamese, Nicaraguan, and Iranian revolutions of more recent times. Mass mobilization for war is what most social revolutions have achieved.

REFERENCES

Anderson, Perry. 1974. *Lineages of the Absolutist State*. London: New Left Books.
Bendix, Reinhard. 1978. *Kings or People: Power and the Mandate to Rule*. Berkeley: University of California Press.
Bendix, Reinhard. 1980. Review of *States and Social Revolutions*. *New Republic* (January 26): 36–38.
Billings, Dwight B. 1980. Review of *States and Social Revolutions*. *Social Forces* 59(1): 292–93.
Collins, Randall. 1981. "Geopolitics and Revolution." Pp. 63–69 in *Sociology Since Midcentury*. New York: Academic Press. Reprinted from *Theory and Society* 9 (1980).
Coser, Lewis A. 1979. "The Sources of Revolt." *New York Times Book Review* (October 31): 13, 44–45.
Dix, Robert H. 1984. "Why Revolutions Succeed and Fail." *Polity* 16(3): 423–46.
Dunn, John. 1982. "Understanding Revolutions." *Ethics* 92(2): 299–315.
Goldfrank, Walter L. 1980. "Macro Mastery." *Contemporary Sociology* 9(3): 386–88.
Goldstone, Jack A. 1980. "Theories of Revolution: The Third Generation." *World Politics* 32 (April): 425–53.

Goldstone, Jack A. 1986. "Revolutions and Superpowers." Pp. 38–48 in *Superpowers and Revolutions,* edited by Jonathan R. Adelman. New York: Praeger.

Goodwin, Jeffrey Roger. 1988. "States and Revolutions in the Third World: A Comparative Analysis." Unpublished Ph.D. dissertation, Department of Sociology, Harvard University.

Himmelstein, Jerome L., and Michael S. Kimmel. 1981. "Review Essay: States and Social Revolutions: The Implications and Limits of Skocpol's Structural Model." *American Journal of Sociology* 86(5): 1145–54.

Huntington, Samuel P. 1968. *Political Order in Changing Societies.* New Haven, CT: Yale University Press.

Kiernan, V. G. 1980. Review of *States and Social Revolutions. English Historical Review* 95 (July): 638–41.

Lowenthal, Richard. 1981. "Were These Revolutions Necessary?" *New York Review of Books* (February 5): 43–45.

McNeill, William H. 1980. Review of *States and Social Revolutions. American Historical Review* 85 (February): 86.

Migdal, Joel S. 1974. *Peasants, Politics, and Revolution: Pressures Toward Political and Social Change in the Third World.* Princeton, NJ: Princeton University Press.

Monas, Sidney. 1980. Review of *States and Social Revolutions. Journal of Modern History* 52 (June): 299–300.

Moore, Barrington, Jr. 1966. *Social Origins of Dictatorship and Democracy: Lord and Peasant in the Making of the Modern World.* Boston: Beacon Press.

Nichols, Elizabeth. 1986. "Skocpol on Revolution: Comparative Analysis vs. Historical Conjuncture." *Comparative Social Research* 9: 163–86.

Paige, Jeffery M. 1975. *Agrarian Revolution: Social Movements and Export Agriculture in the Underdeveloped World.* New York: Free Press.

Popkin, Samuel. 1979. *The Rational Peasant: The Political Economy of Rural Society in Vietnam.* Berkeley: University of California Press.

Scott, James C. 1976. *The Moral Economy of the Peasant.* New Haven, CT: Yale University Press.

Skocpol, Theda. 1979. *States and Social Revolutions: A Comparative Analysis of France, Russia, and China.* Cambridge: Cambridge University Press.

Skocpol, Theda. ed. 1984. *Vision and Method in Historical Sociology.* Cambridge: Cambridge University Press.

Skocpol, Theda, and Meyer Kestnbaum. 1990. "Mars Unshackled: The French Revolution in World-Historical Perspective." Pp. 13–29 in *The French Revolution and the Birth of Modernity,* edited by Ferenc Feher. Berkeley: University of California Press.

Snyder, Richard. 1992. "Explaining Transitions from Neopatrimonial Dictatorships." *Comparative Politics* 24(4): 379–99.

Tilly, Charles, ed. 1975. *The Formation of National States in Western Europe.* Princeton, NJ: Princeton University Press.

Tilly, Charles. 1978. *From Mobilization to Revolution.* Reading, MA: Addison-Wesley.

Tilly, Charles, Louise Tilly, and Richard Tilly. 1975. *The Rebellious Century, 1830–1930.* Cambridge, MA: Harvard University Press.

Trimberger, Ellen Kay. 1978. *Revolution from Above: Military Bureaucrats and Development in Japan, Turkey, Egypt, and Peru.* New Brunswick, NJ: Transaction Books.

Wallerstein, Immanuel. 1974. *The Modern World-System: Capitalist Agriculture and the Origins of the European World-Economy in the Sixteenth Century.* New York: Academic Press.

Walzer, Michael. 1980. "A Theory of Revolution." Pp. 201–23 (chap. 13) of *Radical Principles*. New York: Basic Books.

Wickham-Crowley, Timothy P. 1992. *Guerrillas and Revolution in Latin America: A Comparative Study of Insurgents and Regimes Since 1956*. Princeton, NJ: Princeton University Press.

Wolf, Eric R. 1969. *Peasant Wars of the Twentieth Century*. New York: Harper and Row.

Part I

DOING MACROSCOPIC SOCIAL SCIENCE

1

A critical review of Barrington Moore's *Social Origins of Dictatorship and Democracy*

Social Origins of Dictatorship and Democracy: Lord and Peasant In the Making of the Modern World. By Barrington Moore, Jr. Boston: Beacon Press, 1966.

Many pay lip service to the classical tradition in sociology, but few indeed work in terms of its mandate – which calls upon social scientists to assess, from a comparative and historical perspective, the prospects for freedom, rationality, and democracy in a modernizing world. Of the intrepid few who do consciously carry forward the classical tradition, most elaborate theoretical leads from the enormous scholarly legacy of Max Weber. Barrington Moore, Jr.'s *Social Origins of Dictatorship and Democracy* is therefore all the more unusual and interesting because it is not only a work solidly within the classical sociological tradition, but also the product of a Marxist scholarly perspective. And, leaving aside the literature on imperialism, it is virtually the only well-elaborated Marxist work on the politics of modernization to which one can point.

Social Origins does not postulate one route to the modern world which must be taken by all countries. Nor does it assign the strategic political roles in modernizing revolutions to the bourgeoisie or the proletariat. Yet in deeper and more significant ways, *Social Origins* is a Marxist work. In it Professor Moore relies for theoretical sustenance upon the central conceptions of Marxist political sociology – "the conception of social class as arising out of an historically specific set of economic relationships and of the *class struggle as the basic stuff of politics.*"[1] Writing in a context in which two major alternatives for theories of structural dynamics and social change were recognized by scholars[2] – emphasis on the causal role of ideas or culture or emphasis on the role of economic factors – Professor Moore chose the latter emphasis,[3] despite the fact that

Earlier drafts of this essay have benefited from the comments and criticisms of: Kay Trimberger, John Mollenkopf, Amy Bridges, Atilio Boron, Daniel Bell, George Homans, Mounira Charrad, Joe Bivins, and Bill Skocpol. Needless to say, the present version is entirely the author's own responsibility.

cultural explanations were, in the 1950s and early 1960s, far more popular, indeed virtually orthodox.

Precisely because it is a major creative Marxist work on the sociology of modernization, *Social Origins,* subjected to close critical scrutiny, can tell us much about the potentialities of a Marxist approach.[4] In the pages that follow, I shall present, first, an analytic summary of *Social Origins* which will attempt to order and make explicit its central explanatory variables and arguments, and, then, interrelated criticisms of those elements which, I believe, will point to the necessity for theoretical reorientation.

I. *SOCIAL ORIGINS*: AN ANALYTIC SUMMARY[5]

A. *The moral of the story*

Social Origins of Dictatorship and Democracy is not organized or written in the style of a scientist trying to elaborate clearly and minutely justify a falsifiable *theory* of comparative modernization. It is, rather, like a giant mural painted in words, in which a man who has contemplated the modern histories of eight major nations seeks to convey in broad strokes the moral and factual discoveries that he personally has made, about the various routes to the "world of modern industry" traveled by his "subject" countries, about the roles of landed upper classes and peasantries in the politics of that transformation, and about the consequences of each route for human freedom and societal rationality. For Professor Moore's purpose in writing *Social Origins* is as much moral as theoretical – and it is important that he sees no contradiction between these purposes.

What Moore wrote in a 1958 essay called "Strategy in Social Science" about Karl Marx's fusion of moral passion and scientific objectivity could as well be said about the author of *Social Origins:*

[Marx] started from the conviction that the social institutions of his day were evil. . . . At the same time he thought of himself as a scientist – a savage one to be sure, constantly using hard facts to strip away the veil of hypocrisy and unconscious self-deception that concealed the ugly realities underneath. *For Marx there was no conflict between his position as a moralist and a scientist.* . . . Furthermore, Marx took it for granted that in any society there was a sharp divergence between the values and aspirations expressed in a society and the way the society actually worked. He would have been the last one to deduce social institutions from values. . . .[6]

Thus Professor Moore argues in *Social Origins* that because in

any society the dominant groups are the ones with the most to hide about the way the society works. . . . [V]ery often . . . truthful analyses are bound to have a critical ring, to seem like exposures rather than objective statements, as the term is conventionally used [to denote "mild-mannered statements in favor of the *status quo.* . ."]. . . . For all students of human society, sympathy with the victims of historical processes and skepticism about the victors' claims provide essential safeguards against being taken in by the dominant mythology. A scholar who tries to be objective needs these feelings as part of his ordinary working equipment.[7]

What is the particular truthful message with a critical ring that *Social Origins* attempts to convey? I believe it is the conclusion that "the evidence from the comparative history of modernization" tells us that "the costs of moderation have been at least as atrocious as those of revolution, perhaps a great deal more."[8] This conclusion is argued by Moore in several ways. First, in assessing the evidence of British history, he emphasizes the *legal* violent suffering inflicted on peasants by the enclosure movements; second, in discussing the Indian case, Moore emphasizes the costs in popular suffering of "democratic stagnation," or modernization forgone. Finally, and I believe most important, Moore organizes *Social Origins* around three main "Routes to the modern world," and devotes considerable effort to demonstrating that each has contained a roughly equivalent measure of popular suffering and large-scale collective violence. "A pox on all their houses" is the message about modes of modernization, and the organizing framework of *Social Origins* functions more to facilitate the exposition of this moral conclusion than to clarify or test the (basically Marxist) conceptions of social change and political process which informed Moore's interpretation of "the facts," which to him dictated that moral conclusion.

B. The theoretical argument

Social Origins, in the words of its author,

endeavors to explain the varied political roles played by the landed upper classes and the peasantry in the transformation from agrarian societies . . . to modern industrial ones. . . . [I]t is an attempt to discover the range of historical conditions under which either or both of these rural groups have become important forces behind the emergence of Western parliamentary versions of democracy, and dictatorships of the right and the left, that is, fascist and communist regimes.[9]

The book is organized around the discussion of three distinct Routes to the modern world, each culminating in one of the three societal political outcomes that interest Moore: Western democracy, fascism, and communist dictatorship.[10] The class structures of "agrarian states" undergoing the initial stages of economic modernization are linked to alternate political outcomes via critical political events analyzed as class struggles: "bourgeois revolution" in the case of the three societies that ended up as Western parliamentary democracies (Britain, France, the U.S.A.); "revolution from above" in the case of societies that ended up as fascist dictatorships (Germany, Japan); and "peasant revolution" in the case of the societies (Russia, China) that became Communist dictatorships. Two of Moore's Routes – the Communist and the "Capitalist Reactionary (or Fascist)" – represent genuine theoretical constructs in that they identify patterns of (a) initial class structure, (b) revolutionary political conflict, *and* (c) ultimate systemic political outcome that Moore argues apply to *both* of the two societies classified in each Route. The "Bourgeois Route," on the other hand, is actually a residual category defined only by the twentieth-century political system ("Western democracy") common to its "members." Britain, France, and the United States, as Moore emphasizes, started the modernizing process with very different social structures; and the political upheavals these societies underwent during modernization – the English Civil War, the French Revolution, and the American Civil War – were characterized by very different concrete patterns of class struggle. Moore labels each of these conflicts "bourgeois revolution," but admits that he does so in each case primarily because the conflict in question contributed crucially to the eventual establishment of "bourgeois democracy," not because any one of them constituted simply or mainly a political offensive of a "rising bourgeoisie." Insofar as any theoretically significant common causal pattern is identified as characteristic of the three "bourgeois revolutions," it is "the development of a group in society with an independent economic base, which attacks obstacles to a democratic version of capitalism that have been inherited from the past."[11] In this respect, Moore emphasizes the role of commercial agrarians – gentry in the English Civil War, rich peasants in the French Revolution, and commercial farmers in the American Civil War.

Moore (rather nonsystematically) elaborates and interrelates *three key variables* in order to explain (a) differences among the sequences characteristic of the major Routes, and (b) differences among the "Bourgeois Revolution" cases. His overall "explanation sketch" seems so nonsystematic not only because he fails to define variables and spell out their roles in explaining sequences of structures and events, but also because so much of *Social Origins* is taken up by case accounts for individual countries. This fact has even led one reviewer to assert that Moore's method is "idiographic"! However, appearances can be very deceptive: what Moore really does in the case analyses is to interpret available secondary materials in a way that makes his explanatory and moral concepts seem plausible. It is those concepts that I am attempting to make explicit in this review.

The first key variable is the strength of a bourgeois or commercial impulse. Some degree of commercialization – which for Moore seems to mean *growth of urban-based commodity markets* – is asserted to be operating to undermine and destabilize each agrarian state that Moore discusses. Just as a "rising bourgeoisie" is the prime mover, itself not moved, in virtually every Marxist account of European modernization, so in *Social Origins,* commercialization is an unexplained given. But degrees of strength of the commercial or bourgeois impulse are differentiated and function as the one variable which both cuts across and differentiates all three Routes. According to Moore, "Bourgeois Revolution" countries (seventeenth-century England, eighteenth-century France, nineteenth-century U.S.) are characterized by the presence of a "strong" bourgeois impulse at an early stage of modernization (though the "strong" bourgeois impulse is weakest in France); the bourgeois impulse is of "medium" strength in early modernizing (late eighteenth – mid-nineteenth century) Germany and Japan; and is "weak" in late nineteenth-century China and Russia (and twentieth-century India).

An old-fashioned Marxist might proceed directly from assertions about the strength of the bourgeoisie in relation to other classes to the explanation of patterns and outcomes of class-conflict political struggles (e.g., strong bourgeois impulse → politically aggressive bourgeoisie → bourgeois revolution). But, for Moore, agrarian strata are the strategic actors in the political revolutions from above or below which create the conditions for the development of various forms of political institutions in industrial societies. Therefore, he must identify variables which can explain agrarian strata's (a) political propensities (pro- or anti-liberal/democratic) and (b) opportunities for extra-agrarian class alliances.

The one general pattern of cross-class alliance that Moore discusses is alliance between agrarian and urban upper classes:

The coalitions and countercoalitions that have arisen . . . across these two groups have constituted and in some parts of the world still constitute the basic framework and environment of political action, forming the series of opportunities, temptations, and impossibilities within which political leaders have had to act.[12]

Here the critical thing seems to be the "strength" of the bourgeoisie: if it is "strong," it will set the cultural and political "tone" of any coalition with a landed upper class (i.e., as in England, according to Moore) *no matter who actually holds political office;* if it is only of "medium" strength, the landed upper class will set the tone.

As for the political propensities and capacities of agrarian strata, Moore's elaboration and application to case analyses of two remaining key variables – (1) the form of commercial agriculture: "labor-repressive" versus "market," and (2) "peasant revolutionary potential" – constitute the core of *Social Origins'* analyses of the politics of modernization.

For any Marxist:

It is always the direct relationship of the owners of the conditions of production to the direct producers . . . [t]he specific form in which unpaid surplus labor is pumped out of the direct producers . . . which reveals the innermost secret, the hidden basis of the entire social structure, and with it the political form of the relation of sovereignty and dependence, in short, the corresponding specific form of the state.[13]

Yet Marx himself concentrated on analyzing the capitalist-proletarian relationship, and most Marxist writers since have been content to contrast the exploitative relationship under capitalism (capitalist-worker) with a generic "feudal" lord-peasant exploitative relationship, without attempting to come to grips with the various producer-surplus-controller relationships found in commercial agri-cultures. It is this task that Moore tackles by drawing a distinction between "labor-repressive" and "market" forms of commercial agriculture:

The form of commercial agriculture . . . [is] just as important as commercialization itself. . . .[14]
There are certain forms of capitalist transformation in the countryside that may succeed economically, in the sense of yielding good profits, but which are for fairly obvious reasons unfavorable to the growth of free institutions of the nineteenth-century Western variety. . . .
The distinction I am trying to suggest is one between the *use of political mechanisms* (using the term "political" broadly . . . [to include "traditional relationships and atti-tudes" used by landlords]) on the one hand and *reliance on the labor market,* on the other hand, to ensure an adequate labor force for working the soil and the creation of an agricultural surplus for consumption by other classes.[15]

The "labor-repressive"- versus "market"-commercial agriculture distinction stands at the heart of the explanation of different patterns and outcomes of modernization offered in *Social Origins.* "Market" commercialization created crucial agrarian political allies for "strong" bourgeoisies in England and the (Northern) United States. In contrast, "labor-repressive agrarian systems pro-vide[d] an unfavorable soil for the growth of democracy and [if peasant revolu-tion failed and a moderately strong bourgeoisie existed] an important part of the institutional complex leading to fascism."[16] Why? Moore gives us two main reasons: First:

While a system of labor-repressive agriculture may be started in opposition to the central authority, it is likely to fuse with the monarchy at a later point in search of political support. This situation can also lead to the preservation of a military ethic among the nobility in a manner unfavorable to the growth of democratic institutions.[17]

Second:

At a later stage in the course of modernization, a new and crucial factor is likely to appear in the form of a rough working coalition between influential sectors of the landed upper classes and the emerging commercial and manufacturing interests.[18]
Industrial development may proceed rapidly under such auspices. But the outcome, after a brief and unstable period of democracy has been fascism.[19]

Finally, let me introduce the third key variable, "peasant revolutionary poten-tial." "Reactionary Capitalist" modernization is possible, according to Moore's analysis, only if both "bourgeois" and peasant revolution from below fail to occur. Peasants provide much of the insurrectionary force in both types of revolution. This leads Moore to ask: "what kinds of social structure and histori-cal situations produce peasant revolutions and which ones inhibit or prevent them[?]"[20] A very basic condition for any social revolution, he concludes, is that "commercialization" in an agrarian state must be of such a (moderate or low) strength and form as to leave peasant society basically intact, but "impaired." Beyond that, the interaction of several factors determines whether the peasantry will have a "strong or weak revolutionary potential." Factors conducive[21] to strong potential are: weak and "exploitative"[22] ties to a landed upper class which is not making (or promoting) a successful transition to modern industrialism; and a "radical" form of peasant community solidarity (where "institutional arrangements are such as to spread grievances through the peasant community . . .").[23] Factors tending to produce weak revolutionary potential are: strong ties to the landed upper class, and weak peasant community solidarity, or else a "conservative" form of solidarity (which ties "those with actual and potential grievances into the prevailing social structure").[24] Finally, Moore points out that potentially revolutionary peasants must have non-peasant allies to succeed, but he is not able to provide a general formula for ascertaining who they might be. Still, what made the French Revolution "bourgeois," according to Moore's analysis, was the fact that a peasantry with a significant rich peasant element was able to find Third Estate allies; combined rich peasant and Third Estate interest in promoting private property precluded a collectivist outcome.[25]

Now that an analytic summary has been provided of the Routes and the key variables that Moore uses to explain differences among and within them, it may be helpful to the reader to provide at this point a schematic summary of what has been presented (Table 1.1):

A word should be said about the kind of explanation that Moore appears to be attempting in *Social Origins*. Robert Somers aptly labels it "sequence analysis . . . the systematic study of particular kinds of sequences of events that are assumed to have some kind of causal connection."[26]

The essence of . . . [Moore's] argument[ ] . . . is that certain combinations of factors make certain subsequent events more likely. . . . One wants to know: what are the antecedents or consequences of structure X? Weber has referred to the notion that once certain structures appear, the "die is cast," making it more likely that certain events will occur on the next roll of the dice.[27]

Significantly, Moore does not attain *complete* explanation (or anything approaching it): he tends to *assume* commercialization-flowing-into-industrialization, and focuses on determinants of political institutional outcomes. This really means that he does not explain the *process* of economic development per se, but instead identifies what seem to him probable sequences of three types of states or events – agrarian bureaucratic social structures, revolutions (from above or below), and "modern" political arrangements – with economic development assumed as the continuous process connecting and activating the sequence of structures and events.

Table 1.1. *Categories and explanatory variable clusters in Barrington Moore's Social Origins of Dictatorship and Democracy*

	Route One "Bourgeois Revolution"		Route Two "Reactionary Capitalism"	Route Three "Communism"
*Common starting point:** (except U.S.A.)	Agrarian Bureaucracy		Agrarian Bureaucracy	Agrarian Bureaucracy
Key variable clusters				
Bourgeois impulse:	Strong		Medium-strength	Weak
Mode of commercial agriculture:	Market	Labor-repressive	Labor-repressive	Labor-repressive
Peasant revolutionary potential:	Low	High	Low	High
Critical political event:	Bourgeois Revolution		Revolution from Above	Peasant Revolution
Major systemic political outcome:	Democratic Capitalism		Fascism	Communist Dictatorship
Cases:	Britain U.S.A.	France	Germany Japan	Russia China

*"[P]owerful central governments that we can loosely call royal absolutisms or agrarian bureaucracies established themselves in the sixteenth and seventeenth centuries in all the major countries examined in connection with this study (except of course the United States). . . . [T]he fact forms a convenient if partly arbitrary peg upon which to hang the beginnings of modernization" (*Social Origins*, p. 417).

II. *SOCIAL ORIGINS*: SOME FUNDAMENTAL PROBLEMS

Any thoroughgoing critique is enriched by an alternative perspective, however implicit, on the matters discussed in the work criticized. Later in this essay, I intend to make the major substantive outlines of my own alternative theoretical perspective quite explicit, but at this point it will be useful to contrast my viewpoint in a general way with that of other writers who have criticized *Social Origins*. Writers who have offered theoretical criticisms in reviews of *Social Origins* have, as self-styled Weberians or neo-Weberians, complained either that the book generalizes too much, or that it neglects the independent causal role of ideas, or both.[28] This is not at all the tack that I intend to take. I share Professor Moore's commitment (as expressed in *Social Origins*) to generalizing, structural explanation. My criticisms will be directed at the kind of structural explanations Moore offers, and will center on discussion of four major problem areas: (A) problems with the operationalization of the variable "strength of bourgeois (or commercial) impulse"; (B) difficulties with the distinction between "market" and "labor-repressive" forms of commercial agriculture; (C) inadequacies of class-struggle and class-coalition explanations of political conflicts and societal transformations; and (D) shortcomings inherent in a theoretical focus on exclusively intrasocietal change-producing processes.

A. Bourgeois impulse – the phantom of Social Origins

As was pointed out above in the analytic summary, Professor Moore orders the three Routes according to the relative strength of a commercial or bourgeois impulse. Yet nothing is said about criteria for determining its strength independently from knowledge of the political outcomes (democracy, fascism, communism) to be explained. This would not be of great concern to a reader if no great explanatory weight were assigned to the "strength of bourgeois impulse" factor or if Moore's assertions about the relative strength of the bourgeois impulse could be taken as obvious. Neither condition holds, however.

The bourgeois or commercial impulse, according to its degree of strength, has *indirect effects* on landed class orientations;[29] these, in turn, determine the political outcomes Moore seeks to explain. (Indeed, one of the most ingenious – and, I believe, sound – aspects of *Social Origins* is its deemphasis of direct bourgeois political activity.) One could argue that Professor Moore differentiates England from the other cases primarily in terms of mode of agrarian commercialization, but when it comes to explaining why agrarian bureaucracies with "labor-repressive" agricultures experience (peasant or bourgeois) revolution from below versus revolution from above, the role of a "weak" or "strong" versus "moderate" bourgeois impulse is emphasized along with peasant revolutionary potential. If the impulse is "strong" (as in France), some peasant revolutionaries are likely to be pro-private property, and will find urban allies; if a "strong" impulse is lacking, then, *unless* the impulse is at least of "moderate" strength, the bourgeoisie will not be "worthy" to be an economic[30] junior partner in a reactionary capitalist coalition with a "labor-repressive" landed upper class, and the only possibilities remaining will be peasant revolution or stagnation.

Nor can Moore's statements about degrees of strength of the bourgeois impulse in his various cases simply be taken for granted. By pulling together scattered remarks made by Moore in referring to the "bourgeois impulse," we can infer that, in a systematic assessment of its strength, Moore would consider the numbers, dispersion, and density of upper-class urbanites, apparently excluding urban-dwelling landed gentlemen and concentrating on those town-dwellers engaged in commerce and industry. He also seems to assign importance to evidence of "dependence" on government authority.[31] All this is acceptable and, in principle, potentially operationalizable. But we can only wonder if these implicit criteria were applied independently of results, or consistently. What, for example, are we to make of the fact that the "strong" French bourgeoisie at the end of the *ancien regime* included many professionals, bureaucrats, investors in land (including "feudal" dues), and investors in government-backed securities?[32] Are we really to take it on faith that this "bourgeoisie" was not only "stronger" and more "independent," but considerably more so, than, say, the Russian bourgeoisie in 1910? In assessing the strength of the Russian bourgeoisie, should foreign investments (especially indirect investments) be considered or not?[33] Finally, what are we to make of the fact that the pre-Restoration Japanese commercial class, whose "moderate" strength was supposedly crucial to the explanation of "revolution from above" in Japan, actually played practically no role in industrializing the country, an achievement initiated by bureaucrats who created whole industries administratively without drawing much upon the capital, the personnel, or the political support of the old commercial strata.[34]

B. Market versus labor-repressive commercial agriculture?

Above all because landlords, not bourgeois, are the strategic upper-class political actors in *Social Origins,* much explanatory weight rides on the distinction between modes of agrarian commercialization. At first glance Moore's distinction seems both straightforward and insightful. What better way to extend the Marxist perspective on the politics of modernization than to distinguish between types of agrarian upper-class relations to direct producers, and trace differences in landed upper-class political propensities to that distinction? But the distinction suffers from interrelated logical and empirical difficulties.

Is any propertied upper class ever really free to dispense with political mechanisms "to ensure an adequate labor force . . . and the creation of a . . . surplus"? Does it make sense to lump together under the rubric of "political mechanisms" everything from "customary" landlord/peasant relations to local government and central state functions? What is "the market" abstracted from all such structural underpinnings but a disembodied ideal, nondescriptive of any concrete historical reality?[35]

How does Moore apply the "market" versus "labor-repressive" distinction in practice? In what sense were English landlords – the *only* landed upper class that Moore identifies as market-commercial – landlords who employed Parliamentary decrees to enclose lands, and who used control of parish political offices to regulate the movements of agricultural laborers via administration of justice and the Poor Laws,[36] *less dependent upon political mechanisms* for extracting a surplus from producers than, say, prerevolutionary Chinese landlords, or nineteenth-century Prussian landlords, or post-Restoration Japanese landlords? If one reads carefully, one cannot fail to see that Professor Moore fails to establish empirical grounds for the market versus labor-repressive commercial agriculture distinction at exactly those points in his argument where it carries most explanatory weight – i.e., in distinguishing between English liberalism and German and Japanese authoritarianism.

Because he includes no chapter on Germany in *Social Origins,* Professor Moore provides no systematic description of agrarian class relations East of the Elbe in nineteenth-century Prussia. He *implies* continuity from the feudal past. Yet, by 1820, and increasingly thereafter, East Elbian agriculture was dependent upon hired, not serf, labor; peasant lands had in large part been absorbed by the great estates; and productive techniques were being revolutionized by infusions of Junker and bourgeois capital. Estate magnates controlled local government and were the preponderant class influence in the Prussian state.[37] Moore labels this state of affairs "labor-repressive" commercial agriculture. But how was this Prussian agrarian situation significantly different (in terms of Moore's conceptual distinction) from the English agrarian situation, where landlords rented to farmers who employed agricultural laborers, while gentry and peers together controlled local and central governing institutions?

As for Japan, in his discussion of post-Restoration Japanese agriculture, Moore draws the following conclusion:

> The evidence just reviewed establishes quite clearly that there was a repressive component in the adaptation of the rural upper classes to the rise of commerce and industry. . . . Japanese society in the late nineteenth century may well have generated its own version of the enterprising landlord who so impressed foreign visitors to eighteenth-century England. In Japan, on the other hand, his relationship to the state was almost the reverse of that in England. The British squire used the state to drive off peasant proprietors and keep a few tenants. The Japanese squire did not drive them off the land; instead he used the state, along with more informal levers inherited from earlier times, to squeeze rents out of the peasants and sell the produce on the open market. Hence he was, sociologically speaking, much closer to the commercializing nobleman of eighteenth-century Toulouse than to the corresponding English gentleman.[38]

What is the "evidence" upon which this conclusion is based? Strangely enough, while Moore convincingly shows that Japanese landlords between 1870 and

1930 were making very large profits (above fifty percent of the produce, generally simply in return for providing rental lands), he depicts a situation in which
a market model can perfectly account for the high profits: the Restoration
established law and order, guaranteed property rights, and pegged the land tax
during an inflationary period; an advancing economy created ever increasing
demand for food; productivity increases in rice-culture produced higher outputs;
and population steadily increased. The result of these interacting conditions and
processes? High rents![39] The closest thing to a "political mechanism for extracting surplus" cited by Moore is the Restoration, with its straightforward
order-guaranteeing effects![40] The English state did fully as much for English
landlords. Moore also claims that Japanese landlords relied upon "customary"
ties to extract surpluses, yet "custom" also had its functions in the English countryside.[41]

I conclude that Professor Moore's market versus labor-repressive commercial
agriculture distinction fails to survive close scrutiny. Every property system,
indeed every market, requires political backing. The significant question to ask
is not whether such support is present or absent, but rather *who controls the
political mechanisms and how they are organized.* From this perspective, what
really made England special was the lack of a bureaucratic central authority and
the extent to which landlords dominated both Parliament and the very important
local administrative and sanctioning machineries.

C. The inadequacy of Marxist political sociology

Debates among Marxist theorists about the role of the state have evolved within
unfortunately narrow limits. Virtually all discussion has centered on the problem
of "the capitalist state" (albeit sometimes extremely broadly defined) because it
has been assumed that in precapitalist modes of production (except for the
anomalous and little-analyzed "Asiatic" mode) political and class domination
were undifferentiated. Within the "capitalist state" problematic, given the un-
questioned existence of differentiated state and, ultimately, party structures,
interest has centered on the degree to which, and conditions under which,
political organs are directly staffed by dominant class personnel.

Is the state normally, in Marx and Engels' vivid phrase, "the executive
committee of the bourgeoisie," personally run by dominant class representatives? One exception to this state of affairs unequivocally recognized by Marx
was an exceptional situation of *political* balance of classes which might set the
stage for the personal rule through a bureaucratized state apparatus of a dictator
such as Louis Bonaparte[42] or Bismarck. Yet Marx postulated that even in such
exceptional instances the state continues to function in the long-term, objective
interest of the economically dominant class, even though the political interests
of the dominant class are violated, and the short-term economic interests of
dominant class individuals or subsectors might be compromised.[43]

Since Marx and Engels, the trend in Marxist scholarship has been to place more and more emphasis on the independence of capitalist state structures from direct bourgeois leadership, and focus instead on ways in which seemingly autonomous political structures and processes are invariably constrained to function to create or preserve the capitalist mode of production. Constraining mechanisms emphasized by various authors range from hegemonic ideology,[44] to control by bourgeois personnel of strategic *parts* (but not the whole) of state systems,[45] to the ultimately conditioning effects of economic structures and class struggles.[46] Recently, Nicos Poulantzas has gone so far as to argue that "the . . . State best serves the interests of the capitalist class only when the members of this class do not participate directly in the State apparatus, that is to say when the *ruling class* is not the *politically governing class.*"[47]

But the fatal shortcoming of all Marxist theorizing (so far) about the role of the state is that nowhere is the *possibility* admitted that state organizations and elites might under certain circumstances act *against* the long-run economic interests of a dominant class, or act to create a new mode of production. Here and there in the literature Marxist scholars recognize that royal absolutisms or bureaucratic states have established the conditions for primitive accumulation, or forced industrialization by lagging nations. But no writer has unequivocally accepted the notion of fully independent, non class-conditioned state action even in these instances.[48] Through all of the debates about the political roles of dominant class personnel, Marxist theory has remained frozen within the assumption that "in the last instance" political structures and struggles are determined by the economic.

In *Social Origins,* on the question of the role of the state, Professor Moore breaks with Marxist tradition in that he recognizes and extensively analyzes precapitalist agrarian states. Yet in other important respects Moore remains within the Marxist theoretical tradition, for he retains the fundamental Marxist propensity to explain political struggles and structures as functions of class structures and struggles. Thus, despite occasional psychologistic references to monarchs and exceptional statesmen as strategic individual political actors, when Moore offers sociological explanations for revolutions and political formations, he focuses on landed upper-class *interests* and *activities*. Bourgeois economic activities are treated as contextual influences. Landed upper-class interests are specified by the "market" versus "labor-repressive" distinction. Political successes and failures of landed upper classes depend upon their economic adaptiveness (to commercial agriculture) and their strength relative to peasant and bourgeois class forces. In the final analysis, therefore, each major sociopolitical transformation that does not eliminate a formerly dominant landed upper class (i.e., through peasant revolution from below) must in Moore's scheme somehow be explained as a political action of a landed upper class.

In the pages that follow, I shall focus on three case studies – England, Japan, and Germany – where Moore argues that landed upper-class interests were politically decisive.[49] I have already argued that the market versus labor-repressive distinction between major types of commercial agricultures is highly questionable. Here I shall argue: (a) that the English Revolution and the revolution from above in Japan were not class actions; and (b) that state organization importantly affected the capacity of landed upper strata to preserve their interests during modernization in all three cases.

1. England: Bureaucracy's absence and liberal development. Professor Moore's discussion of the English case centers around two periods – the seventeenth-century English Revolution and the late eighteenth- to middle nineteenth-century transformation of English society from liberal oligarchy to industrial democracy. My comments will follow suit.

Professor Moore presents the English Revolution as a political offensive of mainly "*commercially* minded elements among the landed upper classes, and to a lesser extent among the yeomen" against a would-be absolutist king "and royal attempts to preserve the old [pre-capitalist] order. . . ."[50]

[T]he policy of the leaders of the rebellion was clear and straightforward. They opposed interference with the landlord's property rights on the part of the king and on the part of the radicals from the lower orders. In July 1641, the Long Parliament abolished the Star Chamber, the main royal weapon against enclosing landlords, as well as the general symbol of arbitrary royal power.[51]

My quarrel with this analysis of the English Revolution is that it trivializes what was at issue and omits discussion of a key dimension of the structural situation of the English landed upper class (especially its gentry sector) – a dimension which helped to make the English Revolution possible and which underlay most of the substantive matters at issue.

Moore tends to treat religious and political issues as symbolic of the basic, substantial economic conflict.[52] Yet the Long Parliament in 1641 and after did far more than abolish the Star Chamber and eliminate feudal tenures and royal economic monopolies. It quarreled with the King and his ministers over who should control military forces, the church,[53] the public taxing powers, etc. Parliament had political privileges to defend, and the organizational capacities to do so, not only because English agriculture was commercialized and prosperous, but also because the King had no centralized bureaucratic apparatus at his disposal. A century or so before, the Tudor monarchs who had turned England into a nascent nation-state, had failed to create a civil bureaucracy,[54] making do instead with local church and gentry officials. And there was no standing army. The English Revolution could not have happened if these political conditions had not prevailed; that it did happen was a victory for those within the landed upper class who wanted to maintain and more fully exploit their decentralized and unbureaucratic *political form of class power vis-à-vis* King and commoners. Although urban resources and manpower provided the wherewithal for at least the first stages of Parliament's military battle against the King, gentry of varying economic orientations remained in control of all stages of the legislative and military battles.

To argue that the English Civil War constituted a political rather than a social revolution would be a mere quibble if it made no difference to Moore's major argument in the "England" chapter of *Social Origins:* the argument that the English Revolution *rather directly* established conditions for the gradual capitalist industrialization and political democratization in England. Moore advances this argument only because he does hold that the Civil War *was* a social revolution:

> The outcome of the struggle was an enormous if still incomplete victory for an alliance between parliamentary democracy and capitalism. . . . Both the capitalist principle and that of parliamentary democracy are directly antithetical to the ones they superseded and in large measure overcame during the Civil War: divinely supported authority in politics, and production for use rather than for individual profit in economics. Without the triumph of these principles in the seventeenth century it is hard to imagine how English Society could have modernized peacefully. . . .[55]

Here and there throughout *Social Origins,* Moore speaks of modernizing England as "capitalist" and "democratic."[56] Yet capitalist industrialization[57] did not really get under way in England until the late eighteenth century, and "democracy" cannot reasonably be said to have been established before the late nineteenth century! Moreover, one can sensibly argue that the *direct and immediate* impact of the English Revolution was to retard industrialization[58] and prevent democracy. The landed nobles that ruled nineteenth-century England were most definitely not a "political advance guard for . . . *industrial* capitalism," however friendly they may have been with merchants and bankers. In 1650 upper classes in town and country quite deliberately closed ranks against the Leveller democrats, and renewed democratic offensives were effectively parried until the nineteenth century! In other case studies, Moore calls such an upper-class antidemocratic coalition "reactionary." It existed just as surely in England; the only difference is that in the long run, after industrialization had gathered steam, it failed to prevent gradual concessions to democracy. The answer to why it failed lies as much in class *capacities* as in class *interests.*

"Ruling class" explanations always tend to argue from class interests to intentions to political outcomes: hence Moore's tendency to portray England's landed gentlemen as friendly to industrial capitalism and democracy. An argument which considers political institutional arrangements as an *independent* constraint on class political capacities can make better sense of an ironic situation, like that of modernizing England, in which a class which has won a political battle (here, against royal absolutism and potential bureaucratization) and has a continuing interest in the fruits of that victory (i.e., local-level control of labor-force movements) *consequently* finds itself *unable* to prevent socioeconomic and political changes that gradually undermine its position as a ruling class. Recent analyses[59] of the events surrounding the First Reform Bill

(1832) have argued that the aristocrats who controlled the political process were not trying to "make concessions" to bourgeois democracy, but instead were trying to do the best they could to stave it off *within the limits* of political options *available* to them. Simple repression was not an available option in part because a bureaucracy and standing army were not *already* in existence, in part because they could not be created without violating some interests of the landed upper class (in the process of serving its other interest in repressing bourgeois democracy!). The English landed upper class ruled, but could not fully control events in long-run class interest precisely because "the repressive apparatus of the English state was relatively weak, a consequence of the Civil War [which, ironically, established the landed upper class as a directly ruling class in the first place!], the previous evolution of the monarchy, and of reliance on the navy rather than on the army."[60] These factors belong at the very core of any structural analysis of English development.[61] Turning to the German and Japanese cases, we shall see that the same factors are important there.

2. Japan and Germany: Bureaucracy and revolution from above. Perhaps nowhere in *Social Origins* does Professor Moore strain harder to break the constraints of Marxist political sociology than in his discussion of "revolution from above" in Germany and Japan, and nowhere in his ultimate failure to achieve that *theoretical* breakthrough more costly – costly, that is, in terms of the potential generalizability of his ideas to other case studies of modernization.[62]

The conception of "revolution from above" is Moore's way of dealing with the fact (a difficulty for many traditional Marxist theories of modernization) that no violent popular revolution is necessary "to sweep away feudal obstacles to industrialization . . . as the course of German and Japanese history demonstrates."[63] According to Moore, governments which make a "revolution from above" promote capitalist industrialization by: (1) centralizing and rationalizing the political order; (2) creating "a sufficiently powerful military machine to be able to make the wishes of . . . [the] rulers felt in the arena of international politics";[64] and (3) promoting the spread of national identification and modern skills to the entire population.[65] Moore analyzes the events which for him constitute "revolution from above" (namely: for Japan, the Meiji Restoration; and, for Germany, the Stein-Hardenberg Reforms in Prussia [1807–1814], and Bismarck's Unification [1860s]) in class-instrumentalist terms: "revolution from above" is effected by a coalition of a strong ("labor-repressive") landed upper class and a moderately strong bourgeoisie; the form of modernization chosen was one that kept the landed upper class in the saddle as "ruling class" and prevented basic structural changes. And this retention of *class* power by a "labor-repressive" landed upper class is what ties "revolution from above" to (much later in time) "fascism" in Moore's analysis of Route Two ("Reactionary Capitalist") modernization.

Where the [revolution-from-above class] coalition succeeds in establishing itself, there has followed a period of conservative and even authoritarian government. . . . These authoritarian governments acquired some democratic features. . . . Their history may be punctuated with attempts to extend democracy. . . . Eventually the door to fascist regimes was opened by the failure of these democracies to cope with the severe problems of the day and *reluctance* or *inability to bring about fundamental structural changes.* One factor, but only one, in the social anatomy of these governments has been the *retention of a very substantial share of political power by the landed elite,* due to the *absence of a revolutionary breakthrough by the peasants in combination with urban strata.*[66]

Let us focus on the assertion that revolution from above in Germany and Japan was landed upper-class action. The first point to be made is that the label "revolution from above" fits the facts of the Japanese case much better than those of the German case. The changes wrought by the Meiji Restoration in Japan were far more sudden and sweeping than the piecemeal reforms implemented by political authorities in nineteenth-century Germany. The Meiji reformers completely abolished *daimyo* and (residual) *samurai* rights in land and claims to agrarian income, and launched large-scale industrialization by bureaucratically establishing major industries. In Germany, the Stein-Hardenberg Reforms (1807–1914) abolished hereditary status (estate) monopolies of rights to practice occupations and own landed estates, but did not confiscate, indeed augmented, landed upper-class property. Bismarck's Unification (1860s) created a unified German national market and removed institutional and local obstacles to industrial expansion, but the industries which expanded had been created, and continued to be run, by private entrepreneurs.

Unfortunately, if Moore's label better fits the Japanese case, his *analysis* of "revolution from above" does not. Throughout *Social Origins,* Moore portrays "labor-repressive" landed upper classes as foes of modernization. How is it, that in Japan political representatives of such a landed upper class not only went along with industrialization, but actually spearheaded the process in a situation where the bourgeoisie alone could not have done so? Insofar as Moore senses this implicit contradiction, he deals with it by calling the Japanese reformers "distinguished political leaders" who were "aliens within the aristocracy."[67] Suddenly, structural explanation fails and must be shored up in an ad hoc manner by personalistic explanatory expedients!

But, if Marxist political sociology is supplemented by an understanding of the potential of *bureaucratic political structures* for sustaining cohesive elites with sensitivity to international power balances and loose and pragmatic commitments to *particular forms* of large-scale private property, then such personalistic ad hoc explanatory expedients become unnecessary. Writing on "Elite Revolutions" in Japan and Turkey, Ellen Kay Trimberger provides us with crucial theoretical insights for understanding what Moore calls "revolution from above":

[T]he following conditions are necessary, and perhaps sufficient, to generate revolutionaries [from above] from within the ranks of state bureaucrats:
1) It is only when a bureaucratic elite – or a significant segment of it – forms an
autonomous stratum independent of the economic means of production, that there will be
a possibility of their overthrowing the established regime in order to initiate revolutionary
change. An autonomous bureaucratic stratum is one that gains its status, power, and
wealth primarily from office and *not* from: a) external economic interests in land,
commerce, or industry; or b) dependence upon an economically dominant class of
landowners, businessmen, or industrialists. *Thus it is only in those polities where there
is no consolidated ruling class,* but, rather, where the state bureaucracy is somewhat
independent of the society's productive economic base that revolutionaries may be
generated from within a ruling stratum.
2) An autonomous group of bureaucrats will be impelled to organize a revolutionary
movement and counter-government only when the regime they serve is under an extreme
threat to national sovereignty. . . .
3) Even under the impact of such an extreme external threat, autonomous bureaucrats
will be able to mobilize a revolutionary movement, only if they develop a strong
normative cohesion. . . . Nationalism is the predominate ideological appeal in an elite
revolution. . . .[68]

Trimberger makes better sense of the Meiji Restoration than Moore.[69] In
chapter 5 of *Social Origins,* Moore first analyzes the Restoration as a "feudal
revolution": a staving off by the traditional aristocratic "landed upper class" of
basic social changes which might threaten its position in society. Then he
discusses all the changes actually wrought by the Meiji bureaucrats, switching
in the process from class-instrumentalist language to one in which it is "the
government" that acts. Trimberger, on the other hand, argues that the reformers
were mostly *samurai* officials – men without landed property, who depended
for their livelihood and careers on salaried employment in *han* governments.
And Trimberger emphasizes that it was only because the reformers *were true
bureaucrats,* without landed property or close ties to landowners, that they were
willing to take radical steps in bringing about economic and social transformations.

In contrast to the Meiji Restoration, reform from above in Germany does
seem to fit Moore's class action model. Yet even in this instance, Moore's
analysis would have been strengthened by attention to state organization. The
Stein-Hardenberg reformers, for instance, were not merely exceptional statesmen,[70] they were the cadre of a bureaucratized sector of Prussia's landed upper
class. As *large* landowners, they were careful to protect and enhance the
economic interests of *wealthy* landowners (and wealthy prospective land-
buyers). Yet as men whose careers had been in government service, they were
accustomed to the exercise of political power, and they constituted a status
group, with a common educational background and values, and within which
estate background was relatively unimportant. Finally, and not least important,
they had at their disposal effective (or potentially effective) administrative and
military apparatuses.[71]

At the turn of the nineteenth century, the Prussian nobility was threatened at home by acute economic depression, and from abroad by Napoleon's armies. The brilliantly executed Stein-Hardenberg reforms alleviated the crisis at home – in the interest of the wealthy, noble or not – by freeing the land and met the threat from abroad by reforming the military and generating enough popular support and military participation from the middle class (now free of estate restrictions on mobility) and from the peasantry (now free of feudal personal obligations) to "liberate" German territories in 1814 from French rule or tutelage. The reforms met with resistance from the Junker squirearchy, the local and nonaffluent sector of the noble *estate,* but they constituted a clear-cut case of ruling *class* action to enhance landed upper class and national viability.

The Prussian landed upper class, strengthened by wealthy nonnoble recruits, tightened its grip on the Prussian agrarian economy and polity between 1815 and 1870. Because of its successful adaptation to capitalist agriculture (during the first three-quarters of the nineteenth century), it generally supported measures such as the Zollverein and Bismarck's Unification which furthered the economic development of Germany. It was not until world grain markets were revolutionized in the late nineteenth century that East Elbian landed magnates became foes of free trade, and used their enormous political leverage to prompt German industries into militarist and labor-repressive modes.[72]

Three propositions about the relationship of agrarian state bureaucratization to dominant (landed upper-) class political capacity seem to emerge from the above case discussions:

1. Very weakly bureaucratized state apparatuses can, ironically, be so dominated by landed upper-class interests at all levels that they are rendered virtually useless as instruments of class political response to social crises. That was the case in England. The king and a few top military and political leaders would have been willing to repress middle-class liberal agitation in the 1820s and 1830s, but landed upper-class dominance of decentralized administrative and repressive apparatuses both undercut top leaders' "will" to repress, and closed off their "objective" options.

2. A highly bureaucratic *and centralized* agrarian state which is staffed – especially at the top – by landed notables or men closely tied to landed notables (men who get a substantial part of their income and status from landed wealth) can serve as an especially potent instrument of landed upper-class response to external and internal crises, though the specific, short-run interests of 'weaker' class members (e.g., the Junker squirearchy) may be overridden. Events in nineteenth-century Germany exemplify this proposition.

3. Finally, a highly bureaucratic (though not necessarily centralized) agrarian state which is not directly staffed by landed notables can under extraordinary circumstances, especially foreign threats from more modernized countries, act against the class interests of landed upper strata. That is what happened in Japan.[73]

One might tentatively conclude that, when a society is neither undergoing rapid internal structural change, nor experiencing potentially overwhelming political and/or economic threats from abroad, state and dominant class will be cozy bedfellows, no matter who staffs the state. But if the times are out of joint, it can matter a great deal who staffs the state, and how it is organized. The significance of this for a theory of modernization should be obvious.

D. Wanted: An intersocietal perspective

The primary task undertaken by *Social Origins* is the explanation of changes in political arrangements which accompany the transformation of agrarian states into industrial nations. Significantly, the theoretical variables used to accomplish the task refer exclusively to *intrasocietal structures and processes*. The ubiquitous "motor of social change" is the "commercial impulse," and one must gather from what Moore says of it that it operates inexorably, albeit at different rates and intensities, to undermine every agrarian bureaucracy. Variations of ultimate political outcomes of the modernizing process (Moore's dependent variable) are explained by a combination of the strength of the "commercial impulse" and the type of class structure through which its effects are channeled.

   Given this intrasocietal focus, it is hardly surprising that Moore attempts to justify his selection of cases as follows:

This study concentrates on certain important stages in a prolonged social process which has worked itself out in several countries. . . . The focus of interest is on innovation that has led to political power, not on the spread and reception of institutions that have been hammered out elsewhere, except where they have led to significant power in world politics. The fact that the smaller countries depend economically and politically on big and powerful ones means that the decisive causes of their politics lie outside their own boundaries. It also means that their political problems are not really comparable to those of larger countries. . . .[74]

This statement is of diagnostic interest alone. (For, as all reviewers who have commented on the matter of case selection have recognized, it has no face validity: if one's interest is in powerful innovators, why include India, a poor and weak country whose democratic institutions were implanted via colonization? Clearly, Moore wrote about a group of countries whose modern political arrangements interested him for a melange of moral and theoretical reasons, which is perfectly justifiable in a work whose purpose is to outline, not definitively establish, general hypotheses.) Apparently sensing that his theoretical approach could handle only intrasocietal processes of change, Moore was anxious to establish his cases as societies free from "foreign" influences.

   But, of course, no society is free from foreign influences, and, in his case accounts, Moore is repeatedly forced to refer to "external" conditions or events in order to explain "internal" states or changes. Among the reasons for England's ability to avoid "reactionary capitalist" development were: (1) her status as an island, which allowed her to engage in warfare with the continental monarchies without maintaining a standing army at home, and (2) her status as first modernizer, which facilitated an "imperialism of free trade."[75] Japan's Meiji reformers were responding to threats from more developed nations abroad. ("What prompted this largely feudal revolution [as Moore labels the Restoration] to carry out a program with many undoubtedly progressive features? . . . The foreign threat was decisive. . . .")[76] The Chinese Communists depended for the success of their revolution on "certain fortuitous circumstances, . . . fortuitous in the sense that they did not derive from anything taking place in China itself. . . ."[77]

Can an explanatory factor so systematically resorted to really be "fortuitous"? Moore himself senses the problem. Speaking again of the role of the Japanese invasion in spurring the Chinese Revolution, he writes:

> From the standpoint of Chinese society and politics, the war was an accident. *From the standpoint of the interplay of political and economic forces in the world as a whole, it was scarcely an accident.* Just as the case of the Bolshevik victory in Russia, which some historians see as the accidental outcome of the First World War, the inevitable analytical necessity of isolating certain manageable areas of history can lead to partial truths that are misleading and even false unless and until one subsequently puts them back into their proper context.[78]

A brilliant aperçu. Putting it in my own words, what is required to release forces operating in the international field from the limbo of "fortuity" is a gestalt switch, away from theories which treat social change (here, specifically, modernization) as a process "natural," "directional," "continuous," "necessary," and "immanent"[79] to each and every society (here agrarian bureaucracy) considered, and toward a theory which recognizes that large-scale social change within societies is always in large part caused by forces operating among them, through their economic and political interaction. But, in *Social Origins,* Professor Moore never makes this theoretical gestalt switch.

III. TOWARD AN ALTERNATIVE THEORETICAL APPROACH

To improve upon Professor Moore's analysis of the political accompaniments and results of modernization (industrialization), one must modify his basically Marxist theoretical approach in two ways. First, the independent roles of state organization and state elites in determining agrarian societies and landed upper classes' responses to challenges posed by modernization at home and abroad must be acknowledged and explained.[80] Second, one must break from a focus on exclusively intrasocietal modernizing processes. I have already discussed the first proposed theoretical modification. Let me here further clarify the second, and discuss the interrelation of the two.

A necessary condition of a society's modernization is its incorporation into the historically unique network of societies that arose first in Western Europe in early modern times and today encompasses enough of the globe's population for the world to be viewed for some purposes as if it consisted of a single network of societies.[81]

Modernization is best conceived not only as an intrasocietal process of economic development accompanied by lagging or leading changes in noneconomic institutional spheres, but also as a world-historic intersocietal process. Modernization encompasses the − not necessarily national − industrialization of agrarian societies, and their concomitant transformation into various types of nation-states. Thus modernization involves two major types of developmental structural changes: changes in economic institutions and technology from agricultural to industrial; and changes in political or "integrative" institutions from semibureaucratic and non-mass-mobilizing to some combination of fully bureaucratic and mass-mobilizing (typically through one or more political parties). Both processes occur under the impetus of foreign as well as domestic pressures. Yet the two major types of modernizing changes need not occur simultaneously, or in any single order. Moreover, as economic and political organizations headquartered in the earlier modernized countries achieve the capacity to influence developments on a worldwide scale, the two developmental processes, economic and political, become increasingly disjointed (from the "viewpoint" of a single society). National industrialization becomes increasingly rare, but political control of nonelites remains primarily a nation-state function (though dependent regimes may employ resources from abroad).

Many Marxist works on the consequences of imperialism for "late-modernizing" countries are especially insightful in their analysis of modernization in a twentieth-century world context. But few attempts have been made to apply the intersocietal theoretical perspective on modernization to pre-twentieth-century development. The one major effort that I know of − that of Immanuel Wallerstein[82] − is flawed by its attempt to treat state forms and "strength" (e.g., centralization and bureaucratization) as simple functions of societies' class structures and positions in the world-capitalist economic division of labor.

Actually, prior to the twentieth-century rise of multinational corporations, competition among modernizing societies was mainly the *competition of* (agrarian-state or industrial-nation) *state organizations*. Because economic prowess and political strength were *not* perfectly correlated, structural changes administered "from above" by state elites free from class controls could allow relatively backward agrarian competitors in a modernizing world to gain military strength and time to compensate for relative economic backwardness. So could revolutions "from below" which enthroned political elites willing and able to direct national economic development.

Merely adopting the intersocietal perspective on modernization outlined in the preceding paragraphs would have enormously improved Moore's analysis. It would, for example, have allowed him to clarify in what sense his three Routes actually represent "stages" − as he recurrently wanted to label them.

To a very limited extent these three types – bourgeois revolution culminating in the Western form of democracy, conservative revolutions from above ending in fascism, and peasant revolutions leading to communism – may constitute *alternative routes and choices*. They are much more clearly *successive historical stages*. As such, they display a limited determinate relation to each other. The methods of modernization chosen in one country change the dimensions of the problem for the next countries who take the step, as Veblen recognized when he coined the now fashionable term, "the advantages of backwardness." Without the prior democratic modernization of England the reactionary methods adopted in Germany and Japan would scarcely have been possible. Without both the capitalist and reactionary experiences, the communist method would have been something entirely different, if it had come into existence at all. . . . The historical preconditions of each major political species differ sharply from the others.[83]

In *Social Origins* Moore never explained in what sense "the methods of modernization chosen in one country change the dimensions of the problem for the next countries who take the step." How could he, when his explanatory focus was so exclusively on intrasocietal factors? Breaking from that focus, attending to the economic *and politico-military interactions* among Moore's cases, one might (if there were time and space to develop the arguments at length) resolve the Alternative Routes versus Successive Stages dilemma implicit in *Social Origins*. The revolutionary methods of launching modernization adopted by the "Reactionary Capitalist" and "Communist" national political elites could be interpreted in large part as attempts to maintain substantive national political sovereignty in a modernizing world dominated by the earlier "Bourgeois" (economic and/or political) modernizers. Specifically, the Communist revolutions could be interpreted as attempts also to insulate national economies from a world economy that was becoming so mature as to begin to cut off all opportunities for indigenous entrepreneurial capitalist development, and to "require" instead that politics be put "in command" if the substance of national sovereignty were to be retained. Finally, one could conclude that *national* modernization at this point, insofar as it is possible at all, requires a socialist-mobilizing revolution (with participatory-style, not Western-style, democratization). Today, the price for underdeveloped countries of either Western-style formal democracy or "conservative authoritarian" bureaucratic or military (de facto) dictatorship is stagnation or, at best, partial and warped industrialization through penetration by "multinational" corporate capital. Professor Moore, I think, was groping toward (at least parts of) this conclusion in his Indian case study, but he had no theoretical way to sustain it.

But, if the switch to an intersocietal perspective on modernization solves one problem implicit in *Social Origins* (i.e., the Alternative Routes versus Successive Stages problem), it also raises a host of new issues. In the explanatory scheme of *Social Origins* the variable "strength of bourgeois impulse" serves to gloss over the problem of causes of economic development. By allowing Moore to *assume* that economic development (commercialization-flowing-into-industrialization) is a process, inevitable in the long run, and generated and sustained mainly within potential or actual nation-states, that variable freed Moore to concentrate on (sequence-causal) relationships between intrasocietal class structures and national political outcomes. Alas, as soon as an intersocietal perspective is adopted, *Social Origin's entire structure of assumptions and sequence-explanations collapses.* *National* economic modernization (as the early modernizers knew it) cannot be assumed. Its rate, and indeed the very possibility of its occurrence, are determined by international political-economic conditions. Revolutions from above or below are not only (or perhaps even primarily) responses to intrasocietal developments. Possibilities for continued industrialization and/or democratization in the wake of "bourgeois revolutions" are in part determined by international relationships and conditions, as are needs and opportunities for "fascist" military aggression. By focusing only on internal conditions in explaining his Route sequences, Moore failed to consider variables which condition or determine societal outcomes at each step on the various Ways to the modern world. Switching from an intra- to an intersocietal orientation requires that every causal explanation offered in *Social Origins* be rethought; in that process, some of the sequences fly apart, lose their apparent coherence.

This is especially true for those sequences (i.e., the "Bourgeois" and "Reactionary Capitalist" Routes) which posit direct causal relationships between revolutions and modern political outcomes separated by one or more centuries of time. Unquestionably, something we call "fascism" followed in time revolution or reforms from above in the national histories of Japan and Germany, but, if world-historically specific intersocietal processes provide part of the explanations for the occurrence of both revolution from above and then, later, "fascism" in these two cases, then obviously the connection of the two events becomes less necessary, less generalizable to other cases where revolution from above has occurred or might occur. The solution is not to despair of the possibility of ever generalizing, but to adopt an alternative theoretical perspective which will allow better calculations of how national events really occur, partially determined by internal conditions, partly by external.

In concluding this critical essay, let me emphasize the extent to which Barrington Moore's *Social Origins of Dictatorship and Democracy* constituted, in the intellectual context in which it was conceived, written, and published, an unparalleled positive contribution to the scientific enterprise of understanding modernization. In that context, Professor Moore, and most other social scientists, perceived a choice between explanations of intrasocietal modernization which focused on ideas and values, and explanations which focused on economic factors, as independent variables. By choosing a kind of Marxist approach, Professor Moore made the more valid and fertile choice at a time when all too many others were choosing the other way. One can be effectively critical of *Social Origins* today only insofar as one transcends the theoretical alternatives which originally confronted Moore. I have tried to do so by advocating an approach which simultaneously treats modernization as a world-historical inter-societal process, and insists that economic institutions and state structures are partially independent determinants of societal transformations during modernization.

NOTES

1. Barrington Moore, Jr., "Strategy in Social Science," in *Political Power and Social Theory* (New York: Harper and Row, 1965; first published by Harvard University Press, 1958), p. 116, emphasis added.
2. Tocqueville, Weber, and most modern neo-Weberians all do some nonidealist, structural analyses of political institutions. But, when such authors turn from static analysis to the explanation of social change, including modernization, they generally assign great explanatory significance to ideas and "idea men." Contrast, for example: Weber's analysis of bureaucracy with his discussion of the role of charismatic authority; Tocqueville's comparison of English and French political institutions, with his explanation of the French Revolution; and S. N. Eisenstadt's analysis (in *The Political Systems of Empires*) of historical empire's institutional structures, with his explanations of how they were originally created, and eventually disintegrated. Such authors may seem to emphasize the independent role of politics in social change, but they mean political *ideas,* not political structures.
3. Professor Moore assigns ideas a role as *mediators* between objective situations and behavior, but argues that to "explain behavior in terms of cultural values is to engage in circular reasoning":

    > We cannot do without some conception of how people perceive the world and what they do or do not do about what they see. To detach this conception from the way people reach it, to take it out of its historical context and raise it to the status of an independent causal factor in its own right, means that the supposedly impartial investigator succumbs to the justifications that ruling groups generally offer for their most brutal conduct (*Social Origins,* p. 487).

4. When I refer without qualification to the "Marxist" approach, I mean the "lowest common denominator" of theoretical assumptions made by virtually all writers who would consider themselves, or be considered by responsible others, to be in the Marxist-scholarly tradition. Naturally there are many important differences among such scholars, but I am more concerned with commonalities in this essay.

    Because scholarly and political Marxism are sometimes confused (as for example by Stanley Rothman in his review of *Social Origins* in the *American Political Science Review* 64:1 [March 1970]:61–83), I wish to emphasize that the application to Professor Moore of the label "Marxist" will have absolutely no political connotations in this essay.
5. Reading the following analytic summary is no substitute for reading *Social Origins* itself. The summary presupposes acquaintance with the book.
6. Moore, "Strategy in Social Science," pp. 116–17, emphasis added.
7. Pp. 522–23. All page number references for quotes are to Barrington Moore, Jr., *Social Origins of Dictatorship and Democracy* (Boston: Beacon Press, 1966). A paperback edition was published by Beacon Press in 1967; pagination is the same as in the hardback edition.
8. Ibid., p. 505.
9. Ibid., p. xi.

10. India does not fit well into the theoretical analysis that Moore presents for the three main Routes; hence, I shall have little to say about that case account in this essay. Both India's inclusion in the book, and its classification as a "democracy" seem dubious to me. And Moore's conclusions about India are entirely equivocal.

    Since the United States was never an agrarian bureaucracy or a feudal society, it does not fit well into the overall explanatory scheme of *Social Origins* either. I believe that Moore badly twisted the facts of American history in order to present the Civil War as a "bourgeois revolution." Lee Benson has made a basically sound (though overly rancorous) argument to this effect in his *Toward the Scientific Study of History* (Philadelphia: J. B. Lippincott, 1972), chap. 8, and I will not repeat what would be a similar argument in this essay.

11. *Social Origins,* p. xv.

12. Ibid., p. 423.

13. Karl Marx, *Capital,* Vol. 3 (New York: International Publishers, 1967; originally published, 1894), p. 791.

14. *Social Origins,* p. 420.

15. Ibid., pp. 433–34, italics added. Moore explicitly *excludes* from the category "labor-repressive" agriculture: (1) family farming; (2) "a system of hired agricultural laborers where the workers . . . [have] considerable real freedom to refuse jobs and move about . . ."; and (3) "precommercial and pre-industrial agrarian systems . . . if there is a rough balance between the overlord's contribution to justice and security and the cultivators' contribution in the form of crops" (pp. 434–35). Strictly speaking, it seems to me, (3) should not even be relevant, since the "labor-repressive" versus "market" distinction refers only to commercial agricultures.

16. Ibid., p. 435.

17. Ibid.

18. Ibid., p. 436.

19. Ibid., p. xvi.

20. Ibid., p. 453.

21. *All* "conducive factors" need not be present in any particular case of peasant revolution, according to Moore's argument.

22. On pp. 470–73 of *Social Origins,* Moore develops what I consider to be a naive functionalist definition of "exploitation" in landlord-peasant relationships. He holds that one can objectively measure whether lords (in precommercial agrarian systems) are performing valuable services for "the community" in return for the surpluses they claim. But Moore overlooks the fact that any upper class quite *un*manipulatively creates through its own existence and activities many of the problems that it simultaneously overcomes in "service" to "the community." Thus, if feudal lords had not been wont to fight among themselves, "their" peasants would not have needed the protection for which they supposedly "gave" their surpluses in "fair exchange"!

23. Ibid., p. 475.

24. Ibid., p. 476.

25. I am not going to have much to say about Moore's discussion of "peasant revolutionary potential" in the critical remarks which follow. For three reasons: first, I think Moore is basically on the right track in refusing to focus on peasants alone, or as an aggregate mass; instead, he considers both peasant community social structures and peasant ties to upper strata. Second, what differences I have with Moore on the peasant question stem from my alternative approach to social revolutions, viewed holistically, and those differences are spelled out in a paper delivered at the August 1973 meetings of the American Sociological Association in New York City. Finally, for the theoretical purposes of this paper, it is more important to criticize the way Moore handles upper-class relations to political processes.

26. Robert Somers, "Applications of an Expanded Survey Research Model to Comparative Institutional Studies," in Ivan Vallier, ed., *Comparative Methods in Sociology* (Berkeley and Los Angeles: University of California Press, 1971), p. 392.
27. Ibid., p. 389.
28. See Stanley Rothman, "Barrington Moore and the Dialectics of Revolution: An Essay Review," *American Political Science Review* (March 1970):61–83; and David Lowenthal's Review of *Social Origins* in *History and Theory* 7:2(1968):257–78.

    Most other reviews of *Social Origins* that I have seen have either been, in general, uncritically appreciative, or else have dealt with specific cases or issues (e.g., methodology narrowly defined; viz., Somers, referred to in note 26).
29. Inferring from Moore's analysis: urban markets offer commercial opportunities to agrarian strata, and thus may induce in them promodernizing economic or political attitudes and, especially, behavior.
30. Moore appears to conceive of the bourgeoisie's contribution to "reactionary capitalist' coalitions as solely economic: the bourgeoisie carries on with industrializing the country, while the landed upper class remains in political command.
31. See pp. 174–78; 238–39; 481.
32. See, for example: Alfred Cobban, *The Social Interpretation of the French Revolution* (Cambridge: Cambridge University Press, 1964); Norman Hanson, *A Social History of the French Revolution* (Toronto: University of Toronto Press, 1963), chap. 1; M. Vovelle and D. Roche, "Bourgeois, Rentiers, and Property Owners . . . ," in Jeffry Kaplow, ed., *New Perspectives on the French Revolution* (New York: Wiley, 1965, pp. 25–46; and, above all, George V. Taylor, "Noncapitalist Wealth and the Origins of the French Revolution," *American Historical Review* 72:2(January 1967):469–96.

    For a reinterpretation of the French Revolution which takes account of these facts and which is conformable to the patterns of theoretical reorientation proposed in this essay, see my "A Structural Theory of Social Revolution," a paper presented at the August 1973 Annual Meetings of the American Sociological Association in New York City. [A version of this paper appears as Chapter 6 in this volume.]
33. Precisely because Moore emphasizes the *indirect* political effects of the "bourgeois impulse" via agrarian commercialization, foreign investments cannot simply be ignored. They, as much as indigenous investment, promoted urbanization, industrialization, and the opening of markets for agricultural products. Of course one of the reasons that we do not know how Moore would handle these issues is that he did not include a chapter on Russia in *Social Origins*.
34. See, for example: William W. Lockwood, *The Economic Development of Japan* (Princeton: Princeton University Press, 1968), p. 10 (originally published in hardcover by Princeton in 1954); and Richard Storry, *A History of Modern Japan* (Baltimore: Penguin Books, 1960), p. 121.
35. Indeed the fundamental thrust of Marx's analysis of capitalism is precisely to combat such disembodied, idealistic conceptions of markets!
36. See Karl Polanyi, *The Great Transformation* (Boston: Beacon Press, 1957; first published in 1944), chaps. 7 and 8, and especially p. 94.
37. See Hans Rosenberg, *Bureaucracy, Aristocracy, and Autocracy* (Boston: Beacon Press, 1966; first published in 1958), chap. 9; Hajo Holborn, *A History of Modern Germany, 1648–1840* (New York: Alfred A. Knopf, 1964), pp. 405–10; Theodore S. Hamerow, *Restoration, Revolution, and Reaction* (Princeton: Princeton University Press, 1966), chap. 3; and Theodore S. Hamerow, *The Social Foundations of German Unification, 1858–1871: Ideas and Institutions* (Princeton: Princeton University Press, 1969), chap. 5.
38. *Social Origins*, p. 286.

39. Ibid., pp. 283–86.
40. Ibid., pp. 283–84.
41. See Polanyi, *Great Transformation;* H. J. Habakkuk, "England," in Albert Goodwin, ed., *The European Nobility in the Eighteenth Century* (New York: Harper and Row, 1967), pp. 1–21; F. M. L. Thompson, "The Social Distribution of Landed Property in England Since the Sixteenth Century," *The Economic History Review,* 2d series, 19:3(1966):505–17; F. M. L. Thompson, *English Landed Society in the Nineteenth Century* (London: Routledge & Kegan Paul, 1963); and W. L. Guttsman, *The British Political Elite* (New York: Basic Books, 1963).
42. Karl Marx, " Eighteenth Brumaire of Louis Bonaparte," in Karl Marx and Frederick Engels, *Selected Works* (New York: International Publishers, 1968; "Eighteenth Brumaire" first published in 1852), pp. 95–180.
43. Ibid.
44. Hegemony is an important theme in: Georg Lukács, *History and Class Consciousness* (Cambridge, Mass.: Massachusetts Institute of Technology Press, 1971; this edition first published in 1967); and Antonio Gramsci, *Selections from the Prison Notebooks.* Quintin Hoare and Geoffrey N. Smith, eds. and trans. (New York: International Publishers, 1971).
45. This is perhaps the central argument in Ralph Miliband, The State in *Capitalist Society* (New York: Basic Books, 1969).
46. Nicos Poulantzas, *Political Power and Social Classes* (London: New Left Books, 1973; first published in French in 1968).
47. Nicol [*sic*] Poulantzas, "The Problem of the Capitalist State," *New Left Review,* No. 58 (1969): 73.
48. Either the issue is hedged, or states are labeled according to the historical functions they perform. Thus, in *Political Power and Social Classes,* chap. 3, Nicos Poulantzas labels the European absolutist states that helped create the conditions for the emergence of capitalist economies "capitalist," even though he recognizes that no strong bourgeois class was in existence at the beginning of the transition from feudalism to capitalism in Europe. This approach, it seems to me, confuses causation and objective functioning.
49. In his discussion of peasant political behavior, interestingly enough, Moore does not move directly from class interest to class action; he considers institutional patterns which affect *capacities* to act. I maintain that what is good for lower-class analysis is also good for upper-class analysis.
50. *Social Origins,* p. 14 (italics added).
51. Ibid., p. 17.
52. Ibid.
53. Fights over religious issues in the English Civil War can, I believe, be viewed as political battles: Laudians, Presbyterians, Independents, and the sects differed among themselves not mainly over the content of religious doctrines, but over church organization. These quarrels were all the more intense because, recurrently since the time of Henry VII, monarchs had attempted to use the church hierarchy as a partial substitute for a civil bureaucracy. Of course, if this policy were to work, monarchs had to control clerical appointments. But, often, gentry also claimed that right. And, in the localities, non-upper-class groups increasingly claimed the right to organize their own religous worship.
54. See Christopher Hill, *Reformation to Industrial Revolution* (Baltimore: Penguin Books, 1969), part 2, chap. 1; and Lawrence Stone, "The English Revolution," in R. Forster and J. P. Greene, eds., *Preconditions of Revolution in Early Modern Europe* (Baltimore: Johns Hopkins Press, 1970), pp. 55–108.

Moore equivocates terribly about whether the English monarchy was bureaucratic or not *before* the Civil War. (Compare pp. 2 and 417 with pp. 14 and 22.) His inconsistency on this question suggests the minor explanatory importance he attaches to it.

55. *Social Origins,* pp. 19–20.

56. Ibid., especially p. 294.

57. One might argue that 18th-century England was a *commercial*-capitalist society. But there was nothing inevitable about the transition from agrarian and mercantile commercialism to industrial capitalism. Whether or not agrarian commercialism will spontaneously give rise to industrialism probably depends primarily on the strength of *political controls* available to those with a vested interest in the status quo. Contrast the situation of 18th-century France as described by Taylor, with the situation in England as described by Peter Mathias, *The First Industrial Nation* (New York: Charles Scribner's Sons, 1969).

58. See Christopher Hill, *Reformation to Industrial Revolution* part 4, in conjunction with the evidence in Mathias, *The First Industrial Nation,* chap. 3.

59. See Allan Silver, "Social and Ideological Bases of British Elite Reactions to Domestic Crisis in 1829–1832," *Politics and Society* 1:2(February 1971): 179–202; D. C. Moore, "Concession or Cure: The Sociological Premises of the First Reform Act," *The Historical Journal* 9:1 (1966): 39–59; and D. C. Moore, "The Other Face of Reform," *Victorian Studies* 5:1 (September 1961): 13–34.

60. *Social Origins,* p. 32.

61. In the final pages of his English case analysis, Moore *does* repeatedly mention that the state repressive apparatus was weak. But his emphasis is clearly on the idea that the English landed upper class did not need or desire repression. Moreover, on p. 444 of *Social Origins* he clearly implies that a strong repressive apparatus *could have been created* virtually from scratch if the English landed upper class had needed one. I find that unbelievable, and I am also skeptical about the idea that no repression was "needed." After all, just as aristocrats of the day tended to believe, industrialization and democratization *did destroy* the landed upper class *as a class* with a particular way of life and a hegemonic position in society.

62. On p. 438 of *Social Origins,* Moore suggests in the text and in a footnote that the notion of "authoritarian conservative" or "reactionary capitalist" development might be applicable to Italy, Spain, Poland, Hungary, Rumania, and "much of Latin America," as well as to Germany and Japan. To my knowledge, other researchers have not found it easy to thus extend Moore's analysis. I suspect that the reason is twofold: (1) Moore insists on connecting "reactionary capitalist" development to "fascist" outbursts that were probably world-historically specific occurrences; and (2) Moore assigns an unrealistically important political role to landed upper classes, and systematically underrates the degree to which bureaucratic and military elites are likely to act similarly (across times and countries) regardless of their class backgrounds.

63. Ibid.

64. Ibid., p. 439.

65. Ibid., pp. 438–39.

66. Ibid., pp. 437–38, italics added.

67. Ibid., p. 440.

68. Ellen Kay Trimberger, "A Theory of Elite Revolutions" (paper delivered at the 1970 Meetings of the American Sociological Association), pp. 8–10. A slightly revised version of this paper has been published in *Studies in Comparative International Development* 7:3 (Fall 1972): italics added.

69. For independent confirmation, see John Whitney Hall, *Japan: From Prehistory to Modern Times* (New York: Dell Publishing Company, 1970).

70. *Social Origins,* p. 440.

71. My remarks about the Prussian bureaucratic elite and the Reforms are based upon chaps. 7, 8, and 9 of Hans Rosenberg, *Bureaucracy, Aristocracy, and Autocracy* (Cambridge, Mass.: Harvard University Press, 1958); and upon chap. 13 of Hajo Holburn, *A History of Modern Germany, 1648–1840* (New York: Alfred A. Knopf, 1964).

72. See John R. Gillis, "Aristocracy and Bureaucracy in Nineteenth-Century Prussia," Past and Present, No. 41 (November 1968); 105–129; Theodore S. Hamerow, *Restoration, Revolution, Reaction* (Princeton: Princeton University Press, 1966), chap. 1; Theodore S. Hamerow, *The Social Foundations of German Unification, 1858–1871: Ideas and Institutions* (Princeton: Princeton University Press, 1969), chap. 5; and Alexander Gerschenkron, *Bread and Democracy in Germany* (Berkeley and Los Angeles: University of California Press, 1943).

73. Russian history between 1858 and 1914 shows certain parallels to revolution from above in Japan and Turkey, and there is evidence that the 19th-century Russian bureaucracy was significantly differentiated from the landed upper class. See Walter M. Pintner, "The Social Characteristics of the Early Nineteenth-Century Russian Bureaucracy," *Slavic Review* 29:3 (September 1970): 429–43.

74. *Social Origins,* pp. xii–xiii.

75. Ibid., p. 32.

76. Ibid., pp. 245–46.

77. Ibid., p. 214.

78. Ibid., p. 224, italics added.

79. These adjectives come from Robert A. Nisbet, who has done an extensive analysis and critique of intrasocietal theories of development from which I have learned much. See his *Social Change and History* (London: Oxford University Press, 1969).

80. Two scholars who do focus on the independent role of the state are Reinhard Bendix (see his *Nation-Building and Citizenship*) and Samuel Huntington (in *Political Order and Changing Societies).* Neither, however, seeks to explore systematically the interrelationship of state institutions and class structures. Huntington, especially, fails to take note of class constraints on political elites' freedom of action, even where such constraints blatantly exist.

81. Terence K. Hopkins and Immanuel Wallerstein, "The Comparative Study of National Societies," *Social Science Information* 6 (1967): 39.

82. Immanuel Wallerstein, *Capitalist Agriculture and the Origins of the European World-Economy in the Sixteenth Century* (forthcoming); and "Three Paths of National Development in the Sixteenth Century," *Studies in Comparative International Development.* Wallerstein calls the English state "strong," and implies by the logic of his analysis that the Prussian state should have been very weak.

83. *Social Origins,* pp. 413–14, italics added.

2

Wallerstein's world capitalist system: A theoretical and historical critique

The Modern World-System: Capitalist Agriculture and the Origins of the European World-Economy in the Sixteenth Century. By Immanuel Wallerstein. New York and London: Academic Press, 1974.

Immanuel Wallerstein's *The Modern World-System* aims to achieve a clean conceptual break with theories of "modernization" and thus provide a new theoretical paradigm to guide our investigations of the emergence and development of capitalism, industrialism, and national states. This splendid undertaking could hardly be more appropriately timed and aimed. For quite some time, modernization approaches have been subjected to telling critical attacks (e.g., Gusfield 1967; Frank 1966; Bendix 1967; Tipps 1973; Smith 1973; Tilly 1975, chap. 9). They have been called to task for reifying the nation-state as the sole unit of analysis, for assuming that all countries can potentially follow a single path (or parallel and converging paths) of evolutionary development from "tradition" to "modernity," and, concomitantly, for disregarding the world-historical development of transnational structures that constrain and prompt national or local developments along diverse as well as parallel paths. Moreover, modernization theorists have been criticized for the method of explanation they frequently employ: ahistorical ideal types of "tradition" versus "modernity" are elaborated and then applied to national cases; if the evidence seems to fit, one assumes that a particular historical instance is adequately explained; if not, one looks for the "chance" factors that account for its deviation.

In the opening pages of *The Modern World-System,* and in a related essay

I could not possibly have undertaken the challenging task of writing this review essay without the benefit of intellectual stimulation and thoughtful critical advice from many friends, students, and colleagues, including especially Michael Burawoy, Mounira Charrad, Daniel Chirot, Linda Frankel, Harriet Friedmann, Wally Goldfrank, Peter Gourevitch, Patrice Higonnet, George Homans, David Karen, Victor Perez-Diaz, Bill Skocpol, Dave Slaney, David Stark, Charles Stephen, Charles Tilly, Kay Trimberger, and Jonathan Zeitlin. However, none of these people is responsible for what I have finally decided to say here.

(also published in 1974) called "The Rise and Future Demise of the World Capitalist System," Wallerstein unequivocally defines his approach in direct opposition to these features of modernization theory. Thus in his book he will concentrate on explaining the structure and functioning of capitalism as a world economic system, viewing sovereign states as but "one kind of organizational structure among others within this single social system" (p. 7). Equally important, he intends to avoid the "intellectual dead-end of ahistorical model-building" (1974, p. 388) by grounding his theorizing in an analysis of the historically specific emergence and development of capitalism since the sixteenth century. He hopes thereby to demonstrate "that to be historically specific is not to fail to be analytically universal," that "the only road to nomothetic propositions is through the historically concrete" (1974, p. 391).

Given these very appealing and appropriate intentions of Wallerstein's theoretical program, not to mention the impressive scope of his reading in the works of historians, it is hardly surprising that *The Modern World-System* has met with an uncritically laudatory response from many sociologists. For example, Michael Hechter (1975) in his review of the book for *Contemporary Sociology* suggests that it provides a thoroughly plausible and internally consistent theoretical argument that needs only to be specified and operationalized to provide an adequate guide for fruitful research on development issues. But his assessment is too hasty and superficial. *The Modern World-System* is a theoretically ambitious work that deserves to be critically analyzed as such. And, as I shall attempt to show, Wallerstein's arguments are too misleading theoretically and historically to be accepted at face value. Because *The Modern World-System* does suffer from inadequacies of reasoning and evidence, there may be hypercritical reviews that will use the book's weaknesses as an excuse for dismissing out of hand any such world-historical or Marxist-oriented approach. With such an evaluation I have no sympathy. Like many other important pioneering works, Wallerstein's *Modern World-System* overreaches itself and falls short of its aims. It is therefore incumbent especially upon those of us who are sympathetic to its aims to subject this work to rigorous critical scrutiny. For the true contribution of *The Modern World-System* will lie, not in the proliferation of empirical research based uncritically upon it, but in the theoretical controversies and advances it can spark among its friends. In this spirit, let me begin the necessary process of critique in this review essay.

I

Despite his avowed desire to avoid "abstract model building," Wallerstein in fact deals with historical evidence primarily in terms of a preconceived model of the capitalist world economy. I shall, therefore, start by describing and discussing this model, before proceeding to consider its adequacy for explaining historical developments in early modern Europe.[1]

Wallerstein insists that any theory of social change must refer to a "social system" – that is, a "largely self-contained" entity whose developmental dynamics are "largely internal" (p. 347). For self-containment to obtain, he reasons, the entity in question must be based upon a complete economic division of labor. Leaving aside small-scale, isolated subsistence societies, there have been, he says, only two kinds of large-scale social systems: (1) empires, in which a functional economic division of labor, occupationally not geographically based, is subsumed under an overarching, tribute-collecting imperial state, and (2) world economies, in which there are multiple political sovereignties, no one of which can subsume and control the entire economic system. A world economy should be, in Wallerstein's view, more able than a world empire to experience sustained economic development precisely because economic actors have more freedom to maneuver and to appropriate and reinvest surpluses.

Such a world economy – of which capitalism from the sixteenth century to the present has been (according to Wallerstein) the only long-lasting historical instance – is based upon a geographically differentiated division of labor, featuring three main zones – core, semiperiphery, and periphery – tied together by world market trade in bulk commodities that are necessities for everyday consumption. Each major zone of the world economy has an economic structure based upon its particular mixture of economic activities (e.g., industry plus differentiated agriculture in the core; monoculture in the periphery) and its characteristic form of "labor control" (e.g., skilled wage labor and tenantry in the core; sharecropping in the semiperiphery; and slavery or "coerced cash-crop labor" in the periphery). The different zones are differentially rewarded by the world economy, with surplus flowing disproportionately to the core areas. Moreover, the economic structure of each zone supports a given sort of dominant class oriented toward the world market, as well as states of a certain strength (strongest in the core and weakest in the periphery) that operate in the interests of that class. Finally, according to Wallerstein, the differential strength of the multiple states within the world capitalist economy is crucial for maintaining the system as a whole, for the strong states reinforce and increase the differential flow of surplus to the core zone. This happens because strong states can provide "extra-economic" assistance to allow their capitalist classes to manipulate and enforce terms of trade in their favor on the world market.

II

Let us reflect for a moment upon this model as a whole. Historically, one of the most striking things about capitalism has been its inherent dynamism. From a world-historical perspective, we need to understand how and why capitalism emerged, has developed, and might one day pass from the scene. Wallerstein clearly appreciates the importance of these issues – yet he does not offer very many insights about them, either in *MWS* or in his "Rise and Demise" article (where he sketches an overview of four stages of world capitalist development from the sixteenth century to the present).

For one thing, Wallerstein's theory does not put him in a good position to explain the transition from feudalism to capitalism in Europe. The most obvious difficulty is the lack of any theoretical conception of the dynamics of feudalism, which is neither a "world empire" nor a "world economy" in Wallerstein's terms. To explain what he holds to be the demise of feudalism around 1450, Wallerstein (chap. 1) employs, first, an amalgam of historians' arguments about reasons for the crisis of feudalism (1300–1450) and, then, a series of teleological arguments about how the crisis "had to be solved" if "Europe" or "the system" were to survive. The emergence of the capitalist world system is presented as the solution. Thus in this one instance where Wallerstein actually discusses a supposed transition from one mode of production to another, he uses the language of system survival, even though such language is quite incongruous.

As for how world capitalism develops once it is established, although Wallerstein does assert repeatedly that the system is dynamic, he provides us with no theoretical explanation of why developmental breakthroughs occur. In the "Rise and Demise" article (1974), the momentous consequences of the technological innovations achieved in the Industrial Revolution are much discussed, but not a word is said about the causes of the Industrial Revolution. The only definite dynamics of Wallerstein's world capitalist system are market processes: commercial growth, worldwide recessions, and the spread of trade in necessities to new regions of the globe. Apparently the final demise of the system will come after the market has spread to cover the entire globe and transform all workers into wage laborers. But even the all-important dynamic of global expansion itself depends upon the occurrence of technological innovations – themselves unexplained.

In sharp contrast to his awkwardness and sketchiness in explaining dynamics, Wallerstein is very forceful on the subject of stability of the world capitalist system. In theory, as we have seen, once the system is established, everything reinforces everything else. And Wallerstein consistently employs not only system-maintenance arguments but also direct analogies between the structure of the world capitalist system and the typical structure of political empires (e.g., pp. 349–50) to convey a sense of the massive stability of the whole. For he believes that his model points to the essential structures of world capitalism – to patterns of division of labor and of relationships among states in different economic positions that have endured since the sixteenth century even though the system as a whole has expanded geographically and particular countries have changed positions within the system.

III

Taking our cue from his emphases, then, let us take a close critical look at the ideas about determinants of socioeconomic and political structures that are built into Wallerstein's model of the world capitalist system. We can most readily pinpoint the problematic points, I suggest, if we see that the model is based on a two-step reduction: first, a reduction of socioeconomic structure to determination by world market opportunities and technological production possibilities; and second, a reduction of state structures and policies to determination by dominant class interests.

The ways in which Wallerstein tries to make sense of the differences of economic structure among his three major zones of core, semiperiphery, and periphery lead him to make the first reduction. The crux of the differences is the "mode of labor control" "adopted" in each zone by the dominant classes oriented to the world market. In his theoretical passages addressed to this issue (see esp. chap.2, pp. 87–116), Wallerstein repeatedly implies that the dominant classes choose freely among alternative strategies of labor control by assessing rationally the best means for maximizing profits, given the geographical, demographic, technological, and labor-skill conditions in which they find themselves, and given the profitable possibilities they face for selling particular kinds of products on the world market. Now the curious thing here is that, despite the fact that Wallerstein seems to be placing a great deal of stress on the class structures of the major zones of world capitalism, actually (as far as I can see) he is explaining the fundamental economic dynamics of the system in terms of exactly the variables usually stressed by liberal economists, while ignoring the basic Marxist insight that the social relations of production and surplus appropriation are the sociological key to the functioning and development of any economic system. For this Marxist idea demands that one pay attention to institutionalized *relationships* between producing and surplus-appropriating classes and allow for the ever-present potential of collective resistance from below. Instead, Wallerstein treats "labor control" primarily as a market-optimizing strategy of the dominant class alone.

One major theoretical effect of his reliance on liberal economics is a nonexploitative picture of the process of income distribution within the world system. To be sure, he argues that the forces of the marketplace tend to maintain established differences of "occupational" structure among regions (p. 350). But notice the reason offered: "a capitalist world-economy essentially rewards accumulated capital, including human capital, at a higher rate than 'raw' labor power . . ." (p. 350). Would a liberal economist say anything different, since all that is being argued here is that regions with the scarcer factors of production are differentially rewarded by the market?

Yet, of course, Wallerstein does argue theoretically that the structure and functioning of the world capitalist economy are inherently exploitative. He does so by assigning the international hierarchy of dominating and dominated states (especially core vs. periphery) a crucial mediating role in exacerbating and sustaining overall inequalities in the system as a whole. Thus he writes, "Once we get a difference in the strength of the state-machineries, we get the operation of 'unequal exchange' which is enforced by strong states on weak ones, by core states on peripheral areas. Thus capitalism involves not only appropriation of surplus-value by an owner from a laborer, but an appropriation of surplus of the whole world-economy by core areas" (1974, p. 401).

But, then, how are degrees of state strength and kinds of state economic policies to be explained? Here we arrive at the second reduction built into Wallerstein's model. For in his theory, differences of state strength and policies among states located in different major zones of the world system are explained as the result of differences in regional rates of surplus appropriation and, above all, as the expressions of the different world market interests of the dominant classes within the national political arenas that happen to be located in each major zone (chap. 3, passim). Thus the core area ends up with strong states primarily because there are more plentiful surpluses to tax and because the dominant capitalist classes want state protection for industry and their control of international trade; on the other hand, the periphery ends up with weak or nonexistent states because it reaps less from world trade and because its dominant capitalist classes are interested in profiting from direct dealings with merchants from the core areas. In short, to explain differences in state strength, Wallerstein relies upon arguments about economic conditions and world market interests, largely ignoring other potentially important variables such as historically preexisting institutional patterns, threats of rebellion from below, and geopolitical pressures and constraints.

Given that the economic structure and functioning of the world system have (logically speaking) already been explained in market-technological rather than class terms, Wallerstein *must* make this second reduction, of politics to world market-oriented class interest, in order to be able to assert that the system will be exploitative, and stably so over the long run. For as he points out, if states were equally strong (or potentially equally strong across the major regions), "they would be in the position of blocking the effective operation of transnational economic entities whose locus [*sic*] were in another state. It would then follow that the world division of labor would be impeded, the world-economy decline, and eventually the world-system fall apart" (p. 355). Without a hierarchy of dominating and dominated states corresponding to the existing pattern of economic differentiation, there is no worldwide "unequal exchange" in this theory. Ironically, then, Wallerstein has managed to create a model that simultaneously gives a decisive role to international political domination (curiously enough for a theory that set out to deemphasize the nation-state!) and deprives politics of any independent efficacy, reducing it to the vulgar expression of market-class interests.

Well, so what? Do these theoretical peculiarities matter? Certainly some quite implausible assumptions have to be made to make the model internally consistent. Since everything is directly or indirectly an expression of capitalist class interests (under given technical conditions), we are forced to assume that these classes always get what they want, reshaping institutions and their relations to producing classes to suit their current world market opportunities. At the same time, we must assume that, although all of the variously situated dominant capitalist classes want and are able to maximize their world market trading advantages, nevertheless *only* the core-area capitalists want, need, and get the extra-economic assistance of strong states, while peripheral capitalists do not.

Still, the peculiarities and implausibilities would not matter very much if the model itself were genuinely useful for analyzing and explaining actual historical developments. But I believe that each of the two reductions in Wallerstein's model deprives him of crucial explanatory resources for understanding the patterns of history. Let me argue my case by examining in turn two major early modern European developments that Wallerstein himself stresses in *The Modern World-System:* (1) the resolution of the "crises of feudalism" into opposite socioeconomic structures in Eastern versus Western Europe; and (2) the emergence of monarchical absolutisms. Afterwards I shall draw some tentative conclusions about the overall validity of Wallerstein's model and about a possible alternative approach.

IV

One of the most striking developments in Europe during the "long sixteenth century" (1450–1640) was the divergence of economic patterns between northwestern Europe and Eastern Europe (including, e.g., Poland, Hungary, Livonia, and Germany east of the Elbe River). While in the West serfdom was virtually gone by 1600, and thereafter the commercialization of the social relations of agrarian production and the growth of industries were important trends, in the East the peasants had by 1600 become tied to the land so that labor and dues could be forcibly extracted from them by the landlords, and this so-called second serfdom was accompanied by the decline of towns and indigenous industries under bourgeois control. Moreover during the same general period East and West became more intensively linked through the Baltic trade, in which primary bulk goods, including especially grain, were exported from the East, which in turn imported manufactures, primarily from England and the Netherlands.

Clearly this pattern corresponds very nicely to Wallerstein's model of relations between core and periphery in the emergent capitalist world economy. This in itself is not really surprising, though, since Wallerstein's model, as he fully acknowledges, was originally inspired in part by the work of Marian Malowist, a historian who stresses the importance of the Baltic trade as a contributing cause of the Eastern versus Western divergence. Yet what was for the historian one contributing cause becomes for Wallerstein, given the dictates of his world capitalist system model, *the* theoretically significant explanation. Thus he argues, "The reason why these opposite reactions . . . occurred was because . . . the two areas became complementary parts of a more complex single system, the European world-economy, in which eastern Europe played the role of raw-materials producer for the industrializing west . . ." (p. 95). "The crucial considerations in the form of labor control adopted in eastern Europe were the opportunity of large profit if production were increased (because of the existence of a world market), plus the combination of a relative shortage of labor and a large amount of unused land" (p. 99).

To be really convincing, Wallerstein's explanation should meet two conditions. First, it should be validated (or at any rate not invalidated) by the timing, or sequence, of events; that is, if world trade opportunities really were the decisive cause of the "second serfdom," their availability should precede, or at least fully coincide with, the trends toward enserfment. But actually the process of enserfment was under way in virtually all areas by 1400 (Blum 1957, p. 820), and by "the end of the fifteenth century [i.e., 1500] . . .from the Elbe to the Volga, most of the peasantry were well on the way to becoming serfs" (Blum 1957, p. 821; see also Carsten 1954, chap. 8; Slicher Van Bath 1963, pp. 156–57), whereas Eastern grain exports to the West began expanding significantly around 1500 and achieved their most sudden and sizable growth only between 1550 and 1600 (Malowist 1958, pp. 27–29), *after* the foundations of the coerced labor system were fully established.

Second, and more important, Wallerstein's emphasis on trade opportunities (as well as technical production possibilities) ought to be able to stand critical scrutiny in the light of comparative historical evidence. However, an important article by Robert Brenner (1976) entitled "Agrarian Class Structure and Economic Development in Pre-industrial Europe" strongly suggests that Wallerstein is misguided. Brenner shows that markets cannot solely or primarily explain social-structural transformations or economic developments because, depending upon the preexisting institutional patterns of class relations, different classes may be in the best position to take advantage of available trade opportunities and thereby have their particular positions strengthened. Thus Brenner points out (1976, p. 53) that in parts of northwestern Germany in the 16th century peasants (rather than enserfing lords) took advantage of the new export opportunities "and they appear to have done so after a prolonged period of anti-landlord resistance." As for the Eastern lords, Brenner concludes (1976, p. 53), "No doubt, in this instance, the income from grain produced by serf-based agriculture and sold by export . . . enhanced the class power of the Eastern lords, helping them to sustain their seigneurial offensive. But the control of grain production (and thus the grain trade) secured through their successful enserfment of the peasantry was by no means assured by the mere fact of the emergence of the grain markets themselves." Rather, as even Malowist (Wallerstein's historical source) says (1958, p. 38), "trade developed in a form determined by locally prevalent social and economic circumstances and affected these in turn."

Brenner's carefully crafted comparative historical investigations suggest that to explain the divergences of socioeconomic developments in East versus West we must attend especially[2] to the *"historically specific* patterns of development of the contending agrarian classes and their relative strength in the different European societies: their relative levels of internal solidarity, their self-consciousness and organization, and their general political resources . . ." (1976, p. 52). Thus Brenner makes a case that Eastern peasants were more easily and thoroughly dominated by their landlords because, for various specific historical reasons, they enjoyed much less village community solidarity and local political autonomy than did Western European peasants. The Eastern peasants found it more difficult, especially over the long run, to resist the lords collectively. Consequently, when the Eastern lords attempted to impose coercive controls, initially under conditions of economic crisis and labor scarcity, they succeeded, whereas lords in the West had failed in the same attempt under similar conditions during the 1300s (see Hilton 1969).

Moreover, Brenner goes on to apply his explanatory approach to another issue relevant for Wallerstein's theory: the problem of why English feudal agriculture was transformed in early modern times into an agriculture based primarily on contract rents and wage labor, while French, as well as Eastern European, agriculture was not so transformed. The detailed argument (which I shall not reproduce here) suggests that Wallerstein's theoretical neglect of the independent significance of institutionalized patterns of class relationships deprives him of an important tool for actually explaining, rather than merely asserting, both the "rise of the gentry" and the occurrence of capitalist economic-technological breakthroughs in English agriculture. For, as Brenner argues (1976, p. 37), "[E]conomic development can only be fully understood as the outcome of the emergence of new class relations more favourable to new organizations of production, technical innovations, and increasing levels of productive investment. These new class relations were themselves the result of previous, relatively autonomous processes of class conflict."

V

If Wallerstein's world-market theory prevents him from adequately explaining patterns of economic development in early modern Europe, it leaves him even less able to make sense of the patterns of state development. This was, of course, the era of the initial emergence of absolute monarchies – kingly governments that tried, with varying degrees of success, to impose protobureaucratic administrative controls and coercive monopolies over large populations and territories. Wallerstein recounts the phenomena of absolutism (chap. 3) and tries to subsume them within his theory by invoking the category of the "strong state." According to the theory, let us recall, strong states necessarily grow up in the core zone of the world capitalist economy. Thus Wallerstein asserts, "In the sixteenth century, some monarchs achieved great strength. . . . Others failed. This is closely related . . . to the role of the area in the division of labor within the world-economy. The different roles led to different class structures which led to different politics" (p. 157). "In the core states there evolved relatively strong State systems, with an absolute monarch and a patrimonial State bureaucracy working primarily for this monarch. The venality of office and the development of standing armies based on mercenaries were the critical elements in the establishment of such a bureaucracy" (1972, p. 96). However, Wallerstein's attempt to equate the strong core state and absolute monarchy does not work. The historical evidence simply does not fit the overall pattern implied by the theory, for there were more and stronger absolutisms outside the core than in it.

Economically speaking, both the Netherlands and England were, according to Wallerstein's analysis, core countries. Were they also strong states? The "strong state" is defined theoretically by Wallerstein (p. 355) as strong "vis-à-vis other states within the world-economy including other core states, and strong vis-à-vis local political units within the boundaries of the state . . . also . . . strong vis-à-vis any particular social group within the state." Since the Dutch government was simply a federation of merchant oligarchies, Wallerstein does not even try to convince us that the Netherlands really was a strong state; instead he stresses the economic interdependence of England and the Netherlands and the transitional functions of Dutch economic primacy for the emerging world capitalist system (chap. 4, pp. 199 ff.). But he clearly wants us to believe that the English Tudor state was a strong core state (pp. 231–33) – even though (as he himself admits, pp. 234–35) the English monarchs had no large standing armies and no bureaucratic administration that penetrated the localities. In fact, the English monarchs could rule only through cooperation with locally powerful notables, the county-Parliamentary gentry and the London merchant oligarchy.

What about the true absolute monarchies of Europe, such as the Spanish, the French, and the Swedish? Wallerstein stresses the bureaucratic weight and military aggressiveness of the Spanish state whenever he is trying to account for European domination of the New World and when (chap. 4) he discusses the Hapsburg attempt at empire building within Europe. Then, suddenly, Spain drops out of the picture, even though her monarchy remained thoroughly absolutist and, arguably, just as internationally powerful as the English government throughout the entire historical period under consideration.[3] (Perhaps the English state was more effective in promoting certain protomercantilist policies, but if this alone were used as the index of "state strength," the entire argument would become circular – and, of course, Wallerstein's initial focus on "absolutism" would be belied.) As for France, the theoretically induced dilemma that

Wallerstein faces is how to explain why this country, situated only partly in the core zone, partly in the semiperiphery, actually developed a much stronger state than did either England or the Netherlands. To cope with this dilemma, an alternative ad hoc (and, of course, teleological) explanation of state strength is introduced: France "had to" develop a centralized, bureaucratic monarchy in order to hold together her differently oriented capitalist classes (chap. 5, pp. 263–69, 283 ff.). Similarly, when another, even more blatantly deviant case comes up – that of Sweden, with probably the most powerful and dynamic absolutism of the era (see Anderson 1974, part 1, chap. 7) – Wallerstein introduces still another ad hoc explanation:

The position of Sweden is worth brief attention, as the evolution of Sweden's state machinery approached the model of western Europe rather than that of the periphery, although it was economically very underdeveloped at this time. It was strong, not because its commerce and industry was [*sic*] strong . . .; it was paradoxically rather that its agriculture was weak, and its aristocrats wished to take hold of the profits of other lands for want of being able to create them on their own. . . . As a peripheral state with a weak bourgeoisie, . . . [Sweden] was an arena in which the political power of the aristocracy grew with the economic expansion of the sixteenth century. But the growth of wheat was hindered by the climatic downturn of the time which affected negatively in particular the Scandinavian countries. The nobility hence needed conquest and for that they needed a strong, not a weak, state. Once they had the strong state, they would be able in the seventeenth and eighteenth centuries to use mercantilism as a lever of industrial advance, and hence be spared the fate of Poland. [Pp. 312–13]

But with this final explanatory maneuver, Wallerstein thoroughly contradicts his original assertion that the strongest absolutisms should emerge in the core and certainly not in the periphery. For Sweden demonstrates (as does Prussia, after 1650) that a very strong state can be built on a peripheral agrarian base, and that, once built, it can reshape the economic future of the area in question.

Clearly, neither the differential appearance of absolutist states in early modern Europe nor their effects upon economic development are adequately accounted for by Wallerstein's world capitalist system theory. Better (though not unambiguous or flawless) treatments of patterns of state development are to be found in Anderson (1974) and Tilly (1975). These works suggest that, although no simple or monocausal explanation of state building is possible, two main sets of variables can go a long way toward accounting for the variations. First, internal class structures were important, not because economically dominant classes got automatically what they wanted, but because different patterns of class relationships and alliances – including relationships and alliances involving agrarian feudal classes – created different possibilities for monarchs to extract resources and encouraged them to use available resources in different ways. Second, transnational structures were important, too – including the networks of trade and economic interdependence to which Wallerstein points. But not only these: for an equally if not more important transnational structure was constituted by the system of politico-military interactions among emerging European states. This "European states system" set up pressures, constraints, and opportunities, varying according to the specific geopolitical situation of each country, which helped determine the kinds, strengths, and policies (including economically relevant policies) of the states that developed (or did not develop) in various times and places. Here is a kind of "world system" that Wallerstein seems inclined to emphasize when he contrasts feudal Europe with China in chapter 1; moreover, it resonates with his theoretical stress on "multiple sovereignty" as a defining feature of capitalism. But, unfortunately, the independent reality and effects of a system of militarily competing states cannot be comprehended by a theory that reduces politics to the expression of market situation and class interests; so Wallerstein neglects this explanatory resource as well.

In early modern Europe, incessant military competition among monarchies was an important spur to, and arbiter of, strong state building, for the main use of enlarged royal tax or loan revenues was the building up of standing armies and their deployment in wars. Not surprisingly, those monarchies that found it both necessary and possible to extract the resources (by various means) to build the largest land armies were also the ones that developed the strongest and most bureaucratic administrative machineries (needed to tax the peasants and/or control commerce and/or absorb upper-class subjects). But these were not the countries that found themselves during this period at the center of the nascent capitalist commercial economy. The Netherlands, as Wallerstein himself points out, was a small country whose survival depended upon military balances among her powerful neighbors. And England could remain somewhat aloof from the continental military system (given the nature of the military and naval technology of the times) because of her island situation. Because of their prior political histories and relatively sheltered geopolitical circumstances, England and the Netherlands happened during this period to have governments uniquely responsive to commercial-capitalist interests. These were not bureaucratic governments (even by the standards of the time) and for that very reason they were not so strong (esp. the monarchy over against the dominant classes) as to be able to stifle commercial development or protect the lower classes (as the French monarchy did its peasantry) against encroachments upon their position or very existence by capitalist landlords or bourgeoisies.

Indeed, it was probably one necessary condition (as was England's increasing centrality in world trade) for continuing capitalist development in early modern Europe that England's would-be absolutisms did not, in the final analysis, consolidate themselves. Because they did not, and because England's geopolitical situation allowed her to get along without a military absolutism, agrarian commercialization – which must itself be explained by reference to developments over time of class structure and conflict (see Brenner 1976) – could proceed unhindered, and eventually facilitate the Industrial Revolution. Then, once capitalist relations of production and accumulation were firmly established in England, the dynamics of the European states system ensured that capitalist relations would spread both across Europe and over the entire globe through state initiatives by competing powers and through military conquests, as well as through market expansion.

Interestingly enough, in his detailed historical discussion of England, Wallerstein himself makes points about her geopolitical situation and state structure similar to the ones I have made here. Indeed, the rich historical chapters of *The Modern World-System* (e.g., chaps. 4 and 5) provide many pointers for someone interested in developing new hypotheses about relationships among various dimensions of state strength and processes of capitalist development. The implicit hypotheses do not, however, square very well with Wallerstein's basic model of the world capitalist system. For, if the strongest states are not always in the core and if, in fact, equally strong or stronger states can grow up in the periphery (not to mention the semiperiphery), then according to Wallerstein's own logic (pp. 354–55) the economic division of labor cannot be presumed likely to hold together over time as a "system" and the differential flow of surpluses to the core is likely to be disrupted. Empirically speaking, these disruptive possibilities seem especially likely in later stages of world capitalist development, when strong, noncore states, perhaps created through revolutions from above or below, may be able to initiate rapid industrialization or other programs of economic development. Perhaps we still sense that Wallerstein's vision of an enduring, exploitative division of labor is correct, but in that case the theoretical reasons why it is correct must be found elsewhere than in the market economics and the economic-reductionist political sociology of Wallerstein's own model of the world capitalist system.

Without pretending to offer a fully worked out alternative paradigm, I suggest that, instead of exclusively pursuing Wallerstein's world system approach, we should investigate the world-historical emergence and development of capitalism in terms of hypotheses about variations in both (1) institutionalized class relations of production and exchange, and (2) patterns of state structures and interstate relationships, without simply reducing the latter to the former. To be sure, markets and patterns of trade are bound to be part of the picture, but it seems unlikely that they can be understood in their origin, functioning, or effects except with reference to changes in class and political structures. The alternative picture of world capitalism that is likely to emerge from historical analyses pursued along these lines will probably pertain to intersecting structures (e.g., class structures, trade networks, state structures, and geopolitical systems) involving varying and autonomous logics and different, though overlapping, historical times, rather than a single, all-encompassing system that comes into being in one stage and then remains constant in its essential patterns until capitalism as a whole meets its demise. But this is only meant to be suggestive, not definitive of a true alternative to Wallerstein. Others may prefer to retain his idea of a worldwide economic division of labor and seek to explicate it theoretically and ground it historically in new ways.

Finally, aside from this substantive critique of Wallerstein's approach, two methodological criticisms need to be made. The first has to do with the way Wallerstein handles historical evidence in relation to his theory-building enterprise. In many of the arguments cited in this essay, we have witnessed the major method of argumentation to which Wallerstein resorts: the teleological assertion. Repeatedly he argues that things at a certain time and place had to be a certain way in order to bring about later states or developments that accord (or seem to accord) with what his system model of the world capitalist economy requires or predicts. If the actual causal patterns suggested by historical accounts or comparative-historical analyses happen to correspond with the a posteriori reasoning, Wallerstein considers them to be adequately explained in terms of his model, which is, in turn, held to be supported historically. But if obvious pieces of historical evidence or typically asserted causal patterns do not fit, either they are not mentioned, or (more frequently) they are discussed, perhaps at length, only to be explained in ad hoc ways and/or treated as "accidental" in relation to the supposedly more fundamental connections emphasized by the world-system theory.[4] Frankly, I find this aspect of Wallerstein's approach very disturbing because it has the effect of creating an impenetrable abyss between historical findings and social science theorizing. For, through his a posteriori style of argument, deviant historical cases do not force one to modify or replace one's theory, while even a very inappropriate model can be illustrated historically without being put to the rigorous test of making real sense of actual patterns and causal processes in history. This has been exactly the methodological shortcoming of modernization theories, and it needs badly to be overcome in any new paradigm for development studies!

Which brings me to my second and final methodological point. At the beginning of this review essay I pointed out that Wallerstein hoped to overcome the worst faults of modernization theories by breaking with their overemphasis on national states and their tendency toward ahistorical model building. Ironically, though, he himself ends up reproducing the old difficulties in new ways. Thus strong states and inter*national* political domination assume crucial roles in his theory – though, just like the developmentalists, he reduces politics to economic conditions and to the expression of the will of the dominant groups within each national arena! Moreover, as we have just seen, Wallerstein creates an opposition between a formalistic theoretical model of universal reference, on the one hand, and the particularities and "accidents" of history, on the other hand – an opposition that uncannily resembles the relationship between theory and history in the ideal type method of the modernization approach.

How could these things happen, given Wallerstein's original intentions? The answer, I suggest, is the "mirror image" trap that plagues any attempt to create a new paradigm through direct, polemic opposition to an old one. Social science may, as is often said, grow through polemics. But it can also stagnate through them, if innovators uncritically carry over outmoded theoretical categories (e.g., "system") and if they define new ones mainly by searching for the seemingly direct opposite of the old ones (e.g., "world system" vs. "national system"). For what seems like a direct opposite may rest on similar assumptions, or may lead one (through the attempt to work with an artificial, too extreme opposition) around full circle to the thing originally opposed. The better way to proceed is to ask what new units of analysis – probably not only one, but several, perhaps changing with historical points of reference – can allow one to cut into the evidence in new ways in order to investigate exactly the problems or relationships that the older approaches have neglected.

This review essay has obviously been a very critical one. In it I have grappled with a monumental and difficult book, trying to pinpoint and critically examine the theoretical essentials of its argument. No one should suppose, however, that I am suggesting that we dismiss or ignore Wallerstein's on-going study of the world capitalist system (for this is just the first of four projected volumes). On the contrary, I can think of no intellectual project in the social sciences that is of greater interest and importance. Even if Wallerstein has so far given imperfect answers about the historical development of capitalism, still he has had the unparalleled boldness of vision to raise all the important issues. Even the shortcomings of his effort, therefore, can be far more fruitful for the social sciences than many minute successes by others who attempt much less. No book could have been more deserving of the Sorokin Award than *The Modern World-System* – and no book is more worthy of continued attention and debate.

NOTES

1. This essay does not pretend to present an adequate overview of *The Modern World-System*. A good sense of the scope and richness of the work is conveyed in the reviews by Hechter (1975), Lenzer (1974), and Thomas (1975).
2. Differences of political history and of the relative strength of towns have also to be taken into consideration in order to explain the socioeconomic divergences of East and West. Wallerstein mentions these matters briefly (pp. 97–98); they are discussed at much greater length in Blum (1957). But Brenner (1976, pp. 54–56) raises some important caveats about the influence of towns on the course of agrarian class struggles. His observations suggest that noting the relative strength of towns is no substitute for direct analysis of agrarian class relations.
3. Apparently Wallerstein believes that he need not treat Spain and England as comparable in the same analytic terms. Instead he builds a series of contrasts between Spain as a would-be empire and England as a would-be national state. These arguments are fascinating and ring true in many ways. But they suffer from two difficulties: First, they are usually teleological (and thus credible only if we grant that political rulers were extraordinarily farsighted about the emergence of a world economy, which the Spanish supposedly were trying to subsume and control, while the English supposedly were trying to become a core state). Second, their theoretical status is unclear because Wallerstein has given us no categories for analyzing the politics of European

feudalism; thus, we do not know (except through ad hoc comments) the basis for the "imperial" aspirations of European aristocracies.

4. Why does Wallerstein resort to this a posteriori style of argument? In his "Introduction" he argues that astronomers use this mode of argument to explain the evolution of the universe —a unique system supposedly like the world capitalist system (pp. 7– 8). But, as Friedmann (1976) points out in a brilliant critique of Wallerstein, astronomers do not have historical evidence (not much, anyway) to test their hypotheses, whereas social scientists do. Yet I suggest that the very content of Wallerstein's theory makes it awkward for him to use historical evidence effectively. For historians stress chronologically ordered causal processes, while Wallerstein's world market approach prompts him to stress synchronic interdependencies (see 1974, p. 403) and anticipatory acts on the part of profit-maximizing capitalists and "entrepreneur-like" (p. 60) nation-states.

REFERENCES

Anderson, Perry. 1974. *Lineages of the Absolutist State*. London: New Left.

Bendix, Reinhard. 1967. "Tradition and Modernity Reconsidered." *Comparative Studies in Society and History* 9 (June): 292–346.

Blum, Jerome. 1957. "The Rise of Serfdom in Eastern Europe." *American Historical Review* 62 (July): 807–36.

Brenner, Robert. 1976. "Agrarian Class Structure and Economic Development in Preindustrial Europe." *Past and Present* 70 (February): 30–75.

Carsten, F. L. 1954. *The Origins of Prussia*. London: Oxford University Press.

Frank, André Gunder. 1966. "Sociology of Development and Underdevelopment of Sociology." *Catalyst* 2 (Summer): 20–73.

Friedmann, Harriet. 1976. "Approaches to the Conceptualization of a World System." Unpublished manuscript, Department of Sociology, Harvard University.

Gusfield, Joseph R. 1967. "Tradition and Modernity: Misplaced Polarities in the Study of Social Change." *American Journal of Sociology* 72 (January): 351–62.

Hechter, Michael. 1975. Review Essay on *The Modern World-System. Contemporary Sociology* 4 (May): 217–22.

Hilton, R. H. 1969. *The Decline of Serfdom in Medieval England*. New York: St. Martin's.

Lenzer, Gertrud. 1974. Review of *The Modern World-System. New York Times Book Review* (December 29), pp. 17–18.

Malowist, Marian. 1958. "Poland, Russia and Western Trade in the 15th and 16th Centuries." *Past and Present* 13 (April): 26–39.

Slicher Van Bath, B. H. 1963. *The Agrarian History of Western Europe, A.D. 500– 1850*. London: Arnold.

Smith, Anthony D. 1973. *The Concept of Social Change*. London and Boston: Routledge & Kegan Paul.

Thomas, Keith. 1975. "Jumbo History." *New York Review of Books* (April 17), pp. 26–28.

Tilly, Charles, ed. 1975. *The Formation of National States in Western Europe*. Princeton, N.J.: Princeton University Press.

Tipps, Dean C. 1973. "Modernization Theory and the Comparative Study of Societies: A Critical Perspective." *Comparative Studies in Society and History* 15 (March): 199–226.

Wallerstein, Immanuel. 1972. "Three Paths of National Development in Sixteenth-Century Europe." *Studies in Comparative International Development* 7 (Summer): 95–101.

———. 1974. "The Rise and Future Demise of the World Capitalist System: Concepts for Comparative Analysis." *Comparative Studies in Society and History* 16 (September): 387–415.

3

The uses of comparative history
in macrosocial inquiry

THEDA SKOCPOL AND MARGARET SOMERS

Comparative history is not new. As long as people have investigated social life, there has been recurrent fascination with juxtaposing historical patterns from two or more times or places. Part of the appeal comes from the general usefulness of looking at historical trajectories in order to study social change. Indeed, practitioners of comparative history from Alexis de Tocqueville and Max Weber to Marc Bloch, Reinhard Bendix, and Barrington Moore, Jr., have typically been concerned with understanding societal dynamics and epochal transformations of cultures and social structures. Attention to historical sequences is indispensable to such understanding. Obviously, though, not all investigations of social change use explicit juxtapositions of distinct histories. We may wonder, therefore: What motivates the use of comparisons as opposed to focussing on single historical trajectories? What purposes are pursued – and how – through the specific modalities of *comparative* history?

Certain areas of scholarly endeavor in contemporary social science have given rise to methodological reflection even more sophisticated than the substantive applications of the methods in question, but this has certainly not been the case for comparative history. Despite the steady application of variants of this approach to macrosocial topics such as revolutions, religious evolution, political development, economic "modernization," patterns of collective violence, and the rise and fall of empires, there have been remarkably few efforts to explore the methodological aspects of comparative history as such in any systematic fashion.[1] What is more, the most notable recent discussions by Sewell, Lijphart, and Smelser have all mistakenly tried to collapse distinct types of comparative

An earlier version of this paper was presented at the Session on "Methods of Historical Sociology" at the Annual Meeting of the American Sociological Association, Boston, Massachusetts, August 1979. Thanks go to Bill Skocpol for helping us create the figures in the paper. We are also indebted for comments to Gary Hamilton, Michael Hechter, Lynn A. Hunt, Bruce Johnson, Barbara Laslett, Dietrich Rueschemeyer, and Gilbert Shapiro. The insights of their comments frequently outran our ability to make use of them in moderate revisions; consequently we alone are responsible for the arguments presented here.

history into a single methodological logic.[2] This logic is seen as analogous in all important respects to the mode of hypothesis-testing through multivariate analysis that characterizes those areas of the social sciences where statistical or experimental research designs prevail.[3]

Notwithstanding such attempts at homogenization, there are, in fact, at least three distinct logics-in-use of comparative history. One of them, which we shall label comparative history as *macro-causal analysis,* actually does resemble multivariate hypothesis-testing. But in addition there are two other major types: comparative history as the *parallel demonstration of theory;* and comparative history as the *contrast of contexts.* Each of the three major types of comparative history assigns a distinctive purpose to the juxtaposition of historical cases. Concomitantly, each has its own requisites of case selection, its own patterns of presentation of arguments, and – perhaps most important – its own strengths and limitations as a tool of research in macrosocial inquiry.

The three major logics have enough individual integrity that prototypical recent works of comparative history can be identified as *primarily* embodying one logic or another.[4] We propose to introduce the major types and reflect upon their characteristics by using as our initial examples comparative-historical works that rely primarily upon a single logic. In order to underline that each major methodological logic is compatible with disparate theoretical perspectives and subject matters, we shall use several different studies, varying in these respects, to exemplify each major type of comparative history. As we proceed the reader should bear in mind that in no case will we present full methodological dissections of the works we use as illustrations. For example, many crucial issues about the role of theories and concepts in relation to historical evidence will necessarily be skirted. Our purpose here is strictly to discuss the uses in macrosocial research of comparisons across historical trajectories, and the ways in which such uses influence research designs and the presentation of arguments in scholarly publications.

COMPARATIVE HISTORY AS THE PARALLEL DEMONSTRATION OF THEORY

In this first type of comparative history, the reason for juxtaposing case histories is to persuade the reader that a given, explicitly delineated hypothesis or theory can repeatedly demonstrate its fruitfulness – its ability convincingly to order the evidence – when applied to a series of relevant historical trajectories.

Despite considerable differences of subject-matter and theoretical approach, both S. N. Eisenstadt's *The Political Systems of Empires* and Jeffery M. Paige's *Agrarian Revolution* use comparative history in this way.[5] These books intend above all to convince their readers of the validity of certain theoretical arguments: a structure-functionalist theory of the emergence, persistence, and decline of "centralized historical bureaucratic empires" in the case of Eisenstadt's

Political Systems; an economic-determinist theory of rural class relations and the potential political behavior of cultivating and noncultivating classes in the case of Paige's *Agrarian Revolution.* The primary mode of demonstrating the theory is something other than comparative history in both books. Eisenstadt relies chiefly upon conceptual elaboration and deduction from structure-functionalist premises; Paige spends the first third of *Agrarian Revolution* presenting a logically elegant theoretical model of four types of rural class conflict and a statistical demonstration of its fruitfulness when applied to cross-sectional data on 135 agricultural export sectors in 70 underdeveloped countries. Nevertheless, in both Eisenstadt's and Paige's books, comparative history serves as an ancillary mode of theoretical demonstration. Historical instances are juxtaposed to demonstrate that the theoretical arguments apply convincingly to multiple cases that ought to fit if the theory in question is indeed valid. Cases are selected to cover all possibilities, or to represent a range of sub-types or points on continua. The point of the comparison is to assert a similarity among the cases – similarity, that is, in terms of the common applicability of the overall theoretical arguments that Eisenstadt and Paige are respectively presenting.

The last two-thirds of Jeffery Paige's *Agrarian Revolution* is devoted to in-depth analyses of agrarian class relations and politics in three third-world countries: Peru, Angola, and Vietnam. The broad applicability of Paige's theory is sweepingly demonstrated in this exploration of case histories from Latin America, Africa, and Asia. More interesting still, the three countries Paige discusses serve to illustrate concretely most of the major sub-parts of his overall model of rural class conflict: Peru provides examples of agrarian revolts emerging from commercial haciendas and of reform labor movements on plantations; Angola illustrates the connection of a nationalist revolutionary movement to migratory labor estates; and Vietnam shows to Paige's satisfaction that socialist revolution emerges from a sharecropping agricultural system. Taken together, therefore, Paige's case histories not only repeatedly demonstrate the applicability of his theory, they also enrich his presentation of the alternative possible forms of sociopolitical conflict that the theory is meant to predict and explain.

In *The Political Systems of Empires,* S. N. Eisenstadt repeatedly juxtaposes slices of very diverse historical cases: the ancient empires of Egypt, Babylon, the Incas and the Aztecs; the Chinese Empire; the Persian empires; the Roman and Hellenic empires; the Byzantine empires; certain Hindu states; the Arab caliphate, Arab Moslem states and the Ottoman empire; and various European states and overseas empires. Rhetorically Eisenstadt asks: "Are we justified in grouping these various historically and geographically separate and distinct, societies under one heading, and claiming that they constitute or belong to one type?" "To some extent," Eisenstadt answers, "this whole work will continuously have to substantiate this claim."[6] Indeed, as *Political Systems* proceeds, Eisenstadt alternates back and forth between laying out his theoretical argument and illustrating each part's parallel applicability to aspects of case histories selected from the range of empires included in his type "centralized historical bureaucratic empires" as a whole.[7] It is characteristic of all works of Parallel comparative history to elaborate theoretical models and hypotheses *before* turning to historical case illustrations. Yet whereas Paige does all of his theorizing before discussing the case histories, Eisenstadt develops his theory in stages and divides historical cases into bits and pieces relevant to each theoretical aspect as he presents it. Much more apparently than in Paige's book, therefore, the historical cases in *Political Systems* function strictly to substantiate the completeness of coverage and the consistent applicability of Eisenstadt's theoretical approach.[8]

COMPARATIVE HISTORY AS THE CONTRAST OF CONTEXTS

A second major type of comparative history pursues through the juxtaposition of cases an almost exactly opposite objective from that of Parallel comparative history. The Parallel comparativists seek above all to demonstrate that a theory similarly holds good from case to case; for them differences among the cases are primarily contextual particularities against which to highlight the generality of the processes with which their theories are basically concerned. But scholars such as Clifford Geertz in *Islam Observed,* James Lang in *Conquest and Commerce,* and Reinhard Bendix in *Nation-Building and Citizenship* and *Kings or People* make use of comparative history to bring out the unique features of each particular case included in their discussions, and to show how these unique features affect the working-out of putatively general social processes.[9] Above all, contrasts are drawn between or among individual cases. Usually such contrasts are developed with the aid of references to broad themes or orienting questions or ideal-type concepts. Themes and questions may serve as frameworks for pointing out differences between or among cases. Ideal types may be used as sensitizing devices – benchmarks against which to establish the particular features of each case. Themes, questions, or ideal types may be posed explicitly at the start; or they may be allowed to "emerge" as the historical discussions proceed. Whereas explicit theorizing is characteristic of the Parallel type of comparative history, what matters more in the Contrast-oriented type is that the historical integrity of each case as a whole is carefully respected. For much of the thrust of this variant of comparative history is to suggest that particular nations, empires, civilizations, or religions constitute relatively irreducible wholes, each a complex and unique sociohistorical configuration in its own right.

Books based upon straightforward paired comparisons nicely illustrate the basic essence of Contrast-oriented comparative history. Clifford Geertz's lovely *Islam Observed* is, as its subtitle tells us, about "religious development in Morocco and Indonesia."[10] Geertz wonders what happens in the "modernizing" countries when "established connections between particular varieties of faith and the cluster of images and institutions which have classically nourished them are for certain people in certain circumstances coming unstuck."[11] General answers Geertz finds "not very enlightening" and so he turns to comparative (anthropological) history hoping "to stumble upon general truths while sorting through special cases."[12] In a first chapter tellingly entitled "Two Countries, Two Cultures," Geertz informs us why he finds it fruitful to compare Indonesia and Morocco:

> Their most obvious likeness is . . . their religious affiliation; but it is also, culturally speaking at least, their most obvious unlikeness. They stand at the eastern and western extremities of the narrow band of classical Islamic civilization which, rising in Arabia, reached out along the midline of the Old World to connect them, and, so located, they have participated in the history of that civilization in quite different ways, to quite different degrees, and with quite different results. They both incline toward Mecca, but, the antipodes of the Muslim world, they bow in different directions.[13]

For Geertz, therefore, Indonesia and Morocco are so promising to compare precisely because, through the sharp contrast they offer within Islam, "they form a kind of commentary on one another's character."[14] As Geertz's choice of cases suggests, the task of the Contrast-oriented comparative historian is facilitated when maximally different cases within given bounds are chosen for comparison. Parallel comparative historians seek broad coverage in their selection of cases; Contrast-oriented comparativists may seek this too, but clear-cut differences between or among cases are more important.

James Lang in *Conquest and Commerce* is less explicit than Geertz in justifying the historical comparison he chooses to make, yet in this work as well two cases offer through systematic contrasts a commentary on each other's uniquenesses.[15] Lang is interested in exploring the dissimilar societies that Europeans of different national origins built in the New World. To understand the factors that shaped and perpetuated key differences – from the establishment of colonial empires through to their dismantling by American independence movements – Lang chooses to juxtapose the histories of "Spain and England in the Americas." (Notice that the choice is *not* England and France, or France and Spain, but instead the pair that maximizes the contrast between bureaucratic and commercial contexts.) Lang asks a series of common analytic questions about the historical experiences of English and Spanish America. Indeed, for a reader inspired by the urge to formulate potentially generalizable causal hypotheses, there are many possibilities implicit in Lang's analytic questions. But Lang himself does not pursue these possibilities. For him it is enough to let the questions "reveal dramatically different answers for the two colonial situations."[16]

To see the rationale behind this concern with contrasts that characterizes practitioners of our second major type of comparative history, we can do no better than to turn to Reinhard Bendix. No contemporary scholar has done more to explicate, as well as to apply, the logic of this variant of comparative history.

As Bendix put it in an article meant to introduce his newest book, *Kings or People:*

By means of comparative analysis I want to preserve a sense of historical particularity as far as I can, while still comparing different countries. Rather than aim at broader generalizations and lose that sense, I ask the same or at least similar questions of divergent materials and so leave room for divergent answers. I want to make more transparent the divergence among structures of authority and among the ways in which societies have responded to the challenges implicit in the civilizational accomplishments of other countries.[17]

Bendix's stress here upon making divergences "more transparent" echoes a related argument he made in the Introduction to *Nation-Building and Citizenship:*

Comparative sociological studies . . . increase the "visibility" of one structure by contrasting it with another. Thus, European feudalism can be more sharply defined by comparison, say, with Japanese feudalism, the significance of the Church in Western civilization can be seen more clearly by contrast with civilizations in which a comparable clerical organization did not develop.[18]

Both of Reinhard Bendix's major comparative studies of societal patterns of authority, *Nation-Building and Citizenship* and *Kings or People,* practice the variant of comparative history that he advocates.[19] In each work, general "issues" and "themes" are set out at the beginning (of the book as a whole and at the beginning of each major section). Although to the dissenting eyes of (say) a Marxist or a capitalist world-system theorist, such introductory statements look very much like a full-fledged theory of political development (synthesized from Tocqueville, Hintze, and Weber), Bendix does not present his ideas as an explanation to be tested or applied. Rather he sees them as either "sociological universals" or middle-range ideal types meant to establish a frame of reference for the historical case accounts and comparisons between and among them. In turn, the comparisons reveal the particularities of the cases. In *Nation-Building,* forms of "political modernization" in Western Europe are contrasted to analogous changes (or their absence) in Russia, Japan, and India. And in *Kings or People,* England, France, Imperial Germany and Prussia, Russia, and Japan are discussed in depth and comparatively to show that, although these countries have all experienced epochal transformations in patterns of political legitimation, "[a]uthority in the name of the people has proved as *varied* in practice as the authority of kings" (emphasis added).[20]

Bendix cogently sums up the ambitions – and self-imposed limitations – of the Contrast-oriented type of comparative history:

Comparative analysis should sharpen our understanding of the contexts in which more detailed causal inferences can be drawn. Without a knowledge of contexts, causal inference may pretend to a level of generality to which it is not entitled. On the other hand, comparative studies should not attempt to replace causal analysis, because they can only deal with a few cases and cannot easily isolate the variables (as causal analysis must).[21]

In short, Contrast-oriented comparativists aim to place historical limits on overly generalized theories, but they do *not* aspire to generate new explanatory generalizations through comparative historical analysis.

COMPARATIVE HISTORY AS MACRO-CAUSAL ANALYSIS

Notwithstanding Bendix's strictures, a third group of scholars in fact uses comparative history primarily for the purpose of making causal inferences about macro-level structures and processes. Included here are Barrington Moore, Jr., in *Social Origins of Dictatorship and Democracy;* Theda Skocpol in *States and Social Revolutions;* Frances V. Moulder in *Japan, China and the Modern World Economy;* Robert Brenner in "Agrarian Class Structure and Economic Development in Pre-Industrial Europe"; and Gary G. Hamilton in "Chinese Consumption of Foreign Commodities: A Comparative Perspective."[22]

Barrington Moore, Jr., the dean of contemporary practitioners of Macro-analytic comparative history, provides a rationale for this approach in the Preface to *Social Origins:*

> In the effort to understand the history of a specific country a comparative perspective can lead to asking very useful and sometimes new questions. . . . Comparisons can serve as a rough negative check on accepted historical explanations. *And a comparative approach may lead to new historical generalizations.* In practice these features constitute a single intellectual process and make such a study more than a disparate collection of interesting cases. For example, after noticing that Indian peasants have suffered in a material way just about as much as Chinese peasants during the nineteenth and twentieth centuries without generating a massive revolutionary movement, *one begins to wonder about traditional explanations of what took place in both societies and becomes alert to factors affecting peasant outbreaks in other countries, in the hope of discerning general causes.* Or after learning about the disastrous consequences for democracy of a coalition between agrarian and industrial elites in nineteenth- and early twentieth-century Germany, the much discussed marriage of iron and rye – one wonders why a similar marriage between iron and cotton did not prevent the coming of the Civil War in the United States; *and so one has taken a step toward specifying configurations favorable and unfavorable to the establishment of modern Western democracy* (emphases added).[23]

One notices in Moore's Preface to *Social Origins* much the same suspicion of overly generalized theories that characterizes the work of Reinhard Bendix. As Moore puts it, "too strong a devotion to theory always carries the danger that one may overemphasize the facts that fit a theory beyond their importance in the history of individual countries."[24] "That comparative analysis is no substitute for detailed investigation of specific cases is obvious," Moore declares.[25] Yet it is equally apparent that Moore cares much more than Bendix about using historical comparisons to test the validity of existing theoretical hypotheses and to develop new causal generalizations to replace invalidated ones. The flavor of the intellectual operation involved is effectively conveyed in the above quote. Rather than exploring and contrasting whole histories in terms of pre-given themes, as the Contrast-oriented comparativists do, Macro-analysts like Moore tend to move back and forth between alternative explanatory hypotheses and comparisons of relevant aspects of the histories of two or more cases. As Moore notes, Macro-analysts thus try to specify "configurations favorable and unfavorable" to particular outcomes they are trying to explain.

The logic involved in the use of comparative history for Macro-causal analysis resembles that of statistical analysis, which manipulates groups of cases to control sources of variation in order to make causal inferences when quantitative data are available about a large number of cases. This third variant of comparative history is, indeed, a kind of multivariate analysis to which scholars turn in order to validate causal statements about macro-phenomena for which, inherently, there are too many variables and not enough cases. Macro-analytic comparative historians proceed by selecting or referring to aspects of historical cases in order to set up approximations to controlled comparisons. Always this is done in relation to particular explanatory problems and (one or more) hypotheses about likely causes.

Logically speaking, Macro-analysts proceed according to one of two basic analytic designs, or a combination of these. On the one hand, Macro-analysts can try to establish that several cases having in common the phenomenon to be explained also have in common the hypothesized causal factors, although the cases vary in other ways that might have seemed causally relevant. This approach was once labelled by John Stuart Mill the "Method of Agreement."[26] On the other hand, Macro-analysts can contrast cases in which the phenomenon to be explained and the hypothesized causes are present to other ("negative") cases in which the phenomenon and the causes are both absent, although they are as similar as possible to the "positive" cases in other respects. This procedure Mill called the "Method of Difference."[27] Taken alone, this second approach is more powerful for establishing valid causal associations than is the "Method of Agreement." Sometimes, however, it is possible to combine the two methods by using at once several positive cases along with suitable negative cases as contrasts.

A monumental work of comparative history, Barrington Moore's *Social Origins of Dictatorship and Democracy* primarily uses Mill's Method of Agreement, yet it also argues at times along the lines of the Method of Difference. *Social Origins* identifies three alternative political routes to the modern world: (1) through "bourgeois revolution" to liberal democracy; (2) through "revolution from above" to fascism, and (3) through "peasant revolution" to communism. With the aid of causal variables referring to strengths of bourgeoisies in relation to landlords, to modes of agricultural commercialization, and to types of peasant communities and peasant/landlord relations, Moore seeks to explain why specified sets of major countries have travelled one route rather than the others.[28] *Within* each of his routes, Moore primarily argues along the lines of the Method of Agreement. Each route has two or three nations about

THE METHOD OF AGREEMENT

Case 1	Case 2	Case n
a b c x	d e f x	g h i x
y	y	y

} overall differences

} crucial similarity

THE METHOD OF DIFFERENCE

Positive cases(s)	Negative case(s)
a b c x	a b c not x
y	not y

} overall similarities

} crucial difference

Key:
x = causal variable
y = phenomenon to be explained

Figure 3.1. Two designs for macro-analytic comparative history (from John Stuart Mill)

whose historical development Moore makes a common causal argument, at times using the differences of the cases to eliminate possible alternative arguments. Simultaneously, at the level of comparisons *across* his three major routes, Moore makes some use of the Method of Difference; for as he discusses each particular route, Moore occasionally refers to one or both of the other two routes, using their contrasting developmental patterns to help validate the causal arguments being made for the other route in question. Not only in terms of its substantive scope, therefore, but also in terms of the complexity of its explanatory design, *Social Origins* is a work of virtually unparalleled ambition.

Theda Skocpol's *States and Social Revolutions* is much less ambitious.[29] Yet, especially in its first part on "The Causes of Social Revolutions in France, Russia, and China," it too employs a combination of Mill's analytic approaches, although with more explicit emphasis upon the Method of Difference. Skocpol argues that, despite differences along many dimensions that many theorists of revolution would consider decisive, Bourbon France in the late eighteenth century, late Imperial China after 1911, and Tsarist Russia from March 1917, all experienced social revolutionary crises for similar analytic reasons. By stressing the causal similarities in the face of other potentially important differences, Skocpol makes use of the Method of Agreement. Yet she also proceeds according to the Method of Difference by introducing analytically focussed contrasts between France, Russia, and China, on the one hand, and selected parts of the histories of England, Prussia/Germany, and Japan, on the other. These are suitable controls, Skocpol argues, because they are countries that did *not* undergo successful social-revolutionary transformations even though they were similar in many ways (structurally and historically) to France, Russia, and China. Skocpol uses contrasts to various sets of countries (in various periods of their histories) to validate different specific parts of her causal arguments about France, Russia, and China. For arguments about crises in states as one cause of social-revolutionary crises, she makes contrasts to the Japanese Meiji Restoration and the Prussian Reform Movement; and for arguments about agrarian structures and peasant revolts in revolutions, she makes contrasts to the English Parliamentary Revolution and the (failed) German revolution of 1848–50. In Skocpol's *States and Social Revolutions* only the "positive" cases of social revolution receive extensive discussion. "Negative" – or control – cases are discussed much less fully. For they are introduced strictly for the purpose of helping to validate the main argument about the causes of social revolutions in France, Russia, and China.

As a straightforward comparison of two countries, Frances Moulder's *Japan, China and the Modern World Economy* exemplifies the Method of Difference in action in yet another way.[30] Moulder's explanatory objective is to show that Japan's early, successful breakthrough to modern industrialization, in contrast to China's prolonged stagnation (from the mid-nineteenth to the mid-twentieth centuries), should be attributed *not* to differences between the cultural traditions or domestic economies of the two countries, but rather to the fewer constraints placed upon Japanese development by Western imperialist intrusions.[31] In order to substantiate her causal argument as opposed to alternatives that emphasize domestic differences between Japan and China, Moulder must establish the *similarity* in all apparently causally relevant aspects of the domestic structures of Tokugawa Japan and late Imperial China. And she must also show that Japan and China *differed* (in the appropriate direction and at the relevant times) in terms of the Western intrusions to which they were subjected. Indeed, Moulder's entire book is a closely argued attempt to establish exactly this pattern of many overall similarities and the one crucial difference between Japan and China, its logic being an impeccable application of the Method of Difference.

Like Skocpol's and Moulder's books, two tightly argued articles by Robert Brenner and Gary Hamilton respectively use the Method of Difference to support key explanatory arguments.[32] Even more than the Skocpol and Moulder books, moreover, these articles employ comparative history to refute alternative, competing arguments about their primary concerns. Robert Brenner's article on "Agrarian Class Structure and Economic Development . . ." seeks to explain long-term economic change in late medieval and early modern Europe, in particular "the intensification of serfdom in Eastern Europe in relation to its process of decline in the West" and "the rise of agrarian capitalism and the growth of agricultural productivity in England in relation to their failure in France."[33] Determined to debunk explanations of European economic growth that attribute causal significance to market expansion or to demographic trends, Brenner undermines such arguments by showing that the same putatively causal processes produced different outcomes in different parts of Europe (especially between Eastern and Western Europe, but also between regions of each of these zones). Then Brenner proceeds to argue that variables referring to class relations and the strength of peasant communities versus landlords can better account for the variations in economic development he wants to explain.

In his article on "Chinese Consumption of Foreign Commodities," Gary Hamilton is concerned with what factors influence the non-Western use of Western commodities. The unwillingness of the nineteenth-century Chinese to buy very many Western textile products provides a particularly intriguing problem for analysis. Why this Chinese reluctance? Hamilton outlines at the outset three alternative lines of explanation: faulty marketing and merchandizing arguments, cultural explanations, and a Weberian "status-competition" hypothesis. Methodically, Hamilton makes ingenious use of historical comparisons across space and time to dispose of the first two explanations. He shows that the economic arguments cannot explain why China differed from other non-Western countries in the nineteenth century, and he argues that a Confucian-culture explanation cannot explain why Chinese in earlier historical periods *were* willing to consume foreign products. Finally, Hamilton introduces his preferred status-competition explanation and demonstrates that it can explain the cross-national and cross-temporal variations that its competitors could not. All in all Hamilton is able to make optimally effective use of comparative history as a tool of causal analysis, especially because he ranges freely across cultures and historical epochs in order to find the logically necessary comparisons to further his explanatory argument.

THE TRIANGLE OF COMPARATIVE HISTORY AND SOME WORKS THAT COMBINE LOGICS

Parallel comparative history, Contrast-oriented comparative history, and Macro-analytic comparative history are, therefore, three distinct approaches that actually have been used by historical comparativists. For each of these major types of comparative history, we have reviewed examples of published works that clearly, and virtually exclusively, embody only one of these logics.

Yet it is important to recognize that works of comparative history sometimes *combine* (especially in pairs) the major logics we have reviewed. Two notable,

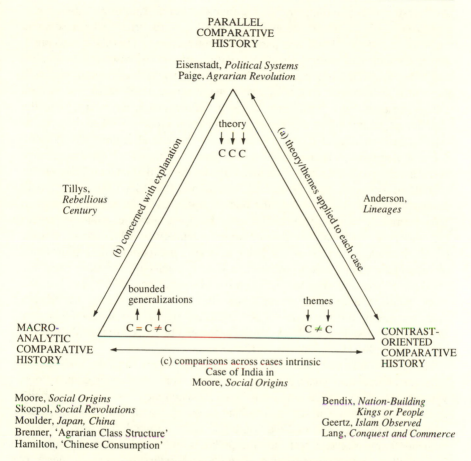

PARALLEL
COMPARATIVE
HISTORY

Eisenstadt, *Political Systems*
Paige, *Agrarian Revolution*

theory
↓ ↓ ↓
C C C

(a) theory/themes applied to each case

(b) concerned with explanation

Tillys,
*Rebellious
Century*

Anderson,
Lineages

bounded
generalizations
↑ ↑
C = C ≠ C

themes
↓ ↓
C ≠ C

MACRO-
ANALYTIC
COMPARATIVE
HISTORY

CONTRAST-
ORIENTED
COMPARATIVE
HISTORY

(c) comparisons across cases intrinsic
Case of India in
Moore, *Social Origins*

Moore, *Social Origins*
Skocpol, *Social Revolutions*
Moulder, *Japan, China*
Brenner, 'Agrarian Class Structure'
Hamilton, 'Chinese Consumption'

Bendix, *Nation-Building
Kings or People*
Geertz, *Islam Observed*
Lang, *Conquest and Commerce*

Figure 3.2. The triangle of comparative history

recently published comparative historical studies that do in fact combine logics
are *Lineages of the Absolutist State* by Perry Anderson and *The Rebellious
Century 1830–1930* by Charles, Louise, and Richard Tilly.[34] As indicated in
Figure 3.2, these works can be located at midpoints on dimensions shared by
pairs of the major logics of comparative history.

A discussion of each of the dimensions of the "Triangle of Comparative
History" in Figure 3.2 can help to further clarify the features of the major types
of comparative history, as well as the characteristics and likely incidence of
works that mix the various possible pairs of types.

To begin with dimension (a) of the Triangle: The Parallel and Contrast-
oriented types of comparative history share the feature that prior general ideas –
theories in the case of the Parallel approach; themes or questions in the case of
the Contrast-oriented approach – are brought to bear on each individual case in

the overall comparative-historical investigation. Perry Anderson's *Lineages of the Absolutist State* sits in the middle of this leg of the triangle because some comparisons in this book are parallel demonstrations of explicit theoretical arguments and other comparisons are contrasts of various cases to one another and to key Marxian concepts. Thus, Parts I and II of *Lineages* commence with theoretical accounts of why absolutist states emerged in Western and Eastern Europe (respectively). Then case histories follow within each part, with the intention of showing how the theoretically general process worked out specifically in each individual country. Even as the theoretical arguments are being demonstrated through such parallel case accounts, contrasts are also being made between East and West and between and among the individual cases. Moreover, Part III of *Lineages* and an appended section called "Two Notes" are both devoted primarily to contrasting the non-European cases of Japan, China, and Turkey among themselves and to European history as a whole. Anderson argues that Turkey and China contrast to European feudalism, while Japan, despite feudal elements, also contrasts to Europe because it experienced no prior mode of production comparable to Western antiquity. Anderson therefore combines Parallel and Contrast-oriented comparative history in complex ways. Yet it is worth noting that there are virtually no elements in *Lineages* of the Macro-analytic strategy of using controlled comparisons to infer causal generalizations. This fact about Anderson's book is nicely signified by its position on the triangle fully opposite the Macro-analytic corner.

As dimension (b) of the triangle indicates, the Macro-analytic and Parallel types of comparative history share a concern with developing explanations, whether causal generalizations or deductively elaborated theories. This shared concern is an objective absent in the Contrast-oriented approach. *The Rebellious Century, 1830–1930* sits mid-way on leg (b) of the triangle because this book combines comparisons to test causal hypotheses with parallel demonstrations of an overall theoretical perspective. *Rebellious Century* examines patterns of collective violence over a century of modern French, German, and Italian history. Within the discussion of each national case, comparisons of regions, times, and various social groups are made to test alternative explanations of how collective violence relates to the expansion of commerce and industry and the rise of national states. This is the distinctively Macro-analytic aspect of *Rebellious Century*. Across the national cases, however, controlled comparisons are not for the most part attempted. Instead, the Tillys primarily argue that a "solidarity" theory of collective violence best covers all three cases, accounting rather well for the changing overall patterns of collective violence in each national history. *Rebellious Century* thus combines the more deductive mode of explanation characteristic of Parallel comparative history with the more inductive style of causal inference characteristic of the Macro-analytic approach. And *Rebellious Century* shows very little concern with using case contrasts to highlight the contextual uniqueness of regions or nations.

Turning to dimension (c) of the triangle, we note that the Contrast-oriented and Macro-analytic variants of comparative history share the feature that direct comparisons between or among historical cases are intrinsic to their respective manner of argumentation – intrinsic to highlighting the unique case contexts in the Contrast-oriented type, and intrinsic to making causal inferences in the Macro-analytic type. This shared feature is absent in the Parallel approach, where theory is applied to case histories one by one. Not incidentally, however, it is difficult to find actual works that successfully mix the Macro-analytic and Contrast-oriented logics of comparative history. Although direct comparisons between and among historical cases are common to both approaches, the comparisons are by definition used for contradictory purposes: inferring causal generalizations across cases as opposed to highlighting the particular features of individual cases. Obviously it is very difficult to use comparisons involving the same cases to do both of these things at once.

The one instance we have discovered of an explicit attempt to do both at once involves the case of India in Barrington Moore's *Social Origins of Dictatorship and Democracy*. In many ways, as Moore himself realizes, India does not conform to the pattern exemplified by most of the other nations he analyzes in *Social Origins* (it was, for example, colonized and had its democratic institutions transmitted from without). And Moore acknowledges that the story of India "constitutes both a challenge to and a check upon the theories advanced in this book as well as others, especially those theories of democracy that were a response to the very different historical experience of Western Europe and the United States."[35] Indeed, to a significant degree Moore appears to use the Indian case as a pure contrast, to place limits upon the generality of the major causal arguments of *Social Origins*. Yet Moore also wants to use India to confirm his causal inferences about the social origins of democracy.[36] In the end, the Indian case has a somewhat ambiguous place in the overall analysis of *Social Origins* precisely because Moore uses it for a mixture of both purposes.

Perhaps *any* "mixed type" work of comparative history will tend to be ambiguous in its message if two (or more) of the major logics are simultaneously applied to the same units of analysis. For not only does Barrington Moore's discussion of India exemplify such ambiguity, so do Parts I and II of Perry Anderson's *Lineages of the Absolutist State*. In these parts, Anderson attempts to show that his theories of the origins and dynamics of Western Absolutism and Eastern Absolutism apply to the various individual "social formations" of Western as opposed to Eastern Europe. And, simultaneously, Anderson contrasts the individual cases among themselves and to the "pure concepts" of Eastern and Western Absolutism. Often the reader finds it hard to tell whether Anderson means to apply a theoretical generalization or to establish the absolute uniqueness of each case.

The Rebellious Century by the Tillys exemplifies a more successful mixture of two distinct logics of comparative history, probably because each of its logics works at a different level of analysis and refers to a separate set of units. Thus the Parallel logic is applied across nations, while the Macro-analytic logic is used within nations to compare groups, regions, and times. No doubt, when *any* combination of pairs of the major logics of comparative history is attempted, the relative segregation of the logics within separate parts or levels of analysis within the work as a whole helps to make such a combination less confusing than it would be if the logics were fused throughout. In any event, the apparent need for segregation in order to avoid ambiguity helps to reinforce the overall argument of this article concerning the distinct integrity and reality of each major logic of comparative history: the Parallel, the Contrast-oriented, and the Macro-analytic. It is to discussion of these that we now return.

STRENGTHS AND LIMITATIONS OF THE MAJOR TYPES

The three major logics of comparative history not only have distinctive purposes, patterns of case selection, and modes of exposition, they also have characteristic strengths and limitations. These are worth assessing for each major type in turn.

The Parallel type can be discussed most briefly because the strictly comparative-historical aspect is least important in this approach. As we have seen, the presentation and clarification of a theory is of overriding importance in works of this type. Juxtaposed case histories are useful insofar as they help to spell out the implications of the theory for specific settings, and insofar as they convincingly demonstrate that the theory covers the full range of cases to which it ought (according to its own claims) to apply. When Parallel comparative history is done well, the reader gains a much fuller understanding (than one would from a general theoretical discussion alone) of how key concepts and variables are operationalized and how the theory works "on the ground" to explain actual historical developments. But no matter how many cases are discussed, the historical analyses themselves do not validate the theory. They can only illustrate and clarify it – and, potentially, refine it. This is because, quite obviously, the cases are selected in the first place in terms of the given theory. And the juxtaposed historical trajectories are not used to establish controls, only to show the theory at work again and again.

Since the juxtaposition of multiple case histories cannot actually strengthen the validation of their theories, practitioners of Parallel comparative history run the risk of being overly repetitive without commensurate methodological gain. Arguably, both Eisenstadt at places in *The Political Systems of Empires* and the Tillys in *The Rebellious Century* fall into this trap. The difficulty of fruitless repetition is particularly striking in *The Rebellious Century,* where exactly the same basic theoretical argument is presented in the introduction and conclusion of the book, in addition to being developed *three times* over in the lengthy core chapters on France, Germany, and Italy. Although the historical cases certainly have intrinsic interest, nothing of any theoretical significance would have been lost had *The Rebellious Century* discussed only one national case rather than three.

Not all works of Parallel comparative history end up seeming repetitious, however. Jeffery Paige's *Agrarian Revolution* cleverly avoids this problem. Because of the complexity of his theoretical argument, in which he predicts several possible historical outcomes, Paige can use the individual case analyses to illustrate different major parts of the overall theoretical argument. Readers are kept interested with varied fare, even as the logical requisites of Parallel comparative history are fulfilled.[37]

Practitioners of Contrast-oriented comparative history stand squarely in the middle between the characteristic disciplinary concerns of social scientists and historians. These comparativists actually care about general issues that cross-cut particular times and places. Indeed, this is what motivates them to do comparative studies rather than single-case historical accounts. Yet Contrast-oriented comparative historians are also profoundly skeptical of received social-scientific theories and uncertain about the prospects for developing any valid macro-level explanatory generalizations at all. Thus they pursue comparative history within the confines of a kind of "self-denying ordinance" against endeavors to develop new explanations. This self-conscious refusal to use comparative history to explain is at once the chief strength and the greatest weakness of the Contrast-oriented approach. It is a strength because the refusal to develop explanations allows Contrast-oriented comparativists to present unbroken accounts of the unique histories of different societies. Historical cases may be used to point out the limits of received general theories, but for the most part the focus is *not* on theories or hypotheses or explanatory problems. Rather it is on the cases themselves and the contrasts between and among them that underline the uniqueness of each. The determined exploration of the unique features of each case leads inevitably toward a kind of descriptive holism. Thus the studies done by Contrast-oriented comparative historians do much to bring out the rich details of diverse societies and cultures and to show how the different spheres of each society and culture inextricably interrelate. Furthermore, Contrast-oriented comparativists take chronology very seriously, emphasizing how sociocultural experiences exhibit continuity over time. It is hardly incidental that Contrast-oriented studies almost always include lengthy, unified case accounts, with events kept strictly in chronological order. Indeed, quite often an unmistakable "genetic determinism" – a tendency to say that earlier, and ultimately the earliest, happenings determine what comes later – creeps into Contrast-oriented presentations. Despite their considerable differences in subject matter and implicit theoretical frameworks, Clifford Geertz's *Islam Observed,* James Lang's *Conquest and Commerce,* Reinhard Bendix's *Kings or People,* and Perry Anderson's *Lineages of the Absolutist State* all exhibit this genetic-determinist proclivity.

Of course the price paid in Contrast-oriented comparative histories is that descriptive holism precludes the development of explanatory arguments, even when these are implicitly present, crying to be drawn out of the comparative-historical materials. Independent and dependent variables are never explicitly distinguished, and the chronological account, "telling the story," is allowed to suffice as the mode of conveying understanding of what happened and why. Worse yet, most (if not all) works of Contrast-oriented comparative history actually smuggle implicit theoretical explanations into their case accounts. Usually this happens through the device of posing common themes or questions to provide the framework for the case accounts and comparisons. In the books of Reinhard Bendix, for example, it is abundantly apparent to any theoretically astute reader that a kind of idealistic Weberian explanation of "modernizing" transformations of political authority structures is being proffered in the introductory sections and throughout the case histories. Bendix makes quasi-explanatory arguments along these lines, and he selects what happenings and aspects of social life to include, or not, in his case histories in a manner appropriate to his implicit theoretical perspective. In a way, there is nothing surprising in this, for it is difficult to see how anyone could survey thousands of years of world history without theoretical guidance. But, of course, the irony is that, like any good Contrast-oriented comparative historian, Bendix disclaims explicit theoretical or explanatory objectives. He presents his themes and concepts as if they were self-evident truths, or else neutral tools, when in fact they imply explanatory hypotheses whose validity could be challenged. Indeed, other comparativists have covered exactly the same ground as Bendix using very different theories or themes.

In short, Contrast-oriented comparative history offers the advantages of holistic, rich descriptions and full, chronological case accounts. Limits to the applicability of received general theories can be dramatically revealed through this approach. But the Contrast-oriented approach can also be theoretically very misleading. For virtually any themes can be brought to bear upon the case materials without being put to any explicit test and without being openly identified as a proto-theory.

Macro-analytic comparative history has the considerable virtue of being the only way to attempt to validate (and invalidate) causal hypotheses about macrophenomena of which there are intrinsically only limited numbers of cases. The problem is that perfectly controlled comparisons are never really feasible. Societies cannot be broken apart at will into analytically manipulable variables; and history rarely, if ever, provides exactly the cases needed for controlled comparisons. Indeed, John Stuart Mill himself despaired of the possibility of effectively applying the analytic methods he discussed to sociohistorical phenomena.[38] And as we have seen, scholars such as Reinhard Bendix have concluded that given the difficulties of doing rigorous causal analysis at the macro level, the attempt should not be made at all.

But complete retreat in the face of the difficulties is surely unnecessary. Even if the validity of macro-level causal hypotheses can never be perfectly established, highly suggestive studies can often be successfully completed. Moreover, macro-causal analysis remains a powerful tool for criticizing and invalidating mistaken theories. As the articles by Robert Brenner and Gary Hamilton clearly show, it is often possible to demonstrate through elementary comparative-historical analysis that widely accepted explanations simply cannot account for variations across times and places. Such critical use of comparative-historical analysis in turn prods social scientists to look for more promising explanatory hypotheses. And insofar as carefully delineated explanatory problems are tackled one by one, considerable progress can usually be made in setting up comparisons across time and/or space to test alternative hypotheses about each problem.

The great comparative historian Marc Bloch once made a statement that could be taken as a maxim for Macro-analytic comparativists, especially in opposition to their Contrast-oriented counterparts: "The unity of place is only disorder," Bloch declared. "Only the unity of problem makes a center."[39] When they ply their trade most thoroughly, Macro-analytic comparative historians take this maxim very seriously. Cases are selected and case materials are manipulated according to the logic of the causal hypotheses being presented and tested. The temptation to narrate unbroken sequences of events about each time and place is resisted when this proves unnecessary for dealing with the explanatory problem at hand. Indeed, from the point of view of Contrast-oriented comparativists (or of traditional historians), Macro-analytic comparative history done well may seem very unaesthetic because in it the unities of time and place are broken. But of course the breaking apart of temporal and geographic unities is exactly what is needed if explanatory problems are to be solved. Unlike Contrast-oriented comparative history, it is arguable that Macro-analytic comparative history is better done in article format rather than in books. For it may be easier in articles to highlight causal arguments, to move freely back and forth across times and places, and to avoid the temptations of presenting lengthy descriptive chronologies for their own sake.[40] Certainly when Macro-analysts do write books, they face the challenge of integrating descriptive accounts with causal arguments. Historical trajectories cannot simply be juxtaposed and contrasted; controlled comparisons (the best approximations possible) must be explicitly presented.

Macro-analytic comparative history has been − and will continue to be − done skillfully. Even so, it is important to recognize that this method offers no automatic or complete solutions to macrosocial explanatory problems. As suggested by the juxtaposition of Marion Levy, Jr.'s study of the "Contrasting Factors in the Modernization of China and Japan"[41] to Frances Moulder's recent (1977) *Japan, China and the Modern World Economy,* it is quite possible for investigators of differing theoretical proclivities to use the same comparative-historical logic to ask about the causes of what is basically the same phenomenon occurring in the same cases, and yet come up with contradictory answers. In both of these studies, the Method of Difference is skillfully employed. The point is that the method itself is no substitute for theory, and cannot in itself guarantee reliable and valid conclusions.

Moreover, even when the conclusions of a Macro-analytic comparative study do seem perfectly sound, there are still unavoidable difficulties about how to generalize the explanation beyond the historical cases actually included in the given study. Can Barrington Moore's arguments be applied to the political development of countries other than the eight actually covered by *Social Origins of Dictatorship and Democracy?* Can Theda Skocpol's arguments about social revolutions in France, Russia, and China be extended to other cases (and failures) of social-revolutionary transformations? The answer is that, because they are largely inductively established, comparative-historical causal arguments cannot be readily generalized beyond the cases actually discussed. In the preface to *Social Origins,* Barrington Moore likens the generalizations his study establishes to "a large-scale map of an extended terrain, such as an airplane pilot might use in crossing a continent."[42] This is an appropriate metaphor. And the reflection it inspires in this context is that no matter how good the map were of, say, North America, the pilot could not use the same map to fly over other continents.

Providing links among valid causal generalizations about different sets of times and places is, ideally, the task of truly "general" theories. Macro-analytic studies cannot completely substitute for general theory-building. Nevertheless, general theories about societal dynamics and epochal transformations are best developed only in close relationship with the findings of Macro-analytic comparative histories. Would-be "universal" theories, developed at high levels of abstraction without any reference to comparative-historical patterns, can end up not explaining *any* causal connections in history very well. But if general theories can be developed in tandem with Macro-analytic investigations, then we should be able, over time, to improve the depth and, especially, the scope of our explanations of societal structures and their historical transformations.

CONCLUSION

In sum, "comparative history" is not a single, homogeneous logic of macrosocial inquiry. Rather it encompasses at least three major logics with distinct purposes, characteristics, strengths, and limitations. Normally, a single investigator pursuing a given comparative-historical study will want and need to use just one of these major logics, or, at most, a carefully combined pair. Comparative historical studies seem to work best when they are done primarily according to one logic or another.

Even so, at the level of the macrosocial enterprise as a whole – the overall quest for understandings about societal orders and social change – the Parallel,

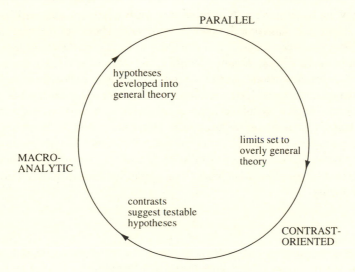

Figure 3.3. A cycle of transitions

Contrast-oriented, and Macro-analytic approaches together form a complementary system. For each type at its own distinctive limits tends to suggest needs and possibilities for studies of the other types. This especially happens, we would argue, in the cycle suggested by Figure 3.3.

Thus Parallel comparative history tends to call forth Contrast-oriented arguments when the need develops to set limits to the scope or claims of an overly generalized social-scientific theory. Contrast-oriented comparative history may give rise to Macro-analytic arguments when juxtapositions of historical trajectories begin to suggest testable causal hypotheses. Finally, too, Macro-analytic comparative history can create a demand for the kind of general theorizing that precedes the construction of a Parallel comparative analysis. This happens when there develops an interest in generalizing causal hypotheses beyond a given set of historical cases, in order to encompass all – or a broader range of – cases exemplifying the phenomenon to be explained. If the new theoretical claims then seem to overreach themselves, the cycle is very likely to begin again.

The arguments of this article about major types of comparative history will, we hope, contribute in several ways to the further development of historically oriented macrosocial research. For one thing, although methodological "recipes" are neither possible nor desirable, future comparative-historical research can surely benefit from a clearer awareness on the part of investigators of the methodological alternatives that have proved fruitful in the past. In addition, the informed appreciation of such research should be enhanced if relevant audiences understand the distinct purposes and characteristics of the major logics of comparative history. For works of different types can then be recognized for what they are and judged in appropriate terms. Finally, and perhaps most important, the time has come for debates to flourish about the practical methods for mediating between theories and historical evidence that actually have been, or might be, used by macroscopically oriented historical sociologists and social historians. Disputes about theoretical paradigms and philosophies of social inquiry cannot substitute for such properly methodological reflections; neither can discussions solely focussed upon quantitative techniques of data analysis. Thus, even if this essay on the uses of comparative history does nothing more than arouse interested skepticism and provoke thoughtful counter-arguments, it will nevertheless have achieved its most basic aim – to encourage methodological reflection by all those who practice or appreciate historically oriented macrosocial inquiry.

NOTES

1. Existing literature on "comparative methods" in sociology has tended either to focus heavily on macrosociological theories and theorists or to emphasize issues of conceptualization and measurement as these especially affect cross-cultural surveys and field research. The former tendency is exemplified by Robert M. Marsh, *Comparative Sociology: A Codification of Cross-Societal Analysis* (New York: Harcourt, Brace and World, 1967); and Ivan Vallier, ed., *Comparative Methods in Sociology: Essays on Trends and Applications* (Berkeley and Los Angeles: University of California Press, 1971). The latter tendency is exemplified by Donald P. Warwick and Samuel Osherson, eds., *Comparative Research Methods* (Englewood Cliffs, N.J.: Prentice-Hall, 1973).
2. William H. Sewell, Jr., "Marc Bloch and the Logic of Comparative History," *History and Theory* 6(2) (1967):208–18; Arend Lijphart, "Comparative Politics and the Comparative Method," *American Political Science Review* 65(3–4) (1971):682–93; and Neil J. Smelser, *Comparative Methods in the Social Sciences* (Englewood Cliffs, N.J.: Prentice-Hall, 1976).
3. This tendency to collapse all comparative history into multivariate analysis has occurred despite the fact that both Max Weber (whose work is extensively surveyed by Smelser) and Marc Bloch (whose methodological views form the basis for Sewell's article) recognized that comparative history could be used not only for hypothesis testing, but also to contrast different societies or cultures and to highlight their respective individual features. Max Weber should be considered a prime practitioner among classical sociologists of the type of comparative history that we will label "Contrast-oriented" and discuss at length below. For Marc Bloch's views on comparative history, see his "A Contribution towards a Comparative History of European Societies," in *Land and Work in Medieval Europe: Selected Papers by Marc Bloch,* trans. J. E. Anderson (New York: Harper and Row, 1967), pp. 44–81.
4. To be sure, the major logics of comparative history are sometimes combined in scholarly works. Later in this paper we will show that well-known recent books by Perry Anderson and Charles, Louise, and Richard Tilly combine different possible pairs of the major types of comparative history.
5. S. N. Eisenstadt, *The Political Systems of Empires: The Rise and Fall of Historical Bureaucratic Societies* (New York: Free Press, 1963); and Jeffery M. Paige, *Agrarian Revolution: Social Movements and Export Agriculture in the Underdeveloped World* (New York: Free Press, 1975).

6. Eisenstadt, *Political Systems,* p. 12.
7. Although Parallel comparative history is Eisenstadt's predominant strategy in *Political Systems,* he also does a bit of causal analysis using an approximation to controlled comparison. Specifically Eisenstadt uses Macro-analytic comparative history when he argues (pp. 106–7) that some societies had one, but not both, necessary conditions to become bureaucratic empires, contrasting these "failed" cases to "successful" ones.
8. An interesting by-product of Paige's willingness to present detailed, integral case accounts (as opposed to Eisenstadt's scattered fragments) is that a reader skeptical of Paige's theory finds it relatively easy (unlike a reader skeptical of Eisenstadt's theory) to use the historical cases to criticize Paige's theory and to tease out alternative explanations. See, for example, Margaret R. Somers and Walter L. Goldfrank, "The Limits of Agronomic Determinism: A Critique of Paige's Agrarian Revolution," *Comparative Studies in Society and History* 21(3) (July 1979):443–58.
9. Full references will be given below as each book is individually discussed or cited.
10. Clifford Geertz, *Islam Observed: Religious Development in Morocco and Indonesia* (Chicago: University of Chicago Press, 1971).
11. *Ibid.,* p. 3.
12. *Ibid.,* p. 4.
13. *Ibid.*
14. *Ibid.*
15. James Lang, *Conquest and Commerce: Spain and England in the Americas* (New York: Academic Press, 1975).
16. *Ibid.,* dust jacket.
17. Reinhard Bendix, "The Mandate to Rule: An Introduction," *Social Forces* 55(2) (December 1976):247.
18. Reinhard Bendix, *Nation-Building and Citizenship* (new enlarged ed.) (Berkeley and Los Angeles: University of California Press, 1977; orig. 1964), pp. 16–17.
19. *Ibid.,* and Reinhard Bendix, *Kings or People: Power and the Mandate to Rule* (Berkeley and Los Angeles: University of California Press, 1978).
20. Bendix, *Kings or People,* p. 5.
21. *Ibid.,* p. 15.
22. Full references will be given below as each work is individually discussed or cited.
23. Barrington Moore, Jr., *Social Origins of Dictatorship and Democracy: Lord and Peasant in the Making of the Modern World* (Boston: Beacon Press, 1966), pp. xiii–xiv.
24. *Ibid.,* p. xiii.
25. *Ibid.,* p. xiv.
26. John Stuart Mill, "Two Methods of Comparison" (excerpt from *A System of Logic,* 1888), in Amatai Etzioni and Frederic L. Du Bow, eds., *Comparative Perspectives: Theories and Methods* (Boston: Little, Brown, 1970), p. 206.
27. *Ibid.,* pp. 207–10.
28. For a summary of the variables, see the table in Theda Skocpol, "A Critical Review of Barrington Moore's 'Social Origins of Dictatorship and Democracy,' " *Politics and Society* 4(3) (Fall 1973):10. Insofar as Moore does *any* of our major kinds of comparative history in *Social Origins,* he uses the Macro-analytic approach. However, it is worth noting that much of *Social Origins* is intended by Moore as straightforward historical analysis of causal sequences specific to the individual countries. As he puts it in the Preface (p. xiii), "the analysis of the transformation of agrarian society in specific countries produces results at least as rewarding as larger generalizations. . . . [F]or any given country one is bound to find lines of causation that do not fit easily into more general theories."

29. Theda Skocpol, *States and Social Revolutions: A Comparative Analysis of France, Russia, and China* (Cambridge and New York: Cambridge University Press, 1979).
30. Frances V. Moulder, *Japan, China and the Modern World Economy: Toward a Reinterpretation of East Asian Development ca. 1600 to ca. 1918.* (Cambridge and New York: Cambridge University Press, 1977).
31. Moulder's book derives its central hypotheses from Immanuel Wallerstein's theory of the capitalist world-economy. For the basic tenets of this theory, see: Immanuel Wallerstein, "The Rise and Future Demise of the World-Capitalist System: Concepts for Comparative Analysis," *Comparative Studies in Society and History* 16(4) (September 1974):387–415; and Immanuel Wallerstein, *The Modern World-System: Capitalist Agriculture and the Origins of the European World-Economy in the Sixteenth Century* (New York: Academic Press, 1974). The theory of the capitalist world-system has been used in conjunction with at least two of the logics of comparative history: Wallerstein himself uses the Parallel approach to show that his overall world-system model can account for the histories of countries in the "core," "semi-periphery," "periphery," and "external" arenas. And Moulder's book shows that Wallerstein's theory is also compatible with a Macro-analytic approach. True, there is only *one* world-economy. But there need not be only one unit of analysis, insofar as causal hypotheses about developments in nations, regions, cross-sections of "world time," etc., can be formulated with the guidance of the theory. Approximations to controlled comparisons may then be possible to test such hypotheses, as Moulder's comparison of Japan and China demonstrates.
32. Robert Brenner, "Agrarian Class Structure and Economic Development in Pre-Industrial Europe," *Past and Present* no. 70 (February 1976):30–75; and Gary G. Hamilton, "Chinese Consumption of Foreign Commodities: A Comparative Perspective," *American Sociological Review* 42(6) (December 1977):877–91.
33. Brenner, "Agrarian Class Structure," p. 47.
34. Perry Anderson, *Lineages of the Absolutist State* (London: New Left Books, 1974); and Charles Tilly, Louise Tilly, and Richard Tilly, *The Rebellious Century, 1830–1930* (Cambridge: Harvard University Press, 1975).
35. Moore, *Social Origins,* p. 315.
36. See especially *ibid.,* pp. 430–32.
37. Another work that uses Parallel comparative history in a non-repetitious and unusually interesting way is *Poor People's Movements* (New York: Pantheon, 1977) by Frances Fox Piven and Richard Cloward. The purpose of this book is to present a theory of the emergence and fate of insurgent movements by non-privileged groups in U.S. society. After the theory is outlined, four cases are presented to illustrate it. Each represents a particular protest movement and a specific "slice in time" from U.S. history between 1930 and the early 1970s. Taken together, the cases add up not only to four separate applications of Piven and Cloward's theoretical perspective on protest movements, but also to a coherent account of the course of U.S. politics since the 1930s, viewed from the bottom up. Piven and Cloward thus uniquely fuse the juxtaposition of cases characteristic of Parallel comparative history with the holism and drama characteristic of an in-depth exploration of a single national experience.
38. Mill, "Two Methods," in Etzioni and Du Bow, eds., *Comparative Perspectives,* pp. 210–13.
39. Marc Bloch, "Une Étude Régionale: Géographie ou Histoire?" *Annales d'Histoire Economique et Sociale* 6 (January 1934):81 (our translation).
40. For examples see the articles cited in note 32 and Theda Skocpol, "France, Russia, China: A Structural Analysis of Social Revolutions," *Comparative Studies in Society and History* 18:2 (April 1976):175–210.

41. Marion J. Levy, Jr., "Contrasting Factors in the Modernization of China and Japan," in Simon Kuznets, Wilbert E. Moore, and Joseph J. Spengler, eds., *Economic Growth: Brazil, India, and Japan* (Durham, N.C.: Duke University Press, 1955), pp. 496–536.
42. Moore, *Social Origins*, p. xiv.

Part II

MAKING SENSE OF THE GREAT REVOLUTIONS

4

Explaining revolutions: In quest of
a social-structural approach

The explanation of revolutions poses a unique challenge for social science. Success depends upon finding some way to hypothesize about complex, large-scale events in which patterned group conflicts and sudden societal transformations intrinsically coincide. Undoubtedly the most difficult cases are social revolutions, in which societal political conflicts occurring in conjuncture with class upheavals from below lead to "rapid, fundamental, and violent domestic change in the dominant values and myths of a society, in its political institutions, social structure, leadership, and government activities and policies" (Huntington, 1968:264). To be sure, the historical occurrences that unequivocally measure up to this definition are few: France, 1789; Russia, 1917; Mexico, 1911–1936; and China, 1911–1949 are the obvious clear-cut instances. Many would argue that a phenomenon of which there are so few instances does not deserve theoretical attention. Yet the enormous impact and continuing historical significance of social revolutions are surely sufficient to override the fact of their generic scarcity and render them a fit object of explanatory effort for social scientists.

What explains revolutions? Why do they (or might they) occur in certain societies at given times, while not in other societies, or at other times in the same societies? Apparently, recent American social science should have much to say in answer to this question, for, like a hundred flowers blooming, theories of revolution have sprung up thick and fast during the past fifteen years. Most recent attempts to explain either revolutions per se, or some broader class of phenomena explicitly conceived as subsuming revolutions, can be identified primarily with one or another of three major approaches: (1) *aggregate-psychological* theories, which attempt to explain revolutions in terms of people's motivations for engaging in political violence or joining oppositional movements; (2) *systems/value-consensus* theories, which attempt to explain revolutions as violent responses of ideological movements to severe disequilibrium in social systems; and (3) *political conflict* theories, which argue that conflict between governments and organized groups contending for political power must be placed at the center of attention.

Yet it will be the burden of argument in this essay that recent social scientific theories of revolution in fact fail to elucidate or explain revolutions. The basic differences are both methodological (in the broad meaning of the term) and substantive. Substantively, the chief difficulty is that existing theories attempt to explain the occurrence of revolutions through hypotheses about the situation and states of mind of rebellious masses or the emergence of consciously revolutionary vanguards, rather than through hypotheses about patterns of institutional development in specific types of complex societies in given sorts of historical circumstances. Methodologically the difficulty lies with attempts to explain revolutions directly in terms of abstract, deductive hypotheses about human behavior or societal processes in general, and to put such hypotheses to statistical tests based on large numbers of units, rather than engaging in comparative-historical analyses to generate and test hypotheses inductively through systematic contrast of the few positive cases of revolution with negative cases of failure or nonoccurrence. Thus I shall be arguing that a major theoretical reorientation – away from social psychological and universalist-deductive modes of explanation, and toward a structural and comparative-historical approach – is required if progress toward the adequate explanation of revolutions is to be made in the social sciences.

AGGREGATE-PSYCHOLOGICAL THEORIES OF REVOLUTION

Aggregate-psychological theorists assume that "revolutions, like all political phenomena, originate in the minds of men . . ." (Schwartz, 1972:58), and so they turn for explanatory power to various theories of motivational dynamics. Some of these theorists (e.g., Geschwender, 1968; Eckstein, 1965; Schwartz, 1971, 1972) rely upon various cognitive psychological theories. But the most prevalent and fully developed type of aggregate-psychological explanation of revolution begins "with the seemingly self-evident premise that discontent is the root cause of violent conflict" (Gurr, 1973:364), and then seeks to explicate this premise with the aid of psychological theories that link frustration to violent, aggressive behavior against the perceived agents of frustration. James Davies (1962, 1969), Ivo and Rosalind Feierabend (1972), the Feierabends and Nesvold (1969, 1973), and Ted Robert Gurr (1968a, 1968b, 1970) have been the leading proponents of this approach. Gurr's book, *Why Men Rebel,* represents the most sophisticated and thoroughly elaborated presentation of a complex model based on frustration-aggression theory. Thus in our discussion of the aggregate-psychological approach to explaining revolutions, we shall focus primarily upon the frustration-aggression variant, and especially upon Ted Gurr's presentations of it.

Frustration-aggression theorists tend to "see" revolutions as just one possible form of violent and illicit political behavior that is fundamentally instigated by a certain frame of mind. Thus Gurr seeks to explain "political violence," by which he means

all collective attacks within a political community against the political regime, its actors – including competing political groups as well as incumbents – or its policies. The concept represents a set of events, a common property of which is the actual or threatened use of violence. . . . The concept subsumes revolution, ordinarily defined as fundamental sociopolitical change accomplished through violence. It also includes guerilla wars, coups d'état, rebellions, and riots. [1970:3–4]

The concerns which dictate this theoretical focus are openly stated:

[A]ll such acts pose a threat to the political system in two senses; they challenge the monopoly of force imputed to the state in political theory; and in functional terms, they are likely to interfere with and, if severe, to destroy normal political processes. [1970:4]

Clearly Gurr is interested in explaining only the "destructiveness" of revolutions, an aspect shared with other types of events, and not the amounts or kinds of societal change that revolutions, specifically, bring about. He focuses upon a style of behavior, "resort to illicit violence," as the defining property that distinguishes these collective events from others. This focus, in turn, "has the crucial theoretical consequence: to direct attention to psychological theories about the sources of human aggression" (Gurr, 1968*b*:247).

Gurr's theory is not mainly psychological in manifest content, however, for he concentrates upon specifying many interrelated societal conditions, which according to his ultimately psychological logic, might operate to initiate and then to focus and channel potentials for collective political violence. Relative deprivation – "a perceived discrepancy between men's value expectations [the goods and conditions of life to which people believe they are rightfully entitled] and their value capabilities [the goods and conditions they think they are capable of attaining or maintaining]" (Gurr, 1970:13) – is specified as the frustrating condition that produces the potential for political violence. Relative deprivation is supposedly to some degree generated in people whenever societies undergo changes. (However, frustration-aggression theorists ultimately specify so many different kinds of social circumstances that might generate feelings of relative deprivation [see especially Gurr, 1970: chaps. 3–5], that the skeptical observer is left wondering whether discontent attributable to relative deprivation could not be attributed by these theorists to any group in any society at any time or place.) Once discontent due to relative deprivation is generated, the magnitudes and forms of collective political violence to which it gives rise depend both upon the intensity and widespreadness among people in society of the feelings of relative deprivation, and upon the effects of various mediating variables that channel and regulate the particular expression of generalized potentials for political violence. Among the important mediating variables that Gurr specifies are cultural conditions such as the degree of legitimation of existing authorities and normative approval for engaging in political violence to express grievances, and institutional conditions such as the degree of organizational strength of dissidents versus regime incumbents (Gurr, 1970: chaps. 6–9).

Still, relative deprivation remains the strategic explanatory variable. For it induces frustration that cannot be entirely suppressed by mediating conditions. Moreover, the possible effects of the mediating variables are all assessed in terms of their imputed psychological impact upon actors already experiencing feelings of relative deprivation – and this gives a distinctive slant to all of Gurr's conclusions about the effects of social conditions. Thus, for example, Gurr concludes that coercive repression is likely to exacerbate political violence, not because he considers government coercion as "political violence" (he does not – he excludes government actions by definition), but because he reasons that government coercion, unless it is extremely intense and totally consistent and efficient, will only increase dissidents' frustration levels and make them even more prone to violence (Gurr, 1970: chap. 8).

Within Gurr's overall model, revolutions in particular are explained merely as responses to widespread and intense relative deprivation that touches *both* "masses" and marginal "elites" in society, thus creating at once both widespread participation in and deliberate organization of violence. Relative deprivation confined merely to the masses would, according to Gurr, produce only "turmoil," since the "ability to rationalize, plan, and put to instrumental use their own and others' discontent is likely to be most common among the more skilled, highly educated members of a society – its elite aspirants" (Gurr, 1968*b*:276).

What does empirical evidence tell us about the validity of frustration-aggression theories? Relative deprivation theorists have collected cross-national aggregate data to test their theories of political violence. Especially noteworthy are the attempts by Gurr (1968*a*) and the Feierabends (1972). On the face of it, "relative deprivation" emerges in these studies as a strong predictor of political violence in a large number of societies around the world. However, Gurr and the Feierabends have not *directly* operationalized their central explanatory variables. While the exact testing of relative deprivation theories, as Davies has aptly argued, requires "the assessment of the state of mind – or more precisely, the mood – of a people" ideally over "an extended period of time in a particular society" (Davies, 1962: 17–18), Gurr and the Feierabends have not taken this approach. As they themselves admit, their studies "resort to an indirect method of measuring psychological variables, employing structural and ecological indicators" (Feierabends and Gurr, 1972:121) for numerous nations for years since World War II. Therefore, the reader must take their theoretical interpretations of the evidence on faith.

A number of researchers have devised more direct tests of relative-deprivation/frustration-aggression theory than those offered by its leading proponents, and these outside investigators have found little empirical support for this approach to explaining political violence. Using survey data on the attitudes as well as the characteristics and situations of Chilean slum dwellers, Alejandro Portes (1971:29) found absolutely no relationship between objective or subjective measures of deprivation and frustration, and declarations of willingness to accept "revolution and revolutionary violence as legitimate means to overthrow an economic and political order." Similarly, in a survey of political attitudes employing Cantril's Self-Anchoring Striving Scale, a subjective "deprivation measure recommended by Gurr," Edward Muller found

little support for an explanation of potential for political violence which ascribes strong – or any – direct effect to relative deprivation, or which casts relative deprivation as an important precondition that might be related to potential for political violence indirectly through effect on a factor such as belief in the legitimacy-illegitimacy of the regime. Relative deprivation . . . was found to be the *least* consequential predictor of potential for political violence. [1972:954]

Finally, David Snyder and Charles Tilly did a study that used objective indicators of relative deprivation, yet improved upon Gurr and the Feierabends by investigating patterns over time. Working with time-series data from France, 1830–1960, Snyder and Tilly (1972) attempted to predict changes in numbers of incidents of collective violence events and participants therein from fluctuations in indices of food prices, prices of manufactured goods, and levels of manufacturing production. They tested a wide variety of models based upon the hypotheses and operationalizations of Gurr, Davies, and the Feierabends, but found no significant relationships.

A few writers, for example Lupsha (1971) and Muller (1972), have responded to the increasingly evident inadequacy of frustration-aggression theories by suggesting that the willingness of individuals to resort to political violence could be better explained by their commitment to moral standards at variance with prevailing ideals or practices in society. Gurr himself (1968a) has accepted "legitimation" as an important "state of mind" variable independent of relative deprivation. Yet, while attention to the moral dimensions of consciousness may produce more powerful theories of the political orientations of individuals, it seems unlikely that any sort of theorizing grounded on the psychological level will produce an adequate explanation of either collective patterns of political violence or revolutions.

For the fundamental difficulty with all aggregate-psychological theories is that they attempt to explain social processes more or less directly on the basis of hypotheses about subjective orientations attributed to aggregates of individuals. Such a theoretical strategy can have even surface plausibility only to the extent that the events to be explained are conceived as the direct manifestations of individual behavior – hence the preferred focus on "political violence." But revolutions, coups, rebellions, even riots, all are events in which not amorphous aggregates but rather collectively mobilized and organized groups engage in violence in the process of striving for objects which bring them into conflict with other mobilized groups. Moreover, the various types of political violence are normally labeled and differentiated not only on the basis of whether primarily skillful and farsighted ("elite") or emotional and shortsighted ("nonelite") people participate in them, but rather on the basis of the social-structural locations of actors and the sociopolitical consequences brought about (or not) by the processes of political conflict. Revolutions above all are not mere extreme manifestations of some homogeneous type of individual behavior. Rather they are complex conjunctures of unfolding conflicts involving differently situated and motivated (and at least minimally organized) groups, and resulting not just in violent destruction of a polity, but also in the emergence of new sociopolitical arrangements. Thus it seems entirely in order to conclude that, even if frustration-aggression theorists could explain either individual predispositions to political violence or sheer aggregate amounts of all types added together (and the studies cited above show that they cannot even do this), they still could not enlighten us as to the causes of revolutions – or any other distinctive form of political conflict.

"To extrapolate from sums or proportions of individual attitudes to the occurrence of structural transformations," says Alejandro Portes (1971:28) in a critique of frustration-aggression theory, "is to accept a naive additive image of society and its structure." In contrast, the two alternative prominent approaches to explaining revolution both employ social-structural logics to correct shortcomings of the aggregate psychological approaches. Thus systems/value-consensus theorists derive their hypotheses about why revolutions happen and what they accomplish by working directly from a theoretical model of an equilibrated social system. And political conflict theorists derive hypotheses about political violence and revolutions from a model of the group political processes that they consider central to all politically organized populations. But even though both of these approaches begin with social-structural perspectives, nevertheless both end up offering fundamental social psychological explanations of the roots of revolutions. Let us investigate why this has happened.

SYSTEMS/VALUE-CONSENSUS THEORIES

While *mass discontent* is the crucial factor for explaining revolutions for frustration-aggression theorists, *systemic crises* and, especially, *revolutionary ideology* are the key factors for systems/value-consensus theorists. In broad outline the systems/value-consensus perspective on revolution is shared by a number of theorists, including, most prominently, the sociological theorist Talcott Parsons (1951: chap. 9), along with his one-time students Edward Tiryakian (1967) and Neil Smelser (1963). However, the perspective has been most thoroughly and judiciously applied specifically to the explanation of political revolutions by the political scientist Chalmers Johnson, in his 1966 book, *Revolutionary Change*. Let us review the argument that Johnson presents.

For Johnson (1966:1) revolution "is a special kind of social change, one that involves the intrusion of violence into civil social relations" which normally function to restrict violence. Like Gurr, then, Johnson makes violence central to his definition of revolution. However, Johnson (1966:57) considers violence not as an emotional urge toward destruction, but rather as a rational strategy intended to accomplish change involving societal reconstruction along with destruction. Therefore, he concludes that the analysis and explanation of revolution must be done with reference to some theory of social structure. Fatefully, though, the sociological theory with which Johnson decides to work is Parsonsian systems theory, and this theory's perspective on societal integration and change inexorably pushes Johnson back toward social-psychological explanations for revolutionary change.

Following the Parsonsians, Johnson (1966:chaps, 2–4) posits that a normal, or crisis-free, society should be conceived as an internally consistent set of institutions that express and specify in norms and roles core societal value-orientations – value-orientations which have also been internalized through processes of socialization to become the personal moral and reality-defining standards of the vast normal majority of the adult members of society. It follows from this conception of the bases of societal integration that close parallels should exist between the dominant world-views of a society and individuals' feelings of personal orientation, and that any objective social-structural crises should automatically be reflected both in the breakdown of the dominant world-views and in the emergence and popular acceptance of an ideology embodying alternative societal value-orientations. Johnson readily accepts these logical consequences of the Parsonsian theory of societal integration.

Thus, according to Johnson, crises in society develop whenever a society's values and environment become significantly "dissychronized." The instigators of crises can be either endogenous innovations (especially of values or technologies) or exogenous influences or intrusions (Johnson, 1966:chap. 4). Yet impetuses to crisis, whatever their source, are always realized via the societal members' experience of disorientation. "The single most generalized characteristic of the disequilibrated system is that values no longer provide an acceptable symbolic definition and explanation of existence" (Johnson, 1966:72–73). As a result "personal disequilibrium" is widely experienced, and there is an increase of individual and group behavior heretofore considered "deviant" in terms of the previous value consensus.

At this point, a revolutionary situation develops only if, and because, ideological movements focused around alternative, innovative value-orientations coalesce and begin to attract large numbers of adherents.

The dynamic element which . . . leads to the development of lines of cleavage is ideology. Without ideology, deviant subcultural groups – such as delinquent gangs, religious sects, and deviant patriotic associations – will not form alliances, and the tensions of the system which led particular groups to form these associations will be dissipated without directly influencing the social structure. [Johnson, 1966:81]

But even given a full-blown revolutionary situation, whether a revolution will actually succeed depends, according to Johnson (1966:91), primarily upon whether or not the legitimate authorities are willing and able to develop policies "which will maintain the confidence of nondeviant actors in the system and its capacity to move toward resynchronization" of values and environment. For Johnson (1966:xiv, 94) insists that authorities can – theoretically speaking – always modify existing values and institutions so as to avert the crisis and the need for revolution.

While the authorities seek to implement policies of "resynchronization," they may of necessity have to rely on coercion to prevent successful revolution. However, Johnson sees this as an entirely chancy situation, and one which cannot last for long. He maintains that a wide variety of "accelerators," which he regards as "not sets of conditions but single events," could at any time "rupture a system's pseudo-integration based on deterrence" (Johnson, 1966:99). He asserts that

superior force may delay the eruption of violence; nevertheless, a division of labor maintained by Cossacks is no longer a community of value-sharers, and in such a situation (e.g., South Africa, today [1966]), revolution is endemic and, *ceteris paribus*, an insurrection is inevitable. [1966:32]

Because he views the "authorities" as necessarily legitimated by consensual societal norms and values, Johnson is most reluctant to admit that a strong, efficient government could repress revolutionary tendencies over a prolonged period—a situation that has, for example, prevailed in South Africa for fifteen years (see Adam, 1971). If Johnson, or any other theorist of the systems/value-consensus persuasion, were ever to admit such a possibility, that would, of course, call into question the basic "value-consensus" model of societal integration and dynamics which underpins this approach to explaining revolutions.

In sum Johnson, like the aggregate psychologists, believes that governments must satisfy their citizens if they are to escape revolution. Only for Johnson it is the citizens' internalized value standards, not merely their customary or acquired appetites, that must be appeased. Further, just as revolutionary movements succeed for the frustration-aggression theorists because they express the anger of the discontented, similarly for the systems/value-consensus theorists they succeed because they allow the disoriented to express commitments to new societal values. In both cases, essentially social-psychological modes of explaining revolutions are grounded on consensual images of societal order and change, the one implicit and utilitarian, the other explicit and moralistic.

Nor has this brand of essentially social-psychological explanation been demonstrated to have any greater empirical validity than frustration-aggression theories. As steps toward more rigorous empirical tests of their theories, Tiryakian (1967:92–95) and Johnson (1966:132, chap. 6) have suggested specific components of indices of "revolutionary potential" or system "disequilibrium." Thus

far, however, no systems/value-consensus theorist has used these or other indicators systematically to test the theory cross-nationally after the manner of the
relative-deprivation theorists.

Perhaps more important, no systems/value-consensus advocate has seriously
confronted historical materials with two straightforward questions: Are revolutions really *made by* ideological movements, consisting of elites and masses
committed to alternative societal values? And are there cases where ideological
movements have been strong – as strong as or stronger than they have been in
successful revolutions – but where no revolution has resulted, even after a
considerable time lag?

Had these simple questions been seriously posed, the answers would by now
have eliminated systems/value-consensus theories as plausible explanations of
revolutions. In the Third World, "disequilibrated social systems" and ideological movements questioning the legitimacy of established authorities and arrangements abound, and yet actual revolutions are rare. It is even more telling to
point out that in no successful revolution to date has it been true that a mass-
based movement sharing a revolutionary ideology has in any sense "made" the
revolution. True enough, revolutionary ideologies and charismatic leaders have
in some instances helped to cement the solidarity of radical vanguards before
and/or during revolutionary crises, and have greatly facilitated the institution of
new national patterns afterward. But in no sense did such vanguards, let alone
vanguards with large, ideologically imbued mass followings, ever create the
essentially politico-military revolutionary crises they exploited. In the French
Revolution the emergence of the revolutionary crisis in 1788–1789 stimulated
the articulation and widespread acceptance of the initial revolutionary ideology,
rather than vice versa as a systems/value-consensus theory of revolution would
suggest (Taylor, 1972). In the Russian Revolution, the Bolshevik ideologues
were but a tiny, faction-ridden sect of the intelligentsia before mid-1917, when
the war-induced collapse of the tsarist government gave them suddenly enhanced opportunities for political leverage and mass manipulation. And in the
Chinese and Mexican revolutions, the ideological movements that ultimately
triumphed in the struggles among competing elites during the revolutionary
interregnums did not even yet exist when the old regimes were toppled in 1911.

Moreover peasants – the most important lower-stratum in revolutionary dramas heretofore – typically have not thought or acted in "revolutionary" ways at
all. Even as they have fueled the greatest social revolutions, peasants – and
often the urban poor as well – have fought for traditional and either specific or
parochial values and goals. As Trotsky perceptively put it, "the masses go into
a revolution not with a prepared plan of social reconstruction but with a sharp
feeling that they cannot endure the old regime" (Trotsky, 1932:x). And it is
usually the concrete aspects of the old regime that they avowedly reject, not its
overall structure and values. Thus peasants have helped to launch revolutions by
seizing the property of landlords in the name of the king and traditional anti-

aristocratic myths (Lefebvre, 1932), or else through appeals to traditional ideals of community justice (L. Tilly, 1971; Chamberlin, 1935:chap. 11; Womack, 1968), while urban workers have tipped the balance in struggles for state power between moderate and radical revolutionary elites in the process of themselves fighting to achieve more immediate goals such as lower food prices (Rudé, 1959) or workers' control of factories (Avrich, 1963).

THE POLITICAL CONFLICT PERSPECTIVE

To explain collective violence and revolutions, aggregate-psychological and systems/value-consensus theorists alike end up focusing on discontent or disorientation and relegating institutional and organizational factors to the role of intervening variables. But writers converging on what I shall call a political conflict perspective (e.g., Oberschall, 1969, 1973; Overholt, 1972; Russell, 1974; Tilly, 1969, 1975) argue that instead there should be an emphasis on the role of organized group conflicts for political goals. The most articulate and prolific spokesman for the new departure is Charles Tilly; moreover, his preliminary statements about revolution (1973, 1974, 1975) demonstrate the internal contradictions that yet remain within this perspective.

The political conflict perspective has developed mainly in critical response to discontent and societal disintegration explanations of political violence. According to Tilly (1975: 484–96), theorists such as Gurr and Davies and Johnson and Smelser have failed to see that political violence is essentially a by-product of omnipresent processes of political conflict among mobilized – that is, organized and resource-controlling – groups and governments. Castigating these theorists for concentrating "their theorizing and their research on individual attitudes or on the condition of the social system as a whole" (1975:488), Tilly contends

that revolutions and collective violence tend to flow directly out of a population's central political process, instead of expressing diffuse strains and discontents within the population; . . . that the specific claims and counterclaims being made on the existing government by various mobilized groups are more important than the general satisfaction or discontent of these groups, and that claims for established places within the structure of power are crucial. [1973:436]

Tilly therefore places "political conflict" at the center of attention. And he proposes to analyze it with the aid of a general model whose major elements are governments ("organizations which control the principal means of coercion") and contenders for power, including both polity members and challengers (Tilly, 1975:501–3). Working with this model and some inductive generalizations about the social structural conditions and European historical trends that have affected the capacities and occasions for groups to mobilize and for governments to repress mobilized contenders, Charles, Louise, and Richard Tilly have recently demonstrated in *The Rebellious Century* (1975) that, for a one-hundred-year period (1830–1930) in France, Italy, and Germany, their approach can make better sense of the overall patterns of incidence of changing forms of collective political violence than can the alternative discontent or social dislocation theories.

Ironically, though, when Tilly turns from criticizing and countering competing explanations of political violence to his own attempt to characterize and explain revolutions in particular, he ends up falling back upon the shopworn hypotheses of relative deprivation and ideological conversion. This happens because of several seemingly innocent pre-theoretical choices made by Tilly before he begins to speculate about the possible causes of revolutions. Although Tilly (1975:485–86) correctly stresses that revolutions are complex events whose occurrence probably depends upon a convergence of several relatively independent processes, nevertheless he chooses to ignore aspects of class conflict and social change and to separate out only the single aspect of struggle for political sovereignty for analytic and explanatory attention. Along with civil wars, international conquests, and national separatist movements, Tilly conceives of revolutions simply as situations of multiple sovereignty:

A revolution begins when a government previously under the control of a single sovereign polity becomes the object of effective, competing, mutually exclusive claims on the part of two or more distinct polities; it ends when a single sovereign polity regains control over the government. [1975:519]

It is easy enough to see that this approach appeals to Tilly because it allows him to generalize from his group conflict model already developed for analyzing political violence: Revolutions can be conceived as a special case of group conflict in which the contenders are both (or all) fighting for ultimate political sovereignty over a population. Yet if what makes revolutionary situations special is precisely *the extraordinary nature of the goal* for which contending groups are struggling, then it naturally seems to follow that what needs to be explained about revolutions is the emergence and appeal of contenders who *intend* to achieve these special goals. And, indeed, when Tilly comes to the point of suggesting causes of revolution, he relies upon social psychological hypotheses to explain the emergence of revolutionary contenders and the increase of their followings. Echoing Chalmers Johnson, Tilly declares (1975:525) that potential contenders are "always with us in the form of millennial cults, radical cells, or rejects from the positions of power. The real question is when such contenders proliferate and/or mobilize." Charismatic individuals and the rise or decline of social groups are possible explanatory factors, Tilly suggests. Yet he notes that one factor is especially important:

The elaboration of new ideologies, new theories of how the world works, new creeds, is part and parcel of both paths to a revolutionary position: the emergence of brand-new challengers and the turning [to revolutionary goals] of existing contenders. [1975:526]

As for "the commitment to the [revolutionary contenders'] claims by a significant segment of the subject population," Tilly suggests (1975:526) that it "is in accounting for the expansion and contracting of this sort of commitment that attitudinal analyses of the type conducted by Ted Gurr, James Davies, and Neil Smelser should have their greatest power." Discontent re-emerges as a central explanatory factor – only with the dependent variable no longer violent behavior but, instead, acquiescence in the support of a revolutionary elite, coalition, or organization.

There is still another tension within the political conflict perspective. On the one hand, because emphasis is placed upon organized political activity, the state becomes central. Indeed Tilly argues that structural transformations of states have provided the opportunities and provocations for a large proportion of violent political conflicts; that agents of the state are the most active perpetrators of violence; and that "war bears a crucial relationship to revolution" both through its impact upon coercive capacities and through its effect on governmental demands upon subject populations (Tilly, 1975:532–37). But, on the other hand, Tilly's stress upon multiple sovereignty as the defining characteristic of revolution trivializes – inadvertently, no doubt – the role of the state. The state is not seen as determining by its own strength or weakness whether or not a revolutionary situation can emerge at all. Instead it is portrayed as an organization competing for popular support on more or less equal terms with one or more fully formed revolutionary organizations or blocs. Societal members are envisaged as able to choose freely and deliberately whether to support the government or a revolutionary organization, with their choices determining whether or not a revolutionary situation develops. Thus, according to Tilly:

> The revolutionary moment arrives when previously acquiescent members of . . . [a] population find themselves confronted with strictly incompatible demands from the government and from an alternative body claiming control over the government – and obey the alternative body. They pay taxes to it, provide men for its armies, feed its functionaries, honor its symbols, give time to its service, or yield other resources, despite the prohibition of a still-existing government they formerly obeyed. Multiple sovereignty has begun. [1975:520–21]

In sum, while the political conflict theorists explicitly reject the notions of discontented or disoriented or morally outraged people directly turning to revolutionary behavior that destroys or overturns the regime or the social system, nevertheless they maintain a largely social-psychological perspective on the causes of revolution. For they retain the image of organized, conscious revolutionaries arising to challenge governmental organizations through appeals for social support from discontented or ideologically converted people.

TOWARD A STRUCTURAL AND COMPARATIVE-HISTORICAL APPROACH

Indeed, if one steps back from the clashes among the leading perspectives on revolution just reviewed, what seems most striking is the sameness of the image of the overall revolutionary process that underlies and informs all three approaches. According to that shared image: First, changes in or affecting societies, social systems, or populations give rise to grievances, social disorientation, or new groups and potentials for collective mobilization. Then there develops a purposive, broadly based movement – coalescing with the aid of ideology and organization – which consciously undertakes to overthrow the existing government, and perhaps the entire social order. Finally, the revolutionary movement fights it out with the "authorities" or the "government" and, if it wins, undertakes to establish its own control, authority, or program of societal transformation. What no one ever seems to doubt is that the basic condition for the occurrence of a revolution is the emergence from society or a people of a deliberate effort, tying together leaders and followers, aimed at overthrowing the existing political or social order. Adherence to this image naturally coaxes even theories intended to be social-structural into social-psychological explanations, for it inexorably pushes analysts' attention toward people's feelings and consciousness – of dissatisfactions and of fundamentally oppositional goals and values – as the central problematic issue in the explanation of revolutions.

But in fact the assumptions about societal order and change that underpin the revolutionary movement image are internally contradictory. If the stability of the core institutions of societies truly rested upon the voluntary support of people who could readily withdraw it and force readjustments if and when those institutions ceased to meet their needs or accord with their values, then revolutions should either happen continually (perhaps every generation, as Thomas Jefferson once proposed) or else, if reform movements were the typical mechanism of adjustment, never at all. On the other hand, if societal order (in general, or in specific types of societies) does *not* rest upon value consensus and/or member satisfactions, if, conversely, institutionalized domination of the many by the few prevails, then revolutions – although according to the existing theoretical perspectives they might be especially "needed" and likely under such circumstances – could hardly develop according to the pattern of the liberal reform movement, in which people coalesce around an explicit program of change and strive to achieve its adoption. For the *normal* functioning of institutionalized domination would surely prevent the emergence of any full-blown, well-organized, and extensively supported movement ideologically and actively committed to revolution. Such a movement would be likely to emerge only *after* a crisis in the normal patterns of state, and perhaps also class, domination, thus rendering the development of such a crisis one of the crucial things to be explained in order to account for revolutions.

Moreover, in any revolutionary crisis, differentially situated and motivated groups become participants in a complex unfolding of multiple conflicts that ultimately give rise to outcomes not originally foreseen or intended by any of the particular groups involved. As the historian Gordon Wood argues:

It is not that men's motives are unimportant; they indeed make events, including revolutions. But the purposes of men, especially in a revolution, are so numerous, so varied, and so contradictory that their complex interaction produces results that no one intended or could even foresee. It is this interaction and these results that recent historians are referring to when they speak so disparagingly of these "underlying determinants" and "impersonal and inexorable forces" bringing on the Revolution. Historical explanation which does not account for these "forces," which, in other words, relies simply on understanding the conscious intentions of the actors, will thus be limited. [1973:129]

Any valid theory of revolution rests on the possibility and the necessity of the analyst "rising above" the participants' viewpoints to find, across given historical instances, similar institutional and historical-circumstantial patterns in the situations where revolutions have occurred and in the processes by which they have developed.

An explanation of revolutions must find problematic, first, the emergence of a revolutionary situation, wholistically conceived, and second, the complex and unintended intermeshing of the various motivated actions of the differentially situated groups which take part in the revolution – an intermeshing that produces overall changes which never correspond to the original intentions of any one group, no matter how "central" it may seem. One can begin to make sense of such complexity only by focusing simultaneously on the interrelated situations of groups within specified societal institutional nexuses, and the interrelations of societies within dynamic international fields. To take such an impersonal and nonsubjective viewpoint – and one which emphasizes patterns of institutionalized relationships among persons, positions, and groups – is to work from what may in some generic sense be called a structural perspective on sociohistorical reality.

How, then, does one proceed from a generalized commitment to such a social-structural frame of reference to the actual development of explanatory hypotheses about revolutions? Shall we plunge directly from our very general notions about how societies are integrated and what revolutionary processes are like, into an attempt to deduce general propositions about some generic revolutionary process conceived to be possible and similar in all times, places, and types of sociopolitical orders? This sort of generalizing, deductive strategy is currently fashionable in social science, and has been the approach followed by all recent theorists of revolution. Thus, for example, Gurr, Johnson, and Tilly alike have attempted to describe and explain revolutions *directly* in terms of general processes occurring within universal entities, individual or collective: that is, relative deprivation leading to frustration and political violence in aggregates of individuals; strains giving rise to value redefinition in social systems; and the occurrence and resolution of multiple sovereignty in polities.

But when it comes to explaining phenomena such as revolutions, the difficulties with such generalizing, deductive strategies for theory-building are threefold. First, highly general theoretical propositions seem to work best in the social sciences, given their existing levels of theoretical development, only to explain phenomena which can be characterized very simply, if not literally, one-dimensionally. But, as virtually all will agree, revolutions are by nature complex and multidimensional.

Second, if one is to take a social-structural approach toward explaining revolutions, one really must theorize in terms of various specific types of societies, for there is little or nothing of any significance that can be said about the political or socio-economic institutions of all kinds of known human societies lumped together. Moreover all successful revolutions to date have occurred in one or another sort of agrarian state, and nothing is to be gained by ignoring this fact in order to develop a theory putatively capable of explaining revolutions in any sort of society from a band or tribe to an advanced industrial nation. If one wishes to generalize from findings about past revolutions in agrarian states to speculation about future possibilities for revolutions in, say, industrial societies, then the more fruitful way to proceed is to attempt to identify the conceivable functional equivalents of, or alternatives for, the causal patterns that can be directly established for revolutionary transformations of agrarian sociopolitical structures.

Third, a primarily deductive and universalizing mode of theory-building makes no real sense for explaining revolutions, because there have been, by any well-focused definition, only a small number of cases, and all of them, as the etiology of the concept "revolution" implies, have occurred during the era of "modernization," in the last several hundred years of world history (Hatto, 1949; Griewank, 1971; Arendt, 1965:chap. 1; Huntington, 1968:chap. 5). Indeed, modernizing trends operative at international as well as intranational levels – for example, commercialization and industrialization, and the rise of national states and of the European states system – have been intrinsically related both to the causes and consequences of revolutions. Of course, to aid in disentangling the multiple, complex processes of revolutions, the investigator can and must make use of whatever available insights there are about human behavior and social processes in general. But the revolutionary processes themselves should be assumed to be, in part, specific to particular, nonuniversal types of sociopolitical structures, and, for the rest, specific to particular sorts of world-historical circumstances.

A critic might well argue at this point that, precisely because they are so few in number and tied to particular world-historical developments, revolutions as such should be studied only by "narrative historians," leaving social scientists free to theorize about more general phenomena. But no such drastic response is necessary. Revolutions *can* be treated as "a theoretical subject." To generalize inductively about them and verify hypotheses about their causes and consequences one can employ the comparative historical method, with selected national historical trajectories as the units of comparison. According to this method – which has a long and distinguished pedigree in social science – one looks for concomitant variations, contrasting cases where the phenomenon one seeks to explain is present with cases where it is absent, controlling in the process for as many sources of extraneous variation as possible by contrasting positive and negative instances which are otherwise as similar as possible

(Nagel, 1950; Sewell, 1967; Smelser, 1971; Smelser, unpublished, 1966; Lijphart, 1971).

As the mode of multivariate analysis to which one necessarily resorts when there are too many variables and not enough cases (Smelser, unpublished, 1966; Lijphart, 1971), comparative analysis is likely to remain the only scientific tool available to the macrosociologist who is interested in national political conflicts and developments, and who is also sensitive to the enormous impacts of world-contextual variables upon national developments (see Hopkins and Wallerstein, 1967). Given the combined variability of "internal" patterns and external situations, analyses of phenomena such as revolutions will make sense only for carefully delineated categories containing a few cases apiece. In contrast to the past practice of the "natural historians" (Edwards, 1927; Brinton, 1938), there should be included in any study both positive and negative cases, so that hypotheses about the causes of the phenomena under investigation can be checked against cases where that phenomenon did not occur (e.g., Skocpol, 1976). Ultimately, cases can be grouped and regrouped in different ways according to what questions are being investigated or according to what hypotheses are being tested, so that the end result of proliferating historically sensitive comparisons will be far richer than the products of studies which try to pretend that historical developments and world contexts are irrelevant.

WHAT ABOUT MARXISM?

On the face of it, there is an already well-established theoretical tradition – Marxism – that seems to meet the need for a historically grounded, social-structural approach to explaining revolutions. In many respects, Marxist explanations of revolutions are exemplary. First, the general image of revolutionary processes to which Marxists adhere emphasizes the importance of social-structural contradictions in generating revolutionary crises:

At a certain stage of their development the material forces of production in society come into conflict with the existing relations of production, or – what is but a legal expression of the same thing – with the property relations within which they had been at work before. From forms of development of the forces of production these relations turn into their fetters. Then comes the period of social revolution. [Marx, in Feuer, 1959:43–44]

Second, Marxists do not assume that all revolutions are, for theoretical purposes, the same. Instead Marxists distinguish between "bourgeois" and "socialist" revolutions according to which mode of production, "feudal" or "bourgeois," is being transformed, and among particular variants of each type of revolution through concrete historical analyses of the forces and relations of production and class structures of the various particular societies in which revolutions have occurred. Finally, Marxists do not fail to treat revolutions as intrinsically related to broader processes of large-scale social change, for they argue that both the causes and consequences of revolutions are directly related to socio-economic developments.

Moreover, some very rich social-historical studies of revolutions have been published in recent years by American social scientists operating within Marxist-derived theoretical frames of reference. Both Barrington Moore, Jr., in his *Social Origins of Dictatorship and Democracy* (1966), and Eric R. Wolf, in his *Peasant Wars of the Twentieth Century* (1969), extended Marxist concepts and hypotheses to analyze revolutions in predominately agrarian countries. Specifically, Moore and Wolf developed path-breaking hypotheses about the historical and social-structural conditions that determine when and how agrarian classes, especially landlords on the one hand, and peasant communities on the other, will engage in collective actions that affect the outcomes of societal political upheavals which occur as agrarian countries are subjected to the effects of capitalist developments. Since peasant revolts have played key roles in every historical instance of social revolution, the advances achieved by Moore and Wolf can and must be incorporated into any historically oriented, social-structural theory of revolutions.

Nevertheless, Marxist-derived theories of revolutionary processes cannot be uncritically accepted as rigorous, empirically validated explanations. The reason why can be straightforwardly stated: The basic Marxist explanation sketch – which argues that revolutions are caused by socio-economic developments that lead to the outbreak of class struggles which, in turn, transform and mark the divide between distinct modes of production – simply does not succeed in laying bare the overall logic of actual historical revolutions. Thus the roles of peasants and urban lower strata, not to mention the dominant strata, in the French, Russian, Mexican, and Chinese revolutions cannot be understood without detailed analysis of the class positions of the various groups, yet political struggles central to these revolutions cannot be comprehended in strictly class terms. Likewise, the causes and consequences of revolutions cannot be comprehended without knowledge of modes of production and their dynamics, yet revolutionary situations involve political-military as well as economic "contradictions." Nor does the juxtaposition of modes of production – feudal/bourgeois for the French and Mexican revolutions, and bourgeois/socialist for the Russian and Chinese – at all adequately characterize the transformations wrought by these revolutions.

Marxist-inspired investigators have rested content with applying or modifying the existing conceptual categories to illuminate the class and group conflicts that occur during revolutions, and have not actually put to empirical test explicit Marxist propositions about the causes of revolutions – using the comparative historical method of checking common patterns identified for positive cases against evidence from similar negative cases. As a result it has been possible for them to downplay for theoretical purposes the very central role of the state in revolutions. In accounting for the causes of revolutions the theoretical emphasis is always placed upon economic developments and class contradictions, while the capacities of political rulers, given the state organizations at hand, to cope with international pressures and, internally, with upper-class political dissidence and lower-class rebellions, are matters often treated descriptively, but never examined theoretically with an eye to identifying the social-structural conditions that might systematically affect such political capacities. Marxist scholars have failed to notice that causal variables referring to the strength and structure of states and the relations of state organizations to class structures may discriminate between cases of successful revolution and cases of failure or nonoccurrence far better than do variables referring to class structures and patterns of economic development alone. Moreover, in their characterizations of the outcomes of revolutions, Marxist-oriented scholars emphasize changes in class structures and even very long-run economic developments, while virtually ignoring the often much more striking and immediate transformations that occur in the structure and functions of state organizations such as armies and administrations, and in the relations between the state and social classes. And, again, this has meant that they have missed identifying the distinctive political-institutional changes that set revolutions apart from nonrevolutionary patterns of national development.

To pull together, then, the strands of the argument made in the course of this review essay: I am suggesting that substantial progress can be made toward explaining revolutions only through a new theoretical strategy – one which synthesizes *an historically grounded, social-structural style of explanation,* akin to the Marxist approach to explaining revolution but differing in substantive emphases, *with a comparative historical method of hypothesis testing,* akin to the statistical techniques idealized by contemporary social scientists, but specifically tailored to handle many variables when there are but a small number of cases. By thus combining, on the one hand, that fusion of theoretical understanding and historical relevance characteristic of a great and enduring macro-theoretical tradition with, on the other hand, the concern of contemporary social science for rigorous hypothesis testing, students of revolution can avoid the twin dangers of abstract, irrelevant theorizing and empirical inadequacy that have long plagued explanatory efforts in this area of inquiry.

REFERENCES

Adam, Herbert. 1971. *Modernizing Racial Domination: South Africa's Political Dynamics.* Berkeley: University of California Press.
Arendt, Hannah. 1965. *On Revolution.* New York: Viking.
Avrich, Paul H. 1963. "Russian factory committees in 1917." *Jahrbücher fur Geschichte Osteuropas* 11:161–182.
Brinton, Crane. 1938. *The Anatomy of Revolution.* New York: Norton.

Chamberlin, William Henry. 1935. *The Russian Revolution, 1917–1921.* New York: Grosset and Dunlap, 1965.

Davies, James C. 1962. "Toward a theory of revolution." *American Sociological Review* 27:5–19.

1969. "The J-curve of rising and declining satisfactions as a cause of some great revolutions and a contained rebellion." Pp. 671–709 in Hugh Davis Graham and Ted Robert Gurr (eds.), *Violence in America.* New York: Signet Books.

Eckstein, Harry. 1965. "On the etiology of internal wars." *History and Theory* 4:133–163.

Edwards, Lyford P. 1927. *The Natural History of Revolution.* Chicago: University of Chicago Press.

Feierabend, Ivo K., and Rosalind L. Feierabend. 1972. "Systemic conditions of political aggression: An application of frustration-aggression theory." Pp. 136–183 in Ivo K. Feierabend, Rosalind L. Feierabend, and Ted Robert Gurr (eds.), *Anger, Violence, and Politics.* Englewood Cliffs, N.J.: Prentice-Hall.

Feierabend, Ivo K., Rosalind L. Feierabend, and Ted Robert Gurr (eds.). 1972. *Anger, Violence, and Politics.* Englewood Cliffs, N.J.: Prentice-Hall.

Feierabend, Ivo K., Rosalind L. Feierabend, and Betty A. Nesvold. 1969. "Social change and political violence: Cross-national patterns." Pp. 606–668 in Hugh Davis Graham and Ted Robert Gurr (eds.), *Violence in America.* New York: Signet Books.

1973. "The comparative study of revolution and violence." *Comparative Politics* 5:393–424.

Feuer, Lewis S. (ed.). 1959. *Marx and Engels: Basic Writings on Politics and Philosophy.* Garden City, N.Y.: Doubleday Anchor.

Geschwender, James A. 1968. "Explorations in the theory of social movements and revolutions." *Social Forces* 42:127–135.

Griewank, Karl. 1971. "Emergence of the concept of revolution." Pp. 13–17 in Bruce Mazlish, Arthur D. Kaledin, and David B. Ralston (eds.), *Revolution: A Reader.* New York: Macmillan.

Gurr, Ted Robert. 1968a. "A causal model of civil strife: A comparative analysis using new indices." *American Political Science Review* 27:1104–1124.

1968b. "Psychological factors in civil violence." *World Politics* 20:245–278.

1970. *Why Men Rebel.* Princeton, N.J.: Princeton University Press.

1973. "The revolution-social-change nexus." *Comparative Politics* 5:359–392.

Hatto, Arthur. 1949. " 'Revolution': An inquiry into the usefulness of an historical term." *Mind* 58: 495–517.

Hopkins, Terence K., and Immanuel Wallerstein. 1967. "The comparative study of national societies." *Social Science Information* 6:25–58.

Huntington, Samuel P. 1968. *Political Order in Changing Societies.* New Haven: Yale University Press.

Johnson, Chalmers. 1966. *Revolutionary Change.* Boston: Little Brown.

Lefebvre, Georges. 1932. *The Great Fear of 1789.* Reprint. New York: Pantheon, 1973.

Lijphart, Arend. 1971. "Comparative politics and the comparative method." *American Political Science Review* 65:682–693.

Lupsha, Peter A. 1971. "Explanation of political violence: Some psychological theories versus indignation." *Politics and Society* 2:89–104.

Moore, Barrington, Jr. 1966. *Social Origins of Dictatorship and Democracy.* Boston: Beacon Press.

Muller, Edward N. 1972. "A test for a partial theory of potential for political violence." *American Political Science Review* 66:928–959.

Nagel, Ernest (ed.). 1950. *John Stuart Mill's Philosophy of Scientific Method*. New York: Hafner.
Oberschall, Anthony. 1969. "Rising expectations and political turmoil." *Journal of Development Studies* 6:5–22.
    1973. *Social Conflict and Social Movements*. Englewood Cliffs, N.J.: Prentice-Hall.
Overholt, William. 1972. "Revolution." In *The Sociology of Political Organization*. Croton-on-Hudson, N.Y.: Hudson Institute.
Parsons, Talcott. 1951. *The Social System*. New York: Free Press.
Portes, Alejandro. 1971. "On the logic of post-factum explanations: The hypothesis of lower-class frustrations as the cause of leftist radicalism." *Social Forces* 50:26–44.
Rudé, George. 1959. *The Crowd in the French Revolution*. New York: Oxford University Press.
Russell, D. E. H. 1974. *Rebellion, Revolution, and Armed Force*. New York: Academic Press.
Schwartz, David C. 1971. "A theory of revolutionary behavior." Pp. 109–132 in James C. Davies (ed.), *When Men Revolt and Why*. New York: Free Press.
    1972. "Political alienation: The psychology of revolution's first stage." Pp. 58–66 in Ivo K. Feierabend, Rosalind L. Feierabend, and Ted Robert Gurr (eds.), *Anger, Violence, and Politics*. Englewood Cliffs, N.J.: Prentice-Hall.
Sewell, William H., Jr. 1967. "Marc Bloch and the logic of comparative history." *History and Theory* 6:208–218.
Skocpol, Theda. 1976. "France, Russia, and China: A structural analysis of social revolutions." *Comparative Studies in Society and History* 18(2):175–210.
Smelser, Neil J. 1963. *Theory of Collective Behavior*. New York: Free Press of Glencoe.
    1971. "Alexis de Tocqueville as a comparative analyst." Pp. 19–47 in Ivan Vallier (ed.), *Comparative Methods in Sociology*. Berkeley: University of California Press.
    Unpubl. "The methodology of comparative analysis."
Snyder, David, and Charles Tilly. 1972. "Hardship and collective violence in France, 1830 to 1960." *American Sociological Review* 37:520–532.
Taylor, George V. 1972. "Revolutionary and nonrevolutionary content in the *Cahiers* of 1789: An interim report." *French Historical Studies* 7:479–502.
Tilly, Charles. 1969. "Collective violence in European perspective." Pp. 1–42 in Hugh Davis Graham and Ted Robert Gurr (eds.), *Violence in America*. New York: Signet Books.
    1973. "Does modernization breed revolution?" *Comparative Politics* 5:425–447.
    1974. "Town and country in revolution." Pp. 271–302 in John Wilson Lewis (ed.), *Peasant Rebellion and Communist Revolution in Asia*. Stanford, Calif.: Stanford University Press.
    1975. "Revolutions and collective violence." Pp. 483–555 in Fred I. Greenstein and Nelson W. Polsby (eds.), *Handbook of Political Science*. Vol. 3. Reading, Mass.: Addison-Wesley.
Tilly, Charles, Louise Tilly, and Richard Tilly. 1975. *The Rebellious Century, 1830–1930*. Cambridge, Mass.: Harvard University Press.
Tilly, Louise. 1971. "The food riot as a form of political conflict in France." *Journal of Interdisciplinary History* 2:23–57.
Tiryakian, Edward. 1967. "A model of societal change and its lead indicators." Pp. 69–97 in Samuel Z. Klausner (ed.), *The Study of Total Societies*. Garden City, N.Y.: Doubleday Anchor.
Trotsky, Leon. 1932. *The Russian Revolution*. Selected and edited by F. W. Dupee. Garden City, N.Y.: Doubleday Anchor, 1959.

Wolf, Eric R. 1969. *Peasant Wars of the Twentieth Century.* New York: Harper and Row.

Womack, John, Jr. 1968. *Zapata and the Mexican Revolution.* New York: Vintage Books.

Wood, Gordon. 1973. "The American Revolution." Pp. 113–148 in Lawrence Kaplan (ed.), *Revolutions: A Comparative Study.* New York: Vintage Books.

Revolutions and the world-historical development of capitalism

THEDA SKOCPOL AND ELLEN KAY TRIMBERGER

Karl Marx's theory of revolutions was elegant, powerful, and politically relevant because it linked the causes and consequences of revolutions directly to the historical emergence and transcendence of capitalism. Nevertheless, events and scholarship since Marx's time show that there is a need for revised ways of understanding revolutions in relation to the world-historical development of capitalism. In the spirit of furthering theoretical efforts to this end, we propose to do two things in this short paper. First, we shall identify the essential elements of Marx's original theory of revolutions and indicate some important ways in which his ideas fail to square with the actual patterns of revolutions as they have occurred historically. Then we shall suggest some alternative analytic emphases that must in our opinion underlie explanations of major types of historical revolutions and efforts to situate them in relation to the development of capitalism. In doing these things, we shall draw especially upon our own comparative historical investigations of social revolutions in France, Russia and China[1] and of bureaucratic revolutions from above in Japan and Turkey,[2] as well as upon the work of scholars such as Immanuel Wallerstein, Otto Hintze, and Daniel Chirot,[3] who have explored transnational aspects of capitalism as a world system.

Earlier versions of this paper were presented at the first annual conference on The Political Economy of the World System at American University on March 31, 1977, and at the session on the "Sociology of the World System" at the 72nd Annual Meeting of the American Sociological Association, Chicago, Illinois, September 5, 1977. Because this paper attempts to highlight central themes of investigations of revolutions that we have pursued over many years, we cannot possibly acknowledge everyone who has helped us. However, we do want to thank Michael Burawoy, Margaret Cerullo, Wally Goldfrank, Jerry Karabel, Judy Stacey, Jeff Weintraub, Jonathan Zeitlin, and the staff of the *Berkeley Journal*, all of whom read earlier drafts of this paper and made criticisms and comments that allowed us to sharpen our arguments – though not always in ways with which they might agree.

I

Before we launch into critical discussion, let us briefly underline some aspects of Marx's approach to revolutions[4] that are still compelling and which we want to recapitulate in our own approach. First, unlike many contemporary academic social scientists, Marx did not try to create a general theory of revolution relevant to all kinds of societies at all times. Instead, he regarded revolutions as specific to certain historical circumstances and to certain types of societies. In accord with this mode of analysis, our arguments about revolutions apply specifically to agrarian states situated in disadvantaged positions within developing world capitalism. It seems to us that revolutions in advanced industrial capitalist or state-socialist societies would have different forms and occur in different ways.

Second, Marx developed a social-structural theory of revolutions which argued that organized and conscious movements for revolutionary change succeed only where and when there is an objectively revolutionary situation, due to contradictions in the larger societal structure and historical situation: thus Marx's oft-quoted saying that men make their own history, but not in circumstances of their own choosing and not just as they please. We have a different conception from Marx about what creates objectively revolutionary crises, but our analysis, like his, hinges on discerning how revolutionary situations arise out of structural relations and historical processes outside of the deliberate control of acting groups.

Third, Marx made class domination central to his conception of social order, and class conflict a defining feature of revolution, and we retain such concerns. In her work on revolutions from above, Trimberger defines revolution as any extra-legal takeover of the state apparatus that destroys the political and economic power of that class which controlled the dominant means of production under the old regime. And in her work on mass-based social revolutions from below, Skocpol defines this particular type of revolution as a sudden, basic transformation of a society's political and socio-economic (including class) structure, accompanied and in part effectuated through class upheavals from below.

Taking off from these continuities with Marx's approach to revolutions, we can now identify various points at which Marx's original theory[5] of revolutions stands in need of revision when juxtaposed to historical revolutions from above and below as we understand them. We shall discuss in turn issues about causes, processes, and outcomes of revolutions.

Causes

Marx held that a revolutionary situation occurs when an existing mode of production reaches the limits of its contradictions. The decisive contradictions are *economic* contradictions that develop between the social forces and the social relations of production. In turn, intensifying class conflict is generated between the existing dominant class and the rising, revolutionary class. Thus Marx theorized that revolutionary contradictions are internally generated within a society. What is more, his perspective strongly suggested that revolutions should occur first in the most economically advanced social formations of a given mode of production.

Actual historical revolutions, though, have not conformed to Marx's theoretical expectations. From the French Revolution on, they have occurred in predominantly agrarian countries where capitalist relations of production were only barely or moderately developed. In every instance, political-military pressures from more economically advanced countries abroad have been crucial in contributing to the outbreak of revolution. Marx began an analysis of uneven world capitalist development, but he did not link this directly to the cause of revolutions. Nor do we agree that the objective conditions within the old regimes that explain the emergence of revolutionary situations have been primarily economic. Rather, they have been *political* contradictions centered in the structure and situation of states caught in cross-pressures between, on the one hand, military competitors on the international scene and, on the other hand, the constraints of the existing domestic economy and (in some cases) resistance by internal politically powerful class forces to efforts by the state to mobilize resources to meet international competition. To mention some examples: the Japanese Meiji Restoration (a bureaucratic revolution from above) occurred because the Tokugawa state (which was already highly bureaucratic) came under severe and novel pressures from imperialist capitalist Western powers; the French and Chinese Revolutions broke out because the Bourbon and Manchu regimes were caught in contradictions between pressures from economically more developed foreign states and resistance from dominant class forces at home; and the Russian Revolution broke out because the Tsarist bureaucracy and military dissolved under the impact of World War I upon economically backward Russia. Thus, it is conflict between nation-states in the context of uneven development of world capitalism that is central to the genesis of revolutions.

Processes

Marx theorized that, given a revolutionary situation, revolutions are fundamentally accomplished through class struggles led by that class which emerges within the womb of the old mode of production and becomes central to the new, post-revolutionary mode of production. Historically, only two classes play this leading revolutionary role. In bourgeois revolutions, a capitalist class that has grown up within feudalism plays the leading role in the revolutionary class conflicts by which feudal relations of production are overthrown and capitalism established instead. In socialist revolutions in advanced capitalist societies, the proletariat plays the leading role. In either type of revolution, the hegemonic revolutionary class may have allies. But such subordinate, allied classes are not capable of becoming nationally organized and self-conscious classes-for-themselves, and consequently they do not control the revolutionary process or outcomes in their own interests, as does the leading revolutionary class.

On the basis of the historical record, two major sets of reservations need to be registered about these ideas of Marx. One point has to do with the relative contributions of class forces and political leaderships to the accomplishment of revolutions. Some revolutions – i.e. revolutions from above – which have had outcomes and consequences that seem quite revolutionary from a Marxist perspective, have not actually been made by class forces or through class struggles; instead, bureaucratic-military political elites have reorganized states and used state power to effect socio-economic structural transformations. For example, the Meiji Restoration in Japan – a revolution from above which destroyed the economic and political power of the traditional aristocracy and created a centralized state apparatus used to initiate successful capitalist development – was led by samurai bureaucrats in control of military and organizational resources, but with no personal control over, or vested interest in, the agrarian economy. These bureaucratic revolutionaries acted in response to nationalist movements among the traditional aristocracy demanding an end to Western intervention in Japan, but such domestic conflict excluded the mass of the peasantry and was quite different from Marx's notion of class struggle.[6] Other revolutions – especially social revolutions such as the French, Russian, Chinese, Mexican, Vietnamese and Angolan – have been effected in part through class struggles. But here, too, state-building leadership groups have played very central roles.[7] How, for example, could the processes and outcomes of the Russian, Chinese and Vietnamese revolutions be understood without attention to the contribution of Leninist-Communist parties, or the French Revolution without attention to the role of the Jacobins and Napoleon? In both revolutions from above and social revolutions from below, political leadership emerged from the ranks of educated strata already oriented toward government service in the pre-capitalist, statist old regimes. During the revolutionary crises, these leaderships struggled to reorganize state power on a basis that would defend revolutionary changes against international enemies and enhance national autonomy vis-à-vis foreign states. In short, we are arguing that it does not make sense to try to reduce the contribution of revolutionary parties or bureaucratic-military elites to that of merely representing and acting along with class forces, since these specifically political forces have been uniquely responsible for consolidating revolutions by establishing new state organizations.

The second point to be made in reaction to Marx's views on the processes of revolutions has to do with which classes actually are central to revolutions. In our view, revolutionary leadership has never come from those who controlled the means of production. Hence, we find no instance of a class-conscious capitalist bourgeoisie playing the leading political role in a revolution (though of course some revolutions have contributed in their outcomes to the further or future growth of capitalism and bourgeois class dominance). Moreover, because social revolutions from below have occurred in agrarian states situated in more or less disadvantaged positions within developing world capitalism, their successful occurrence has not been determined by the struggle of proletarians against capitalists, but rather by the class struggles of peasants against dominant landed classes and/or colonial or neo-colonial regimes.[8]

Outcomes

Finally, we arrive at the issue of what revolutions immediately accomplish, once they have successfully occurred. Marx held that revolutions mark the transition from one mode of production to another, that they so transform class relations as to create conditions newly appropriate for further economic development. Superstructural transformations of ideology and the state also occur, but these were seen by Marx as parallel to and reinforcing the fundamental changes in class relations.

Yet, historically, revolutions have changed state structures as much as, or more than, they have changed class relations of production and surplus appropriation. In all of the cases of revolution from above and below that we studied, state structures became much more centralized and bureaucratic. Moreover, Third World revolutions since World War II have broken or weakened the bonds of colonial or neo-colonial dependency above all by creating truly sovereign and, in some cases, mass-mobilizing national governments.[9] Equally important, the effects that revolutions have had upon the subsequent economic development of the nations they have transformed have been traceable not only to the changes in class structures but also to the *changes in state structures and functions* that the revolutions accomplished. As Immanuel Wallerstein has very aptly argued, "development [i.e., national economic development] does require a 'breakthrough.' But it is a political breakthrough that in turn makes possible the far more gradual economic process."[10]

II

If Marx's original, elegant theory is no longer entirely adequate, then how can we make sense in new ways of revolutions in relation to the development of capitalism? Obviously, we are not going to be able to provide complete answers here. But we can propose three analytic principles that we have found especially useful in our own efforts to explain revolutions from above and below in agrarian states situated within developing world capitalism. These are: (1) a non-reductionist conception of states; (2) social-structural analyses of the situation of the peasantry within the old and new regimes (and for cases of social revolution from below, in relation to the organized revolutionary leadership); and (3) a focus on international military competition among states within the historically developing world capitalist economy. Let us elaborate each point in turn.

The state

We believe that states should be viewed theoretically as conditioned by, but not entirely reducible in their structure or functioning to, economic and/or class interests or structures. States are neither mere instruments of dominant class forces nor structures simply shaped by objective economic constraints. Rather, states are fundamentally administrative and military organizations that extract resources from society and deploy them to maintain order at home and to compete against other states abroad. Consequently, while it is always true that states are greatly constrained by economic conditions and partly shaped and influenced by class forces, nevertheless, state structures and activities also have an underlying integrity and a logic of their own, and these are keyed to the dynamics of international military rivalries and to the geo-political as well as world-economic circumstances in which given states find themselves.

This conception of states[11] helps to make sense of certain of the facts about the causes of revolutions that seemed so jarring when placed in juxtaposition with Marx's original notions. For if states are coercive organizations not reducible to class structures, then it makes sense that processes that serve to undermine state strength should be crucial in bringing about revolutions from below, while revolutions from above are based upon political reorganization within a state that is already strong and autonomous over against class forces. In all of the five countries that we have studied most intensively – France, Russia, China, Japan and Turkey – there were, prior to the revolutions, relatively centralized and partially bureaucratic monarchical states, none of which had been incorporated into a colonial empire. As they came under pressure in a capitalist world, these states had the capacity to try to mobilize national resources to stave off foreign domination – something that occurred through revolution from above in Japan and Turkey, whereas the old regimes broke down completely in France, Russia, and China, clearing the way for revolutions from below. Thus, Trimberger has demonstrated how in Japan the separation of samurai bureaucrats from control over the means of production and the absence of a consolidated landed class able to exert political influence permitted military bureaucrats to undertake under foreign pressure a revolution from above without mass participation, which destroyed the traditional aristocracy and polity, and established a modern state that fostered capitalist development. With more difficulty and less success, a similar process took place in Turkey. And Skocpol has shown how in Bourbon France and Imperial China politically powerful landed classes were able to limit the autonomy of civil and military state bureaucrats, undermining the effectiveness of their attempts at modernizing reforms and causing the disintegration of centralized repressive controls over the lower classes. In Russia, the landed nobility was much less politically powerful vis-à-vis reforming state authorities, but the agrarian class structure nevertheless limited Russia's ability to prepare for the exigencies of modern warfare, so that the Tsarist state was overwhelmed and destroyed in World War I. The theoretically relevant point that applies to all of these cases regardless of the various patterns is that if one treats states theoretically as potentially autonomous even vis-à-vis the existing class structure and dominant class, then one can explore the dynamic *interactions* between the state organizations and dominant class interests. In situations of intense foreign politico-military pressure, these interactions can become contradictory and lead either to state action against dominant class interests or to dominant class forces acting in ways that undermine the state. Thus, the non-reductionist theoretical approach to the state helps make sense of the specifically political crises that launch revolutions.

This conception of the state also helps to render understandable those aspects of the processes and outcomes of revolutions that Marx's class conflict theory of revolutions seems to downplay or ignore. Revolutions are not consolidated until new or transformed state administrative and coercive organizations are securely established in the place of the old regime. Consequently, it makes sense that political leaderships – parties or bureaucratic/military cliques – that act to consolidate revolutionized state organizations should play a central role in revolutionary processes. And if states are extractive organizations that can deploy resources to some extent independently of existing class interests, then it makes sense that revolutions create the *potentials* for breakthroughs in national economic development in large part by giving rise to more powerful, centralized, and autonomous state organizations. This was true for all of the revolutions from above and below that we studied, although the potential for state-guided or initiated national economic development was more thoroughly realized in Japan, Russia, and China than it was in France and Turkey. Thus, the actual realization of the revolution-created potential depends upon the international and world-historical economic constraints and opportunities that are specific to each case after the revolution.[12]

The situation of the peasantry

In addition to looking at states as relatively autonomous and in dynamic interrelation with dominant classes, one should also pay careful attention to the situation of the peasantry in relation to the state and dominant class. Historically, mass-based social revolutions from below have successfully occurred only if the breakdown of old-regime state organizations has happened in an agrarian socio-political context where peasants, as the majority, producing class, possess (or obtain) sufficient local economic and political autonomy to revolt against landlords. Such results occurred successfully in the French, Russian, and Chinese Revolutions alike. By contrast (as Skocpol has argued), the German Revolution of 1848–50 was condemned to failure by the lack of socio-political conditions conducive to peasant rebellion East of the Elbe. And it was certainly an important condition for revolutions *from above* in Japan and Turkey that peasants in those countries remained immured within traditional structures not conducive to widespread revolts against landlords.

What is more, the varying outcomes of successful social revolutions are significantly affected by the specific way in which the peasantry becomes involved in the overall revolutionary process, and by the nature of its relationship to the state organizations of the new regime. For, although Marx was mistaken to slight the revolutionary potential of the peasantry, he was not wrong in arguing that the peasantry is incapable of becoming a nationally self-organized class for itself. Even when peasants have local community organizations that afford them strong collective solidarity against landlords, they still lack the interest or ability to organize parties or armies that can compete effectively for state power at the national level. Thus, even during successful revolutions, peasants always end up being mobilized or incorporated into revolutionary parties and/or states. Yet the exact way in which this happens – whether, for example, by political organization and persuasion by a peasant-oriented revolutionary party, as in China and Vietnam, or by coercive and bureaucratic domination from above after the initial consolidation of revolutionary state power, as in Russia – makes an important difference for the character of the new regime. Skocpol[13] develops this argument at length for Russia and China in particular, arguing that overall features of the two communist systems (such as degrees and kinds of socio-economic stratification and of state coerciveness and administrative centralization) can be traced in large part to the relationships established between peasants and state-building parties during the revolutionary processes.

The international state system

Finally we arrive at an analytic emphasis that can help make sense of the entire context within which the causes and outcomes of revolutions have been shaped and their consequences determined. In its theoretical essentials, this point has two parts: (a) capitalism should be conceived not only as a mode of production based upon a relationship between wage labor and accumulating capital, but also as a world economy with various zones that are interdependent and unequal[14]; and (b) capitalism from its inception has developed within, around, and through a framework of "multiple political sovereignties" – that is, the system of states that originally emerged from European feudalism[15] and then expanded through the incorporation of pre-existing imperial states, and through colonization followed eventually by decolonization, to cover the entire globe as a system of nations. We must emphasize that, in our view, this changing international system of states was not originally created by capitalism, and throughout modern world capitalist history represents an analytically autonomous level of transnational reality, *interdependent* in its structure and dynamics with the world economy, but not reducible to it. Indeed, just as capitalist economic development has spurred transformations of states and the international states system, so have these "acted back" upon the course of capital accumulation within nations and upon a world scale.[16]

The significance of international military competition for helping to cause the revolutions from above and below that we have studied has been amply alluded to in our discussion of the state. Similarly, John Dunn's studies[17] of contemporary revolutions have led him to argue that "the great bulk of revolutionary success in the twentieth century has been intimately related to either of two very undomestic processes: world war and decolonization,"[18] both developments within the international state system of world capitalism.

The analysis of capitalism as a world system and of revolution as generated by state competition and state formation within this system also provides a framework from which to interpret the results of revolutions, and helps us to understand why there has been continual disillusionment when revolutionary outcomes have failed to mesh with ideological claims. Although there have been important variations in the state structures that have emerged from revolutions, all revolutions during the evolution of world capitalism have given rise to more bureaucratized and centralized states. While not completely rejecting analyses that stress impetuses toward post-revolutionary bureaucratization traceable to influences of the old regime or revolutionary parties, our analysis does shift the emphasis to the necessity faced by the revolutionized regimes of coping with international pressures comparable to those that helped to create the revolutionary crises in the first place. It is not just revolutions from above, but all revolutions that have become "bureaucratic revolutions" – in the specific sense of creating larger, more centralized, and more autonomous state organizations than existed under the old regimes.[19] Revolutionary leaders have sought to enhance national standing and have seen the state apparatus as the most important tool to achieve this, especially where the state could be used to guide or undertake national industrialization. International pressures have been more effective in determining the outcomes of revolutions than intra-national pressures for equality, participation and decentralization. Even in China, where organized interests have fought for more equality and participation, China's vulnerable international situation has always encouraged centralization and bureaucracy.

How are we, finally, to reason about the consequences of revolutions for the development of capitalism and its eventual transformation into socialism? For Marx, this problem could be straightforwardly handled: some revolutions (i.e., bourgeois revolutions) established capitalism, while others (i.e., socialist revolutions) abolished capitalism and created the conditions for the rapid emergence of communism. Marx's "mode of production" was at least implicitly identified with the socio-economic arrangement of a nation-state unit, and the major types of revolutions – bourgeois and socialist – were seen as succeeding each other as given nations developed through major stages from feudalism to capitalism to socialism. Subsequently, Lenin and Trotsky stressed the idea that the capitalist stage (and bourgeois revolution) could be in a sense compressed or skipped over if the proletariat rather than the bourgeoisie took the leading role in a backward country among a set of neighbor countries where revolutions would probably occur roughly simultaneously.

But actual revolutions have not readily conformed to the types and sequences originally projected by Marx or his successors. Certainly no country has had two successive revolutions, one bourgeois and the other socialist, and even revolutions that bear certain superficial resemblances to the "bourgeois" and "socialist" types do not really fit. Revolutions from above and below that have functioned to further bourgeois-capitalist development have not been "made by" class conscious bourgeoisies; as for "socialist revolutions," there have been revolutions made in part through class revolts from below that have culminated in the abolition of private property and the bourgeois class. Yet these have occurred in "backward" agrarian countries, and not solely or primarily through proletarian class action. The outcomes of these revolutions can be described as "state socialist" in the sense that party-states have taken direct control of national economies. Yet these regimes act, so to speak, in the place of the bourgeoisie to promote national industrialization and do not conform to (or converge upon) Marx's original vision of socialism or communism.

From the perspective that capitalism is transnational in scope, we see why Marx's original typology of revolutions cannot hold. Since revolutions have occurred only in specific countries within the capitalist world economy and the international state system, and at particular times in their world-historical development, it follows that no single revolution could possibly either fully establish capitalism or entirely overcome capitalism and establish socialism. Yet some theorists of the "world capitalist system" have taken a position on the consequences of revolutions that we find equally inadequate. For example, Immanuel Wallerstein has argued that the occurrence of national revolutions which abolish capitalist private property in favor of state ownership and control of the means of production has not altered the basic economic structure and dynamics of the world capitalist system.[20] We agree with Wallerstein that state ownership is not socialism, and that no alternative world socialist economy has yet been created. But one can agree with these conclusions while still maintaining that state-socialist revolutions such as the Russian and Chinese have made a real difference for world capitalism because they have culminated in regimes that place unusual and/or extreme restrictions on flows of international trade and private capital investment. To be sure, these restrictions are not absolute and, of course, they vary from one state-socialist country to another. But surely it matters for the structure, dynamics, and longevity of the world capitalist system that, for example in China, a state-socialist revolution occurred rather than a military coup culminating (as in Brazil) in a regime willing to collaborate intimately with foreign investors and willing to promote industrialization for export rather than for furthering more equal internal consumption. We agree with Daniel Chirot, who argues that even if "no unified communist international system exists, this does not lessen the long-range revolutionary threat to the system posed by the communist powers," since "as long as the main goal of [communist] revolutionaries . . . is closure to capitalist influence, the presence of a complete new alternative system is not necessary."[21]

In the final analysis, though, we must always keep in mind that even if revolutions of some types – such as state socialist – do, relatively speaking, disrupt world capitalism (i.e., more than either non-revolutions or non-state socialist revolutions), this does not mean that they simultaneously build socialism. To do this they must *also* promote socio-political equality within and between nations. Both the capitalist world economy and the international state system have pressured revolutionized countries in ways that make more equalitarian patterns difficult to achieve or sustain. Still, some revolutions have done better than others, and different international circumstances provide only part of the reasons. World systems analyses must be supplemented by comparative-historical studies of intra-national structures and struggles. The specific societal configurations of state, economic, and class forces make a great difference in structuring the type of revolutionary outbreak and its consequences for both national and world-capitalist development. Undoubtedly, the equalitarian tendencies of the "state socialist" revolutions of China and Cuba (for example) have been constrained and limited by the necessities of competition and survival in a capitalist world. Nevertheless, the internal class and political struggles that gave rise to those equalitarian tendencies in China and Cuba did make a difference compared to other state socialist revolutions (such as Russia) and compared to other revolutions that did not abolish private property. It was Marx himself who originally made the analysis of such struggles central to our understanding of revolutions. In this he still has the last word.

NOTES

1. Theda Skocpol, "France, Russia and China: A Structural Analysis of Social Revolutions," *Comparative Studies in Society and History* 18 (April 1976), pp. 175–210; Skocpol, "Old Regime Legacies and Communist Revolutions in Russia and China," *Social Forces* 55 (December 1976), pp. 284–315; Skocpol, *States and Social Revolutions* (New York and London: Cambridge University Press, 1979).
2. Ellen Kay Trimberger, "A Theory of Elite Revolutions," *Studies in Comparative International Development* 7 (Fall 1972), pp. 191–207; Trimberger, "State Power

and Modes of Production: Implications of the Japanese Transition to Capitalism," *The Insurgent Sociologist* 7 (Spring 1977), pp. 85–98; Trimberger, *Revolution From Above: Military Bureaucrats and Modernization in Japan, Turkey, Egypt, and Peru* (New Brunswick, N.J.: Transaction Books, 1978).

3. Immanuel Wallerstein, *The Modern World-System: Capitalist Agriculture and the Origins of the European World-Economy in the Sixteenth Century* (New York: Academic Press, 1974); Wallerstein, "The Rise and Future Demise of the World Capitalist System: Concepts for Comparative Analysis," *Comparative Studies in Society and History* 16 (September 1974), pp. 387–415; Otto Hintze, "Economics and Politics in the Age of Modern Capitalism," 1929, in Felix Gilbert (ed.), *The Historical Essays of Otto Hintze* (New York: Oxford University Press, 1975), pp. 422–452; Daniel Chirot, *Social Change in the Twentieth Century* (New York: Harcourt Brace Jovanovich, 1977).

4. Our understanding of Marx's theory of revolutions is synthesized from wide reading in his writings, and we will not give references each time we discuss his views. Important texts for understanding Marx on revolutions include: "The Communist Manifesto," *The German Ideology,* Preface to "A Contribution to the Critique of Political Economy," *The Eighteenth Brumaire of Louis Bonaparte,* and *The Class Struggles in France.* All of these are widely reprinted.

5. In this paper we are deliberately *not* exploring all of the changing emphases to be found in writings on revolution by Marxists since Marx. Nor are we exploring the many nuances to be found in Marx's own writings. Our purpose is to highlight crucial issues for further theorizing about revolutions. Since Marx's ideas are relatively widely known (and, in our view, still the most powerful ideas available about revolutions), we are using the rhetorical device of juxtaposing our arguments and sense of the historical evidence to the central thrust of Marx's theory.

6. Trimberger 1972, 1977, 1978, *op. cit.*

7. This is suggested not only by our own work, but also by Eric Wolf in his "Conclusion" to *Peasant Wars of the Twentieth Century* (New York: Harper and Row, 1969); and John Dunn, in *Modern Revolutions* (New York and London: Cambridge University Press, 1972).

8. Again, beyond our work, see Barrington Moore, Jr., *Social Origins of Dictatorship and Democracy* (Boston: Beacon Press, 1966); Wolf, *op. cit.*; Gerard Chaliand, *Revolution in the Third World: Myths and Prospects* (New York: Viking, 1977).

9. See Dunn 1972, *op. cit.,* and Chaliand, *op. cit.*

10. Immanuel Wallerstein, "The State and Social Transformation: Will and Possibility," *Politics and Society* 1 (May 1971), p. 364.

11. Our argument about states resonates closely with Otto Hintze, "Military Organization and the Organization of the State," 1906, in Felix Gilbert (ed.), *The Historical Essays of Otto Hintze* (New York: Oxford University Press, 1975), pp. 178–215; and Charles Tilly (ed.), *The Formation of National States in Western Europe* (Princeton, N.J.: Princeton University Press, 1975); and it extends recent tendencies within Marxist scholarship (e.g., Nicos Poulantzas, *Political Power and Social Classes* (London: New Left Books, 1973); Perry Anderson, *Lineages of the Absolutist State* (London: New Left Books, 1974); and Fred Block, "The Ruling Class Does Not Rule: Notes on the Marxist Theory of the State," *Socialist Revolution* 7 (May–June 1977), pp. 6–28; to view state organizations and their "managers" as capable of independent initiatives vis-à-vis dominant classes. For a general survey of recent Marxist ideas on the state, see David Gold, Clarence Lo, and Erik Wright, "Recent Developments in Marxist Theories of the Capitalist State," *Monthly Review* (October 1975), pp. 29–43; (November 1975), pp. 36–51.

12. See Susan Eckstein, "How Economically Consequential Are Revolutions?: A Comparison of Mexico and Bolivia," Paper presented at the 70th Annual Meeting of the American Sociological Association, August 27, 1975; and Eckstein, "The Impact of Revolution: A Comparative Analysis of Mexico and Bolivia," Beverly Hills, Calif.: Sage Publications (Contemporary Political Sociology Series), 1975.
13. Skocpol, December 1976, *op. cit.;* and Skocpol, forthcoming, *op. cit.,* chapter 4.
14. Wallerstein, *The Modern World System,* 1971; and September 1974, *op. cit.*
15. Anderson, *op. cit.;* Tilly, *op. cit.*
16. See Hintze 1929, *op. cit.*
17. Dunn 1972, *op. cit.,* and Dunn, "The Success and Failure of Modern Revolutions," Paper presented at the Workshop on the Sources of Radicalism and the Revolutionary Process, Research Institute on International Change, Columbia University, May 7, 1975.
18. Dunn 1975, *op. cit.,* p. 17.
19. Chaliand, *op. cit.*
20. Wallerstein, "Dependence in an Interdependent World: The Limited Possibilities of Transformation Within the Capitalist World Economy," *African Studies Review* 17 (April 1974), pp. 1–25; Wallerstein, September 1974, *op. cit.*
21. Chirot, *op. cit.,* pp. 232–233.

6

France, Russia, China: A structural analysis of social revolutions

'A revolution', writes Samuel P. Huntington in *Political Order in Changing Societies,* 'is a rapid, fundamental, and violent domestic change in the dominant values and myths of a society, in its political institutions, social structure, leadership, and government activities and policies'.[1] In *The Two Tactics of Social Democracy in the Democratic Revolution,* Lenin provides a different, but complementary perspective: 'Revolutions', he says, 'are the festivals of the oppressed and the exploited. At no other time are the masses of the people in a position to come forward so actively as creators of a new social order'.[2]

Together these two quotes delineate the distinctive features of *social revolutions.* As Huntington points out, social revolutions are rapid, basic transformations of socio-economic and political institutions, and – as Lenin so vividly reminds us – social revolutions are accompanied and in part effectuated through class upheavals from below. It is this combination of thoroughgoing structural transformation and massive class upheavals that sets social revolutions apart from coups, rebellions, and even political revolutions and national independence movements.

If one adopts such a specific definition, then clearly only a handful of successful social revolutions have ever occurred. France, 1789, Russia, 1917, and China, 1911–49, are the most dramatic and clear-cut instances. Yet these momentous upheavals have helped shape the fate of the majority of mankind, and their causes, consequences, and potentials have preoccupied many thoughtful people since the late eighteenth century.

Nevertheless, recently, social scientists have evidenced little interest in the study of social revolutions as such. They have submerged revolutions within

This article represents a shortened and revised version of a paper presented at the Session on Revolutions of the 1973 Meetings of the American Sociological Association. For criticism, advice (not all of it heeded), intellectual stimulation and encouragement offered to the author in the long course of preparing this paper, thanks go to: Daniel Bell, Mounira Charrad, Linda Frankel, George Homans, S. M. Lipset, Gary Marx, John Mollenkopf, Barrington Moore, Jr., Bill Skocpol, Sylvia Thrupp and Kay Trimberger.

more general categories – such as 'political violence', 'collective behavior', 'internal war', or 'deviance' – shorn of historical specificity and concern with large-scale social change.[3] The focus has been mostly on styles of behavior common to wide ranges of collective incidents (ranging from riots to coups to revolutions, from panics to hostile outbursts to 'value-oriented movements', and from ideological sects to revolutionary parties), any of which might occur in any type of society at any time or place. Revolutions tend increasingly to be viewed not as 'locomotives of history', but as extreme forms of one or another sort of behavior that social scientists, along with established authorities everywhere, find problematic and perturbing.

Why this avoidance by social science of the specific problem of social revolution? Ideological bias might be invoked as an explanation, but even if it were involved, it would not suffice. An earlier generation of American social scientists, certainly no more politically radical than the present generation, employed the 'natural history' approach to analyze handfuls of cases of great revolutions.[4] In large part, present preoccupation with broader categories can be understood as a reaction against this natural history approach, deemed by its critics too 'historical' and 'a-theoretical'.

In the 'Introduction' to a 1964 book entitled *Internal War,* Harry Eckstein defines 'a theoretical subject' as a 'set of phenomena about which one can develop informative, testable generalizations that hold for all instances of the subject, and some of which apply to those instances alone'.[5] He goes on to assert that while 'a statement about two or three cases is certainly a generalization in the dictionary sense, a generalization in the methodological sense must usually be based on more; it ought to cover a number of cases large enough for certain rigorous testing procedures like statistical analysis to be used'.[6] Even many social scientists who are not statistically oriented would agree with the spirit of this statement: theory in social science should concern itself only with general phenomena; the 'unique' should be relegated to 'narrative historians'.

Apparently it directly follows that no theory specific to social revolution is possible, that the *explanandum* of any theory which sheds light on social revolutions must be something more general than social revolution itself. Hence the efforts to conceptualize revolution as an extreme instance of patterns of belief or behavior which are also present in other situations or events.

This approach, however, allows considerations of technique to define away substantive problems. Revolutions are not just extreme forms of individual or collective behavior. They are distinctive conjunctures of socio-historical structures and processes. One must comprehend them as complex wholes – however few the cases – or not at all.

Fortunately social science is not devoid of a way of confronting this kind of problem. Social revolutions *can* be treated as a 'theoretical subject'. To test hypotheses about them, one may employ the comparative method, with national historical trajectories as the units of comparison. As many students of society have noted, the comparative method is nothing but that mode of multivariate analysis to which sociologists necessarily resort when experimental manipulations are not possible and when there are 'too many variables and not enough cases' – that is, not enough cases for statistical testing of hypotheses.[7] According to this method, one looks for concomitant variations, contrasting cases where the phenomena in which one is interested are present with cases where they are absent, controlling in the process for as many sources of variation as one can, by contrasting positive and negative instances which otherwise are as similar as possible.

Thus, in my inquiry into the conditions for the occurrence and short-term outcomes of the great historical social revolutions in France, Russia and China, I have employed the comparative historical method, specifically contrasting the positive cases with (a) instances of non-social revolutionary modernization, such as occurred in Japan, Germany and Russia (up to 1904), and with (b) instances of abortive social revolutions, in particular Russia in 1905 and Prussia/Germany in 1848. These comparisons have helped me to understand those aspects of events and of structures and processes which distinctively rendered the French, Chinese and Russian Revolutions successful social revolutions. In turn, the absence of conditions identified as positively crucial in France, Russia and China constitutes equally well an explanation of why social revolutions have not occurred, or have failed, in other societies. In this way, hypotheses developed, refined, and tested in the comparative historical analysis of a handful of cases achieve a potentially general significance.

EXPLAINING THE HISTORICAL CASES: REVOLUTION IN MODERNIZING AGRARIAN BUREAUCRACIES

Social revolutions in France, Russia and China occurred, during the earlier world-historical phases of modernization, in agrarian bureaucratic societies situated within, or newly incorporated into, international fields dominated by more economically modern nations abroad. In each case, social revolution was a conjuncture of three developments: (1) the collapse or incapacitation of central administrative and military machineries; (2) widespread peasant rebellions; and (3) marginal elite political movements. What each social revolution minimally 'accomplished' was the extreme rationalization and centralization of state institutions, the removal of a traditional landed upper class from intermediate (regional and local) quasi-political supervision of the peasantry, and the elimination or diminution of the economic power of a landed upper class.

In the pages that follow, I shall attempt to explain the three great historical social revolutions, first, by discussing the institutional characteristics of agrarian states, and their special vulnerabilities and potentialities during the earlier world-historical phases of modernization, and second, by pointing to the peculiar characteristics of old regimes in France, Russia and China, which made them uniquely vulnerable among the earlier modernizing agrarian states to social-revolutionary transformations. Finally, I shall suggest reasons for similarities and differences in the outcomes of the great historical social revolutions.

An agrarian bureaucracy is an agricultural society in which social control rests on a division of labor and a coordination of effort between a semi-bureaucratic state and a landed upper class.[8] The landed upper class typically retains, as an adjunct to its landed property, considerable (though varying in different cases) undifferentiated local and regional authority over the peasant majority of the population. The partially bureaucratic central state extracts taxes and labor from peasants either indirectly through landlord intermediaries or else directly, but with (at least minimal) reliance upon cooperation from individuals of the landed upper class. In turn, the landed upper class relies upon the backing of a coercive state to extract rents and/or dues from the peasantry. At the political center, autocrat, bureaucracy, and army monopolize decisions, yet (in varying degrees and modes) accommodate the regional and local power of the landed upper class and (again, to varying degrees) recruit individual members of this class into leading positions in the state system.

Agrarian bureaucracies are inherently vulnerable to peasant rebellions. Subject to claims on their surpluses, and perhaps their labor, by landlords and state agents, peasants chronically resent both. To the extent that the agrarian economy is commercialized, merchants are also targets of peasant hostility. In all agrarian bureaucracies at all times, and in France, Russia and China in non-revolutionary times, peasants have had grievances enough to warrant, and recurrently spur, rebellions. Economic crises (which are endemic in semi-commercial agrarian economies anyway) and/or increased demands from above for rents or taxes might substantially enhance the likelihood of rebellions at particular times. But such events ought to be treated as short-term precipitants of peasant unrest, not fundamental underlying causes.

Modernization is best conceived not only as an *intra*-societal process of economic development accompanied by lagging or leading changes in non-economic institutional spheres, but also as a world-historic *inter*-societal phenomenon. Thus,

a necessary condition of a society's modernization is its incorporation into the historically unique network of societies that arose first in Western Europe in early modern times and today encompasses enough of the globe's population for the world to be viewed for some purposes as if it consisted of a single network of societies.[9]

Of course, societies have always interacted. What was special about the modernizing inter-societal network that arose in early modern Europe was, first, that it was based upon trade in commodities and manufactures, as well as upon strategic politico-military competition between independent states,[10] and, second, that it incubated the 'first (self-propelling) industrialization' of England after she had gained commercial hegemony within the Western European-centered world market.[11]

In the wake of that first commercial-industrial breakthrough, modernizing pressures have reverberated throughout the world. In the first phase of world modernization, England's thoroughgoing commercialization, capture of world market hegemony, and expansion of manufactures (both before and after the technological Industrial Revolution which began in the 1780s), transformed means and stakes in the traditional rivalries of European states and put immediate pressure for reforms, if only to facilitate the financing of competitive armies and navies, upon the other European states and especially upon the ones with less efficient fiscal machineries.[12] In the second phase, as Europe modernized and further expanded its influence around the globe, similar militarily compelling pressures were brought to bear on those non-European societies which escaped immediate colonization, usually the ones with pre-existing differentiated and centralized state institutions.

During these phases of global modernization, independent responses to the dilemmas posed by incorporation into a modernizing world were possible and (in some sense) necessary for governmental elites in agrarian bureaucracies. Demands for more and more efficiently collected taxes; for better and more generously and continuously financed militaries; and for 'guided' national economic development, imitating the available foreign models, were voiced within these societies especially by bureaucrats and the educated middle strata. The demands were made compelling by international military competition and threats. At the same time, governmental leaders did have administrative machineries, however rudimentary, at their disposal for the implementation of whatever modernizing reforms seemed necessary and feasible (at given moments in world history). And their countries had not been incorporated into dependent economic and political positions in a world stratification system dominated by a few fully industrialized giants.

But agrarian bureaucracies faced enormous difficulties in meeting the crises of modernization. Governmental leaders' realm of autonomous action tended to be severely limited, because few fiscal or economic reforms could be undertaken which did not encroach upon the advantages of the traditional landed upper classes which constituted the major social base of support for the authority and functions of the state in agrarian bureaucracies. Only so much revenue could be squeezed out of the peasantry, and yet landed upper classes could often raise formidable obstacles to rationalization of tax systems. Economic development might mean more tax revenues and enhanced military prowess, yet it channelled wealth and manpower away from the agrarian sector. Finally, the mobilization of mass popular support for war tended to undermine the traditional, local authority of landlords or landed bureaucrats upon which agrarian bureaucratic societies partly relied for the social control of the peasantry.

Agrarian bureaucracies could not indefinitely 'ignore' the very specific crises, in particular fiscal and martial, that grew out of involvement with a modernizing world, yet they could not adapt without undergoing fundamental structural changes. Social revolution helped accomplish 'necessary' changes in some but was averted by reform or 'revolution from above' in others. Relative stagnation, accompanied by sub-incorporation into international power spheres, was still another possibility (e.g., Portugal, Spain?). Social revolution was never deliberately 'chosen'. Societies only 'backed into' social revolutions.

All modernizing agrarian bureaucracies have peasants with grievances and face the unavoidable challenges posed by modernization abroad. So, in some sense, potential for social revolution has been built into all modernizing agrarian bureaucracies. Yet, only a handful have succumbed. Why? A major part of the answer, I believe, lies in the insight that 'not oppression, but weakness, breeds revolution'.[13] It is the breakdown of a societal mode of social control which allows and prompts social revolution to unfold. In the historical cases of France, Russia and China, the unfolding of social revolution depended upon the emergence of revolutionary crises occasioned by the incapacitation of administrative and military organizations. That incapacitation, in turn, is best explained not as a function of mass discontent and mobilization, but as a function of a combination of pressures on state institutions from more modernized countries abroad, and (in two cases out of three) built-in structural incapacities to mobilize increased resources in response to those pressures. France, Russia and China were also special among all agrarian bureaucracies in that their agrarian institutions afforded peasants not only the usual grievances against landlords and state agents but also 'structural space' for autonomous collective insurrection. Finally, once administrative/military breakdown occurred in agrarian bureaucracies with such especially insurrection-prone peasantries, then, and only then, could organized revolutionary leaderships have great impact upon their societies' development – though not necessarily in the ways they originally envisaged.

BREAKDOWN OF SOCIETAL CONTROLS: FOREIGN PRESSURES AND ADMINISTRATIVE/MILITARY COLLAPSE

If a fundamental cause and the crucial trigger for the historical social revolutions was the incapacitation of administrative and military machineries in modernizing agrarian bureaucracies, then how and why did this occur in France, Russia and China? What differentiated these agrarian bureaucracies which succumbed to social revolution from others which managed to respond to modernizing pressures with reforms from above? Many writers attribute differences in response to qualities of will or ability in governmental leaders. From a sociological point of view, a more satisfying approach might focus on the interaction between (a) the magnitude of foreign pressures brought to bear on a modernizing agrarian bureaucracy, and (b) the particular structural characteristics of such societies that underlay contrasting performances by leaders responding to foreign pressures and internal unrest.

Overwhelming foreign pressures on an agrarian bureaucracy could cut short even a generally successful government program of reforms and industrialization 'from above'. Russia is the obvious case in point. From at least the 1890s onward, the Czarist regime was committed to rapid industrialization, initially government-financed out of resources squeezed from the peasantry, as the only means of rendering Russia militarily competitive with Western nations. Alexander Gerschenkron argues that initial government programs to promote heavy industry had succeeded in the 1890s to such an extent that, when the government was forced to reduce its direct financial and administrative role after 1904, Russia's industrial sector was nevertheless capable of autonomously generating further growth (with the aid of foreign capital investments).[14] Decisive steps to modernize agriculture and free peasant labor for permanent urban migration were taken after the unsuccessful Revolution of 1905.[15] Had she been able to sit out World War I, Russia might have recapitulated the German experience of industrialization facilitated by bureaucratic guidance.

But participation in World War I forced Russia to fully mobilize her population including her restive peasantry. Army officers and men were subjected to years of costly fighting, and civilians to mounting economic privations – all for nought. For, given Russia's 'industrial backwardness . . . enhanced by the fact that Russia was very largely blockaded . . .', plus the 'inferiority of the Russian military machine to the German in everything but sheer numbers . . . , military defeat, with all of its inevitable consequences for the internal condition of the country, was very nearly a foregone conclusion'.[16] The result was administrative demoralization and paralysis, and the disintegration of the army. Urban insurrections which brought first middle-strata moderates and then the Bolsheviks to power could not be suppressed, owing to the newly-recruited character and war weariness of the urban garrisons.[17] Peasant grievances were enhanced, young peasant men were politicized through military experiences, and, in consequence, spreading peasant insurrections from the spring of 1917 on could not be controlled.

It is instructive to compare 1917 to the Revolution of 1905. Trotsky called 1905 a 'dress rehearsal' for 1917, and, indeed, many of the same social forces with the same grievances and similar political programs took part in each revolutionary drama. *What accounts for the failure of the Revolution of 1905 was the Czarist regime's ultimate ability to rely upon the army to repress popular disturbances.* Skillful tactics were involved: the regime bought time to organize repression and assure military loyalty with well-timed liberal concessions embodied in the October Manifesto of 1905 (and later largely retracted). Yet, it was of crucial importance that the futile 1904–05 war with Japan was, in comparison with the World War I morass, circumscribed, geographically peripheral, less demanding of resources and manpower, and quickly concluded once defeat was apparent.[18] The peace treaty was signed by late 1905, leaving the Czarist government free to bring military reinforcements back from the Far East into European Russia.

The Russian Revolution occurred in 1917 because Russia was too inextricably entangled with foreign powers, friend and foe, economically and militarily more powerful than she. Foreign entanglement must be considered not only to explain the administrative and military incapacitation of 1917, but also entry into World War I. That involvement cannot be considered 'accidental'. Nor was it 'voluntary' in the same sense as Russia's entry into the 1904 war with Japan.[19] Whatever leadership 'blunders' were involved, the fact remains that in 1914 both the Russian state and the Russian economy depended heavily on Western loans and capital. Moreover, Russia was an established part of the European state system and could not remain neutral in a conflict that engulfed the whole of that system.[20]

Foreign pressures and involvements so inescapable and overwhelming as those that faced Russia in 1917 constitute an extreme case for the earlier modernizing agrarian bureaucracies we are considering here. For France and China the pressures were surely no more compelling than those faced by agrarian bureaucracies such as Japan, Germany and Russia (1858–1914) which successfully adapted through reforms from above that facilitated the extraordinary mobilization of resources for economic and military development. Why were the Bourbon and Manchu regimes unable to adapt? Were there structural blocks to effective response? First, let me discuss some general characteristics of all agrarian states, and then point to a peculiar structural characteristic shared by Bourbon France and Manchu China which I believe explains these regimes' inability to meet snow-balling crises of modernization until at last their feeble attempts triggered administrative and military disintegration, hence revolutionary crises.

Weber's ideal type of bureaucracy may be taken as an imaginary model of what might logically be the most effective means of purposively organizing social power. According to the ideal type, fully developed bureaucracy involves the existence of an hierarchically arrayed officialdom, where officials are oriented to superior authority in a disciplined manner because they are dependent for jobs, livelihood, status and career-advancement on resources and decisions channelled through that superior authority. But in preindustrial states, monarchs found it difficult to channel sufficient resources through the 'center' to pay simultaneously for wars, culture and court life on the one hand, and a fully bureaucratic officialdom on the other. Consequently, they often had to make do with 'officials' recruited from wealthy backgrounds, frequently, in practice, landlords. In addition, central state jurisdiction rarely touched local peasants or communities directly; governmental functions were often delegated to landlords in their 'private' capacities, or else to non-bureaucratic authoritative organizations run by local landlords.

Inherent in all agrarian bureaucratic regimes were tensions between, on the one hand, state elites interested in preserving, using, and extending the powers of armies and administrative organizations and, on the other hand, landed upper classes interested in defending locally and regionally based social networks, influence over peasants, and powers and privileges associated with the control of land and agrarian surpluses. Such tensions were likely to be exacerbated once the agrarian bureaucracy was forced to adapt to modernization abroad because foreign military pressures gave cause, while foreign economic development offered incentives and models, for state elites to attempt reforms which went counter to the class interests of traditional, landed upper strata. Yet there were important variations in the ability of semi-bureaucratic agrarian states to respond to modernizing pressures with reforms which sharply and quickly increased resources at the disposal of central authorities. What can account for the differences in response?

Not the values or individual qualities of traditional bureaucrats: Japan's Meiji reformers acted in the name of traditional values and authority to enact sweeping structural reforms which cleared the way for rapid industrialization and military modernization. Russia's Czarist officialdom was renowned for its inefficiency and corruption, and yet it implemented basic agrarian reforms in 1861 and 1905 and administered the first stages of heavy industrialization.

Leaving aside value-orientations and individual characteristics, we must look at the class interests and connections of state officials. *The adaptiveness of the earlier modernizing agrarian bureaucracies was significantly determined by the degree to which the upper and middle ranks of the state administrative bureaucracies were staffed by large landholders.* Only state machineries significantly differentiated from traditional landed upper classes could undertake modernizing reforms which almost invariably had to encroach upon the property or privileges of the landed upper class.

Thus, in an analysis of what she calls 'elite revolutions" in Japan (1863) and Turkey (1919), Ellen Kay Trimberger argues that segments of the traditional leaderships of those agrarian bureaucracies were able to respond so effectively to intrusions by more modern powers only because 'the Japanese and Turkish ruling elites were political bureaucrats without vested economic interests. . . .'[21] Similarly Walter M. Pintner concludes from his careful research into 'The Social Characteristics of the Early Nineteenth-Century Russian Bureaucracy' that:

By the end of the eighteenth century the civil bureaucracy in the central agencies, and by the 1850s in the provinces also, was an essentially self-perpetuating group. Recruits came from a nobility that was in large measure divorced from the land, and from among the sons of nonnoble government workers (military, civil, and ecclesiastical). . . . What is important is that the state's civil administration, even at the upper levels, was staffed with men who were committed to that career and no other and who seldom had any other significant source of income. The competence, efficiency, and honesty of the civil service were undoubtedly very low, . . . however, it should have been a politically loyal instrument, and indeed it proved to be when the tsar determined to emancipate the serfs and assign to them land that was legally the property of the nobility.[22]

But where – as in Bourbon France and late Manchu China – regionally-based cliques of landed magnates were ensconced within nominally centralized administrative systems, the ability of the state elites to control the flow of tax resources and implement reform policies was decisively undermined. By their *resistance* to the mobilization of increased resources for military or economic purposes in modernization crises, such landed cliques of officials could engender situations of acute administrative/military disorganization – potentially revolutionary crises of governmental authority.

The French monarchy struggled on three fronts throughout the eighteenth century.[23] Within the European state system, France's 'amphibious geography' forced her to compete simultaneously with the great continental land powers, Austria and (after mid-century) Prussia, and with the maritime powers, above all, Britain. Britain's accelerating commercial and industrial development put France at ever increasing disadvantage in trade and naval strength and the extraordinary efficiency of Prussia's bureaucratic regime, its special ability to extract resources from relatively poor people and territories and to convert them with minimal wastage to military purposes, tended to compensate for France's advantages of national wealth and territorial size. And the French monarchy had to fight on a 'third front' at home – against the resistance of its own privileged strata to rationalization of the tax system.

Perceptive as he was in pointing to rationalization and centralization of state power as the most fateful outcomes of the French Revolution, Alexis de Tocqueville[24] surely exaggerated the extent to which monarchical authority already exhibited those qualities before the Revolution. To be sure:

At first view France, the historic center of continental statecraft, presents the picture of a clear, homogeneous and consistent governmental structure. The king was the sole legislator, the supreme chief of the administrative hierarchy and the source of all justice. . . . All authority was delegated by the crown, and its agents, whether ministers, provincial intendants or subdelegates, were its mandatories. . . . In the matter of justice the council of state, acting as the king's private court, could override judgements of all ordinary courts. The sovereign's *parlements,* the intermediary and lower courts pronounced justice in the king's name, and even the seigneurial, municipal, and ecclesiastical courts were subject to his control . . . The Estates General were no more and the few remaining provincial estates were reduced to pure administrative bodies.[25]

Such was the system in theory, an absolute monarch's dream. But in practice? Quite aside from general qualities which set the French administrative system in the eighteenth century in sharp contrast to the Prussian – as 'more disjointed, less uniform, less effectively geared by control devices, above all less firmly co-ordinated by a single driving purpose penetrating the entire administrative hierarchy'[26] – the system afforded landlords (and wealth-holders generally) strategic points of institutional leverage for obstructing royal policies.

A substantial number of the First and Second Estates was obviously still trying to live in terms of the old feudal structure that had lost its functional justification at least two centuries before . . . [T]he residue is not hard to identify or describe. Characteristically it was composed of the larger landowners, but not the princes of the realm nor even the constant residents at Versailles. The latter had obviously, if not necessarily willingly, cast their lot with the King. Similarly, many of the lesser nobles had, whether from ambition or necessity, taken service in the army or, occasionally, in the administration. The remaining survivors of the old feudal classes, however, tended to live on their properties in the provinces, serve and subvert the local bureaucracy, seek preferment in the Church, and find expression and defense of their interests through the provincial estates and *parlements*.[27]

The *parlements,* or sovereign courts, nominally a part of the administrative system, were the most avid and strategically located of the institutional defenders of property and privilege. 'The French monarchy never remedied its fatal error of having sold judicial offices just at the moment when it became master of the political machine. The monarch was almost completely powerless in the face of his judges, whom he could not dismiss, transfer, or promote'.[28]

Magistrates of the *parlements* varied markedly in the length of their noble pedigrees, but virtually all were men of considerable wealth, '. . . for their fortunes included not only their offices, in themselves representing large investments, but also a formidable accumulation of securities, urban property, and rural seigneuries'.[29] As courts of appeal for disputes about seigneurial rights, the *parlements* played a crucial role in defending this 'bizarre form of property' held by noble and bourgeois alike.[30] 'Indeed, without the juridical backing of the parlements the whole system of seigneurial rights might have collapsed, for the royal officials had no interest in the maintenance of a system which removed income from those who were taxable into the hands of those who could not be taxed'.[31]

Not surprisingly, given their property interests and extensive connections with non-magisterial propertied families, the *parlementaires* were avid defenders of the rights and privileges of the upper classes in general. 'By their remonstrances and by their active participation in the surviving provincial estates the magistrates proceeded to uphold . . . opposition to undifferentiated taxation, encroachments on seigneurial autonomy, and ministerial assaults on the fortress of regional particularism.'[32] By their dogged defense of tax and property systems increasingly inadequate to the needs of the French state in a modernizing world, the *parlements* throughout the eighteenth century repeatedly blocked attempts at reform. Finally, in 1787–88, they '. . . opened the door to revolution'[33] by rallying support against now indispensable administrative fiscal reforms, and by issuing the call for the convening of the Estates General.

France fought at sea and on land in each of the general European wars of the eighteenth century: the War of the Austrian Succession; the Seven Years War; and the war over American Independence. In each conflict, her resources were strained to the utmost and her vital colonial trade disrupted, yet no gains, indeed losses in America and India, resulted.[34] The War for American Independence proved to be the last straw. '[T]he price to be paid for American Independence was a French Revolution':[35] royal treasurers finally exhausted their capacity to raise loans from financiers, and were forced (again) to propose reforms of the tax system. The usual resistance from the *parlements* ensued, and an expedient adopted by Calonne in an attempt to circumvent it – the summoning of an

Assembly of Notables in 1787 – only provided privileged interests yet another platform for voicing resistance. A last-ditch effort to override the *parlements* (by Brienne in 1787–88) crumbled in the face of concerted upper-class defiance, popular demonstrations, and the unwillingness of army officers to direct forcible suppression of the popular resistance.[36]

The army's hesitance was especially crucial in translating fiscal crises and political unrest into general administrative and military breakdown. Recruited from various privileged social backgrounds – rich noble, rich non-noble, and poor country noble – the officers had a variety of long-standing grievances, against other officers and, significantly, against the Crown, which could never satisfy them all.[37] But it is likely that the decisive explanation for their behavior lies in the fact that they were virtually all privileged, socially and/or economically, and hence identified during 1787–88 with the *parlements*. In her *Armies and the Art of Revolution,* Katharine Chorley concludes from comparative historical studies that, in pre-industrial societies, army officers generally identify with and act to protect the interests of the privileged strata from which they are recruited. During its opening phases, until after the King had capitulated and agreed to convene the Estates General, the French Revolution pitted all strata, led by the privileged, against the Crown. The army officers' understandable reluctance to repress popular unrest during that period created a general crisis of governmental authority and effectiveness which in turn unleashed social divisions, between noble and non-noble, rich and poor, that made a subsequent resort to simple repression by the Old Regime impossible.

The officers' insubordination early in the Revolution was all the more easily translated into rank-and-file insubordination in 1789 and after, because of the fact that French soldiers were not normally insulated from the civilian population. Soldiers were billeted with civilians, and those from rural areas were released during the summers to help with the harvest at home. Thus, during 1789, the *Gardes Françaises* (many of whom were married to Parisian working-class women) were won over to the Paris revolution in July, and peasant soldiers spread urban news in the countryside during the summer and returned to their units in the autumn with vivid tales of peasant revolt.[38]

Like the Bourbon Monarchy, the Manchu Dynasty proved unable to mobilize resources sufficient to meet credibly the challenges posed by involvement in the modernizing world. '[T]he problem was not merely the very real one of the inadequate resources of the Chinese economy as a whole. In large measure the financial straits in which the Peking government found itself were due to . . . [inability to] command such financial capacity as there was in its empire'.[39] Part of the explanation for this inability lay in a characteristic which the Chinese state shared with other agrarian states: lower and middle level officials were recruited from the landed gentry, paid insufficient salaries, and allowed to engage in a certain amount of 'normal' corruption, withholding revenues collected as taxes from higher authorities.[40] Yet, if the Manchu Dynasty had encountered the forces of modernization at the height of its powers (say in the early eighteenth century) rather than during its declining phase, it might have controlled or been able to mobilize sufficient resources to finance modern industries and equip a centrally controlled modern army. In that case, officials would never have been allowed to serve in their home provinces, and thus local and regional groups of gentry would have lacked institutional support for concerted opposition against central initiatives. But, as it happened, the Manchu Dynasty was forced to try to cope with wave after wave of imperialist intrusions, engineered by foreign industrial or industrializing nations anxious to tap Chinese markets and finances, immediately after a series of massive mid-nineteenth-century peasant rebellions. The Dynasty had been unable to put down the Taiping Rebellion on its own, and the task had fallen instead to local, gentry-led, self-defense associations and to regional armies led by complexly interrelated gentry who had access to village resources and recruits. In consequence of the gentry's role in putting down rebellion, governmental powers formerly accruing to central authorities or their bureaucratic agents, including, crucially, rights to collect and allocate various taxes, devolved upon local, gentry-dominated, sub-district governing associations and upon provincial armies and officials increasingly aligned with the provincial gentry against the center.[41]

Unable to force resources from local and regional authorities, it was all Peking could do simply to meet foreign indebtedness, and after 1895 even that proved impossible.

Throughout the period from 1874 to 1894, the ministry [of Revenue in Peking] was engaged in a series of largely unsuccessful efforts to raise funds in order to meet a continuing series of crises – the dispute over Ili with Russia, the Sino-French War [1885], floods and famines, the Sino-Japanese War [1895]. . . . After 1895 the triple pressure of indemnity payments, servicing foreign loans, and military expenditures totally wrecked the rough balance between income and outlay which Peking had maintained [with the aid of foreign loans] until that time.[42]

The Boxer Rebellion of 1900, and subsequent foreign military intervention, only further exacerbated an already desperate situation.

Attempts by dynastic authorities to remedy matters through a series of 'reforms' implemented after 1900 – abolishing the Confucian educational system and encouraging modern schools,[43] organizing the so-called 'New Armies' (which actually formed around the nuclei of the old provincial armies),[44] transferring local governmental functions to provincial bureaus,[45] and creating a series of local and provincial gentry-dominated representative assemblies[46] – only exacerbated the sorry situation, right up to the 1911 breaking point. 'Reform destroyed the reforming government'.[47] With each reform, dynastic elites thought to create powers to counterbalance entrenched obstructive forces, but new officials and functions were repeatedly absorbed into pre-existing local and (especially) regional cliques of gentry.[48] The last series of reforms, those that created representative assemblies, ironically provided cliques of gentry with legitimate representative organs from which to launch the liberal, decentralizing 'Constitutionalist movement' against the Manchus.

What ultimately precipitated the 'revolution of 1911' was a final attempt at reform by the central government, one that directly threatened the financial interests of the gentry power groups for the purpose of strengthening central government finances and control over national economic development:

> The specific incident that precipitated the Revolution of 1911 was the central government's decision to buy up a [railroad] line in Szechwan in which the local gentry had invested heavily. . . . The Szechwan uprising, led by the moderate constitutionalists of the Railway Protection League, sparked widespread disturbances that often had no connection with the railway issue. . . .[49]

Conspiratorial groups affiliated with Sun Yat Sen's T'eng Meng Hui, and mainly composed of Western-educated students and middle-rank New Army officers, joined the fray to produce a series of military uprisings. Finally,

> . . . the lead in declaring the independence of one province after another was taken by two principal elements: the military governors who commanded the New Army forces and the gentry-official-merchant leaders of the provincial assemblies. These elements had more power and were more conservative than the youthful revolutionarists of the T'eng Meng Hui.[50]

The Chinese 'Revolution of 1911' irremediably destroyed the integument of civilian elite ties – traditionally maintained by the operation of Confucian educational institutions and the central bureaucracy's policies for recruiting and deploying educated officials so as to strengthen 'cosmopolitan' orientations at the expense of local loyalties – which had until that time provided at least the semblance of unified governance for China. 'Warlord' rivalries ensued as gentry interests attached themselves to regional military machines, and this condition of intra-elite disunity and rivalry (only imperfectly and temporarily overcome by Chiang Kai-Shek's regime between 1927 and 1937)[51] condemned China to incessant turmoils and provided openings (as well as cause) for lower-class, especially peasant, rebellions and for Communist attempts to organize and channel popular unrest.

PEASANT INSURRECTIONS

If administrative and military breakdown in a modernizing agrarian bureaucracy were to inaugurate social revolutionary transformations, rather than merely an interregnum of intra-elite squabbling, then widespread popular revolts had to coincide with and take advantage of the hiatus of governmental supervision and sanctions. Urban insurrections provided indispensable support during revolutionary interregnums to radical political elites vying against other elites for state power: witness the Parisian *sans culottes'* support for the Jacobins;[52] the Chinese workers' support for the Communists (between 1920 and 1927);[53] and the

Russian industrial workers' support for the Bolsheviks. But fundamentally more important in determining final outcomes were the peasant insurrections which in France, Russia and China constituted irreversible attacks on the powers and privileges of the traditional landed upper classes.

Agrarian bureaucracy has been the only historical variety of complex society with differentiated, centralized government that has, in certain instances, incubated a lower-class stratum that was *simultaneously strategic* in the society's economy and polity (as surplus producer, payer of rents and taxes, and as provider of corvée and military manpower), and yet *organizationally autonomous* enough to allow the 'will' and 'tactical space' for collective insurrection against basic structural arrangements.

How have certain agrarian bureaucracies exemplified such special propensity to peasant rebellion? As Eric Wolf has pointed out, 'ultimately, the decisive factor in making a peasant rebellion possible lies in the relation of the peasantry to the field of power which surrounds it. A rebellion cannot start from a situation of complete impotence. . . .'[54] If they are to act upon, rather than silently suffer, their omnipresent grievances, peasants must have 'internal leverage' or 'tactical mobility'. They have this to varying degrees according to their position in the total agrarian social structure. Institutional patterns which relate peasants to landlords and peasants to each other seem to be the co-determinants of degrees of peasant 'tactical mobility'. Sheer amounts of property held by peasants gain significance only within institutional contexts. If peasants are to be capable of self-initiated rebellion against landlords and state officials, they must have (a) some institutionally based collective solidarity, and (b) autonomy from direct, day-to-day supervision and control by landlords in their work and leisure activities. Agricultural regimes featuring large estates worked by serfs or laborers tend to be inimical to peasant rebellion – witness the East Elbian Junker regime[55] – but the reason is not that serfs and landless laborers are economically poor, rather that they are subject to close and constant supervision and discipline by landlords or their agents. If large-estate agriculture is lacking, an agrarian bureaucracy may still be relatively immune to widespread peasant rebellion if landlords control sanctioning machineries,[56] such as militias and poor relief agencies, at local levels. On the other hand, landlords as a class, and the 'system' as whole, will be relatively vulnerable to peasant rebellion if: (a) sanctioning machineries are centralized; (b) agricultural work and peasant social life are controlled by peasant families and communities themselves. These conditions prevailed in France and Russia and meant that, with the incapacitation of central administrative and military bureaucracies, these societies became susceptible to the spread and intensification of peasant revolts which in more normal circumstances could have been contained and repressed.

It is worth emphasizing that peasant actions in revolutions are not intrinsically different from peasant actions in 'mere' rebellions or riots. When peasants 'rose' during historical social revolutionary crises, they did so in highly traditional rebellious patterns: bread riots, 'defense' of communal lands or customary rights, riots against 'hoarding' merchants or landlords, 'social banditry'. Peasants initially drew upon traditional cultural themes to justify rebellion. Far from becoming revolutionaries through adoption of a radical vision of a desired new society, 'revolutionary' peasants have typically been 'backward-looking' rebels incorporated by circumstances beyond their control into political processes occurring independently of them, at the societal 'center'.[57]

In the highly abnormal circumstances of social revolution, administrative breakdown, political rebellions of marginal elites, and peasant insurrections *interacted* to produce transformations that none alone could have occasioned or accomplished. Because peasants could rebel on their own in France and Russia, they did not have to be *directly mobilized* by urban radicals. In China, such mobilization was ultimately necessary, but it was for the most part a military mobilization which conformed with important modifications to an age-old pattern of elite/peasant coordination of effort to accomplish 'dynastic replacement'. As we shall see, China is the exception that proves the rule about peasant insurrectionary autonomy and social revolution.

At the end of the Old Regime, 'France was unique in Europe in that seigneurial privilege co-existed with a free peasantry owning a good deal of land'[58] and largely controlling the process of agrarian production. Averaging across regions, peasants owned about one-third of the land,[59] subject to tithes, taxes, and seigneurial dues, and peasants probably cultivated most of the remainder as renters or sharecroppers (*métayers*), for large landowners rarely directly exploited their own holdings.[60] The development of regional and national markets for grain and other agricultural products, a process directly and indirectly encouraged by government activities,[61] spurred class differentiation within the ranks of the peasantry and fueled intra-village tensions. *Laboureurs* (rich peasants) with sufficient land and equipment could profit from rising prices for grain and land, but swelling masses of smallholders with insufficient land to support families were hard-pressed by rising rents and by bread prices that outstripped wage rates for agricultural or industrial labor.[62] Nevertheless, virtually all peasants shared resentment of taxes, tithes, and seigneurial dues, and community institutions reinforced propensities and capacities to act together against common enemies.

One important effect of the traditional agricultural system was to foster a strong community-feeling in the village. The management of the open fields required uniformity of cultivation and the commons were administered by the village as a whole . . . and the allocation of taxes was a matter of common concern. The village shared rights which it might have to defend in the courts. . . . In a system both traditional and partly communal there was little scope for individualism, and peasants, while recognizing the private ownership of land, were inclined to regard the harvest as the property of the community.[63]

Big landlords in France exercised few local governing functions. Parish priests and rich peasants might exercise preponderant influence in village assemblies and on the local governing councils established in 1787, but in general peasant communities looked after their own affairs.[64] Seigneurs or their agents still exercised prerogatives of 'feudal' justice on their estates, but military forces to back up judicial decisions, and, in general, to enforce order were controlled by the Intendants, administrative agents of the central government.[65]

Peasant participation in the Revolutionary drama began in the spring of 1789 with bread riots, a long-established form of popular response to conditions of grain scarcity and high bread prices.[66] The winter of 1788 had been unusually severe, and an industrial depression had been underway since 1786.[67] 'Irrespective of political events, there would have been widespread rioting and disorder in France during the summer of 1789'.[68] But then, '. . . under the impact of economic crisis and political events, the peasant movement developed from early protests against prices, through attacks on enclosure, gaming [*sic*] rights, and royal forests, to a frontal assault on the feudal land system itself'.[69]

Not that Third Estate spokesmen deliberately sought to stir up or mobilize the peasantry: leaders of the Third Estate were as anxious to protect property as were nobles; indeed many owned or administered seigneurial rights.[70] Rather, the political events leading up to the calling and convening of the Estates General, and then to the fall of the Bastille and the assertion of national sovereignty by the Assembly, *accelerated and focused* the peasant rebellion in indirect ways. The convening of the Estates General, involving as it did the process of drawing up the *cahiers,* encouraged all Frenchmen to ruminate upon their social and political grievances and raised widespread hopes that they would be acted upon. The spread of anti-aristocratic rhetoric by Third Estate spokesmen encouraged peasants to symbolize their own difficulties in terms of an 'aristocratic plot'.[71] And, finally, divisions within the elite, pitting Crown and central administration against the privileged, and the Third against the Second Estate, served to disorganize the army.[72] At first, officers were reluctant to repress popular demonstrations; later lines of command were entirely muddled, as rank-and-file soldiers became politicized, and as the 'municipal revolution' caused intendants to abandon their posts and national guards to claim sole jurisdiction in matters of maintaining popular order. 'Within the space of a few weeks the royal government lost control over the provinces, for in matters of importance the towns henceforth took their orders only from the Assembly'.[73] The Assembly, in turn, could not encourage systematic repression of peasant revolts by the urban national guards without playing into the hands of the Crown and the conservative nobles and hence jeopardizing all that had been gained in July, 1789.[74] Thus, the peasantry, during the spring and summer of 1789 (and, in fact, thereafter for several years) was left largely free to push rebellion in rural areas beyond the largely ritualized form of the bread riot and was encouraged by what it perceived of urban upheavals to focus its attack upon *one* of its traditional enemies in particular: the seigneur.

The real enemy of the majority of the peasants was the large landowner, noble, bourgeois or *laboureur* (yeoman farmer), whose acquisitiveness was threatening them with expropriation. But the main landowner in the village was often the seigneur, who was also responsible for the . . . burden of seigneurial dues. It was not difficult to lay most economic grievances at the seigneur's door. Royal taxation would have been lighter if the nobility had paid its full share. . . . The tithe, in very many cases, went not to the local *curé*, but to maintain the aristocratic abbot of an almost empty monastery in luxury at Versailles, while the impoverished contributors had to make supplementary grants to maintain the village church. The countryman thus found himself locked in a circle of frustration of which privilege seemed to hold the key to every door. Consequently, the village was able, for a time, to submerge its internal divisions in a common assault on the privileges of the nobility. . . . [T]he insurgent peasants made not for their seigneur's valuables but for their feudal title-deeds.[75]

The 'choice' of enemy was encouraged by the fact that urban forces had also singled him out, but mainly it was inherent in the agragrian structure of the Old Regime. That structure '. . . tended to maintain the cohesion of the rural community in opposition to the landed nobility'[76] yet rendered the landed noble (and other owners of seigneurial rights) dependent upon sanctioning machineries controlled from the center. When those machineries ceased to function effectively, the fate of seigneurial property was sealed.

Historians agree that the Russian Emancipation of the serfs in 1861, intended by the Czar as a measure to stabilize the agrarian situation, actually enhanced the rebellious potential of the ex-serfs. Heavy redemption payments and inadequate land allotments fuelled peasant discontent. More important, legal reinforcement of the *obshchina*'s (peasant commune's) authority over families and individuals fettered ever-increasing numbers of peasants to the inadequate lands, reinforced collective solidarity, retarded the internal class differentiation of the peasantry, and left communes largely free to run their own affairs subject only to the collective fulfillment of financial obligations to the state.[77] Estate owners were deprived of most direct authority over peasant communities.[78]

Not surprisingly, given this agrarian situation, widespread peasant rebellions erupted in Russia in 1905, when the Czarist regime simultaneously confronted defeat abroad and an anti-autocratic movement of the middle classes, the liberal gentry, and the working classes at home. 'Economic hardship created a need for change; peasant tradition, as well as revolutionary propaganda, suggested the remedy [i.e., attacks on landlords and land seizures]; official preoccupation and indecisiveness invited the storm; and soon the greatest disturbance since the days of Pugachev was under way'.[79]

In the wake of the unsuccessful Revolution of 1905, the Czarist regime abandoned its policy of shoring up the peasant commune. It undertook the break-up of repartitional lands into private holdings and implemented measures to facilitate land sales by poorer peasants and purchases by richer ones.[80]

Between 1905 and 1917, these measures, in tandem with general economic developments, did something to alleviate agrarian stagnation, promote permanent rural migration to urban industrial areas, and increase class differentiation and individualism in the countryside.[81] However, by 1917, little enough had been accomplished – only one-tenth of all peasant families had been resettled on individual holdings[82] – that peasant communities engaged in solidary actions against both landlords and any rich peasant 'separators' who did not join their struggle.

'Any shrewd observer of Russian conditions who weighed the lessons of the agrarian disorders of 1905 could have foreseen that a breakdown of central power and authority was almost certain to bring an even greater upheaval in its train'.[83] And, indeed, between the spring and the autumn of 1917, 'side by side with the mutiny of the Russian army marched a second great social revolutionary movement: the seizure of the landed estates by the peasantry'.[84]

The peasant movement of 1917 was primarily a drive of the peasantry against the *pomyeschik* class. Among the cases of agrarian disturbance, violent and peaceful, 4,954, overwhelming the largest number, were directed against landlords, as against 324 against the more well-to-do peasants, 235 against the Government and 211 against the clergy.[85]

The broad general result of the wholesale peasant land seizure of 1917 was a sweeping levelling in Russian agriculture. The big latifundia, even the small estate, ceased to exist. On the other hand landless or nearly landless peasants obtained larger allotments.[86]

For the peasants simply applied traditional communal repartitional procedures to lands seized from the landlords. Their revolt, together with the Bolsheviks' victory, '. . . sealed forever the doom of the old landed aristocracy'.[87]

The Chinese case presents decisive contrasts with France and Russia but nevertheless confirms our general insight about the importance of structurally conditioned 'tactical space' for peasant insurrection as a crucial factor in the translation of administrative/military breakdown into social revolution.

Except in infertile and marginal highland areas, Chinese peasants, though mostly family smallholders or tenants,[88] did not live in their own village communities clearly apart from landlords.

The Chinese peasant . . . was a member of two communities: his village and the marketing system to which his village belonged ['typically including fifteen to twenty-five villages . . .' dependent on one of 45,000 market towns]. An important feature of the larger marketing community was its elaborate system of stratification. . . . Those who provided *de facto* leadership within the marketing community *qua* political system and those who gave it collective representation at its interface with larger polities were gentrymen – landed, leisured, and literate. . . . . It was artisans, merchants, and other full-time economic specialists, not peasants, who sustained the heartbeat of periodic marketing that kept the community alive. It was priests backed by gentry temple managers . . . who gave religious meaning to peasants' local world.[89]

Voluntary associations, and clans where they flourished, were likewise contained within marketing communities, headed and economically sustained by gentry. Thus kinship, associational and clientage ties cut across class distinctions between peasants and landlords in traditional China. Gentry controlled at local levels a variety of sanctioning machineries, including militias and other organizations which functioned *de facto* as channels of poor relief.[90]

Not surprisingly, therefore, settled Chinese peasant agriculturalists did not initiate class-based revolts against landlords, either in pre-modern or in revolutionary (1911–49) times. Instead, peasant rebellion manifested itself in the form of accelerating rural violence and social banditry, spreading outward from the mountainous 'border areas' at the edges of the empire or at the intersections of provincial boundaries. Social banditry invariably blossomed during periods of central administrative weakness or collapse and economic deflation and catastrophe. Precisely because normal traditional Chinese agrarian-class relations were significantly commercialized, local prosperity depended upon overall administrative stability, and peasants were not cushioned against economic dislocations by kin or village communal ties. During periods of dynastic decline, local (marketing) communities 'closed in' upon themselves normatively, economically, and coercively,[91] and poorer peasants, especially in communities without well-to-do local landed elites, lost property and livelihood, and were forced to migrate. Such impoverished migrants often congregated as bandits or smugglers operating out of 'border area' bases and raiding settled communities. Ultimately they might provide (individual or group) recruits for rebel armies led by marginal elites vying for imperial power.[92]

The nineteenth and the first half of the twentieth centuries constituted a period of dynastic decline and interregnum in China, complicated in quite novel ways by Western and Japanese economic and military intrusions. Peasant impoverishment, local community closure, spreading social banditry and military conflicts among local militias, bandit groups, and warlord and/or 'ideological' armies, characterized the entire time span, and peaked during the mid-nineteenth and mid-twentieth centuries.

The Communist movement originated as a political tendency among a tiny fraction of China's nationalist and pro-modern intellectual stratum and created its first mass base among Chinese industrial workers concentrated in the treaty ports and to a lesser degree among students and southeast Chinese peasants. But after 1927, the Chinese Communists were forced out of China's cities and wealthier agrarian regions by Kuomintang military and police repression. Would-be imitators of the Bolsheviks were thus forced to come to terms with the Chinese agrarian situation. This they did initially (between 1927 and 1942) by recapitulating the experiences and tactics of traditional rebel elite contenders for imperial power in China. Scattered, disorganized and disoriented Communist leaders, along with military units (which had split off from KMT or warlord armies) of varying degrees of loyalty, retreated to mountainous border areas, there often to ally with already existing bandit groups.[93] Gradually the fruits of raiding expeditions, plus the division and weakness of opposing armies, allowed the 'Communist' base areas to expand into administrative regions.

Only after a secure and stable administrative region had finally been established in Northwest China (after 1937) could the Communists finally turn to the intra-market-area and intra-village political organizing that ultimately bypassed and then eliminated the gentry, and so made their drive for power unique in China's history. Before roughly 1940, ideological appeals, whether 'Communist' or 'Nationalist' played little role in mediating Communist elites' relations to peasants, and spontaneous class struggle, fuelled from below, played virtually no role in achieving whatever (minimal) changes in agrarian class *relations* were accomplished in Communist base areas.[94] To be sure, ideology was important in integrating the Party, an elite organization, and in mediating its relationship with the Red Army. But until Party and Army established relatively secure and stable military and administrative control over a region, Communist cadres were not in a position to penetrate local communities in order to provide organization, leadership, and encouragement for peasants themselves to expropriate land. This finally occurred in North China in the 1940s.[95] Once provided with military and organizational protection from landlord sanctions and influence, peasants often reacted against landlords with a fury that exceeded even what Party policy desired. Perhaps Communist ideological appeals were partially responsible for peasant insurrection. More likely, even at this stage, the Communist organizations' important input to local situations was not a sense of grievances, or their ideological articulation, but rather simply *protection* from traditional social controls: William Hinton's classic *Fanshen: A Documentary of Revolution in a Chinese Village* vividly supports such an interpretation.[96]

Even to gain the military strength they needed to defeat the Kuomintang, the Chinese Communists had to shove aside – or encourage and allow peasants to shove aside – the traditional landed upper class and establish a more direct link to the Chinese peasantry than had ever before been established between an extra-local Chinese rebel movement and local communities.[97] The Chinese Communists also established more direct links to peasants than did radical elites in Russia or France. The Chinese Revolution, at least in its closing stages, thus has more of the aspect of an elite/mass movement than the other great historical social revolutions. Yet the reasons for this peasant mass-mobilizing aspect have little to do with revolutionary ideology (except in retrospect) and everything to do with the 'peculiarities' (from a European perspective) of the Chinese agrarian social structure. That structure did not afford settled Chinese peasants institutional autonomy and solidarity against landlords, yet it did, in periods of political-economic crisis, generate marginal poor-peasant outcasts whose activities exacerbated the crises and whose existence provided potential bases of support for oppositional elite-led rebellions or, in the twentieth-century world context, a revolutionary movement. Thus Chinese Communist activities after 1927 and ultimate triumph in 1949 depended directly upon *both* the insurrectionary potentials and the blocks to peasant insurrection built into the traditional Chinese social structure.

RADICAL POLITICAL MOVEMENTS AND
CENTRALIZING OUTCOMES

Although peasant insurrections played a decisive role in each of the great historical social revolutions, nevertheless an exclusive focus on peasants – or on the peasant situation in agrarian bureaucracies – cannot provide a complete explanation for the occurrence of social revolutions, even given administrative/ military collapse. In pre-modern times, France, Russia and China were recurrently rocked by massive peasant rebellions,[98] yet peasant uprisings did not fuel structural transformations until the late eighteenth century and after. Obviously agrarian bureaucracies were exposed to additional and unique strains and possibilities once English and then European commercialization-industrialization became a factor in world history and development. The stage was set for the entry of marginal elites animated by radical nationalist goals.

Who were these marginal elites? What sectors of society provided the social bases for nationalist radicalisms? *Not* the bourgeoisie proper: merchants, financiers and industrialists. These groups have had surprisingly little *direct* effect upon the politics of modernization in any developing nation, from England to the countries of the Third World today. Instead, their activities, commerce and manufacturing, have created and continuously transformed, indeed revolutionized, the national and international *contexts* within which bureaucrats, professionals, politicians, landlords, peasants, and proletarians have engaged in the decisive political struggles. To be sure, in certain times and places, the 'bourgeois' commercial or industrial context has been pervasive enough virtually to determine political outcomes, even without the overt political participation of bourgeois actors. But such was not the case in the earlier modernizing agrarian bureaucracies, including France, Russia and China.

Instead, nationalist radicals tended to 'precipitate out' of the ranks of those who possessed specialized skills and were oriented to state activities or employments, but either lacked traditionally prestigious attributes such as nobility, landed wealth, or general humanist education, or else found themselves in situations where such attributes were no longer personally or nationally functional. Their situations in political and social life were such as to make them, especially in times of political crises, willing to call for such radical reforms as equalization of mobility opportunities, political democracy, and (anyway, before the revolution) extension of civil liberties. Yet the primary orientation of these marginal elites was toward a broad goal that they shared with all those, including traditionally prestigious bureaucrats, whose careers, livelihoods, and identities were intertwined with state activities: the goal of extension and rationalization of state powers in the name of national welfare and prestige.

In Bourbon France, radicals (of whom the Jacobins were the most extreme) came primarily from the ranks of non-noble, non-wealthy lawyers, professionals, or state functionaries, and disproportionately from the provinces.

The royal bureaucracy, with its host of minor juridico-administrative officers, the professional civil servants of the great ministeries, the crowds of lawyers, the doctors, surgeons, chemists, engineers, lower army officers . . . all of these formed a social nexus which provided the men who did most of the work of government as well as of the professions, but who were kept out of the higher offices by lack of *noblesse* or of sufficient wealth to purchase it, and humiliated socially by the thought that they belonged to a lower caste.[99]

In the market towns and small administrative centers a new class of bourgeois (that is, non-noble) lawyers had grown up to defend the interests of the provincial members of the monarchial society. It was they who seem to have suffered most, or at least most consciously, from the delaying and obfuscating tactics of the aristocratic courts and therefore best understood the pall that privilege cast over all administrative efforts at reform. Through the famous corresponding societies, these provincial critics exchanged ideas and laid the intellectual foundation for much that happened in 1789 and after.[100]

In Russia, by 1917, the revolutionary sects, such as the Bolsheviks and the Left Social Revolutionaries, constituted the surviving politically organized representatives of what had earlier been an outlook much more widespread among university-educated Russians: extreme alienation, disgust at Russia's backwardness, preoccupation with public events and yet refusal to become involved in the round of civil life.[101] As Russia underwent rapid industrialization after 1890, opportunities for university education were extended beyond the nobility – a circumstance which helped to ensure that universities would be hotbeds of political radicalism – yet, before long, opportunities for professional and other highly skilled employments also expanded. Especially in the wake of the abortive 1905 Revolution, Russia's university-educated moved toward professional employments and liberal politics.[102] Yet when events overtook Russia in 1917, organized radical leadership was still to be found among the alienated intelligentsia.

In China, as in Russia, radical nationalist modernizers came from the early student generations of university-educated Chinese.[103] Especially at first, most were the children of traditionally wealthy and prestigious families, but urban and 'rich peasant' backgrounds, respectively, came to be overrepresented in the (pre-1927) Kuomintang and the Communist elites.[104] With the abolition of the Confucian educational system in 1904, and the collapse of the imperial government in 1911, even traditionally prestigious attributes and connections lost their meaning and usefulness. At the same time, neither warlord regimes, nor the Nationalist government after 1927 offered much scope for modern skills or credentials; advancement in these regimes went only to those with independent wealth or personal ties to military commanders. Gradually, the bulk of China's modern-educated, and especially the young, came to support the Communist movement, some through active commitment in Yenan, others through passive political support in the cities.[105]

Two considerations help to account for the fact that radical leadership in social revolutions came specifically from the ranks of skilled and/or university-educated marginal elites oriented to state employments and activities. First, agrarian bureaucracies are 'statist' societies. Even before the era of modernization official employments in these societies constituted both an important route for social mobility and a means for validating traditional status and supplementing landed fortunes. Second, with the advent of economic modernization in the world, state activities acquired greater-than-ever objective import in the agrarian bureaucratic societies which were forced to adapt to modernization abroad. For the concrete effects of modernization abroad first impinged upon the state's sphere, in the form of sharply and suddenly stepped up military competition or threats from more developed nations abroad. And the cultural effects of modernization abroad first impinged upon the relatively highly educated in agrarian bureaucracies, that is upon those who were mostly either employed by the state or else connected or oriented to its activities. (This is obvious for Russia and China. Consider as well the fascination of educated French officials and laymen during the eighteenth century with British economic and political models and ideas.)[106] Understandably, as agrarian bureaucracies confronted modernization abroad, the state was viewed by virtually everyone, from conservative reformers to radicals and revolutionaries, as the likely tool for implementation of reforms at home and enhancement of national standing in the international context. This was true for eighteenth-century France, as well as for pre-revolutionary Russia and China. Edward Fox has remarked on the irony of the fact that

> in the middle of what has been described as the 'democratic revolution,' an entire generation of gifted social critics and publicists should all but unanimously demand the royal imposition of their various programs of reform. In the theoretical and polemical literature of the time, the 'absolute' monarchy was criticized for its failure to exercise arbitrary power. To Frenchmen of the *ancien régime*, it was the monarchy that represented what was modern and progressive and political 'liberties' that appeared anachronistic. . . . For virtually all the inhabitants of continental France, fiscal and judicial reforms were far more urgent issues than the development of political liberty; and the monarchy was the obvious agency for their implementation. Only the King's failure to live up to their expectations drove his subjects to intervene.[107]

   The earlier modernizing agrarian bureaucracies that (to varying degrees) successfully adapted to challenges from abroad did so either through revolution, or basic reforms 'from above' or social revolution 'from below'. Either traditional bureaucrats successfully promoted requisite reforms or else their attempts precipitated splits within the upper class which could, if the peasantry were structurally insurrection-prone, open the door to social revolution. In the context of administrative/military disorganization and spreading peasant rebellions, tiny, organized radical elites that never could have created revolutionary crises on their own gained their moments in history. As peasant insurrections undermined the traditional landed upper classes, and the Old Regime officials and structures tied to them, radical elites occupied center stage, competing among themselves to see who could seize and build upon the foundations of central state power.

'A complete revolution', writes Samuel Huntington, '. . . involves . . . the creation and institutionalization of a new political order'.[108] A social revolution was consummated when one political elite succeeded in creating or capturing political organizations – a revolutionary army, or a revolutionary party controlling an army – capable of restoring minimal order and incorporating the revolutionary masses, especially the peasantry, into national life. No political elite not able or willing to accept the peasants' revolutionary economic gains could hope to emerge victorious from the intra-elite or inter-party conflicts that marked revolutionary interregnums. Elites with close social or politico-military ties to traditional forms of landed upper-class institutional power (i.e., the privileged rentier bourgeoisie of France, the Kerensky regime in Russia, the [post-1927] Kuomintang in China) invariably lost out.

The historical social revolutions did not culminate in more liberal political arrangements. At opening stages of the French, Russian (1905) and Chinese revolutions, landed upper-class/middle-strata political coalitions espoused 'parliamentary liberal' programs.[109] But events pushed these groups and programs aside, for the organized elites who provided the ultimately successful leadership in all social revolutions ended up responding to popular turmoil – counterrevolutionary threats at home and abroad, peasant anarchist tendencies, and the international crises faced by their societies – by creating *more* highly centralized, bureaucratized and rationalized state institutions than those that existed prior to the revolutions. This response, moreover, was entirely in character for elites adhering to world views which gave consistent primacy to organized political action in human affairs.[110]

The strengthening and rationalizing of central state powers was the result of the French Revolution as surely as of the Russian and Chinese. In assessing the basic changes wrought by the French Revolution, Franklin Ford assigns greatest importance, after the elimination of the estate system, to administrative, political and military transformations. After 1789, 'citizen' masses were incorporated into politics, at least symbolically, and via the *'levée en masse'* into the national army. More important, France

came out of the revolutionary-Napoleonic crisis with its administrative organization profoundly and . . . irreversibly altered. . . . After 1815, France retained a set of budgetary procedures, a network of departmental prefects, and a system of centrally appointed judges in the place of the deficit financing ex post facto, the quaint chaos of provincial powers, and the court system based on ownership of office with which the old monarchy had lived for centuries.[111]

Within France, Napoleon on the whole maintained the civil equality won during the Revolution, at least in the restricted sense in which birth conferred no formal privilege. Such of the legacy of the Enlightenment as related merely to national efficiency, for example internal free trade and advanced technical education, became a permanent part of French society. But much that the Enlightenment regarded as essential disappeared, notably freedom of the press and freedom from arbitrary arrest. In many respects

Napoleonic France was closer than the France of Louis XV to Montesquieu's conception of despotism.[112]

The 'liberal' reforms which were put forward in all the historical social revolutions alike were guarantees of equal personal rights for all citizens. Alone they are not enough to warrant labelling any political regime 'liberal.'

Thus, what changed most thoroughly in *all* of the historical social revolutions was the mode of societal control of the lower strata. Landed upper classes lost (at least) their special socio-political authority and their roles in controlling the peasantry (however feebly) through local and regional quasi-political institutional arrangements – the *parlements* and seigneurial courts in France; *zemstvos* and landed estates in Russia; clans, associations, sub-district, district and provincial governments in China. The peasantry and the urban lower strata were directly incorporated into now truly *national* polities and economies, institutionally and symbolically.

But wasn't the French Revolution a 'bourgeois' revolution, in contrast to the 'communist' Chinese and Russian Revolutions? Throughout, this essay has emphasized patterns common to all three of the great historical revolutions, thus violating much of the common wisdom about the special 'bourgeois' nature of the French Revolution. The traditional argument about the French Revolution holds that it was in some sense made by a 'strong' bourgeois economic class, and 'cleared the way' politically, judicially and socially for capitalist industrialization in France.

Proponents of the view that the French Revolution was a 'bourgeois revolution' can point to evidence which seems to support their position. The French Revolution did *not* result in the complete elimination of property-owning upper classes.[113] Neither did political elites take direct control of the economy to spur national industrialization. Regional, estate and guild barriers to the formation of a national market were eliminated. And, in time, France did undergo capitalist industrialization.

Yet there are equally important facts which contradict the thesis of the 'bourgeois revolution'. Before the Revolution, French 'industry' was overwhelmingly small-scale and non-mechanized,[114] and commercial and financial capital coexisted non-antagonistically, indeed symbiotically, with the more settled and prestigious 'proprietary' forms of wealth (land, venal office, annuities).[115] During the Revolution, political leadership for the Third Estate was overwhelmingly recruited from the ranks of professionals (especially lawyers), office-holders, and intellectuals, not commercial or industrial bourgeois. The men who ruled France after the Revolution were bureaucrats, landowners, soldiers, commercial and financial capitalists, much as before.[116] Economically relevant reforms enacted during the Revolution were largely the culmination of '. . . the century old movement [started by Colbert] for the abolition of internal customs . . . [a movement] . . . led throughout, and ultimately brought to success, not by the representatives of commercial and industrial interests, but by reforming officials'.[117]

From the point of view of what might have optimized conditions for French national industrialization, the French Revolution seems best interpreted as either overwrought or premature. A few ministerial reforms under the Old Regime might well have optimized chances for France quickly to emulate British industrial developments (especially since Old Regime officials were leaning toward a system of international free trade, as exemplified by the Commercial Treaty of 1786). Social revolution in France, as in Russia and China, strengthened national political institutions, equipped them to mobilize people and resources to meet the crises of modernization, to guarantee order at home, and to counter foreign threats. Yet in Russia and China, emerging from revolutionary crises in the twentieth century, strengthened national political institutions could be used *directly* to promote industrialization building upon enterprises already implanted by foreign capital and employing models and advanced technologies from abroad. But in post-Revolutionary France, resources mobilized by strengthened national institutions were dissipated in the adventuristic Napoleonic Wars, while France lost ground against her chief economic competitor, Great Britain. The outcome could hardly have been different. A French economy consisting entirely of small-scale agricultural and (mostly non-mechanized) industrial units could hardly be directed from above (as the Jacobin interlude proved),[118] especially when foreign models of large-scale industry were as yet in world history entirely lacking.

The French Revolution was remarkably similar to the Russian and the Chinese in its basic *causes* – failure of Old Regime officials to mobilize sufficient national resources to promote national economic development and/or counter military competition or threats from more developed nations abroad – and in its *structural dynamics* – peasants and marginal political elites against a traditional landed upper class. That *outcomes* differed – that in France no communist party emerged to fully displace landed wealth, collectivize agriculture, and direct industrialization – is not only attributable to factors stressed by traditional theories of revolution, such as the shape of the pre-revolutionary class structure[119] and the established ideological aims of avowed revolutionary elites, but also to the *opportunities* and *requirements* for state initiatives in industrialization presented by the *world* political economy *at the time* each agrarian bureaucratic society was incorporated into a modernizing world and experienced social revolutionary transformation 'in response'.

Let me sum up what this essay has attempted to do. To explain the great historical social revolutions, I have, first, conceptualized a certain type of society, the agrarian bureaucracy, in which social control of the lower strata (mainly peasants) rests with institutions locally and regionally controlled by landed upper classes, together with administrative and military machineries centrally controlled; and second, I have discussed differences between agrarian bureaucracies which did and those which did not experience social revolutions in terms of (a) institutional structures which mediate landed upper-class relations to state apparatuses and peasant relations to landed upper classes and (b) types and amounts of international political and economic pressures (especially originating with more developed nations) impinging upon agrarian bureaucracies newly incorporated into the modernizing world. According to my analysis, social revolutions occurred in those modernizing agrarian bureaucracies – France, Russia and China – which *both* incubated peasantries structurally prone to autonomous insurrection *and* experienced severe administrative and military disorganization due to the direct or indirect effects of military competition or threats from more modern nations abroad.

In the process of elucidating this basic argument, I have at one point or another alluded to evidence concerning Prussia (Germany), Japan (and Turkey), and Russia in 1905. Obviously the coverage of these and other 'negative' cases has been far from complete. Yet partial explanations have been offered for the avoidance of social revolution by Prussia/Germany, Japan and Russia through 1916. Japan and Russia escaped administrative/military collapse in the face of moderate challenges from abroad because their traditional governmental elites were significantly differentiated from landed upper classes. Prussia lacked a structurally autonomous, insurrection-prone peasantry, and therefore when, in 1848, the King hesitated for a year to use his armies to repress popular disturbances, the Junker-led army, manned by peasants from the estates east of the Elbe, remained loyal and intact until it was finally used to crush the German Revolutions during 1849–50.

This comparative historical analysis has been meant to render plausible a theoretical approach to explaining revolutions which breaks with certain long-established sociological proclivities. While existing theories of revolution focus on discontent, and its articulation by oppositional programs or ideologies, as the fundamental cause of revolutions, I have emphasized mechanisms and dynamics of societal social control through political and class domination. Moreover, while other theories view the impact of modernization (as a cause of revolution) in terms of the effects of processes of economic development on class structures, 'system equilibrium', or societal members' levels of satisfaction, my approach focuses on the effects of modernization – viewed also as an inter-societal politico-strategic process – upon adaptive capacities of the agrarian bureaucratic states and upon the opportunities open to political elites who triumph in revolutions.

Obviously, thorough testing of these ideas will require more precise delineation of concepts and the extension of hypotheses derived from this analysis to new cases. But I have made a start. And I hope that especially those who disagree with my conclusions will themselves turn to historical evidence to argue their cases. Social science can best grow through the interplay of theory and historical investigation, and comparative historical analysis represents one indispensable tool for achieving this.

NOTES

1. Samuel P. Huntington, *Political Order in Changing Societies* (New Haven: Yale University Press, 1968), p. 264.
2. Stephan T. Possony, ed., *The Lenin Reader* (Chicago: Henry Regnery Company, 1966), p. 349.
3. For important examples see: Ted Robert Gurr, *Why Men Rebel* (Princeton, N.J.: Princeton University Press, 1970); Neil J. Smelser, *Theory of Collective Behavior* (New York: The Free Press of Glencoe, 1963), and Harry Eckstein, 'On the Etiology of Internal Wars', *History and Theory* 4(2) (1965).
4. Crane Brinton, *The Anatomy of Revolution* (New York: Vintage Books, 1965; original edition, 1938); Lyford P. Edwards, *The Natural History of Revolution* (Chicago: University of Chicago Press, 1971; originally published in 1927); George Sawyer Petee, *The Process of Revolution* (New York: Harper and Brothers, 1938); and Rex D. Hopper, 'The Revolutionary Process', *Social Forces* 28 (March, 1950): 270–9.
5. Harry Eckstein, ed., *Internal War* (New York: The Free Press, 1964), p. 8.
6. *Ibid.*, p. 10.
7. See: Ernest Nagel, ed., *John Stuart Mill's Philosophy of Scientific Method* (New York: Hafner Publishing Co., 1950); Marc Bloch, 'Toward a Comparative History of European Societies', pp. 494–521 in Frederic C. Lane and Jelle C. Riemersma, eds., *Enterprise and Secular Change* (Homewood, Ill.: The Dorsey Press, 1953); William H. Sewell, Jr., 'Marc Bloch and the Logic of Comparative History', *History and Theory* 6(2) (1967): 208–18; Neil J. Smelser, 'The Methodology of Comparative Analysis', (unpublished draft); and S. M. Lipset, *Revolution and Counterrevolution* (New York: Anchor Books, 1970), part I.
8. In formulating the 'agrarian bureaucracy' societal type concept, I have drawn especially upon the work and ideas of S. N. Eisenstadt in *The Political Systems of Empires* (New York: The Free Press, 1963); Barrington Moore, Jr., in *Social Origins of Dictatorship and Democracy* (Boston: Beacon Press, 1967); and Morton H. Fried, 'On the Evolution of Social Stratification and the State', pp. 713–31 in Stanley Diamond, ed., *Culture in History* (New York: Columbia University Press, 1960). The label 'agrarian bureaucracy' is pilfered from Moore. Clear-cut instances of agrarian bureaucratic societies were: China, Russia, France, Prussia, Austria, Spain, Japan, Turkey.
9. Terence K. Hopkins and Immanuel Wallerstein, 'The Comparative Study of National Societies', *Social Science Information* 6 (1967): 39.
10. See Immanuel Wallerstein, *The Modern World System: Capitalist Agriculture and the Origins of the European World-Economy in the Sixteenth Century* (New York and London: Academic Press, 1974).
11. E. J. Hobsbawm, *Industry and Empire* (Baltimore, Md.: Penguin Books, 1969).
12. See Walter L. Dorn, *Competition for Empire, 1740–1763* (New York: Harper and Row, 1963; originally, 1940).
13. Christopher Lasch, *The New Radicalism in America* (New York: Vintage Books, 1967), p. 141.
14. Alexander Gerschenkron, 'Problems and Patterns of Russian Economic Development', pp. 42–72 in Cyril E. Black, ed., *The Transformation of Russian Society* (Cambridge, Mass.: Harvard University Press, 1960).

15. Geroid Tanquary Robinson, *Rural Russia Under the Old Regime* (Berkeley and Los Angeles: University of California Press, 1969; originally published in 1932), Chap. 11.

16. William Henry Chamberlin, *The Russian Revolution,* Volume I (New York: Grosset and Dunlap, 1963; originally published in 1935), pp. 64–5.

17. Katharine Chorley, *Armies and the Art of Revolution* (London: Faber and Faber, 1943), Chap. 6.

18. *Ibid.,* pp. 118–9.

19. In 1904, '[t]he Minister of Interior, von Plehve, saw a desirable outlet from the [turbulent domestic] situation in a "little victorious war" ' (Chamberlin, *op. cit.,* p. 47).

20. See: Leon Trotsky, *The Russian Revolution* (selected and edited by F. W. Dupee) (New York: Anchor Books, 1959; originally published in 1932), Volume I, Chap. 2; and Roderick E. McGrew, 'Some Imperatives of Russian Foreign Policy', pp. 202–29 in Theofanis George Stavrou, ed., *Russia Under the Last Tsar* (Minneapolis: University of Minnesota Press, 1969).

21. Ellen Kay Trimberger, 'A Theory of Elite Revolutions', *Studies in Comparative International Development* 7(3) (Fall, 1972): 192.

22. Walter M. Pintner, 'The Social Characteristics of the Early Nineteenth-Century Russian Bureaucracy', *Slavic Review* 29(3) (September, 1970): 442–3. See also, Don Karl Rowney, 'Higher Civil Servants in the Russian Ministry of Internal Affairs: Some Demographic and Career Characteristics, 1905–1916', *Slavic Review* 31(1) (March, 1972): 101–10.

23. Dorn, *op. cit.;* and C. B. A. Behrens, *The Ancien Regime* (London: Harcourt, Brace, and World, 1967).

24. Alexis de Tocqueville, *The Old Regime and the French Revolution* (New York: Anchor Books, 1955; originally published in French in 1856).

25. Dorn, *op. cit.,* p. 23.

26. *Ibid.,* p. 30.

27. Edward Whiting Fox, *History in Geographic Perspective: The Other France* (New York: W. W. Norton, 1971), p. 69.

28. Dorn, *op. cit.,* p. 26.

29. Franklin L. Ford, *Robe and Sword* (New York: Harper and Row, 1965; originally published in 1953), p. 248.

30. Alfred Cobban, *The Social Interpretation of the French Revolution* (Cambridge: Cambridge University Press, 1968), Chaps. 4 and 5. There is growing agreement among historians that, at the end of the *Ancien Régime,* there was, 'between most of the nobility and the proprietary sector of the middle classes, a continuity of investment forms and socio-economic values that made them, economically, a single group. In the relations of production they played a common role. The differentiation between them was not in any sense economic; it was juridical'. From George Taylor, 'Noncapitalist Wealth and the Origins of the French Revolution', *American Historical Review* 72(2) (January, 1967): 487–8. Similar views are expressed by J. McManners, 'France', pp. 22–42 in Albert Goodwin, ed., *The European Nobility in the Eighteenth Century* (New York: Harper and Row, 1967; originally published in 1953); and Behrens, *op. cit.,* pp. 46–84.

31. Alfred Cobban, *A History of Modern France, Volume I: 1715–1799* (Baltimore, Md.: Penguin Books, 1963; originally published in 1957), p. 155.

32. Ford, *op. cit.,* p. 248.

33. Cobban, *A History . . . ,* p. 68.

34. Dorn, *op. cit.*

35. Cobban, *A History . . . ,* p. 122.

36. Jean Egret, *La Pré-Revolution Française, 1787–1788* (Paris: Presses Universitaires de France, 1962).
37. Chorley, *op. cit.,* pp. 138–9.
38. *Ibid.,* p. 141.
39. Albert Feuerwerker, *China's Early Industrialization* (New York: Atheneum, 1970; originally published in 1958), p. 41.
40. Chung-li Chang, *The Chinese Gentry* (Seattle: University of Washington Press, 1955); Ping-ti Ho, *The Ladder of Success in Imperial China* (New York: Columbia University Press, 1962); and Franz Michael, 'State and Society in Nineteenth Century China', *World Politics* 7 (April, 1955): 419–33.
41. Philip Kuhn, *Rebellion and Its Enemies in Late Imperial China* (Cambridge, Mass.: Harvard University Press, 1970).
42. Feuerwerker, *op. cit.,* pp. 40–1.
43. Mary C. Wright, ed., *China in Revolution: The First Phase, 1900–1913* (New Haven: Yale University Press, 1968), pp. 24–6.
44. Yoshiro Hatano, 'The New Armies', pp. 365–82 in Wright, ed., *op. cit.;* and John Gittings, 'The Chinese Army', pp. 187–224 in Jack Gray, ed., *Modern China's Search for a Political Form* (London: Oxford University Press, 1969).
45. John Fincher, 'Political Provincialism and the National Revolution', in Wright, ed., *op. cit.,* p. 202.
46. Fincher, *op. cit.;* and P'eng-yuan Chang, 'The Constitutionalists', in Wright, ed., *op. cit.*
47. Wright, ed., *op. cit.,* p. 50.
48. Fincher, *op. cit.*
49. Wright, ed., *loc. cit.*
50. John King Fairbank, *The United States and China* (third edition) (Cambridge, Mass.: Harvard University Press, 1971), p. 132.
51. Martin C. Wilbur, 'Military Separatism and the Process of Reunification Under the Nationalist Regime, 1922–1937', pp. 203–63 in Ping-ti Ho and Tang Tsou, eds., *China in Crisis,* Volume I, Book I (Chicago: University of Chicago Press, 1968).
52. Albert Soboul, *The Sans Culottes* (New York: Anchor Books, 1972; originally published in French in 1968); and George Rudé, *The Crowd in the French Revolution* (London: Oxford University Press, 1959).
53. Jean Chesneaux, *The Chinese Labor Movement, 1919–1927* (Stanford: Stanford University Press, 1968).
54. Eric R. Wolf, *Peasant Wars of the Twentieth Century* (New York: Harper and Row, 1969), p. 290.
55. In 1848 the East Elbian region of 'Germany' escaped general peasant insurrection, and the Prussian armies that crushed the German Revolutions of 1848 were recruited from the East Elbian estates, officers and rank-and-file alike. See: Theodore Hamerow, *Restoration, Revolution, Recreation* (Princeton, N.J.: Princeton University Press, 1958); and Hajo Holborn, *A History of Modern Germany, 1648–1840* (New York: Alfred A. Knopf, 1963).
56. 'Sanctioning machineries' are organizations which control forceful or remunerative sanctions. 'Social control' also involves normative pressures, but to be truly binding, especially in hierarchical situations, these must typically be 'backed up' by application or credible threat of application of force or manipulation of needed remuneration.
57. See Wolf, *op. cit.,* 'Conclusion'; and Moore, *op. cit.,* Chap. 9 and 'Epilogue'.
58. Norman Hampson, *A Social History of the French Revolution* (Toronto: University of Toronto Press, 1963), p. 23.
59. Ernest Labrousse, 'The Evolution of Peasant Society in France from the Eighteenth

Century to the Present', pp. 43–64 in E. M. Acomb and M. L. Brown, Jr., eds., *French Society and Culture Since the Old Regime* (New York: Holt, Reinhart and Winston, 1966); Georges Lefebvre, 'Repartition de la Propriété et de l'Exploitation Foncières à la Fin de l'Ancien Régime', pp. 279–306 in Georges Lefebvre, *Études sur la Revolution Française* (Paris: Presses Universitaires de France, 1963); Albert Soboul, *La France à la Veille de la Revolution: Aspects Economiques et Sociaux* (Paris: Centre de Documentation Universitaire, La Sorbonne, 1960), Chap. 6; and Hampson, *op. cit.*, p. 23.

60. Alun Davies, 'The Origins of the French Peasant Revolution of 1789', *History* 49(165): (February, 1964): 25; and Henri Sée, *Economic and Social Conditions in France During the Eighteenth Century* (New York: F. S. Crofts, 1931), pp. 3–4.

61. Louise Tilly, 'The Food Riot as a Form of Political Conflict in France', *The Journal of Interdisciplinary History* 11(1) (Summer, 1971): 23–57.

62. Davies, *op. cit.;* Georges Lefebvre, *The French Revolution,* Volume I (New York: Columbia University Press, 1962), pp. 47–9; and Albert Soboul, 'Classes and Class Struggles During the French Revolution', *Science and Society* 17(5) (Summer, 1953): 243–4.

63. Hampson, *op. cit.,* p. 24; also see Albert Soboul, 'The French Rural Community in the Eighteenth and Nineteenth Centuries', *Past and Present,* Number 10 (November, 1956): 78–95.

64. Soboul, 'French Rural Community . . . ,' 80–1.

65. J. S. Bromley, 'The Decline of Absolute Monarchy', in J. M. Wallace-Hadrill and J. McManners, eds., *France: Government and Society* (London: Methuen, 1957).

66. Tilly, *op. cit.*

67. Lefebvre, *op. cit.,* Chap. 8.

68. Hampson, *op. cit.,* p. 69.

69. George Rudé, *The Crowd in History* (New York: Wiley, 1964), p. 103.

70. Alfred Cobban, *The Social Interpretation . . . ,* Chap 5.

71. Lefebvre, *loc. cit.*

72. Chorley, *op. cit.,* Chap. 8.

73. Hampson, *op. cit.,* p. 78.

74. Lefebvre, *op. cit.,* p. 129.

75. Hampson, *op. cit.,* p. 27.

76. Soboul, 'French Rural Community . . .', p. 85.

77. Terence Emmons, 'The Peasant and the Emancipation', and Francis M. Watters, 'The Peasant and the Village Commune', both in Wayne S. Vucinich, ed., *The Peasant in Nineteenth-Century Russia* (Stanford: Stanford University Press, 1968); and Robinson, *op. cit.*

78. Jerome Blum, *Lord and Peasant in Russia* (Princeton, N.J.: Princeton University Press, 1961), pp. 598–9; and Robinson, *op. cit.,* pp. 78–9.

79. Robinson, *op. cit.,* p. 155.

80. *Ibid.,* pp. 188–207.

81. Gerschenkron, *op. cit.,* pp. 42–72.

82. Robinson, *op. cit.,* pp. 225–6.

83. Chamberlin, *op. cit.,* p. 257.

84. *Ibid.,* p. 242.

85. *Ibid.,* p. 252.

86. *Ibid.,* p. 256.

87. *Ibid.*

88. R. H. Tawney, *Land and Labour in China* (Boston: Beacon Press, 1966; originally published in 1932), Chap. 2.

89. G. William Skinner, 'Chinese Peasants and the Closed Community: An Open and Shut Case', *Comparative Studies in Society and History* 13(3) (July, 1971): 272–3.
90. Kuhn, *op. cit., passim.*
91. Skinner, *op. cit.,* pp. 278ff.
92. See: Skinner, *op. cit.,* Kuhn, *op. cit.;* and George E. Taylor, 'The Taiping Rebellion: Its Economic Background and Social Theory', *Chinese Social and Political Science Review* 16 (1933): 545–614.
93. See: Mark Selden, *The Yenan Way in Revolutionary China* (Cambridge, Mass.: Harvard University Press, 1971), Chaps. 1–2; Dick Wilson, *The Long March 1935* (New York: Avon Books, 1971); and Agnes Smedly, *The Great Road: The Life and Times of Chu Teh* (New York: Monthly Review Press, 1956).
94. Selden, *op. cit.;* Franz Schurmann, *Ideology and Organization in Communist China* (second edition) (Berkeley and Los Angeles: University of California Press, 1968), pp. 412–37; Ilpyong J. Kim, 'Mass Mobilization Policies and Techniques Developed in the Period of the Chinese Soviet Republic', pp. 78–98 in A. Doak Barnett, ed., *Chinese Communist Politics in Action* (Seattle: University of Washington Press, 1969).
95. Selden, *op. cit.;* and Schurmann, *op. cit.*
96. William Hinton, *Fanshen: A Documentary of Revolution in a Chinese Village* (New York: Vintage Books, 1968; first published in 1966).
97. Schurmann, *op. cit.,* pp. 425–31.
98. See, for example, Roland Mousnier, *Peasant Uprisings in the Seventeenth Century: France, Russia and China* (New York: Harper and Row, 1972; originally published in French, 1967).
99. Cobban, *A History* . . . , p. 134. See also: Hampson, *A Social History* . . . , p. 60; and Georges Lefebvre, *The French Revolution,* Volume I (New York: Columbia University Press, 1962), p. 45.
100. Fox, *op. cit.,* pp. 89–90.
101. George Fischer, 'The Intelligentsia and Russia', pp. 253–73 in Black, ed., *op. cit.*
102. George Fischer, 'The Russian Intelligentsia and Liberalism', pp. 317–36 in Hugh McLean, Martin Malia and George Fischer, eds., *Russian Thought and Politics – Harvard Slavic Studies, Volume IV* (Cambridge, Mass.: Harvard University Press, 1957); and Donald W. Treadgold, 'Russian Radical Thought, 1894–1917', pp. 69–86 in Stavrou, ed., *op. cit.*
103. John Israel, 'Reflections on the Modern Chinese Student Movement', *Daedalus* (Winter, 1968): 229–53; and Robert C. North and Ithiel de Sola Pool, 'Kuomintang and Chinese Communist Elites', pp. 319–455 in Harold D. Lasswell and Daniel Lerner, eds., *World Revolutionary Elites* (Cambridge, Mass.: The M.I.T. Press, 1966).
104. North and Pool, *op. cit.*
105. John Israel, *Student Nationalism in China: 1927–1937* (Stanford: Hoover Institute Publications, 1966).
106. See: Fox, *op. cit.,* Chap. 4, and Behrens, *op. cit.*
107. Fox, *op. cit.,* p. 90.
108. Huntington, *op. cit.,* p. 266.
109. See: Hampson, *A Social History* . . . , Chap. 2; Sidney Harcave, *The Russian Revolution of 1905* (London: Collier Books, 1970; first published in 1964); and P'eng-yuan Chang, 'The Constitutionalists', pp. 143–83 in Wright, ed., *op. cit.*
110. On the Bolsheviks, see Robert V. Daniels, 'Lenin and the Russian Revolutionary Tradition', pp. 339–54 in McLean, Malia and Fischer, eds., *op. cit.* Daniels argues that 'the more autocratic societies like pre-revolutionary Russia . . . prompted

historical theories which put a premium on individual will, power and ideas . . . ',
p. 352.

111. Franklin L. Ford, 'The Revolutionary-Napoleonic Era: How Much of a Water-shed?' *American Historical Review* 69(1) (October, 1963): 22–3.
112. Norman Hampson, *The Enlightenment* (Baltimore: Penguin Books, 1968), p. 262.
113. Hampson, *A Social History* . . . , Chap. 10.
114. See, *op. cit.*, pp. 172–3.
115. George V. Taylor, 'Noncapitalist Wealth and the Origins of the French Revolution', *American Historical Review* 72(2) (January, 1967): 469–96.
116. Cobban, *Social Interpretation* . . . , Chaps. 12 and 13.
117. *Ibid.*, p. 70.
118. On the difficulties with attempts to impose economic controls during the Jacobin ascendance, see: Soboul, *The Sans Culottes,* 'Conclusion'; and Moore, *op. cit.*, pp. 70–92.
119. Normally 'class structure' is analyzed only or mainly with reference to the mode of production of a society, but state organization and activities influence patterns of stratification as well. State influences were crucial in creating social forces that played key roles in the great historical social revolutions.

Part III

A DIALOGUE ABOUT CULTURE AND IDEOLOGY
IN REVOLUTIONS

7

Ideologies and social revolutions: Reflections on the French case

WILLIAM H. SEWELL, JR.

This article was inspired – perhaps I should say provoked – by Theda Skocpol's *States and Social Revolutions*.[1] I believe that her book deserves the general acclaim it has received as a model of comparative historical analysis and as a brilliant contribution to the sociology of revolutions. But I also believe that Skocpol's treatment of the role of ideology in revolution is inadequate. This article begins by developing an alternative to Skocpol's conception of ideology, then demonstrates how this alternative conception can help to illuminate the history of the French Revolution, and concludes with some suggestions for future comparative studies of revolutions.

Skocpol's goal in *States and Social Revolutions* is to specify, by means of a comparative historical analysis, the causes and the outcomes of the three great social revolutions of modern times: the French, the Russian, and the Chinese. She analyzes revolutions from what she terms a "non-voluntarist, structuralist perspective,"[2] emphasizing three fundamental structural relations: (1) between classes (especially landlords and peasants), (2) between classes and states, and (3) between different states in international relations. To summarize a very complex and subtle argument, Skocpol sees a particular combination of conditions as being conducive to social revolution: (1) well-organized and autonomous peasant communities, (2) a dominant class of absentee agricultural rentiers who are highly dependent on the state, and (3) a semibureaucratized state that falls behind in military competition with rival states. When these three conditions are present, as they were in different ways in France, Russia, and China, the result can be social revolution – a breakdown of the state, a peasant uprising, a transformation of class relations, and, eventually, a massive consolidation of bureaucratic power in a new state.

One of Skocpol's most important contributions to the history and sociology

I would like to thank Keith Baker, Richard Eaton, Dale Eickelman, Neil Fligstein, Peter Machinist, Sarah Maza, William Reuss, Renato Rosaldo, Theda Skocpol, and Norman Yoffee for comments on earlier drafts. An earlier version of this article was presented at the American Historical Association meetings in Los Angeles in 1981.

of revolutions is her approach to the problem of multiple causation. All serious analysts agree that the causes of revolutions are complex. But in the face of this complexity they usually employ one of two strategies: a "hierarchical" strategy of asserting the primacy of some type of cause over the others, or a "narrative" strategy of trying to recount the course of the revolution in some semblance of its real complexity. The trouble with both the usual strategies is that they are, literally, insufficiently analytical. The narrative strategy discusses different causal features of the revolutionary process only as they make themselves felt in the unfolding of the story. Consequently, causes tend to get lost in a muddle of narrative detail and are never separated out sufficiently to make their autonomous dynamics clear. The problem with the hierarchical strategy is that while it successfully specifies the causal dynamics of one factor, it tends to subordinate the roles of other factors, either treating them only as background (as most studies of revolution have done with the problem of the international setting) or conflating them with the chosen causal factor. Here the obvious example is the way that Marxist theories of revolution have tended to view the state as simply an expression of class power, rather than as a distinctive institution with its own interests and dynamics.

Skocpol's strategy is to insist that causation is a matter of "conjunctural, unfolding interactions of originally separately determined processes."[3] Although I might prefer "autonomously determined" to "separately determined," I believe that Skocpol's strategy is an inspired compromise, one that combines the best features of both the usual approaches while avoiding their faults. It appropriates the conceptual power of the hierarchical strategy and applies it to not one but several causal processes; but it also appropriates the narrative strategy's emphasis on sequence, conjuncture, and contingency. By proceeding in this way, Skocpol manages to specify the distinct causal contributions of class, state, and international structures and processes to the outbreak and outcome of revolutions, while at the same time respecting the unique and unfolding concatenation of causal forces in each of the revolutions she studies. I have nothing but admiration for the way she solves the problem of multiple causation. My quarrel with her is that she has not made her causation multiple enough – that she has not recognized the autonomous power of ideology in the revolutionary process. In her account, ideology remains conflated with class struggle or state consolidation, just as the state has usually been conflated with class in Marxist theories of revolution. One of the tasks of this paper is to trace out the autonomous dynamics of ideology in the case of France, and to indicate how ideology fit into "the conjunctural unfolding of interacting processes" known as the French Revolution. But doing this, as I hope to demonstrate, does more than add one more "factor" that can account for some portion of the change that took place. It also leads to a fundamentally different conceptualization of the process of revolution.

Skocpol systematically rejects ideological explanations of revolution. Her principal argument for doing so is that the ideologies of revolutionary leaders serve as very poor predictors of "revolutionary outcomes." As she puts it, "any line of reasoning that treats revolutionary ideologies as blueprints for revolutionary outcomes cannot sustain scrutiny. . . ." Leaders "have typically ended up accomplishing very different tasks and furthering the consolidation of quite different kinds of new regimes from those they originally (and perhaps ever) ideologically intended."[4] This is true, of course, and it certainly is sufficient ground for dismissing any argument that the ideology of revolutionary leaders provides a sufficient explanatory blueprint for the regimes that emerge from revolutionary struggles. But Skocpol goes on to make the entirely unwarranted conclusion that ideologies are of *no* explanatory value. "It cannot be argued," she writes, "that the cognitive content of . . . ideologies *in any sense* provides a predictive key to . . . the outcomes of the Revolutions."[5] This is an extreme position and a very difficult one to sustain, even for so careful and systematic a thinker as Skocpol. One example will suffice to make this clear. A glaring difference between the outcomes of the French and Russian Revolutions was that private property was consolidated in France and abolished in Russia. Can this difference be explained without taking into account the different ideological programs of the actors in the French and the Russian Revolutions? In one of the most awkward and least convincing passages in the book, Skocpol attempts to do so. But she cannot explain the contrast without introducing ideology surreptitiously, in the guise of "world-historical context." She assures us that because "there were no world-historically available models for state-controlled industrialization" at the time of the French Revolution, "no communist-style, mass-mobilizing political party could consolidate state power."[6] In Russia, by contrast, "there were world-historically available models of state control over industries."[7] In other words, socialism, an ideology invented in the nineteenth century, was not available in 1789 but was well-known by 1917. This is an obvious truism, but it does point toward something important about the difference between the French and Russian Revolutions. The leaders of the French Revolution, to the last man, not only were not socialists, but were adherents of a particular "world-historically available model," which featured the collectivization of the means of production. In short, Skocpol's invocation of differing world-historical contexts turns out to introduce, although in a highly obfuscated form, the crucial difference between French and Russian revolutionary ideologies.

This obfuscation marks a sharp departure from the usual lucidity of Skocpol's argument. Similarly, her steadfast denial of the importance of ideology marks a departure from her otherwise rather catholic explanatory strategy. For example, when she determines that class antagonisms and struggles cannot by themselves explain the outbreak or the outcomes of revolutions, she does not conclude that they are of *no* explanatory value. Rather, she incorporates them as one of several important factors that *together* explain the outbreak and consequences of social revolutions.

What accounts for this uncharacteristic and unsatisfactory treatment of ideology? I suspect that Skocpol's refusal to include ideology in her explanatory package derives from her rejection of naive voluntarist theories of revolution. To admit that ideologies have a strong causal impact on revolutions would appear to give people's conscious intentions a much more significant role in the revolutionary process than Skocpol thinks they deserve. Although I would allow a somewhat greater role than Skocpol does for conscious choice, I think her distrust of naive voluntarist explanations is well placed. What I dispute is that building ideological factors into the explanation necessarily entails a surrender to naive voluntarism.

Although Skocpol is concerned to give a "structural" explanation of revolutions, her own account of ideology has not taken into account the (broadly speaking) "structuralist" mood that has come to dominate recent thinking about ideology. Theorists as diverse as Louis Althusser, Michel Foucault, Clifford Geertz, and Raymond Williams, to name only a few, have shifted the emphasis from highly self-conscious, purposive individuals attempting to elaborate or enact "blueprints" for change, to the relatively anonymous and impersonal operation of "ideological state apparatuses," "epistemes," "cultural systems," or "structures of feeling."[8] For these theorists, the coherence and the dynamics of an ideological formation (under whichever title) are sought in the interrelations of its semantic items and in their relation to social forces, not in the conscious wills of individual actors. Ideologies are, in this sense, anonymous, or transpersonal.

Ideology, then, should be conceived in structural terms. However, I hesitate to use Skocpol's term "nonvoluntarist." Ideological utterances, like all other forms of social action, require the exercise of human will. To say that an ideology "is structured" or "is a structure" is not to say that it is inaccessible to human volition, but that ideological action is shaped by preexisting ideological (and other) realities. All social structures (of which ideological structures are a subcategory) are, as Anthony Giddens has pointed out, "dual" in character.[9] That is, they are at once constraining and enabling. They block certain possibilities, but they also create others. Ideological structures undergo continuous reproduction and/or transformation as a result of the combined willful actions of more or less knowledgeable actors within the constraints and the possibilities supplied by preexisting structures. It is, consequently, not quite right to speak of ideological structures as "nonvoluntary" or "nonvoluntarist," since both the reproduction and the transformation of these structures are carried out by a very large number of willful actors. Ideological structures are, however, anonymous. The whole of an ideological structure (with its inevitable contradictions and discontinuities) is *never* present in the consciousness of any single actor – not even a Robespierre, a Napoleon, a Lenin, or a Mao – but in the collectivity. An ideological structure is not some self-consistent "blueprint," but the outcome of the often contradictory or antagonistic action of a large number of actors or groups of actors. If anonymous ideological structures in this sense do not seem quite parallel to the "nonvoluntarist" state, class, and international structures analyzed by Skocpol, this is because, in my opinion, she has a far too reified conception of social structure. State, class, and international structures are in fact characterized by the same anonymity, duality, and collectivity as ideological structures. They, too, are reproduced and/or transformed by willful actors, acting within the constraints and possibilities imposed by preexisting structures, not by some reified extrahuman forces. By defining ideology in structural terms, and by de-reifying class, state, and international structures, all four types of structures can be encompassed by a single, consistent conceptual framework.

It is necessary, then, to replace Skocpol's somewhat naive voluntarist conception of ideology with a conception of ideology as an anonymous and collective, but transformable, structure. But this is not the only way in which Skocpol's conception of ideology must be revised. Ideology must also, as most recent theorists have insisted, be understood as constitutive of the social order. While agreeing, in one way or another, that social being determines consciousness, recent theorists would also insist that consciousness simultaneously determines social being. Ideology must be seen neither as the mere reflex of material class relations nor as mere "ideas" which "intellectuals" hold about society. Rather, ideologies inform the structure of institutions, the nature of social cooperation and conflict, and the attitudes and predispositions of the population. All social relations are at the same time ideological relations, and all explicit ideological discourse is a form of social action. What all of this suggests is a very different and far more complex object of study than Skocpol takes up in her fairly cursory discussions of revolutionary ideology. It is not enough to treat ideology as a possible causal factor explaining some portion of the change wrought by revolution. If society is understood as ideologically constituted, then adding ideology to the account will also mean rethinking the nature, the interrelations, and the effects on the revolution of state, class, international, and other structures. Moreover, the replacement of one socio-ideological order by another also becomes a crucial dimension of the change that needs to be explained, one no less important than the replacement of one class system by another or one state apparatus by another.

I believe that a view of ideology as anonymous, collective, and as constitutive of social order is not only superior to Skocpol's view of ideology but actually more consonant with a structural approach to revolution. This is a contention that cannot be demonstrated by theoretical argument alone. I will therefore try to demonstrate it briefly in practice by sketching an account of ideological change in the French Revolution.

THE IDEOLOGY OF THE OLD REGIME

As usual, any account of the French Revolution must begin with the Old Regime. The ideological foundations of the French Old Regime were complex and contradictory. The complexities and contradictions were of two distinguishable types: those internal to the traditional ideology of the French monarchical state, and those introduced during the eighteenth century by the new Enlightenment ideological discourse.

The traditional ideology of the Old Regime was itself made up of disparate materials arising out of various discourses in different historical eras. It was composed of feudal, Catholic, constitutional, corporate, and juristic elements, fused only imperfectly in a sometimes precarious absolutist synthesis under the centralizing monarchs of the seventeenth century. To characterize a highly complex set of ideas very briefly, this synthesis pictured society as a set of privileged corporate bodies held together by the supreme will of a semisacerdotal king.[10]

The units of the kingdom were not individual subjects, but corporate bodies of widely varying kinds – including the three estates of the realm, the provinces, the chartered cities, trade guilds, universities, academies, religious orders, chartered companies, and numerous bodies of magistrates. Privilege was the key to the corporate conception of the social order. Privilege, in the seventeenth or eighteenth century, had a meaning very close to its etymological roots: "private law" (from the Latin *privus* and *legum*). Each of the corporate bodies that composed the state had particular indemnities, advantages, customs, and regulations – in short, a set of laws peculiar to itself – that set it apart from the rest of the population. It was these privileges that defined it as a distinct corporate body and gave it a definite place in the state. Left to themselves, these diverse corporate bodies would inevitably fall into disunity. Concerned above all with maintaining their privileges against the claims of rivals, the corporate bodies were bound to quarrel among themselves over jurisdiction and precedent. It was the royal will that welded them together into a unified state. The various corporate bodies were themselves only subordinate members of the political body of the state. The king, as head of this body, kept a proper balance between the members by regulating and adjudicating privilege and by maintaining the rightful hierarchy. In contrast to the partial and self-interested concerns of the subordinate corporate bodies, the king was concerned with the welfare of the state as a whole. Because his was the only truly public will, it was by rights absolute. The king was the supreme legislator, the font of justice and honor, and the embodiment of the majesty and glory of the state.

The king's position of supremacy was justified largely on religious grounds: the monarch ruled by "divine right." He was placed in his position by the will of God, and was owed obedience as God's representative.[11] The king's extraordinary quasi-sacerdotal quality was made evident in the royal coronation ritual – the French call it the *sacre* – which marked the king's elevation to his high office.[12] One of the crucial phases of the ceremony was the anointment of the king's head and body with chrism (holy oil) miraculously preserved from the original seventh-century *sacre* of Clovis. Thereafter, the king took communion, receiving not only the consecrated host of the layman, but the consecrated wine normally reserved to the priest. The king was, in fact, the only layman in the realm who ever took communion "in both species," as it was called. These two holy substances, the chrism and the consecrated wine, raised the king forever from the ranks of laymen, transforming him into an earthly representative of divine power and providing him with a priestly aura. It was this God-given power that made the king's will supreme in the state. Corresponding to this intimate relationship between spiritual power and public authority at the pinnacle of the political order was a pervasive intermingling of secular and religious idioms at all levels of society. Such corporate bodies as trade guilds and cities had their own patron saints whose feast days were celebrated with appropriate pomp and display, and the ritual of most corporate bodies included common masses and worship. Moreover, the entry of a person into a corporate body normally involved the swearing of a religious oath. In this sense, the bonds that united members of a corporate body were spiritual as well as legal, just as the royal power that welded all the corporate bodies into a single state was spiritual in origin.[13]

This ideology was intimately linked with the institutional structure of the French state. As Tocqueville long ago observed, the Old Regime state was composed of several distinct historical layers – a feudal layer dating from the early middle ages, a corporate layer dating from the rise of cities, guilds, and estates in the high middle ages, a magisterial layer dating from the proliferation of venal office in the sixteenth and seventeenth centuries, and a bureaucratic layer dating from the administrative centralization of Richelieu and Louis XIV.[14] Each of these successive forms of the state had superseded, but not abolished, the earlier forms. Thus, the officials of Louis XIV could establish the hegemony of the central government over feudal seigneurs, chartered cities, provinces, and assorted bodies of magistrates, depriving them of much of their public power. But it could not do away with them entirely.[15] The beauty of the idea of privilege was that it brought together all of the diverse rights and duties of these established institutions under a single operative concept, one that simultaneously gave state recognition to their autonomy within their own sphere and limited them to the role of quasi-private, partial bodies. It rendered the whole range of established institutions dependent on the king – cast as the guarantor of privilege – while leaving the direction of the state entirely in his hands.

It is important to recognize, however, that the absolutist state and its ideology, while greatly enhancing the power of the king, nevertheless embodied a historic compromise. The price of the king's theoretically absolute power was his recognition of the privileges of preexisting institutions. He had the power to regulate and adjudicate privileges, and, as the head of the state and the font of honor, to create new institutions and to grant new privileges. He also had the formal power to abolish privileges as well as to create them, but this power was severely circumscribed in practice. Any wholesale abolition of privileges by the king would violate his own raison d'être and thus jeopardize his "absolute" power. The corporate ideology of the absolute monarchy rendered it absolute only within a system of essentially fixed privileges.[16]

The retention of corporate privileges, however residual under the reign of a powerful monarch such as Louis XIV, was of crucial importance for the politics of the eighteenth century. Under the far less effective Louis XV and Louis XVI, bodies whose powers had been diminished almost to the vanishing point by Louis XIV could return to vigor and claim broad public functions. Thus the eighteenth-century parlements were able to use their right of remonstrance to assert (not always successfully) an important role in royal legislation. And in the ultimate crisis of 1787–89, the king found himself forced to call the Estates General, an old corporate institution with a claim to very broad public powers. Under the firm hand of Louis XIV, the internal contradictions of the corporate monarchical ideology were not salient. But in times of crisis or weakness of royal power, the suppressed claims of corporate bodies could burst forth and challenge the absolute supremacy of the king.

The internal contradictions of the corporate monarchical ideology were complicated by the development of the new centralized royal administration. The relation of the administration to the monarchical ideology was highly paradoxical. On the one hand, the idea of corporate privilege was a crucial device for one of the administration's most important tasks: subordinating all institutions to the royal will. Moreover, the king's ability to create the centralized administration depended on his extraordinary position as ruler by divine right. The rational and centralized royal administration was in a sense the highest expression of the supremacy of the royal will over the defective and partial wills of the myriads of corporate bodies. On the other hand, the corporate ideology of absolutism could not give a coherent account of the structure of the administrative system, whose officers, far from becoming a privileged corporate body, instead remained royal servants, revocable at the will of the king, and whose purposes and activities tended to undermine the particularism intrinsic to the corporate view of society. It was in the context of a monarchical state whose practices were expanding beyond their own ideological foundations that the ideology of the French Enlightenment emerged.

The Enlightenment contradicted the ideology of the monarchical state in both of its essentials. First, where the monarchical ideology saw divine spirit as the ultimate source of the social order, the Enlightenment insisted on a purely naturalistic account of the world. Social order was derived from natural phenomena, and was to be understood in terms of the operation of natural laws. Second, where the monarchical ideology pictured society as composed of a multitude of particular corporate bodies, each with its own specific privileges, the Enlightenment insisted on the universal applicability of reason to human affairs. It had scorn for all privilege, no matter how ancient or venerable. Considered as a body of abstract doctrines, the Enlightenment appears as a direct assault on the ideology of the French monarchical system.

Yet few contemporaries regarded it as such. In fact, the new Enlightenment ideas, vocabulary, metaphors, and prejudices were adopted rapidly and enthusiastically by the social and economic elites of the Old Regime, the very groups who had the greatest stake in the existing system. The Enlightenment became the compulsory style of the most exclusive and prestigious Parisian salons and won many converts in the upper circles of the army, the magistracy, the royal bureaucracy, the Court nobility, and even the Church. It was embraced with particular fervor by certain members of the royal bureaucracy. Although many bureaucrats continued to conceive of state and society in traditional terms, there was a strong affinity between the bureaucracy and the Enlightenment. Enlightenment notions of reason and natural law provided bureaucrats with a fully elaborated discourse in terms of which they could justify their attempts to promote administrative uniformity and abolish entrenched privileges. The epitome of the Enlightenment bureaucrat was Turgot, whose distinguished administrative career was capped by a brief term (1774–76) as controller general (head administrative officer of the crown), when he attempted wholesale legislative abolition of privileges.[17] But even after Turgot had been driven from office and most of his innovations reversed, his successors continued to pursue a less radical version of his reform program. It is perhaps not surprising that royal bureaucrats, whose position and mission lacked any coherent justification within the terms of the corporate monarchical ideology, should have adopted the Enlightenment so enthusiastically. But at least the terminology of the Enlightenment was embraced by the leading defenders of corporate privilege as well. The Parlement of Paris, in its blistering remonstrances against Turgot's reform edicts, laced its rhetoric with appeals to nature and reason.[18] In fact, in the last two decades of the Old Regime, virtually all shades of political opinion drew, to a greater or lesser extent, on the Enlightenment idiom.[19]

By the end of the Old Regime, the French political system did not have a single ideology. Rather, it had two sharply divergent yet coexisting ideologies that differed not only in their policy implications, their modes of thought, and their pictures of society, but in their ultimate metaphysical foundations. The ideology of the Enlightenment was, of course, elaborated largely in opposition to the corporate monarchical ideology. It is therefore tempting to characterize the corporate monarchical ideology alone as the true ideology of the Old Regime and to see the Enlightenment as a proto-revolutionary force, a powerful solvent of Old Regime principles that was already at work within the very integument of the Old Regime state. But this would be to read history backwards. The corporate monarchical ideology and the Enlightenment ideology were *both* working parts of the Old Regime as it existed in the 1770s and 1780s. Since these ideologies differed on so many points, it is fair to say that there was an ideological contradiction at the core of the state. But there is no reason to believe that the contradictions weakened the state or hastened its fall. There is, after all, no necessary connection between the ideological consistency and the stability of states. The admirably stable British state of the eighteenth and nineteenth centuries was hardly famous for its ideological consistency. One could even argue that the coexistence of corporate and Enlightenment ideologies contributed to the stability of the Old Regime French state; that the smooth functioning of a state structured in this particular way was actually enhanced by the simultaneous availability of both corporate-monarchical and rational-universal principles. But even if one admits that the split ideological personality of the Old Regime state was bound to give way eventually to some more coherent ideological formation, it certainly need not have led to a revolution. Elements of the two ideologies might have been combined in any number of stable amalgams, just as they were in so many European states in the nineteenth century.

IDEOLOGY AND THE REVOLUTIONARY CRISIS

The Old Regime state was thrown into crisis by impending bankruptcy, not by its split ideological personality. But once the crisis had begun, ideological contradictions contributed mightily to the deepening of the crisis into revolution. The crisis was propelled by two overlapping but distinguishable politico-ideological processes: the disintegration of the absolutist synthesis and the development of a radical Enlightenment program. The central issue around which both of these ideological processes revolved was the calling of the Estates General.

In order to resolve the financial crisis, the king had no alternative to imposing far-reaching reforms that would abolish many hitherto sacrosanct privileges – especially the nobility's and the clergy's exemptions from taxation. But to do this meant to revoke the implicit compromise on which the absolutist synthesis rested – the guarantee of corporate privileges in return for renunciation of corporate claims to public authority. Any foreseeable resolution of the financial crisis was therefore certain to rupture the existing mode of government. The question was whether it would do so to the benefit of the king's powers or to those of the privileged corporate groups. In the event, the weakened king could not impose reforms against the resistance of the privileged groups. Instead, they forced him to call the Estates General, which was the supreme embodiment of corporate power.[20] The Estates General was composed of representatives of the three estates of the realm: the Clergy, the Nobility, and the Third Estate. According to ancient constitutional principle, the king could not impose new taxes without its consent, and it in turn could demand redress of grievances from the king before consenting to new levies. The "absolute" monarchs of the seventeenth and eighteenth centuries had, of course, imposed new taxes repeatedly without calling the Estates General; in fact, the Estates had not met since 1614. But like all the other political powers of corporate bodies, which its existence had both epitomized and protected, the Estates General had never been abolished in principle, only suspended in practice. Its calling in 1788 marked the end of absolutism and the consequent resurgence of the corporate claims so long suppressed by the absolute monarchs.

Nowhere was the ideological character of the revolutionary crisis so clearly displayed as on the question of the Estates General. After all, in 1788 the Estates General had only an ideological existence. As a functioning institution it had disappeared in 1614. The necessity of reviving the Estates General was an *ideological* necessity. In order to unify their resistance to the king and give it a coherent justification, the insurgent parlements, assemblies of notables, and provincial estates had to call for restitution of the only body with a powerful claim to represent all corporate interests simultaneously. But the revival of a long absent institution meant that it had to be reconstituted from scratch. After nearly one and three-quarters centuries, there were no living memories of an Estates General and no precedents sufficiently authoritative to determine its composition and procedures. In these circumstances it is hardly surprising that the way in which this phantom institution was to be fleshed out became the topic of an immense and unprecedented ideological debate.

If the calling of the Estates General was determined by the logic of disintegration of the absolutist ideological synthesis, the ensuing debate was dominated by the emergence of an Enlightenment alternative to the increasingly disjointed corporate and absolutist discourse. While the Estates General was obviously corporate in its external form, the calling of the Estates could also be interpreted in Enlightenment terms – as a consultation of the national will or as an invitation to revise the social contract. Moreover, since the electorate was supposed to formulate and discuss its grievances for the meeting of the Estates, censorship was suspended. This lifting of the usual limits on political discourse was greeted with an avalanche of pamphlets and newspapers advancing theories and proposals of every description. The most influential of the pamphlets was the Abbé Sieyès's *What Is the Third Estate?* which mounted a thorough and passionate attack on the whole system of privilege, denouncing the aristocrats as enemies of the Nation and arguing that the Assembly of the Third Estate was in fact a fully sovereign National Assembly.[21] Thus, by the time the Estates General met, in May of 1789, a fundamental recasting of the state in Enlightenment terms was already on the agenda, and many of the Third Estate representatives were inclined to see their estate as the germ of a National Assembly rather than as a subordinate part of an ancient corporate body.

Up to the crisis of 1787, the ideology of the Old Regime had been character-

ized by a twofold but apparently stable contradiction: a contradiction between a
dominant absolutist and a subordinate corporate conception of the state, and a
second contradiction between this absolutist synthesis and the ideology of the
Enlightenment. The royal bankruptcy and the ensuing crisis led to a disaggrega-
tion of this complex and contradictory ideological formation into its elements –
absolutist and corporate ideologies that were groping for satisfactory self-
definitions in the new circumstances, and an Enlightenment revolutionary ideology whose proponents were now searching to recast the political world in its
mold. The crisis of the Old Regime state liberated Enlightenment ideology from
its ambiguous partnership with absolutism and made possible an attempt to
reorder the state fundamentally in Enlightenment terms. The drift of events over
the spring and summer of 1789 continued to undermine the plausibility of the
corporate and absolutist alternatives, while enhancing that of the revolutionary
alternative. The Third Estate's arrogation of the title "National Assembly," the
Tennis-Court Oath, the defection of "patriot" nobles and clergy to the National
Assembly, the taking of the Bastille and the consequent municipal revolutions,
the spreading peasant revolts: each of these familiar events increased the supremacy of the revolutionary Enlightenment ideology over its rivals. But it was
not until the night of August fourth that they were finally swept from the field.

The night of August fourth was the crucial turning point of the Revolution
both as a class struggle and as an ideological transformation. These two aspects
of the night of August fourth were intimately linked. By decreeing the end of
the seigneurial system, the National Assembly was recognizing the peasants'
victory over the feudal lords, attempting to satisfy the peasants and thereby win
their firm adherence to the Revolution. But the reforms of August fourth dismantled much more than seigneurialism. Thanks to a combination of astute
planning on the part of the patriot faction and a wave of magnanimous radicalism that swept over the deputies, the Assembly abolished the entire privileged
corporate order. The way in which this happened is significant: privileges were
renounced amid joyous weeping by those who had been their beneficiaries.
Great seigneurial landowners proposed abolition of seigneurial dues, representatives of the clergy offered up their tithes, representatives of the provinces and
the cities renounced provincial and municipal privileges, and so on. The result
was a holocaust of privilege. By the morning of August fifth, the entire array of
corporate institutions and the privileges that had fixed their place in the state had
been formally annihilated. What remained was the uncluttered Enlightenment
ideal of equal individual citizens governed by laws that applied to all and
represented by a National Assembly that expressed their general will.

The specifically ideological component of the night of August fourth must be
emphasized. This component can be seen above all in the enthusiasm that swept
through the Assembly. By early August, the National Assembly had been living
a deep ideological contradiction for nearly three anguished months. It had
embarked on the construction of a new political order based on Enlightenment

political theory, yet it had done so within the shell of a theoretically absolute monarchical regime and surrounded by a privileged corporate society that contradicted the Assembly's enunciated principles. It had consistently taken whatever steps were necessary to protect its position against the king, but it had so far held back from any systematic attack on the old social system – partly out of fear, partly out of regrets for an old order that had treated most representatives well, and partly out of sheer prudence. It was, of course, the exigencies of the peasants' class struggle that dictated abolition of seigneurial privileges. But this first breach in the system of privilege led immediately to a sweeping abolition of privileges that were by no means threatened by the peasant rebellion. Once the Assembly was forced to destroy one complex of privileges, it was moved forward by an overwhelming urge for ideological consistency and destroyed them all. The mood of the Assembly on the night of August fourth – the transports of lofty emotion, the tears of joy – reveal the meaning of its actions. It was at last forsaking the murky paths of ideological compromise and stepping forward into the clear light of revolutionary purity. By annihilating privilege, the Assembly was declaring the nation to be genuinely transformed, cutting it loose from its decaying moral and metaphysical moorings and setting it on a firm course of reason and natural law. The representatives' rapture in the midst of these events is understandable: they were participating in what seemed to them a regeneration of the world.[22]

The regeneration was metaphysical as well as institutional. When the Assembly destroyed the institutional arrangements of the Old Regime, it also destroyed the metaphysical assumptions on which they had been based. No longer was the social order derived from divine will operating through the media of king, Church, religious oath, and common worship. The destruction of privilege meant the destruction of the entire spirit-centered conceptual world from which privilege had derived, and its replacement by a new natural world. On the night of August fourth the accent was on destruction of the old institutional order, but the Assembly swiftly followed with a solemn Declaration of the Rights of Man and Citizen, which set forth the metaphysical principles of the new order – "the natural, inalienable, and sacred rights of man." The Assembly's first priority after the night of August fourth was to formulate a proper metaphysical foundation for the state. Only after this had been accomplished did it begin the long and arduous task of writing a new constitution.

Skocpol, of course, recognizes the central importance of the night of August fourth. It was then, above all, that Marx's "gigantic broom" swept away the "medieval rubbish" that had hitherto cluttered the French state.[23] The problem is that she reduces August fourth to an outcome of the peasant revolt. She fails to recognize that it was a crucial turning point in two quite distinct revolutionary processes: a class process of peasant revolt and an ideological process of conceptual transformation. Its role was very different in the two processes. The night of August fourth began the *closure* of the peasants' class struggle. By assenting to the destruction of the seigneurial system, the National Assembly legitimized and effectively quieted the peasant revolt. While the peasants remained restive for some time, refusing to pay their former lords the fees enacted by the Assembly for redemption of seigneurial dues, and often resisting the payment of taxes as well, the peasant problem dwindled steadily in significance. It was essentially terminated in 1793 when redemption payments were abolished.

The role of August fourth in the ideological transformations of the French Revolution was very different. August fourth marked the end of one ideological dynamic – the tension between Enlightenment and corporate monarchical principles. But it also inaugurated another: the elaboration of Enlightenment metaphysical principles into a new revolutionary social and political structure. The peasant revolt contributed mightily to the destruction of the Old Regime. It dictated the destruction of seigneurialism and it made the country ungovernable – thus paralyzing the Old Regime state and giving the National Assembly the opportunity to assume power. But after August 1789, the peasant revolt had only a limited role in determining the shape of the new regime and the nature of the conflicts that drove the Revolution forward. These were determined by a quite different array of forces, including the pressures of international war and the need to consolidate state power which Skocpol rightly emphasizes. But the conflicts were also shaped crucially by the metaphysical and ideological redefinitions that occurred in August and September of 1789. These created a new framework of rhetoric and action and a new set of political issues that dominated the subsequent unfolding of the Revolution. This ideological dynamic, which Skocpol's account of the Revolution misses, will be the subject of the following section.

THE ELABORATION OF REVOLUTIONARY IDEOLOGY

The developmental dynamics of revolutionary ideology changed drastically when the Enlightenment idiom became the dominant idiom of government. One of the remarkable features of the night of August fourth was the unanimity of the Assembly's actions, a unanimity that lasted through the adoption of the Declaration of the Rights of Man and Citizen. As long as Enlightenment principles were viewed essentially in opposition to the corporate-monarchical principles of the Old Regime, they seemed uniform and consistent. But once the corporate-monarchical ideology was driven from the field, the contradictory possibilities inherent in the Enlightenment began to emerge. The ideology embraced by the National Assembly on August fourth and then enshrined in the Declaration of the Rights of Man and Citizen was highly abstract and general. It was, thus, less a blueprint than a set of architectural principles that could be applied to the construction of quite different sociopolitical orders. The ideological dynamics of the Revolution arose out of the elaboration of practical plans from these abstract revolutionary principles. It would be impossible, in a brief paper, to recount the ideological history of the French Revolution – and point- less besides, given the vast existing scholarship on the subject.[24] Instead, I will try to indicate four important general features of the Revolution's ideological dynamic: first, the progressive radicalization of ideology from 1789 to 1794; second, the production of rival ideological variants; third, the ideological re- structuring of a vast range of social life; and, finally, the emergence of politi- cally crucial but quite unanticipated ideological outcomes.

Radicalization

The progressive radicalization of the Revolution from 1789 to the Terror of 1793–94 is one of the most familiar features of French Revolutionary history. Here Skocpol essentially accepts the now dominant interpretation which sees the outbreak of international war as the crucial factor leading to the Terror.[25] According to this interpretation, the exigencies of war – enforcing conscription, assuring supplies for the troops, maintaining discipline in the sometimes balky provinces – gave an advantage to the "Mountain" (the radical faction in the National Convention), which alone was willing to adopt the extreme measures necessary to save the Revolution. The result was the emergence of a virtual dictatorship by the Convention's Committee of Public Safety, staffed by Monta- gnards, with Robespierre as its leading figure. At the same time, the war crisis also fueled radicalization by mobilizing the sans-culottes – the common people of Paris – whose fanatic republicanism was colored by economic grievances against the rich. The sans-culottes and the Mountain forged an uneasy but powerful alliance, with the insurrectionary sans-culottes repeatedly purging or intimidating the moderate faction in the legislature, while the Mountain passed legislation guaranteeing low bread prices and permitted the sans-culottes to harass the wealthy. As long as the war crisis continued, the sans-culottes, the Mountain, and the Committee remained united. But with the definitive victories of the French armies in the spring of 1794, this radical alliance came apart, and in the end Robespierre was abandoned by the sans-culottes and was executed by vote of his erstwhile collaborators in the Convention. According to this interpretation, the radicalization of the Revolution resulted from a particular conjuncture of class struggles and legislative struggles under the goad of the war emergency.

Although the period of the Terror was also a period of tremendous ideological radicalism, most historians have treated ideology either in instrumental terms – as an arm of factional struggle – or as a reflection of the actors' class positions. Recently, however, François Furet has put forward a new interpretation of the ideology of the Terror that replaces the conventional class and political dynamic with an internal ideological dynamic. In *Penser la Révolution française*,[26] Furet denies the conventional explanation that the Terror was a response to the national peril,[27] and denies that class interests played a decisive role in revolutionary struggles for power.[28] Instead, he sees the Terror as developing inevitably out of the ideology of the Revolution. The revolutionaries had borrowed from Rousseau a highly abstract notion of popular sovereignty which insisted on the unity of the general will. Furet points out that this notion of the general will could not be sustained without its Manichean double: the idea of an "aristocratic plot." If a united popular will did not always manifest itself clearly in the cacophony of revolutionary debate, this was not because of a real disunity, but because of the lies and deceptions of the people's enemies, who wished to restore the Old Regime by treachery. Given the primacy of this abstract notion of the unified people's will, dissent was understood not as a normal fact of political life, but as a plot, a manifestation of treason against the people and the Revolution, and dissenters had to be destroyed to maintain the virtue – indeed the very existence – of the revolutionary state. According to Furet, the Terror was generated by a continuing dialectic between the notion of the general will and the aristocratic plot, and was implicit in revolutionary ideology from the beginning. Although the Terror developed through the "circumstances" of the war and attending political struggles, its dynamic was essentially internal and ideological.[29]

In sharp contrast to Skocpol, Furet insists on the collective and anonymous character of this ideological dynamic. He goes to some length, for example, to argue that Robespierre's personal characteristics are irrelevant to his role in the Revolution. Robespierre was a dominant figure not because he was "the incorruptible," nor because of his unique political talents, but because he succeeded in "becoming an *embodiment*" of revolutionary ideology.[30] Revolutionary ideology itself, not Robespierre, was the significant historical actor. "The Revolution," as Furet puts it, "would speak *through* him. . . . He was the *mouthpiece* of its purest and most tragic discourse."[31] The discourse of the Jacobins during the Terror, thus, was not a voluntary creation of Robespierre, or Saint-Just, or Marat, or any other revolutionary leader, but the completion of a semiotic circuit already operating since the summer of 1789.

This account of the radicalization of the Revolution marks an important advance. Its insistence on the anonymity of the ideological dynamic supplies a crucial corrective to Skocpol's interpretation. But it is marred by an extreme causal monism. For Furet, the ideological dynamic was not just autonomous, but absolute. Political power having been "vacated by the traditional authorities" in 1789,[32] it was not a class or a party but an *ideology* that seized power. "The Revolution," according to Furet, "placed the symbolic system at the center of political action";[33] it established "a world where mental representations of power governed all actions, and where a network of signs completely dominated political life."[34] From 1789 to 1794, ideology broke loose from social moorings, and its dynamic utterly dominated over social and political existence. Class, warfare, and political factionalism were not constraints shaping ideological developments, but mere grist for the ideological mill. Not until the Thermidorian reaction did civil society reemerge with "its unwieldiness, its conflicting interests, and its divisions."[35] This claim that 1789 established a kind of semiotic despotism transcending all social constraints is untenable. Instead of demonstrating how the ideological dynamic interacted with class struggles, the international system, political alliances, and the exigencies of state building, Furet lapses into a causal monism worthy of the most economistic of Marxists. Surely an adequate explanation of the radicalization of the Revolution must admit *both* that class struggles and the exigencies of war pushed the Revolution to ever more radical measures, *and* that the nature of these measures and the way in which struggles and exigencies were interpreted and acted upon were largely determined by the structure of revolutionary ideology.

Ideological variants

While the general drift of revolutionary ideology from 1789 to 1794 was certainly in a radical direction, this was the outcome not of some necessary elaboration of inherent tendencies, but of a succession of sharply contrasting rival ideological variants. These variants were elaborated by different political factions, each of which sketched out a different blueprint from a common set of revolutionary principles. There were Constitutional Monarchist, Girondin, Jacobin, and sans-culotte variants of revolutionary ideology – and, subsequently, Thermidorian and Napoleonic variants as well.

Each of these variants was developed in opposition to some other variant or variants. They consequently underwent continuous revision according to the vicissitudes of factional struggle. None of the factions ever succeeded in holding the field unchallenged, not even – perhaps least of all – the Jacobins. This, of course, meant that no faction was ever in a position to impose its own ideological blueprint on state and society. Thus, the question Skocpol poses as a test of the effect of ideology in the French Revolution – Does the Jacobin ideology accurately predict the outcomes of the Revolution? – turns out to be a very poor test. Even if it were possible in principle for a revolutionary group successfully to impose its ideological blueprint on a society (and I do not for a moment believe that it is) neither the Jacobins nor any other faction in the French Revolution held power long enough or firmly enough to have done so. The reshaping of state and society was the outcome of an evolving struggle between political factions, each of which was attempting to construct society according to its own evolving plan.

Each variant of revolutionary ideology can be conceptualized as a systematic transformation of existing rival variants. Thanks to the work of Albert Soboul, this process of transformation can be demonstrated most clearly for the sans-culottes.[36] The sans-culottes had two class-based predilections that colored virtually all of their thought and actions: a hostility to the rich that arose from their relative poverty, and a collectivism that, as I have argued elsewhere, derived from the corporate or guild values of the prerevolutionary urban *menu peuple*. The sans-culottes' transformations of revolutionary ideology can be seen, for instance, in their notions of "aristocracy" and of "the aristocratic plot." In the discourse of the Constitutional Monarchists, the distinction between "the aristocracy" and "the people" was above all legal: "aristocrats" were those who had privileges that separated them from the common people and the common law. In Girondin and Jacobin discourse, the distinction became increasingly political: "aristocrats" were those who opposed the Revolution, or who opposed the radicalization of the Revolution. The sans-culottes, while accepting both of these prior notions, added important nuances of their own: "aristocrats" were also the rich, who lived better than they and cared more about their gold than about the republic; or the haughty, who put on airs, wore breeches instead of the baggy trousers of the common people, wore powdered wigs, or spoke in a "distinguished" fashion.[37] The sans-culottes, in joining the common campaign against "aristocrats," redefined them in a way that reflected their own class resentments. A similar transformation took place in the sans-culottes' notion of the aristocratic plot. The Girondins and Jacobins alike attributed all types of political opposition and administrative difficulties to the aristocratic plot. But for the sans-culottes, the aristocratic plot was also responsible for high prices of foodstuffs. Aristocrats were systematically withholding grain from the market in order to starve out the patriotic sans-culottes and reduce them to slavery.[38]

The sans-culotte conception of the aristocratic plot was based on a distinctive conception of the economy. The economic policy of all revolutionary governments, whether headed by Constitutional Monarchists, Girondins, or Jacobins, was to establish free trade in all commodities and to leave individuals free to pursue their own self-interest – thereby releasing the natural laws of political economy whose operation would lead to prosperity and universal well-being. The sans-culottes opposed the establishment of free trade, but they based their agitation on an equally naturalistic political economy of their own. According to the sans-culottes, nature was bountiful, providing sufficient food to assure the subsistence of all. If prices rose so high as to reduce the people to hunger, this could only be the result of speculation by evil aristocrats, who hoarded grain in order to enrich themselves and to starve the true patriots. To ensure proper circulation of nature's bounty, it was necessary to institute price controls and to enforce them by a policy of terror against speculators.

The sans-culottes also transformed the revolutionary conception of property to make it fit with their conception of the economy. The Jacobins and Girondins saw property as the absolute possession of individuals, who were free to dispose of it as they saw fit. But the sans-culottes saw proprietors – especially proprietors of foodstuffs – as mere trustees of goods that in the final analysis belonged to the people as a whole.[39] Hence the people had the right to set prices at a level that would assure the subsistence of all. This view of property owners as trustees was closely related to a view of elected officials as "mandatories." The sans-culottes reduced the notion of political representation almost to the vanishing point. As opposed to the Girondins, who saw the individual citizen's chief role as casting a vote to choose members of a representative body, who would then rationally determine the general will and enact it into law, the sans-culottes believed that the people as a whole, acting through their local sectional assemblies, should constantly, collectively, and unanimously express their general will, maintaining continual surveillance over all their "mandatories" and immediately replacing those who deviated from the general will. Just as proprietors were continuously responsible to the whole of the people for the good and honest management of the means of collective subsistence, so the "mandatories" were continuously responsible for the correct expression of the collective will.[40] In both cases the sans-culottes were suspicious of mechanisms that alienated power from the direct control of the people, and they utilized terror as the means of enforcing what they saw as the general will.

This sketch makes it clear that the ideology of the sans-culottes was distinct from that of other revolutionary factions. But it also demonstrates that the sans-culotte ideology was constructed out of the same terminology and the same essential set of concepts: popular sovereignty, natural law, the general will, representation, virtue, property, aristocracy, the people. The ideologies of the sans-culottes, the Jacobins, the Girondins, and all other factions were each transformations of one another; they were formed in the continuing dialogue and conflict of mutual struggle, shaped out of common materials by the strategic choices, the presuppositions, and the interests of each faction. They can be seen as distinct but related explorations of the possibilities – and the constraints – inherent in the structures of French Revolutionary ideology.

Ideological restructuring of social life

French Revolutionaries of all factions were acutely aware that the whole of social life was infused with ideological significance, and were therefore determined to restructure society from top to bottom and across the board. Indeed, I would insist that this totality of revolutionary ambition be included as part of any meaningful definition of "social revolution." The French, Russian, and Chinese Revolutions were "social" not only because they included revolts from below and resulted in major changes in the class structure, but because they attempted to transform the entirety of people's social lives – their work, their religious beliefs and practice, their families, their legal systems, their patterns of sociability, even their experiences of space and time. Of course, the collapse of the Old Regime state made reforms of many social institutions imperative. The peasant uprisings had shattered rural property relations of the Old Regime; the events of the summer of 1789 had destroyed discipline in the army; and on the night of August fourth the National Assembly had abolished the tithes and tax privileges of the clergy and had dismantled the old legal and administrative system, with its venal magistrates and its widely varying municipal and provincial privileges and customs. The revolutionary legislators therefore had no choice but to elaborate reforms for all of these institutional sectors. Moreover, the exigencies of state consolidation and class struggles set important limits on how these reforms would be structured. The new system of rural property, for example, could not recognize seigneurial rights, and the new legal system could not be administered by magistrates whose purchased offices conferred nobility. Yet, as I will attempt to demonstrate, the particular shape of the reformed institutions was largely determined by revolutionary ideology.

Moreover, the revolutionaries were by no means content to reform only those areas of social life where the collapse of the Old Regime had destroyed existing institutional arrangements. Their revolution recognized a new metaphysical order; wherever existing social practices were based on the old metaphysics they had to be reconstituted in new rational and natural terms. This involved legislative intervention into many institutional spheres and social practices that had survived the upheavals of 1789 intact and whose continuation would have posed no threat to the consolidation of the revolutionary regime. Two examples were enactment of a new system of weights and measures and adoption of a new revolutionary calendar. The new metric system replaced a confused welter of local weights and measures with a uniform system based entirely on decimal calculation and facts of nature. The meter, the unit of length, was set at exactly one ten-millionth of the distance from the North Pole to the equator. Zero degrees and 100 degrees temperature were defined by the freezing and boiling points of pure water at sea level. Other measures were derived from these. The liter was defined as 100 cubic centimeters; the gram as the mass of a cubic centimeter of water at the melting point; the calorie as the quantity of heat required to raise a cubic centimeter of water one degree in temperature; and so on. Where the old systems had been arbitrary, clumsy, heterogeneous, and based on the tyranny of local custom, the new system measured out the world in terms at once uniform, rational, easily manipulable, and based on immutable facts of nature.[41]

If the metric system was intended to impose a new naturalistic conception of quantity, the revolutionary calendar was intended to transform the population's experience of time. Except for the names of the months, which were Roman, the old calendar was entirely Christian. The years were counted from the birth of Jesus; the week of seven days was terminated by a day of worship; each day was associated with a different saint; and the yearly round of seasons was marked by religious festivals: Christmas, Lent, Easter, the Assumption, All Souls, and so on. The very passage of the days, thus, was a continuing reminder of the cosmic drama of Christianity. The revolutionary calendar, which was introduced in 1793 and remained in use for thirteen years, wiped out all this Christian symbolism. The "French Era" was proclaimed to have begun at the autumnal equinox on September 22, 1792, which coincided with the proclamation of the French Republic. Years were thenceforth to be numbered by their distance from this beginning, rather than from the birth of Christ. Weeks were increased to ten days, with each day denominated by its number – Primidi, Duodi, Tridi, and so forth, up to Decadi, the day of rest, which now came every ten days rather than every seven. (The Republic was, among other things, a speed-up.) Three Decadis (also the term for the ten-day week) made up a revolutionary month, and the remaining five days each year were set aside as a Republican festival, called the *sans-culottides,* to commemorate the patriotic deeds of the sans-culottes. The months were named for their natural climatic characteristics: Vendémaire, Brumaire, and Frimaire, the months of vintage, fog, and frost (September 22–December 20); Nivose, Pluviose, and Ventose, the months of snow, rain, and wind (December 21–March 20); Germinal, Floréal, and Prairial, the months of germination, flowers, and meadows (March 21–June 18); and Messidor, Thermidor, and Fructidor, the months of harvest, heat, and fruit (June 19–September 16). Finally, each day of the year was given the name of a plant (turnip, chicory, heather), of some other product of nature (honey, cork, beeswax), or of an animal (hog, ox, cricket), just as each day under the old calendar had been the day of a particular saint. The Decadis, the days of rest, were named for implements of labor that were used the other nine days to transform natural objects into useful goods – pickaxe, shovel, mattock, and so on.[42] This revolutionary calendar established an entirely new framework for reckoning the passage of time, one that was based on, and therefore called to mind, nature, reason, and virtuous republican deeds.

Reforms of weights and measures and of the calendar were only the beginning of the revolutionaries' wide-ranging attempts to recast the social order – and indeed the physical order – in the new metaphysical mold. The revolutionaries reformed educational and scientific institutions. They eliminated earlier forms of address, substituting the universal terms *citoyen* and *citoyenne* for the hierarchy of status-bound terms from the Old Regime. They redefined marriage as a purely civil contract, rather than a sacrament, and therefore permitted divorce. They made birth, marriage, and death civic rather than religious events, and required that they be duly enregistered by the civil authorities. They changed the punishment meted out to criminals, among other things making decapitation the universal form of capital punishment rather than an exclusive privilege of the nobility. The list goes on and on. These reforms absorbed an enormous amount of the revolutionaries' energy and made significant contributions to the overall pattern of revolutionary outcomes. And they are incomprehensible except as a result of revolutionary ideology.

If many of the revolutionary reforms seem to be explicable in purely ideological terms, ideology also had a role in shaping even those reforms which were powerfully influenced by class struggles and struggles for consolidation of the state. One example is the reform of territorial administration. The provinces, which were the units of territorial administration under the Old Regime, were stripped of their sundry privileges on the night of August fourth. Before long, however, the provinces themselves were abolished and replaced by new units called departments. Unlike the provinces, which varied from immense and internally differentiated territories such as Languedoc or Burgundy to tiny and homogeneous ones such as Foix or Aunis, the departments were drawn up to be approximately equal in size and population. The uniformity of the departments was motivated in part by the goal of state consolidation; homogeneous territorial units made possible a simpler and more efficient state apparatus. But the motivations were also ideological. The geographic uniformity of the departments reiterated and established the equality and uniformity of citizens' rights everywhere in the French nation. Moreover, the new departments were named for natural features of the territory – the High Alps, the Low Alps, and the Jura; the Seine, the Garonne, the Loire, and the Moselle; the Moors, the mouths of the Rhone, the North Coast, Land's End, and so on.[43] The administrative units of the French state were henceforth "natural" divisions of the territory, not an accumulation of dynastic accidents.

The role of ideology was equally important in the National Assembly's disastrous attempt to reform the Church. On the night of August fourth, representatives of the clergy renounced tithes and tax privileges, thus necessitating important reforms in Church organization. But it was by no means inevitable that these reforms would drive the Church into counterrevolution. The reform of the Church revolved around three issues: finances, church government, and oaths.[44] The financial issues were the most practically exigent, but also gave rise to the least controversy. Since tithes had been abolished, some new means of supporting the clergy had to be devised. The Assembly's solution was to make clergy paid state officials. This new demand on the public budget was more than compensated for by expropriation of the Church's vast landholdings. Since the old taxes were virtually uncollectible and new taxes had not yet been imposed, sale of Church lands was the only practical means available to the state to finance the costly reforms of the early Revolution. The expropriation of Church land was accepted with surprisingly little protest – in part, perhaps, because the state salaries for parish priests were considerably more generous than their prerevolutionary earnings.

Reforms in Church government were derived more from ideological than from practical political necessity. Their essential features were a redefinition of parishes and episcopal sees to make them correspond to the communes and departments of the new civil administrative system, and the provision that priests and bishops, like other governmental officials, were to be elected by popular suffrage. The reasoning of the National Assembly on this issue is clear enough: if priests and bishops were to become public servants, they should be chosen by the same methods as legislators, judges, mayors, and councilmen. This proposal posed serious problems for priests, however, since it seemed to require an obedience to popular will that contradicted their obedience to bishops and the pope. Reforms of Church government, therefore, threatened to drive a wedge between the Church and the Revolution in a way that expropriation of Church lands did not.

The issue that precipitated an open break, however, was the far more abstract, purely ideological, issue of oaths. This issue went straight to the core of the metaphysical transformation of 1789. The religious vow or oath had been an essential metaphysical constituent of Old Regime society. An oath was a crucial part of the royal coronation; guild members swore an oath upon entering the body of guild masters; it was the vows taken in ordination that transformed laymen into members of the First Estate. These oaths were sworn to God, and were therefore permanent; as the metaphor put it, they made an indelible impression on the soul of the swearer. It was largely through the medium of religious oaths that spirit structured the social order of the Old Regime. The Revolution based the social order on reason and natural law rather than divine spirit, on dissoluble contracts rather than permanent religious oaths. It therefore could not tolerate oaths that claimed to establish perpetual obligation or that recognized an authority superior to the French nation. Thus it dissolved all monasteries and convents and released monks and nuns from their "perpetual" vows. (It was this same impulse that led to making marriage a purely civil and dissoluble contract rather than a sacrament.)

Finally, the National Assembly, in 1791, imposed a civic oath – a kind of public vow of adherence to the social contract – on all priests. The civic oath was a simple and superficially innocuous affair: "I swear to be faithful to the Nation and the Law, and the King, and to maintain with all my power the constitution of the kingdom."[45] The problem was that it seemed to a majority of the clergy to contradict the oath of obedience to ecclesiastical authority, and therefore ultimately to the pope, which they had sworn upon ordination. They therefore refused to take the oath, were suspended from their parishes, and were driven either into exile or into open defiance of the Revolution. The attempt to impose the civic oath on the clergy was one of the greatest political disasters of the Revolution. The alienation of the clergy, whose prestige and influence in many rural parishes was enormous, also alienated much of the rural population. It created a continual source of disorders – clandestine masses, baptisms, and marriages performed by nonjuring priests, riots when "constitutional" priests were introduced into parishes, and so on. In the west of France, these conflicts led to the famous Vendée rebellion of 1793, which plunged the Republic into civil war at the same time that the allied monarchical forces were advancing on Paris.[46] The attempt to reform the Church, hence, set in motion one of the major dynamics that led to political polarization, radicalization, and the Terror. More clearly than any other episode of the Revolution, perhaps, it demonstrates the importance of ideology as a determinant of the course of Revolutionary history.

Unanticipated ideological outcomes

It should be clear by now that the content of revolutionary ideology is crucial to any adequate explanation of the course of the French Revolution. But this does not exhaust the role of ideology in the Revolution. Enlightenment political ideology was itself transformed by the struggles of the Revolution, and among the most important (indeed, world-historically important) outcomes of the Revolution were certain new ideological discourses. Like many of the political outcomes Skocpol discusses, these ideological outcomes were shaped by the exigencies of revolutionary struggles, and therefore were not and could not have been foreseen by revolutionary actors.

One of the most important ideological products of the Revolution was the idea of revolution itself. Before 1789, the meaning of the word "revolution" in political discourse, was, in the words of the Académie Française, "vicissitude or great change in fortune in the things of the world." As an example of its use the dictionary gave the following sentence: "The gain or loss of a battle causes great revolutions in a state."[47] A revolution was, thus, any sudden change in a state – anything from a fundamental reordering of a state's constitution to the mere loss of a battle or fall of a ministry. Before 1789, the word also had connotations of recurrence. The political philosophers of the age were fond of observing that all states are subject to revolutions in the course of time – that is, to unforeseeable changes in fortune, in circumstances, or in their constitutions. Revolution, as the word was used in the Old Regime, was a recurring fact of political life, an inevitable result of the instability of all human institutions.

It was the events of 1789 to 1794 that introduced the modern notion of revolution to the world. Revolution came to mean not any sudden change in the affairs of the state, but something much more specific: the overthrow of one government by the people and its replacement by another government. Revolution was henceforth inseparable from the exercise of popular sovereignty. (It is only in the context of this definition that the modern distinction between revolution and coup d'état makes sense.) Before 1789, a revolution was something that happened to the state – it was unpredictable, a kind of chance occurrence that was bound to happen now and again, but not something that could be foreseen and planned for. The decisive interventions of the Parisian people during 1789 – the taking of the Bastille in July of 1789 and the removal of the king from Versailles to Paris in the "October days" – were in fact quite unplanned; they were revolutions in the old sense. But they gave rise to a concept of popular insurrection that made possible deliberate and concerted uprisings later – the Revolution of August 10, 1792 that deposed the king, and the insurrection that purged the Girondins from the Convention on June 2, 1793.

After 1789, revolution became something that people did to the state consciously and with forethought. This new concept of revolution had an enormous impact on subsequent history. Protecting the state against revolution became one of the cardinal concerns of governments, and, at the same time, some people became self-conscious planners and fomenters of revolution. Before 1789 there could be revolutions, but the nouns "revolutionary" or "revolutionist" did not exist. It was only after 1789 that self-conscious revolutionaries made their entrance onto the stage of the world and, consequently, into the world's dictionaries. Skocpol rightly points out that both states and revolutionaries have vastly overestimated the latter's powers. With rare exceptions "revolutions are not made; they come."[48] But there can be no denying that the idea of revolution as a planned event has transformed politics – not only in France, but in the entire world.

Another crucial ideological discourse produced by the French Revolution was Nationalism. The idea of the nation was central to the political theory of the Revolution from the beginning. Originally it was bound up with the theory of the social contract. The nation was the body created by the social contract. Its bonds of solidarity were voluntarily created and were maintained by formal political and legal institutions. Sieyès's definition of the nation was typical: "a body of associates living under common laws and represented by the same legislature."[49] This conception of the nation suffered from one very serious weakness: it was highly abstract and rational, and therefore proved incapable of inspiring passionate emotional commitment to the state on the part of the mass of citizens. This was a crucial problem once war began, since the government had to motivate the citizens to take up arms and risk death in defense of the Revolution. The traditional focus of emotional loyalty to the state had been the monarch. But the king was already in disgrace and in virtual captivity when the war broke out in 1792; he could not serve as a symbol of loyalty to the Revolution. In their attempts to raise the ardor of the populace, the revolutionaries made plenty of appeals to the social contract, the law, liberty, and the constitution. But on the whole these proved less effective than invocations of the *Patrie*.

"*La Patrie*" was a complex notion. Originally signifying the land where one had been born, during the eighteenth century it came to be linked to the idea of liberty. To be a "patriot" by 1789 meant not only to love one's native country but to love liberty as well.[50] The *Patrie* was, consequently, an ideal emotional symbol of the revolution, associating the primordial loyalties of birth with the revolutionary regime and revolutionary ideals. Over time, however, the *Patrie* or Nation came to be defined increasingly in terms of land and blood. An example was the emergence of the idea that France was endowed with "natural frontiers" (the Alps, the Mediterranean, the Pyrenees, the Atlantic, the Channel, and the Rhine) – an idea that led the French Republic to annex the entire West Bank of the Rhine with its vast German- and Flemish-speaking population as an integral part of France. But the definition of the nation in terms of land and blood went farthest in Germany, where French nationalism and French domination led to an explosion of nationalist thought and agitation, and where the liberal connotations of the nation were much less salient. In Germany the nation could be thought of as a primordial fact of nature prior to all social contracts or constitutions. For example, by 1813 the German nationalist Josef Görres could speak of the "common tie of blood relationship" that "united all members of the nation. . . . This instinctive urge which binds all members into a whole is the law of nature and takes precedence of all artificial treaties. . . . The voice of nature in ourselves warns us and points to the chasm between us and the alien."[51] As this quotation makes clear, the form of nationalism that became ubiquitous in the nineteenth and twentieth centuries was already present by the end of the Revolutionary and Napoleonic wars.

Two features of this emerging nationalist discourse should be stressed. First, for all of its contrast with the political ideas of the Enlightenment, it, too, was based on the Enlightenment's naturalistic metaphysics. It defined the nation and citizenship in terms of the natural substances land and blood, and it conceived of the loyalty of the national land and blood as natural. Second, it had no notable theorists. It was an anonymous discourse that arose out of the demands of the situation and the possibilities of preexisting ideology rather than being formulated systematically by some theoretician.

Nationalism and the new concept of revolution were certainly two of the most significant unanticipated ideological outcomes of the French Revolution, but they were not the only ones. The concepts of political terror and of what Marxists eventually dubbed the "vanguard revolutionary party" were both produced in the years 1789 to 1794. Conservative political thought was a product of the Revolution no less than revolutionary political thought. The horrifying example of the French Revolution was the inspiration for the theories of Burke, Bonald, and de Maistre, and for the conservative political regimes of all the European states of the Restoration era. Socialism, as I have argued elsewhere, must be seen as a somewhat more distant response to the social and ideological changes introduced by the French Revolution.[52] The French Revolution also produced a new consciousness of history and a new concept of the social order; it stands at the origin of modern social and historical thinking.[53] The French Revolution was an ideological event of the first magnitude. If anything, its ideological outcomes were even more important than its class or state-building outcomes.

CONCLUSION

What implications does this account of ideology in the French Revolution have for the comparative analysis of revolutions? I think it suggests four things. First, that ideology plays a crucial role in revolutions, both as cause and as outcome. Second, that to understand this role, we must adopt a much more robust conception of ideology than Skocpol's – one that treats ideology as anonymous, collective, and constitutive of social order. Third, that this conception makes it possible to analyze ideology in a fashion consonant with Skocpol's "structural" approach. And fourth, that such an analysis suggests hypotheses that could profitably be investigated comparatively. The first three propositions I shall take as sufficiently demonstrated. The fourth needs some elaboration.

Although the specific ideological developments of the French Revolution cannot be expected to recur elsewhere, the French case suggests a number of things to look for in other revolutions. Did other old-regime states contain such deep ideological contradictions? (Perhaps the existence of a reforming bureaucracy in old-regime Russia or of western-educated officials in old-regime China were signs of this kind of contradiction.) Were political crises more likely to develop into social revolutions where such ideological contradictions existed? How common were metaphysical revolutions of the sort that occurred in France in August of 1789? (The tremendous artistic and cultural ferment that followed the Bolshevik Revolution certainly suggests something of the kind in the Russian Revolution.) Were revolutions that included such metaphysical transformations likely to be more radical or more social than those that did not? Under what conditions did revolutions generate a large number of ideological variants? What determined the extent to which revolutionaries attempted to restructure a wide range of social life? How commonly did such attempts lead to resistance that crucially affected the course and outcome of the revolution? (Collectivization of agriculture in the Soviet Union appears on the surface to be such a case.) How did the struggles and exigencies of the revolution lead to the development of unanticipated ideological discourses? Why did some revolutions (such as the Russian) lead to an extended ideological freeze, while others (such as the French and the Chinese) led to the continued production of new ideological variants for decades after the apparent consolidation of the revolution? Such questions are no less susceptible to comparative study than the questions Skocpol asked about old-regime state and agrarian structures, international pressures, peasant uprisings, and processes of state consolidation. They certainly belong on the agenda for future comparative histories of revolution.

NOTES

1. Theda Skocpol, *States and Social Revolutions: A Comparative Analysis of France, Russia, and China* (Cambridge, 1979).
2. Ibid., p. 33.
3. Ibid., p. 320, n. 16.
4. Ibid., pp. 170–71.
5. Ibid., p. 170. Emphasis mine.
6. Ibid., p. 234.
7. Ibid., p. 235.
8. Louis Althusser, "Ideology and Ideological State Apparatuses," in *Lenin and Philosophy* (London, 1971), pp. 123–73; Michel Foucault, *The Order of Things: An Archaeology of the Human Sciences* (New York, 1970), and "What Is an Author?" in *Language, Counter-Memory, Practice: Selected Essays and Interviews,* trans.

Donald F. Bouchard and Sherry Simon (Ithaca, N.Y., 1977), pp. 113–38; Clifford Geertz, *The Interpretation of Cultures* (New York, 1973); Raymond Williams, *Marxism and Literature* (Oxford, 1977).

9. Anthony Giddens, *New Rules of Sociological Method* (London, 1976), p. 161.
10. See esp. Roland Mousnier, "Les concepts d'ordres, d'états, de fidelité, et de monarchie absolue en France de la fin du XVe siècle à la fin du XVIIIe siècle," *Revue historique* 502 (April–June 1972): 289–312; and William H. Sewell, Jr., "Etat, Corps and Ordre: Some Notes on the Social Vocabulary of the French Old Regime," in *Sozialgeschichte Heute, Festschrift für Hans Rosenberg zum 70. Geburtstag,* ed. Hans-Ulrich Wehler (Göttingen, 1974), pp. 49–68.
11. The definitive statement of this theory was by Bishop Bossuet. Jacques Benigne Bossuet, *Politique tirée des propres paroles de l'Ecriture sainte,* ed. Jacques Le Brun (Geneva, 1967).
12. G. Père, *Le sacre et le couronnement des rois de France, dans leurs rapports avec les lois fondamentales* (Paris, 1922).
13. This is set forth more systematically in Sewell, "Etat, Corps, and Ordre."
14. Alexis de Tocqueville, *The Old Regime and the French Revolution,* trans. Stuart Gilbert (Garden City, N.Y., 1955).
15. Skocpol's discussion of this pattern is excellent (*States and Social Revolutions,* pp. 52–54).
16. See Roland Mousnier and Fritz Hartung, "Quelques problèmes concernant la monarchie absolue," *Relazioni del X Congresso Internazionale di Scienze Storiche,* 6 vols. (Florence, 1955), 4:1–55.
17. On Turgot and his ministry, see Douglas Dakin, *Turgot and the Ancien Regime in France* (London, 1939; reprint, New York, 1965); Edgar Faure, *La disgrace de Turgot* (Paris, 1961); and Keith Michael Baker, *Condorcet: From Natural Philosophy to Social Mathematics* (Chicago, 1975), pp. 55–72.
18. These remonstrances are available in Jules Flammermont, ed., *Remontrances du Parlement de Paris au XVIIIe siècle,* vol. 3 (Paris, 1898).
19. See Keith Michael Baker, "French Political Thought at the Accession of Louis XVI," *Journal of Modern History* 50 (June 1978): 279–303. The mixing of corporate and Enlightenment language and ideas among the provincial elites of the Old Regime is massively documented in Daniel Roche, *Le siècle des lumières en province: Académies et académiciens provinciaux, 1680–1789,* 2 vols. (Paris and The Hague, 1978).
20. The best account is Jean Egret, *La pré-révolution française, 1787–1788* (Paris, 1962); English trans., *The French Prerevolution, 1787–1788* (Chicago, 1977).
21. Emmanuel Joseph Sieyès, *Ou'est-ce que le Tiers Etat?* ed. Roberto Zapperi (Geneva, 1970).
22. This interpretation of the night of August fourth was originally worked out by Keith Baker and myself in a course on the French Revolution which we taught jointly at the University of Chicago in 1973. Detailed accounts are Patrick Kessel, *La nuit du 4 août 1789* (Paris, 1969); and Jean-Pierre Hirsch, *La nuit du 4 août* (Paris, 1978).
23. Skocpol, *States and Social Revolutions,* pp. 183–85.
24. The great general histories of the Revolution include Albert Mathiez, *The French Revolution* (New York, 1964); Georges Lefebvre, *The French Revolution,* 2 vols. (New York, 1964); and Albert Soboul, *The French Revolution, 1787–1799,* trans. Alan Forest and Colin Jones (New York, 1975). See also, Crane Brinton, *The Jacobins* (New York, 1930); M. J. Sydenham, *The Girondins* (London, 1961); J. M. Thompson, *Robespierre and the French Revolution* (London, 1952); Albert Soboul, *Les sans-culottes parisiens en l'an II: Mouvement populaire et gouverne-*

ment révolutionnaire, 2 juin 1793–9 thermidor an II, 2d ed. (Paris, 1962); the central section of this book has been translated into English as *The Parisian Sans-Culottes in the French Revolution, 1793–1794* (Oxford, 1964); Albert Mathiez, *Girondins et Montagnards* (Paris, 1930); *Etudes robespierristes*, 2d ed., 2 vols., (Paris, 1927); and *La réaction thermidorienne* (Paris, 1929).

25. Skocpol, *States and Social Revolutions*, pp. 185–93. On the effects of the war on radicalization, see, e.g., Lefebvre, or Soboul, *The French Revolution*.
26. François Furet, *Penser la Révolution française* (Paris, 1978), trans. Elborg Forster, as *Interpreting the French Revolution* (Cambridge, 1981).
27. Furet, *Interpreting the French Revolution*, pp. 61–63.
28. Ibid., p. 51.
29. Ibid., p. 63.
30. Ibid., p. 56.
31. Ibid., p. 59, 61; emphasis mine.
32. Ibid., p. 43.
33. Ibid., p. 51.
34. Ibid., p. 48.
35. Ibid., p. 78.
36. Soboul, *The Parisian Sans-Culottes;* and Walter Markov and Albert Soboul, eds., *Die Sansculotten von Paris, Dokumente zur Geschichte der Volksbewegung, 1793–1794* (Berlin, 1957).
37. Soboul, *The Parisian Sans-Culottes*, pp. 19–23.
38. Ibid., pp. 53–68. This idea was, in fact, a politicized version of the idea of a *"pacte de famine"* – a famine plot – which was already widespread among the popular classes during grain shortages of the Old Regime. Steven L. Kaplan, *The Famine Plot Persuasion in Eighteenth-Century France* (Philadelphia, 1982).
39. William H. Sewell, Jr., *Work and Revolution in France: The Language of Labor from the Old Regime to 1848* (Cambridge, 1980), pp. 112–13; and Soboul, *The Parisian Sans-Culottes*, pp. 464–67.
40. Soboul, *The Parisian Sans-Culottes*, p. 109. For an analysis of the Girondin concept of representation, see Keith Michael Baker, *Condorcet: From Natural Philosophy to Social Mathematics* (Chicago, 1975), pp. 303–16.
41. Legislation on the metric system is reprinted in John Hall Stewart, *A Documentary Survey of the French Revolution* (New York, 1951), pp. 503–6, 555–60, 754–58. How serious the legislators were about exact correspondence with nature is demonstrated by the law of 19 Frimaire, Year VIII (December 10, 1799) where the previously decreed length of the meter was lengthened slightly to fit the latest measurements of the meridian (p. 757).
42. Ibid., pp. 507–15.
43. Ibid., pp. 137–41.
44. For an excellent brief discussion of these reforms, see M. J. Sydenham, *The French Revolution* (New York, 1965), pp. 74–78.
45. Stewart, p. 233.
46. The best account is Charles Tilly, *The Vendée* (Cambridge, Mass., 1964).
47. *Le dictionnaire de l'Académie françoise*, 2 vols. (Paris, 1694).
48. Skocpol, quoting Wendell Phillips, *States and Social Revolutions*, p. 17. The Iranian revolution has made Skocpol question the universality of this claim. Theda Skocpol, "Rentier State and Shi'a Islam in the Iranian Revolution," *Theory and Society* 11 (1982): 265–84.
49. Sieyès, p. 126.
50. Jacques Godechot, "Nation, patrie, nationalisme et patriotisme en France au XVIIIe siècle," *Annales historiques de la Révolution française* 206 (1971): 481–501; Robert

R. Palmer, "The National Idea in France before the Revolution," *Journal of the History of Ideas* 1 (1940): 95–111.

51. Quotes in Hans Kohn, *Prelude to Nation-States: The French and German Experience, 1789–1815* (Princeton, N.J., 1967), pp. 294–95.

52. Sewell, *Work and Revolution in France*.

53. Here it is significant that the first uses of the term "social science" were in France in the 1790s (Keith Michael Baker, "The Early History of the Term 'Social Science,' " *Annals of Science* 20 [1969]: 211–26).

Cultural idioms and political ideologies in the revolutionary reconstruction of state power: A rejoinder to Sewell

It is a rare pleasure in intellectual life to have one's work confronted in a simultaneously appreciative and challenging fashion. I am indebted to William Sewell for offering an analytically sophisticated and historically grounded critique of the way *States and Social Revolutions* addresses the problem of ideology.[1] He rightly points out that I treated the issues too cursorily and relied upon a notion of ideologies as deliberate blueprints for change that leaves untouched many of the ways in which ideas may affect the course of revolutions. Sewell offers instead "a much more robust conception of ideology . . . that treats ideology as anonymous, collective, and constitutive of social order."[2] According to Sewell, this way of understanding ideology is consonant with the overall structural analysis of *States and Social Revolutions,* and it can guide us toward wise questions and answers about the role of ideological transformations in the French Revolution and beyond.

If *States and Social Revolutions* "provoked" Sewell to write the preceding article, his able discussion has in turn encouraged me to think through more carefully how the analysis of ideologies should – and should not – be incorporated into future historical and comparative work on revolutions. Perhaps surprisingly, given my reputation for "structural determinism." I shall suggest that we need a less "anonymous" approach than Sewell advocates. I certainly agree with Sewell that culture is "transpersonal," but I want to register profound reservations about the use of anthropological conceptions of cultural systems in analyzing the contributions made by cultural idioms and ideological activities to revolutionary transformations.

A NONINTENTIONALIST AND STATE-CENTERED APPROACH TO REVOLUTIONS

Few aspects of *States and Social Revolutions* have been more misunderstood than its call for a "nonvoluntarist," "structuralist" approach to explaining social revolutions. "Nonintentionalist at the macroscopic level" might have been a better way to label my approach. For the point is simply that no single acting group, whether a class or an ideological vanguard, deliberately shapes the complex and multiply determined conflicts that bring about revolutionary crises and outcomes. The French Revolution was not made by a rising capitalist bourgeoisie or by the Jacobins; the Russian Revolution was not made by the industrial proletariat or even by the Bolshevik party. If the purpose is to explain in cross-nationally relevant terms why revolutions break out in some times and places and not others, and why they accomplish some changes and not others, we cannot achieve this by theorizing as if some grand intentionality governs revolutionary processes. This point was (and is) worth making, because much social-scientific and historiographical work on revolutions is pervaded by untenable intentionalist assumptions. Sewell and I apparently agree that these misleading assumptions need to be rooted out.

Rather than seeking to ground the causes of social revolutions and their outcomes in hypostatized interests or outlooks, *States and Social Revolutions* focused on "structures," or patterned relationships beyond the manipulative control of any single group or individual. Such social structures, understood in historically concrete ways, give us the key to the conflicts among groups that play themselves out in revolutions, producing results outside of the intentions of any single set of actors. Yet, of course, social structures – such as landlord-peasant relationships, or ties that bind monarchs and administrative officials – are not themselves actors. They are, as Sewell rightly says, both enabling and constraining, and they are produced and reproduced only through the conscious action of the concrete groups and individuals that relate to one another in the relevant patterned ways. Since the historical case studies of *States and Social Revolutions* are replete with groups acting for material, ideal, and power goals, it should be apparent that I never meant to read intentional group action out of revolutions – only to situate it theoretically for the explanatory purposes at hand.

While the nonintentionalism of *States and Social Revolutions* has frequently been misunderstood or misrepresented, the book's substantive theoretical message has been more obvious to readers. Class structures and conflicts, I argued, are not the only or the basic "structural" keys to revolutionary causes or outcomes. Analysts need to focus more directly on the international relationships of states to one another, and on the relationships of old-regime rulers and revolutionary state builders to dominant and subordinate classes. Class conflicts as such, especially conflicts pitting peasants against landlords and existing agrarian property relations, certainly entered into the processes of revolution in France, Russia, and China. But one must constantly focus on the direct and indirect interactions of class struggles with the primary conflicts in these revolutions – the conflicts surrounding the breakdown of the administrative and coercive organizations of the old-regime monarchical states, and the subsequent, often highly protracted conflicts over the kinds of new state organizations that would be successfully consolidated in the place of the prerevolutionary regimes. Thus, in France, peasant revolts in 1789 both grew out of and accelerated the collapse of monarchical absolutism. And rural property relations – indeed, all property relations in revolutionary France – were practically and legally transformed from 1789 through the Napoleonic settlement, not only according to the vagaries of class struggles but also in relation to the needs, opportunities, and constraints faced by successive sets of political leaders seeking to reconstruct the French polity and the administrative and military apparatuses of a centralized national state.

REVOLUTIONS AS IDEOLOGICAL REMAKINGS OF THE WORLD

Perhaps it was unfortunate that I was so preoccupied in *States and Social Revolutions* with reworking class analysis in relation to a state-centered understanding of revolutions. As a result, I did less than I might have done to rework in analogous ways an alternative strand of theorizing about social revolutions – one that sees them not as class conflicts but as ideologically inspired projects to remake social life in its entirety.

One modern scholar who takes this approach is Michael Walzer. He defines revolutions as "conscious attempts to establish a new moral and material world and to impose, or evoke, radically new patterns of day-to-day conduct. A holy commonwealth, a republic of virtue, communist society – these are the goals revolutionaries seek."[3] Walzer explains varying revolutionary outcomes by analyzing the relationships between the classes that revolt against old regimes and the ideologically inspired vanguards that attempt to use terror to construct revolutionary utopias under their own hegemony. In his view, some modern revolutions – the ones he likes better, such as the English and the French – have resulted in "Thermidor," in which the revolutionary class was able to depose the ideological vanguard. Others – especially communist-led revolutions in countries with peasant majorities – have resulted in the permanent institutionalization of vanguard power through continuing moralistic and coercive efforts to remake the world according to an ideological vision.

Sewell also understands the essence of revolution as an ideologically inspired attempt to remake all of social and cultural life. Witness his description of the night of August 4, 1789: "The representatives' rapture . . . [was] understandable: they were participating in what seemed to them a regeneration of the world." Sewell clearly joins the historical actors he describes in this perception. "The regeneration was metaphysical as well as institutional," he says. From August 1789 on, the French peasantry, one class apparently not gripped by Enlightenment ideas, drops out of the story of the French Revolution, which thenceforth becomes in Sewell's telling "the elaboration of Enlightenment metaphysical principles into a new revolutionary social and political structure." To be sure, various factions and social strata, from the Constitutional Monarchists to the Girondins to the Jacobins to the *sans-culottes*, continue to contend. But they are simply elaborating different ideological variants from a shared set of revolutionary principles. For August 4, 1789 "marked the end of . . . the tension between Enlightenment and corporate monarchical principles," and from then on the "Enlightenment idiom became the dominant idiom of government," creating "a new framework of rhetoric and action and a new set of political issues that dominated the subsequent unfolding of the revolution."

It is worth underlining how and why Sewell's understanding of revolution as an ideological remaking of the world contrasts to Walzer's intentionalist version of this perspective. Sewell does not claim that a particular ideological vanguard took control on August 4 and tried to remake France after that. His argument is more "impersonal," "anonymous," "collective" than Walzer's. Because Walzer's theory of revolutions is so thoroughly intentionalist, he is forced to designate a particular group as the carrier of the ideological project to remake the world in each revolution. For France, he designates those Jacobins who conducted the Terror. But what are we then to do with the other political leaderships and groups that made ideological arguments in the French Revolution? According to Sewell, what came to the fore in August 1789 was a new ideological idiom, a new set of principles of discourse and action, under the aegis of which many contending groups then proceeded to wage political struggles. In contrast to Walzer, Sewell's approach has the important advantage that we can talk about contending and successive "ideological variants" developed by different groups of actors.

THE DISADVANTAGES OF AN ANTHROPOLOGICAL UNDERSTANDING OF CULTURAL SYSTEMS

But Sewell's approach also has important drawbacks, centering on the unconvincing attempt he makes to portray August 1789 as *the* ideologically pivotal moment of the French Revolution. If Sewell's understanding of ideology improves upon Walzer by allowing for many groups to elaborate related ideological discourses, it suffers in being unrealistically totalistic and synchronous. This reflects what I will label Sewell's "cultural system" understanding of ideology. As he puts it, ideology is "constitutive of social order," and "if society is understood as ideologically constituted," then "it is not enough to treat ideology as a possible causal factor explaining some portion of the change wrought by revolution." Instead, "the replacement of one socio-ideological order by another . . . becomes a crucial dimension of the change that needs to be explained" for any given revolution.

Who thinks about cultural meanings in this way? Who treats culture as "constitutive of social order" – which means fusing into one concept both social relations and meaningful discourse pertaining to a social world holistically conceived? Anthropologists, of course. Their fieldwork experiences and disciplinary tasks have given a certain plausibility to this conception. For they have immersed themselves in the social activities and the talk of strange communities for relatively short periods of time and then come back to tell Western academics what they learned. Analysis of cultural systems has been their way to do this. Lately, due above all to the inspired writing and broad intellectual influence of Clifford Geertz, anthropological approaches to cultural analysis have been seeping into neighboring disciplines.[4] No discipline has been more eager than history to borrow, adapt, and deploy Geertzian approaches to cultural analysis.[5] And William Sewell, himself profoundly influenced by Geertz, has been one of the most able agents of this cross-disciplinary intellectual movement.[6]

Dangerous pitfalls lurk when students of complex, changing, highly stratified sociopolitical orders rely upon anthropological ideas about cultural systems.[7] It is all too easy to suppose the existence of integrated patterns of shared meanings, total pictures of how society does and should work. Given the impossibility of face-to-face fieldwork contact with diverse societal groups acting and arguing in real time, there is an inevitable temptation to read entire systems of meaning into particular documents – such as the Abbé Sieyès's *What Is the Third Estate?* Most risky of all, one is tempted to treat fundamental cultural and ideological change as the synchronous and complete replacement of one society-wide cultural system by another. Thus: on the night of August 4, corporate monarchical political culture was swept from the field and the logic of the Enlightenment took over.

TOWARD A MORE HISTORICALLY GROUNDED APPROACH

The influence of "the Enlightenment" on "the French Revolution" is hardly a new historiographical topic; generations of historians (and others) have weighed in on this question and no doubt will continue to do so.[8] As I survey the ongoing debates, certain substantive conclusions seem tentatively established and particular ways of posing the issues seem more fruitful than others. Surely the whole drift of research and debate has been away from any inclination to conflate the Enlightenment – a transnational intellectual movement dealing with basically metaphysical issues – with the French Revolution as a series of social and political conflicts that occurred in only one of the many nations affected by, and contributing to, the Enlightenment.[9] Many cultural changes that occurred in France around the time of the Revolution might well have occurred in one way or another anyway; thus a careful analyst has no warrant to attribute them to "revolutionary" anything. Meanwhile, the particular versions of Enlightenment ideas elaborated in Old Regime and revolutionary France were affected by the political institutions and conflicts of the time, just as the politics was influenced by Enlightenment ideas. Yet there was no simple fusion of Enlightenment and politics. Given the nature of Enlightenment thought itself, there hardly could have been. Again and again, intellectual historians have pointed out the variety of implicit and explicit political views held by the *philosophes,* including Rousseau, and have underlined their reluctance to prescribe any particular political reforms or institutional arrangements.[10] Sewell knows all of this, and reports some of it. But does he realize how problematic these realities make his attempt to turn "Enlightenment principles" into a governing "ideology" that could structure political arguments and actions in revolutionary France from August 1789?

Historians, sociologists, and political scientists are not well served by supposing that sets of ideas – whether intellectual productions or cultural frameworks of a more informally reasoned sort – are "constitutive of social order." Rather, multiple cultural idioms coexist, and they arise, decline, and intermingle in tempos that need to be explored by intellectual and sociocultural historians. At any given time, cultural idioms are drawn upon by concretely situated actors as they seek to make sense of their activities and of themselves in relation to other actors. To be sure, it will make a difference which idiom or mixture of idioms is available to be drawn upon by given groups. Indeed, the very definitions of groups, their interests, and their relations to one another will be influenced by cultural idioms. But the choices and uses of available idioms – and the particular potentials within them that are elaborated – will also be influenced by the social and political situations of the acting groups, and the tasks they need to accomplish in relation to one another.

I prefer to reserve the term "ideology" for idea systems deployed as self-conscious political arguments by identifiable political actors. Ideologies in this sense are developed and deployed by particular groups or alliances engaged in temporally specific political conflicts or attempts to justify the use of state power. Cultural idioms have a longer-term, more anonymous, and less partisan existence than ideologies. When political actors construct ideological arguments for particular action-related purposes, they invariably use or take account of available cultural idioms, and those idioms may structure their arguments in partially unintended ways. Yet they may also develop new ideological arguments in response to the exigencies of the unfolding political struggle itself. By thus separately conceptualizing "cultural idioms" and "ideologies," one can hope to attend to the interplay of the nonintentionalist and intentionalist aspects of ideas in revolutions much as I tried to do in *States and Social Revolutions* by examining class and state structures in relation to the goals and capacities of acting groups.[11]

Substantively speaking, the analysis of cultural idioms and ideologies in social revolutions deserves treatment analogous to the analysis of class relations and class conflicts: both phenomena must be studied in relation to the central drama of the breakdown and rebuilding of state organizations. Sewell asserts that a huge range of reforms introduced by French revolutionaries "are incomprehensible except as a result of [Enlightenment] revolutionary ideology." I do not agree (and I am not even exactly sure what this statement means). Although many reforms were indeed conceptualized in the light of certain understandings of Enlightenment ideals, the reforms figured in ongoing political struggles and typically helped (as much as possible in given circumstances) to strengthen the authority of the French national state in relation to the Church and particular private groups ranging from the wealthy and privileged to local communities. How, for example, could we understand the introduction of the revolutionary calendar – a reform that Sewell labels "purely ideological" – outside of this political context?

From the foregoing perspective, issues of political ideology in the French Revolution need to be approached somewhat differently from the way Sewell approaches them. Enlightenment principles were only one of the various cultural idioms that coexisted in France from the Old Regime through the Revolution, and there certainly was never any pivotal moment at which the Enlightenment became embodied in an overarching political ideology (or even a system of ideological variants) that took over French politics. The Old Regime itself (as Sewell acknowledges at points and forgets at others) was not associated with a single overarching ideological system. Within ruling circles, corporatist, Catholic, and absolutist principles coexisted with various borrowings from the Enlightenment; and popular groups had their own "little cultures," blends of even more diverse elements tied to particular localities and occupational communities.

After a decade of ideologically passionate revolutionary struggles, moreover, eclecticism continued to prevail in the official imagery of the French new regime. Napoleon deliberately melded together bureaucratic personnel and symbols from all political factions under the aegis of a highly generalized French nationalism. Unlike Sewell, I see no basis for attributing "nationalism" (even unintentionally) to some Enlightenment-inspired cultural code, and it seems to me that the most important ideological fact about Napoleonic rule was precisely its deliberate amalgamation of nationalism with contradictory strands of revolutionary political symbolism in order to help stabilize a bureaucratic-authoritarian state without the aid of an hegemonic political party.

As for the struggles of the revolution itself, the early leaders used shifting combinations of corporate-representational and Enlightenment ideas to challenge, first, monarchical absolutism and then "privilege." They also seem to have fashioned a quite new conception of unified national-popular sovereignty that grew from the exigencies and opportunities of the initial political struggle itself – a conflict pitting assemblies of elected representatives against the monarch. From the summer of 1789 onward, as Sewell rightly says, many of the deliberately planned institutional changes were influenced by (various readings of) the thought of the Enlightenment. But we need to ask pointed questions about how and through precisely whose efforts this happened – and with what varying degrees and kinds of success.

From the time of the initial elections to the Estates General, the revolutionary process itself was bringing to the fore strategically located leaders who were prone to draw inspiration from various readings of Enlightenment ideas. More than in most social revolutions, political leaders in the French Revolution engaged in continuous talk about reconstructing institutions. This was, after all, a revolution unusually centered in the urban politics of elected assemblies, dominated by lawyers and other literate elites. The research of George Taylor has given us clues to why this pattern of political organization gave unusual leverage to Enlightenment-inspired politicians.[12]

But we should not make the mistake of assuming that the talkers and the legislators could ever straightforwardly shape outcomes according to Enlightenment principles. After all, some of the most moralistic attempts to apply Enlightenment principles – such as the revolutionary calendar and the Cult of the Supreme Being – failed to become permanently institutionalized. The "logic of the Enlightenment" will not tell us why. Nor will it tell us why successive leaderships in the French Revolution understood the political potentials of Enlightenment ideals quite differently. Instead, for each phase of the Revolution, we need to examine the possibilities for consolidating various forms and functions of state power and consider how those possibilities interacted with the specific ideas and modes of political action available to particular groups.[13]

Throughout the Revolution, not only various readings of Enlightenment precepts but other existing and emergent stands of meaningful discourse were repeatedly mobilized for political purposes. These included corporatist-representational ideas deployed by Constitutional Monarchists; traditional norms of social solidarity and "just prices" used by the *sans-culottes* and by peasants engaged in a variety of struggles against high prices, dues, tithes, and taxes; and Catholic and monarchical principles advocated by the Vendean rebels and other counterrevolutionaries. Emergent conceptions of national sovereignty and rights were elaborated both by the French and by their diverse foreign antagonists in the unending European wars of this period. With all of these ideologically self-conscious forces at work, the French Revolution's "outcomes" obviously cannot be attributed simply to the efforts made by Paris-centered assemblies and vanguard committees to apply in practice their Enlightenment-influenced conceptions of societal regeneration. Sewell would agree with this point. But neither can the outcomes be attributed to the impersonal working out of the logic of an impersonal Enlightenment cultural code.

Instead, the outcomes of the French Revolution – ranging from private property to administrative rationalization to the Concordat with the Catholic church – were nonintentionally shaped by the interactions of all of the intentionally mobilized political discourses that figured in the conflicts to displace and replace the Old Regime. A full analysis of the many ways that cultural idioms figured in the political arguments of the French Revolution, as well as in the shaping of its complex and contradictory outcomes, requires attention to much more than just Enlightenment discourse treated as if it were a cultural system "constitutive of social order." It requires that we examine very concretely the consciousness and talk of particularly situated acting groups, and that we take seriously the essentially political tasks they were trying to accomplish during the Revolution. From this perspective, Enlightenment discourses – plural – emerge as important idioms, but not the only idioms, used in the political ideologies developed by revolutionary state builders in France from 1789 until the collapse of the Terror. Recognizing this, we can do a more historically grounded job of explaining the culturally conditioned choices of these conscious actors – and a better job of explaining the successes and failures of their ideas and arguments within the overall context of multiple cultural idioms and contending ideologies that constituted the ideational aspect of the French Revolution.

FROM THE FRENCH CASE TO COMPARATIVE STUDIES

Sewell suggests at one point that the "totality of revolutionary ambition," the will to "transform the entirety of people's social lives – their work, their religious beliefs and practice, their families, their legal systems, their patterns of sociability, even their experiences of space and time" – "be included as part of any meaningful definition of 'social revolution.' " In my view, this would impose a misreading of the French Revolution, an inappropriate conflation of the Enlightenment and the Revolution, onto a concept that needs to allow more room for the analysis of variations across modern history. In any given revolution, there may well be actors struggling to reconstruct social life as a whole in moral, even metaphysical terms. But rather than assume this by definition, we need to understand why and how such efforts have played more prominent roles in some social revolutions – such as the French Revolution and in the contemporary Iranian revolution, for example – than in others – such as the Mexican revolution.[14]

Epochal and transnational intellectual transformations – such as the Enlightenment and the proliferation of modernist and militant-traditionalist discourses within contemporary Islam – do not in and of themselves "cause" social revolutions to happen. But they probably do independently affect the scope of transformations that revolutionary politicians attempt to institute when they rise to state power amidst ongoing social revolutions. The political organizations available to contending leaderships in revolutions also affect the scope of transformations attempted. Groups organized in Leninist fashion are especially prone and able to act as totalitarian vanguards in Walzer's sense. And I have already suggested that the French Revolution gave unusual opportunities for planning sociopolitical reconstructions to assemblies of legislators. But there have been modern social revolutions, such as the Mexican, fought out primarily by contending armies rather than by Leninist parties, militant clerics, or well-read legislators. Partly as consequence, I would hypothesize, these revolutions have allowed less political space for moralistic efforts to remake all of social life. The reconstruction of national politics as such, drawing upon and melding together strands from cultural idioms appealing to various social forces in the revolutionary alliance, has been the primary ideological accomplishment of such nonmetaphysical social revolutions.

Sewell concludes his essay with some tantalizing suggestions of questions about ideology that belong on the agenda for future comparative studies of revolutions. Although I would not frame all of the queries in quite the same way, I agree wholeheartedly that the time has come for *comparative* analysts – not just students of single revolutions – to probe the patterns of interrelation among cultural idioms, political ideologies, and the politics of revolutionary transformations. Comparative history is just as useful for pinpointing unique patterns as it is for teasing out causal regularities.[15] It may turn out that patterns of culture and ideology are causally unique to each revolution, but that would not make them the less significant. As a comparative historical sociologist who has analyzed causal regularities in modern social revolutions, I continue to believe that struggles over the organization and uses of state power are at the heart of all revolutionary transformations. Yet each revolution has its own idioms of politics, and these must be deciphered with the aid of the best strategies of cultural analysis we students of society – historians, anthropologists, sociologists, and political scientists alike – can devise.

NOTES

1. Theda Skocpol, *States and Social Revolutions: A Comparative Analysis of France, Russia, and China* (Cambridge, 1979).
2. All quotations from Sewell from William H. Sewell, Jr., "Ideologies and Social Revolutions: Reflections on the French Case," in this volume.
3. Michael Walzer, "A Theory of Revolution," *Marxist Perspectives,* no. 5 (Spring 1979), p. 30.
4. For a widely read statement of this approach, see Clifford Geertz, *The Interpretation of Cultures* (New York, 1973).
5. See Ronald G. Walters, "Signs of the Times: Clifford Geertz and the Historians," *Social Research* 47 (Autumn 1980): 537–56.
6. See the discussion of history and cultural anthropology in William H. Sewell, Jr., *Work and Revolution in France* (Cambridge, 1980), pp. 10–13.
7. I do not mean to imply that anthropologists cannot do an excellent job of analyzing ideologies in complex societies. An exemplary piece of work on cultural idioms and ideological variants in a revolutionized nation is Michael M. J. Fischer, *Iran: From Religious Dispute to Revolution* (Cambridge, Mass., 1980). My remarks here are in part an attempt to conceptualize the kind of approach Fischer uses so that it can be generalized to other historical contexts.
8. A (somewhat dated) overview of generations of historiography on this topic appears in William F. Church, ed., *The Influence of the Enlightenment on the French Revolution,* 2d ed. (Lexington, Mass., 1974). Recent scholarship includes the important works by Keith Baker and Daniel Roche cited by Sewell. See also the useful discussion in Robert Darnton, "In Search of the Enlightenment: Recent Attempts to

Create a Social History of Ideas," *Journal of Modern History* 43, no. 1 (March 1971): 113–32.

9. See Roy Porter and Mikulas Teich, eds., *The Enlightenment in National Context* (Cambridge, 1981).

10. Arguments along this line appear in Darnton; Alfred Cobban, "The Enlightenment and the French Revolution," pp. 305–15 in *Aspects of the Eighteenth Century,* ed. Earl R. Wasserman (Baltimore, 1965); and Norman Hampson, *The Enlightenment* (London, 1968).

11. Although he does not use the terminology I offer here, an example of the kind of analysis I have in mind appears in Alvin Gouldner, "Stalinism: A Study of Internal Colonialism," pp. 209–59 in *Political Power and Social Theory,* vol. 1, ed. Maurice Zeitlin (Greenwich, Conn., 1980). Marxism is treated as a cultural idiom that predisposed all of its adherents against viewing the peasantry as an autonomous or modernizing force. Then Gouldner shows how Stalinist ideology, forged under particular Russian circumstances in the 1920s, took the *potential* antipeasant bias in Marxism to a violent extreme. Gouldner also discusses how, under very different circumstances of political struggle in relation to Confucian cultural legacies, the Chinese Communists came to see the peasantry in a more positive light as objects of revolutionary persuasion.

12. George Taylor, "Revolutionary and Nonrevolutionary Content in the *Cahiers* of 1789: An Interim Report," *French Historical Studies* 7 (Spring 1972): 479–502.

13. In addition to Taylor, see the discussion of the political adaptation of Rousseau's ideas by Brissot, Robespierre, and Saint-Just in Norman Hampson, "The Enlightenment in France," pp. 48–52 in Porter and Teich.

14. On the Mexican case, see John Dunn, *Modern Revolutions* (Cambridge, 1972), chap. 2; and Walter L. Goldfrank, "Theories of Revolution and Revolution without Theory: The Case of Mexico," *Theory and Society* 7 (January–March 1979): 135–65.

15. See Marc Bloch, "A Contribution towards a Comparative History of European Societies," pp. 44–81 in *Land and Work in Medieval Europe: Selected Papers by Marc Bloch,* trans. J. E. Anderson (1928; New York, 1967); William H. Sewell, Jr., "Marc Bloch and the Logic of Comparative History," *History and Theory* 6, no. 2 (1967): 208–18; and Theda Skocpol and Margaret Somers, "The Uses of Comparative History in Macrosocial Inquiry," *Comparative Studies in Society and History* 22, no. 2 (April 1980): 174–97.

Part IV

FROM CLASSICAL TO CONTEMPORARY SOCIAL REVOLUTIONS

9

What makes peasants revolutionary?

The centrality of peasants in modern revolutions was underscored for the first time in contemporary North American scholarship by Barrington Moore, Jr., in *Social Origins of Dictatorship and Democracy: Lord and Peasant in the Making of the Modern World*. Eloquently, the opening sentences of Moore's chapter on "The Peasants and Revolution" declared that the "process of modernization begins with peasant revolutions that fail. It culminates during the twentieth century with peasant revolutions that succeed" (Moore, 1966: 453). *Social Origins* in fact proved uncannily prescient and timely in its emphasis on the revolutionary potential of the peasantry. When Moore's great opus was in preparation during the 1950s and early 1960s, neither Marxism nor orthodox social science paid much heed to the roles of agrarian classes in "the making of the modern world." The peasantry, especially, was spurned as the repository of conservatism and tradition, of all that needed to be overcome by a revolutionary bourgeoisie or proletariat, or by a modernizing elite. But once the United States became tragically engaged from the mid-1960s in a military effort to stymie the Vietnamese Revolution, U.S. scholars quite understandably became fascinated with the revolutionary potential of the peasantry – especially in the Third World. The questions addressed by Moore's chapter on peasants in *Social Origins* – "what kinds of social structures and historical situations produce peasant revolutions and which ones inhibit or prevent them" (Moore, 1966: 453) – were immediately relevant for an entire nascent genre of research and theorizing on peasants and revolution.

The first major contribution to this new literature, written in the heat of the movement against U.S. involvement in Vietnam, was Eric R. Wolf's 1969 book *Peasant Wars of the Twentieth Century*. Studies undertaken by younger scholars emerged during the 1970s: Joel S. Migdal's *Peasants, Politics, and Revolutions: Pressures toward Political and Social Change in the Third World* (1974);

This essay is an extended and modified version of an article that originally appeared in *Comparative Politics*, 14, 3 (1982).

Jeffery M. Paige's *Agrarian Revolution: Social Movements and Export Agriculture in the Underdeveloped World* (1975); and James C. Scott's *The Moral Economy of the Peasant* (1976), the last of which was extended into a theory of peasant-based revolutions in a recent article (1977a) "Hegemony and the Peasantry."[1] In contrast to the Old World frame of reference predominant in Moore's *Social Origins,* the works of Wolf, Migdal, Paige, and Scott share a principal focus on Third World revolutions, the natural result of the Vietnam-era preoccupations out of which they developed.[2] Nevertheless, variations of method and substantive focus are immediately noticeable. Eric Wolf seeks to generalize inductively about peasant-based revolutions on the basis of in-depth histories of six twentieth-century cases: Mexico, Russia, China, Vietnam, Algeria, and Cuba. Joel Migdal elaborates a systematic theory of how imperialistic modernizing forces impinge on peasant villages and how peasants, in turn, are likely to respond economically and politically. This theory is illustrated with bits and pieces of secondary evidence gleaned from fifty-one published village studies in Asia and Latin America, as well as with primary evidence from Migdal's own field experiences in Mexico and India. James Scott's ideas on peasant revolutions are widely but impressionistically based, illustrated by examples from publications on revolutions ranging from the seventeenth-century English case to the recent Chinese and Vietnamese Revolutions. Finally, Jeffery Paige's study is the most methodologically elaborate. It combines a quantitative analysis of agrarian movements between 1948 and 1970 in 135 agricultural export sectors, with in-depth historical accounts of agrarian movements in three countries – Peru, Angola, and Vietnam. All of this evidence is used to test an explicit formal theory of rural class conflict in the contemporary underdeveloped world.

The works of Wolf (1969a), Migdal (1974), Paige (1975), and Scott (1977a) cry out for discussion as a set. By looking at these works together, and by weighing the relative merits and common limits of their arguments, we can readily lay bare the state of current knowledge on peasants and revolution and indicate unresolved issues and potentially fruitful paths for future research. I shall review and evaluate what these scholars have to say in answer to three major questions: (1) which peasants are most prone to revolution and why? (2) what roles do political and military organizations play in peasant-based revolutions? (3) does capitalist imperialism create conditions for peasant-based revolutions – and, if so, how? These organizing questions will take us to the heart of the basic arguments of the four authors – and into the thick of the often sharp differences among them.

What is more, these questions will focus our attention on historical and cross-societal variations in the social and political factors that contribute to peasant-based revolutions, rather than prompt us to dwell on ahistorical conceptions of the nature of "the peasant" as a supposedly general human type. Some of the recent debates between those who see peasants as inherently moral communitarians (e.g., Scott, 1976) versus those who insist that they are inherently individualistic and competitive rational individuals (e.g., Popkin, 1979) have had the unfortunate effect of drawing attention away from the *sharply varying* social structures and political situations within which peasants and potential revolutionary organizers or allies of peasants have actually found themselves. As our joint interrogation of Wolf, Migdal, Paige, and Scott will underline, it is quite fruitless to predict peasant behavior or its revolutionary (or nonrevolutionary) effects on the basis of *any* broad speculation about the nature of the peasantry. Varying social structures, political configurations, and historical conjunctures constitute much more appropriate terms of analysis and explanation.

WHICH PEASANTS ARE MOST PRONE TO REVOLUTION, AND WHY?

Our excursus through the recent literature on peasants and revolution starts with a question that will eventually reveal itself to be too narrowly framed. All the same, it is a revealing place to begin because three of our authors split sharply in their answers.[3] Eric Wolf and James Scott argue different variants of one polar position – that the peasants most prone to revolution are village dwellers who possess landed property. In contrast, Jeffery Paige argues that smallholding peasants are normally conservative and quiescent, whereas *propertyless* laborers or sharecroppers, cultivators who earn income from wages not land, are more likely to become revolutionary.

The key issue in explaining revolutions for James Scott (1977a) is whether or not a lower class has the cultural and social-organizational autonomy to resist "the impact of hegemony ruling elites normally exercise" (Scott, 1977a: 271). Despite their localism and traditionalism, precapitalist peasant smallholders, sharecroppers, or tenants are in Scott's view unusually likely to enjoy such autonomy. Their village-and kin-based social networks promote local communal solidarity, even as their worldviews and values are inherently in tension with dominant-class culture. Moreover, the immediate processes of economic production are directly controlled by the peasants themselves. "If this analysis is accurate," Scott concludes:

it implies that we are often likely to find the strongest resistance to capitalism and to an intrusive state among the more isolated peasantries with entrenched precapitalist values. While the values that motivate such peasantries are thus hardly socialist values in the strict, modern use of that word, their tenacity and the social organization from which they arise may provide the social dynamite for radical change. The situation of immigrant workers and landless day laborers . . . may well seem more appropriate to strictly socialist ideas, but their social organization makes them less culturally cohesive and hence less resistant to hegemony (Scott, 1977a: 289).

Wolf (1969a) tends to agree with Scott about the kinds of peasants most likely to become involved in revolutions, but he provides a different analysis of the reasons why. Impressed by the obstacles that poverty and vulnerability to repression can place in the way of political involvement by peasants, Wolf argues that most poor peasants and landless laborers are unlikely initiators of rebellion. They are usually closely tied to or dependent upon landlords, and cannot rebel unless outside forces intervene to mobilize and shield them. In contrast, says Wolf, much greater "tactical leverage" to engage in rebellion is normally possessed by smallholders or tenants who live in communal villages outside direct landlord control, and by peasants (even poor ones) who live in geographically marginal areas relatively inaccessible to governmental authorities. As Wolf concludes: "ultimately, the decisive factor in making a peasant rebellion possible lies in the relation of the peasantry to the field of power which surrounds it. A rebellion cannot start from a situation of complete impotence" (Wolf, 1969a: 290). Thus, for Wolf, the crucial insurrectionary capacities possessed by communal, property-holding peasants are not cultural as Scott would have it, but lie instead in the material and organizational advantages their situation offers for collective resistance against outside oppressors.

The way Jeffery Paige (1975) approaches the issue of which sorts of peasants are most prone to revolution differs considerably from the approaches of Scott and Wolf. Instead of speaking of peasant villages facing outside forces, Paige organizes his argument strictly around class relations between lower-class laboring "cultivators" and upper-class "noncultivators" who appropriate surplus income from agricultural production in established capitalist enclaves of underdeveloped countries. Paige hypothesizes about the political effects of different sources of income from export-zone agricultural production. His basic model (see Figure 9.1) is a fourfold box which holds that certain organizational forms of agricultural production are typically associated with alternative combinations of cultivator and noncultivator income from land or wages or capital. In turn, different kinds of agrarian politics are expected to occur for each combination of income sources.

This discussion will deal only with two out of four of Paige's theoretical boxes – namely the top two, where the "noncultivators" are landed upper classes that derive income through politically enforced ownership of large amounts of land. One of the most insightful features of Paige's argument is his insistence that patterns of agrarian class conflict are dependent not only on the characteristics and situations of the lower classes themselves, but equally on the characteristics and situations of the upper, noncultivating classes. For example, Paige argues that agrarian revolution is potentially on the agenda only when noncultivators derive their income from land rather than capital, because only then are the upper classes forced by their structural position to refuse incremental, reformist concessions. This turns class conflicts with cultivators into a zero-sum game, in which control of property and state power are inherently at issue. Whether or not one fully accepts the substance of Paige's argument,[4] the class-relational logic of his analysis is exemplary: whether peasants become

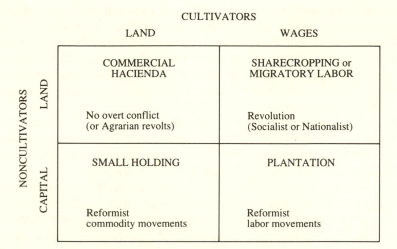

Figure 9.1. Paige's theory of rural class conflict: combinations of cultivator and noncultivator income, typical forms of agricultural organization, and expected forms of agrarian
social movements. *Source:* Adapted from Paige, *Agrarian Revolution,* Figure 1.1.

revolutionary depends as much on the interests and capacities of their class
opponents as it does on the interests and capacities of the peasants themselves.

Agrarian conflict also depends in Paige's model upon the likely political
behavior of different kinds of lower-class cultivators – and with respect to
this matter Paige arrives at opposite conclusions from Scott and Wolf. When
smallholding peasants who derive their livelihood from land ownership are
dominated by a landed upper class, Paige holds that the normal result will be an
absence of overt conflict. Propertyless laborers, instead, are the ones Paige
deems likely to make revolutions against landed upper classes. Landholding
peasants are hypothesized to be mutually isolated and economically competitive
among themselves, averse to taking risks, and strongly dependent upon rich
peasants and landed upper classes. Wage-earning cultivators are held to be
solidary, willing to take risks, and autonomous from upper-class controls; thus
they are structurally inclined to give deliberate support to revolutionary political
movements. Specifically, Paige argues that migratory laborers will tend to
ally with native communities to support anticolonialist, nationalist movements,
whereas sharecroppers (especially in decentralized agricultural systems such as
wet-rice agriculture) will support class-conscious revolutionary socialist movements.[5]

Nothing better illustrates the contradictory lines of reasoning embodied in
Eric Wolf's versus Jeff Paige's theories than the contrasting conclusions these
authors draw from the rural social basis of the Vietnamese Revolution. Eric
Wolf (1969a: ch. 4) locates the areas of strongest support for the Communist-
led revolution disproportionately in northern and central Vietnam, in certain

mountainous regions populated by ethnic minorities, and (during the 1960s) in those areas of southern Vietnam differentially populated by smallholding peasants. Wolf reasons that these were areas where peasants could safely provide solidary support, relatively free from French, landlord, or U.S. repressive power. In southern Vietnam, Wolf says, village communities were unstable and therefore more difficult for the Communists to organize. Moreover, landlords and their allies were quite strong in the South.

Paige, on the other hand, tries (1975: ch. 5) to make a sharp theoretical distinction between areas of Vietnam that provided strong "spontaneous" social support for revolutionary socialism and geographically marginal areas where Communist forces flourished during the military phases of the revolution. Using this distinction, Paige argues that the earliest, historically consistent agrarian support for the Communists was centered in the export-oriented, rice sharecropping areas of the Mekong delta in southern Vietnam – precisely where, according to his analysis, the cultivating lower strata consisted of workers without secure landholdings, who were paid in crop shares and condemned to common low status in an export economy dominated by large landholders, creditors, and merchants. The southern Vietnamese sharecroppers, Paige reasons, had a strong interest in, and capacity for, collective revolutionary action, whereas smallholding peasants in central and northern Vietnam were dominated by village notables and divided against one another by competition for land and village resources.

Thus, the available answers to our first organizing question – which peasants are most prone to revolution, and why? – are without doubt strikingly contradictory. Who is right? Or, to put it another way, whose way of posing the issues and developing an explanation is more valid and fruitful? If explicit, thorough reasoning and methodological sophistication were sufficient to ensure correctness in social science, our vote of confidence would automatically go to Jeffery Paige, for his *Agrarian Revolution* is an unusually meticulous piece of scholarship. Nevertheless, I believe that Paige's argument is open to serious question – especially on the issue of which peasants are most prone to revolution.

As we have already noted, Paige's model predicts that in an agrarian system where both the upper classes and the lower classes derive their incomes from land, there should normally be "little or no peasant political activity" (Paige, 1975: 41). However, Paige is quickly forced to note that although "the combined political characteristics of upper and lower classes dependent on land seem to suggest that few rebellions of any kind should take place, periodic uprisings have been a constant part of manorial economies from the German peasant wars to the Bolivian revolution of 1952" (Paige, 1975: 41–42). He admits that these historical realities "do seem to contradict the principle that peasants should lack the coherent political organization necessary to oppose the landlords" (Paige, 1975: 42). But there is no real contradiction, claims Paige, because in the cases at issue the peasants are always helped by breakdowns of state power or by outside political allies: "Peasant rebellions in commercial hacienda systems depend on the weakening of the repressive power of the landed aristocracy, the introduction of organizational strength from outside the peasant community, or both" (Paige, 1975: 42). Even when such facilitating factors intervene, the peasants still are not "truly revolutionary," Paige asserts. His explanation has several steps:

Many peasant revolts which occur when a landed upper class has been critically weakened are little more than simultaneous land rushes by thousands of peasants bent on obtaining land that they may legally regard as theirs. . . . (Paige, 1975: 42–43).
    The land seizures, in turn, may destroy the rural class structure and end the political power of the landed upper class. . . . (Paige, 1975: 45).
    [Nevertheless,] even after the landed class has been weakened to the point that it can be liquidated by widespread peasant land seizures, the peasants themselves still lack the internal political organization to seize state power. . . . (Paige, 1975: 43).
    In fact the peasants are seldom the beneficiaries of the political changes they set in motion . . . [R]eform or socialist parties . . . [provide] the political organization and opposition to the landed elite that the peasants themselves . . . [cannot] sustain. It is, therefore, usually those parties that fill the political vacuum left by the departure of the landlords (Paige, 1975: 45).

I have quoted at such length because it is very important to note what Paige is doing here. In the course of elaborating a theoretical category in which "little or no peasant political activity" is expected, Paige recounts evidence of revolts and (in effect) revolutionary overturns of landed upper classes and states that support them. Indeed, by the end of the discussion, Paige offers a formulation that is really quite different from the theoretical prediction of no political activity with which he began; instead Paige states that "the characteristic forms of political behavior in systems in which both the upper classes and the lower classes are dependent on income from land *are, alternatively, political apathy or agrarian revolt*" (Paige, 1975: 45, emphasis added). What is more, although he never says so explicitly, Paige surely realizes that under appropriate military conditions such "agrarian revolts" can have truly revolutionary consequences. All of this is said not to contradict theoretical expectations, because the peasants are only revolting for immediate objectives (such as driving out the landlords and taking their property!) and are not deliberately trying to reorganize national politics, and because the revolts of the peasants can only spread and achieve lasting results when military breakdowns or outside organizers intervene to help the peasantry.

Nothing said by Paige in all of this maneuvering to deal with the revolts of landed peasants is wrong historically. But it should not escape the reader's attention that Paige has now set formidably high standards for an agrarian cultivating class to qualify as truly revolutionary. Our curiosity should be thoroughly aroused: do migratory laborers and sharecroppers meet these standards in Paige's theoretical discussion and empirical accounts?

According to Paige, the "typical form of social movement in systems dependent on landed property and wage labor is revolutionary. Such movements involve not only violent conflict over landed property and direct attack on the rural stratification system, but also a coherent political effort to seize control of the state by force . . . [L]ong guerilla wars are the likely result" (Paige, 1975: 58). Yet Paige carefully distinguishes between two subtypes in this "land and wages" category. In the first subtype, where migratory labor estates are involved, the "workers themselves are too divided to provide the coherent political organization necessary for armed insurrection" (Paige, 1975: 68). Thus, "only in colonial areas where the estate system has not completely eliminated the power of the indigenous landed classes can a revolutionary nationalist movement occur" (Paige, 1975: 70). In such cases, organized nationalist parties and armies created by indigenous elites can intervene to organize the migratory laborers who, otherwise, like peasants "on a commercial hacienda . . . [are] incapable of providing the organizational strength to oppose the power of the landlords" (Paige, 1975: 70). Obviously, therefore, for the revolutionary nationalist variant of his "land and wages" category, Paige fails even to assert that there are dynamics among the cultivators themselves different from those found in the "land and land" category. A critic can justly point out that the differences in political behavior between smallholding peasants and migratory laborers seem to depend not so much on the income sources of the cultivators themselves as upon the larger societal and political contexts within which these agrarian lower classes are located.

But when we arrive in *Agrarian Revolution* at discussions of the truly revolutionary landless cultivators – sharecroppers in systems of decentralized wet-rice agriculture – then military factors and organized political parties suddenly take on very different roles from those they play in agrarian revolts or merely nationalist revolutions. *Socialist* revolutions are, for Paige, genuinely class-based affairs. To be sure, organized ideological parties are also involved in these revolutions – namely, Communist parties and ideologies. But Paige baldly maintains that these parties bear a unique relationship to sharecropper tenant supporters: ". . . [A]reas of tenancy have shown a pronounced attraction to left-wing, particularly Communist, ideologies and a surprising potential for powerful political organization. . . . *Unlike the politics of peasants dependent on individual subsistence plots, these political affiliations are internally generated, not introduced by outside urban-based parties*" (Paige, 1975: 62, emphasis added).

"In the case of decentralized sharecropping systems the organization is based on a Communist party *organized from within* the worker community" (Paige, 1975: 70, emphasis added). In short, Paige would have us believe that parties involved in organizing smallholders or migratory laborers come to them from without, whereas Communist parties organizing rice sharecroppers somehow emerge from within as pure expressions of cultivators' class interests and their conscious revolutionary determination to overthrow landlords and the state.

A moment's reflection will reveal the unbelievability of Paige's bizarre theoretical treatment of revolutionary Communism in Vietnam and in other rice sharecropping systems. Asian Communist parties, like all modern political parties from reformist to socialist to nationalist, have been created and led by urban-educated–middle-class people.[6] In no sense are they the autonomous organizational creations of agrarian lower classes. Sometimes these parties have operated in the countryside primarily as political mobilizers, without deploying their own military forces. At other times – especially during armed guerilla struggles for revolutionary power – Asian Communist parties have combined political and military mobilization of peasants and workers. Invariably, Communist parties *come to* agrarian lower classes in search of their support for national political objectives that go well beyond the immediate goals of the vast majority of the peasants, whether smallholders or sharecroppers. In Vietnam, the Communists had anticolonial, nationalist objectives as well as the "revolutionary-socialist" goals exclusively stressed by Paige.[7] And the survival of the Vietnamese Communist party from 1930, let alone its ultimate victories in northern and then southern Vietnam, is simply incomprehensible as the product of anything less than widespread social support among many different kinds of Vietnamese peasants, not to mention Vietnamese workers and middle classes.

Paige's climactic argument about the social basis of Vietnamese Communism refers to southern Vietnam in the early- to mid-1960s – and here peculiarities and contradictions abound. For Vietnam as a whole Paige dismisses nonsharecropping areas of Communist strength as indicators of military presence rather than political appeal. Yet for southern Vietnam he uses (Paige, 1975: 329–33) as his indicator of Communist political appeal an index of the geographical locations of assassinations of village notables and chiefs by the (Communist-led) National Liberation Front. But assassinations, surely, are an expression of combined political and military struggle. Even more important, assassinations would logically seem to reveal those localities where Communists were *contesting for control,* not the places where such control was already securely possessed. Indeed, Paige's own historical discussion reveals a well-known fact about politics in southern Vietnam. It was always an arena of uphill struggle for the Communists, and not only because of French and then U.S. military strength. Even in those localities with Paige's theoretically appropriate proto-revolutionary class relations, the Communists had to compete for power not only with local repressive organizations controlled by landlords, but also with two powerful nonrevolutionary sects, the Cao Dai and the Hoa Hao.[8] The Hoa Hao, according to Paige's own data, did just as well among the rice sharecroppers as the Communists. This sect was ultimately eclipsed only after the assassination of its leader and much governmental repression; until then it was much more truly a spontaneous peasant organization than the Communists ever were. Yet Paige's theory cannot make sense of the Hoa Hao. For the theory predicts only "revolutionary socialist" politics for the rice sharecroppers of the Mekong delta.

In sum, Jeffery Paige's arguments about the political capacities of landholding versus landless peasants do not hold up in the face of critical scrutiny. Paige
theoretically posits a kind of "revolutionary socialist" agrarian lower class that
probably does not exist in reality. Certainly Paige provides no valid evidence
that cultivators in this category can organize themselves selfconsciously to
attack class relations and the state, for the presence among the sharecroppers of
Communist slogans and activities is his prime empirical indicator of revolutionary socialism.[9] A close, skeptical reading of *Agrarian Revolution* suggests that
either peasant smallholders or landless laborers can end up playing important
parts in revolutions. This is hardly the conclusion entailed by Paige's model;
thus one is forced to wonder about its fruitfulness. Income sources in the
abstract are not valid predictors of the political interests and capacities of
agrarian classes.

In *Social Origins,* Barrington Moore presents (1966: 475–76) a distinction
between contrasting sorts of local community solidarity: "conservative solidarity," in which peasant smallholders, tenants, or laborers are dominated by rich
peasants or landlords who control the resources and organizational levers of
village society; versus "radical solidarity," in which peasants themselves share
resources and run village organizations which can be set in opposition to
landlords or the state. Paige's attempt to derive degrees of solidarity among
cultivators directly from their sources of income in land versus wages blinds
him analytically to the possibility of "radical solidarity" among smallholding
peasants.[10] Yet in sociohistorical situations where such solidarity has existed
(for example, Russia and Mexico), communities of landholding peasants have
been collectively able and willing to revolt against landlords and the state. Thus,
James Scott and Eric Wolf are correct to argue that communities of peasant
smallholders have at times fuelled revolutionary overturns of dominant classes
and the state.

This brief detour into Barrington Moore's *Social Origins* suggests the kind of
analytic approach necessary to improve upon Paige: a social-structural approach
that looks closely at institutionalized economic and political relations between
landed upper classes and agrarian lower classes, on the one hand, and institutionalized relations among the peasants themselves, on the other. Much more
than James Scott, Eric Wolf resembles Moore in using such a social-structural
approach. Scott may be right in some of his assertions about the revolutionary
potential of peasant communities, but his primarily cultural approach leads him
to romantic, ahistorical assertions about the peasantry in general. To read Scott
(especially 1976 and 1977b) is to get the impression that all peasant villages are
basically the same: communal, subsistence-oriented, nonexploitative, culturally
in tension with outside dominant classes, and economically on the defensive
against encroaching capitalism or imperialism. But as demonstrated by Paige's
astute and detailed analysis (1975: 285–300) of the villages of central and
northern Vietnam, exploitative and competitive internal divisions and class

tensions can readily exist within subsistence-oriented villages with communal resources. Imperialist pressures can exacerbate internal divisions and exploitation.[11] And as the comparative-historical investigations of both Barrington Moore and Eric Wolf document, the structural variations of class and community arrangements within agrarian societies are very great. These variations, in turn, determine different landlord and peasant responses to capitalism and different patterns of agrarian politics from case to case. James Scott's transhistorical cultural approach cannot descriptively handle – let alone explain – such variations of structures and outcomes.

Eric Wolf, however, *is* sensitive to the full range of social-structural and political issues that must be taken into account to explain peasant-based revolutions. Although there is nothing rigorous about his answers, Wolf inquires about peasants' property holdings, about their relations to one another and to landlords and – perhaps just as important – about their relations to the state and to organized political and military forces challenging state power. In these final emphases Wolf goes beyond even Barrington Moore. Wolf's notion of "tactical mobility" for the peasantry encompasses many of the same concerns addressed by Moore's discussion of conservative versus radical forms of village solidarity. Yet Wolf is alluding to more than whether peasants are collectively solidary and free from tight controls by landlords. His concept also inquires into the relative freedom of peasants from state repression, either by virtue of their marginal geopolitical location, or as a result of the intervention of armed revolutionaries to shield the peasants.

In a sense Eric Wolf's explanatory approach is too complex and vague to be more than a set of analytic pointers. It tells us to pay attention to political and military as well as socioeconomic relationships. It also suggests that we must examine more than the situation of the peasantry and the agrarian economy alone, if we are to understand peasant participation in revolutionary transformations. Taking heart from these pointers, we should now bracket the debate over which kinds of peasants are most prone to revolution and move on to examine directly how broader political and economic forces are implicated in peasant-based revolutions.

WHAT ROLES DO POLITICAL AND MILITARY ORGANIZATIONS PLAY IN PEASANT-BASED REVOLUTIONS?

Joel Migdal's *Peasants, Politics, and Revolution* (1974) has not been discussed in any detail so far, yet this is a good time to bring up some of its key arguments. By highlighting the centrality of political organizations in revolutions, Migdal achieves among our authors a unique angle of vision on the questions of how and why peasants become revolutionary.

Wolf (1969a), Scott (1977a), and Paige (1975) alike tend to envisage revolutions as (in one way or another) made by class forces – although Wolf, it is true, does begin to bring states, parties, and armies into the picture in ways alluded to above. Certainly Jeffery Paige strives mightily for pure economic and class reductionism. Reformist, socialist, nationalist, and Communist parties abound in his empirical data and illustrative historical accounts, but such parties are never there as independent variables, only as indicators of economically determined political conflicts. Agrarian income sources and class relations are supposed to explain reforms, revolts, and revolutionary movements. Despite his sharp differences with Paige, James Scott also belittles the causal importance of political organizations in peasant revolutions. Scott grants that a "revolution to be successful may . . . require a disciplined party or army in addition to an aroused peasantry" (1977a: 292) because only such extra-peasant forces can provide "the coordination and tactical vision" (1977a: 294) necessary to overcome peasant fragmentation and achieve national state power. Scott nevertheless celebrates the indispensable revolutionary force of autonomous peasant violence. He maintains that "the spontaneous action of the peasantry in many revolutionary movements . . . has forced the issue and mobilized its would-be leadership . . ." (Scott, 1977a: 295), adding that "more often than not it has been the autonomous . . . action of the peasantry that has *created* the revolutionary situations . . ." (Scott, 1977a: 295–96). Institutionalization of peasant politics, argues Scott, is very likely to undercut revolution: "There is . . . no a priori reason for assuming that the outside leadership of the peasantry will be more militant than its clientele. . . . In fact, one would expect that the more organized, the more hierarchical, and the more institutionalized a peasant . . . movement becomes . . . the more likely it will become woven into the established tapestry of power" (Scott, 1977a: 296).

In contrast, Joel Migdal asserts that the peasant revolutions of the twentieth century have been propelled by armed revolutionary parties that have directly mobilized peasant support. Such "revolutionary movements," Migdal points out, "are created by the impetus of those from outside the peasant class . . . [T]he participation of peasants in revolutionary organizations is preceded by the development of an organizational superstructure by students, intellectuals, and disaffected members of the middle class" (Migdal, 1974: 232). To be sure, peasants must also be involved in the revolutionary process. Yet for Migdal the issue is not how agrarian class relations themselves generate revolutionary movements, nor how peasant spontaneity creates revolutionary situations and prods radical elites to make revolutions. Rather, Migdal seeks to explain how social exchanges between revolutionary parties and local peasant populations can be established – exchanges so stable and mutually rewarding as to account for sustained peasant support and "participation in institutionalized revolutionary movements" (Migdal, 1974: 228–29).

Underlying Migdal's approach to peasant revolutionary involvement is his strong belief that twentieth-century peasant revolutions differ fundamentally from revolutions and revolts in previous times: "In the last fifty years, peasants in certain areas have engaged in prolonged national struggles to change the system of government and the distribution of power. These movements have not been based on a sudden burst of violence after frustration has built as was often true of the spasmodic, anomic peasant rebellions of past centuries. Rather, peasants in these cases have engaged in long drawn-out revolutions in a variety of institutionalized ways – as political cadres, as disciplined soldiers, as loyal suppliers of food, money, and shelter, and as active and passive members of a host of revolutionary organizations and groups" (Migdal, 1974: 226). "Why," Migdal wonders, "has the character of . . . [peasant] participation changed from the more eruptive, anomic qualities of the French Revolution . . . and the Russian Revolution to the organized aspects of the Chinese and Vietnamese Revolutions?" (Migdal, 1974: 227). Migdal never answers this question very satisfactorily. His book argues at length that peasants in the twentieth-century Third World face an unprecedented economic crisis due to pressures from imperialism. Participation in organized revolutionary movements which offer programs to address local peasant problems is said to be one way that peasants can try to cope with the unprecedented crisis. But Migdal never compares, for example, prerevolutionary French and Russian peasants to Chinese and Vietnamese peasants. He does not show that the economic difficulties faced by these two sets of peasants were different in ways that could explain "anomic" versus "institutionalized" forms of revolutionary participation.

Even if Migdal fails to explain adequately why peasants have historically participated in revolutions in different ways, he still points toward a distinction that needs to be made. The distinction is *not* really between twentieth-century and pre-twentieth-century peasant-based revolutions. Migdal is mistaken to argue that peasants participated in the French and Russian Revolutions as "eruptive" masses of "anomic" frustrated individuals. On the contrary, peasants in those revolutions were well organized at local levels and pursued their goals in a very determined, sustained fashion over a period of years (see Skocpol, 1979: ch. 3). The same can be said for the village-based supporters of Emiliano Zapata in the Mexican Revolution, which also fits the same overall pattern as the French and Russian cases (see Wolf, 1969a: ch. 1). The pattern of these revolutions has been one of the breakdown of the old-regime state, followed by widespread local peasant revolts that undercut landed upper classes and conservative political forces. Organized revolutionaries have then consolidated new state organizations, *not* by politically mobilizing the peasantry, but rather by more or less coercively imposing administrative and military controls on the countryside.

A contrasting pattern of peasant-based revolution is exemplified by the Chinese, Vietnamese (and perhaps Cuban) Revolutions, and by the revolutionary anticolonial movements of Portuguese Africa.[12] Here peasants have been directly mobilized by organized revolutionary movements, either before (Cuba; Portuguese Africa) or after (China; Vietnam) the collapse of effective state power in the preexisting regime. Because of this direct mobilization, peasant resources and manpower have ended up participating in the build up of new-regime social institutions and state organizations. Peasant participation in this revolutionary pattern is less spontaneous and autonomous than in the first pattern. But the results can be much more favorable to local peasant interests, because during the revolutionary process itself direct links are established between peasants and revolutionary political and military organizations.[13]

Once we make the distinction between these two alternative scenarios for peasant-based revolutions, many apparent disagreements among scholars about such issues as "which peasants are revolutionary" and "what roles are played by organized political forces" tend to dissolve. Basic explanatory questions can also be sorted out in terms of their applicability to one pattern or the other. It should be clear that autonomous peasant villages are more likely to play a pivotal role in the first revolutionary pattern, where widespread local revolts accelerate the downfall of the old regime and *indirectly* condition the consolidation of the new regime. Without being willing to call them revolutionary, Jeffery Paige (1975) describes instances of this pattern under his category of "agrarian revolt." Moreover, much of what Eric Wolf (1969a) has to say in his "Conclusion" and virtually all of what James Scott has to say in "Hegemony and the Peasantry" (1977a) fits this first pattern of peasant-based revolution. By contrast, Joel Migdal (1974) deals mainly with the second pattern, as does Paige (1975) in his "revolutionary nationalism" category.

When peasants are directly mobilized into revolutionary politics (according to the second pattern), then autonomous villages are not causally important. What is more, many different kinds of peasants – subsistence smallholders in marginal areas; landless laborers or tenants; even solidary villages of peasants, or else of landlords and peasants together – can potentially be mobilized by revolutionary movements. In my view, there has been too much of a tendency in the literature to suppose that the adherence of peasants to organized revolutionary movements must be explained by the economic interests and social circumstances of the peasants themselves. Even Joel Migdal succumbs to this tendency when he argues (1974: 229–30) that peasants undergoing the most rapid, disruptive exposure to newly penetrating market forces will be the ones most likely to respond to organized political movements that offer solutions to their market-induced woes. But there is no reason at all to suppose that peasants in traditional social structures are free from experiences of poverty, class exploitation, and political insecurity.[14] There is no reason why organized revolutionary movements, once on the scene, cannot appeal to many different kinds of agrarian cultivators, including traditional ones. This certainly was what the Vietnamese Communists succeeded in doing: in mountainous areas, they mobilized minority ethnic groups, peasants and notables together, by appealing to their fears of ethnic exploitation; in northern Vietnam, they mobilized peasants by displacing the French and by shoving aside within the communal villages exploitative landlords and Confucian notables; and in southern Vietnam they mobilized peasants, including Paige's rice sharecroppers, by seizing and redistributing large landholdings and by organizing local associations to support peasant livelihood and defend their possession of the redistributed land.[15]

Insofar as the occurrence – or success – of peasant-based revolution depends upon the direct mobilization of peasants by revolutionary movements, then the sheer availability and viability of such movements becomes decisive – just as much as the condition of the peasants themselves. Migdal, in fact, correctly points out that a crucial "factor determining the probability of peasants' participation in revolutionary movements is the degree to which revolutionary leadership appears, with an organizational framework capable of absorbing peasants and then expanding power through their recruitment" (Migdal, 1974: 232). Moreover, given that "revolutionary movements are created by the impetus of those . . . outside the peasant class," Migdal admits that "exogenous factors," beyond the scope of his analysis of peasant villages per se, "determine in which countries such outside revolutionaries will appear and where they will provide a high degree of revolutionary leadership in those countries in which they do appear" (Migdal, 1974: 232, 235).

Perhaps the most important questions to ask about the emergence and growth of institutionalized revolutionary alliances between peasants, on the one hand, and political parties and armies, on the other, refer not to the peasants themselves, but to the circumstances that produce organized revolutionaries and allow them to operate effectively in the countryside. Under what social-structural and world-historical conditions have nationalist and/or Communist parties emerged *and become willing and able to address themselves to rural populations?* Have colonial situations been more amenable to this development than neocolonial situations? How have variations in colonial situations and processes of decolonization helped to produce or inhibit the formation of agrarian revolutionary alliances? What social-structural, historical, and (even) cultural factors can help us understand why Asian Communists have been more willing to attempt peasant mobilization than have, say, Latin American Communists or Communists in Moslem countries? Answers to questions such as these may turn out to explain more about the occurrence of peasant-based revolutions of the second pattern than any amount of investigation of the peasant situation as such.[16] For impoverished and exploited peasants in many places may potentially be amenable to revolutionary mobilization – if a revolutionary organization can establish itself with some minimal security in the countryside, and if its cadres can address peasant needs successfully. But this process cannot begin to get underway unless such a revolutionary leadership emerges in colonial or national politics, finds itself unable to achieve power in the cities alone, and proves militarily and politically capable of operating in the countryside.

Once a political movement is in contact with the countryside, there may be only some possible policies that will work to mobilize the peasantry, given on the one side – the constraints faced by revolutionaries – and on the other side – the specific features of local class, community, and political arrangements among the peasantry. In Joel Migdal's book (1974: chs. 9–10), reformist, conservative, and revolutionary political organizations are treated as if they make the same kinds of appeals to the peasantry – namely, the offering of selective economic incentives to individuals and small groups. To some extent this may be true. Yet, compared to nonrevolutionary politicians, revolutionaries may offer distinctive kinds of benefits to peasants, and they certainly demand more costly kinds of support from peasants in return. Nonrevolutionary politicians are well advised to offer modest, economic benefits to particular individuals and subgroups, playing them off against others *within* the peasantry. Revolutionaries must attempt to stimulate demand for, and then supply, more *collective* benefits (even if just at local levels). *Class* benefits – such as redistributed land or local political power – can tend to unite peasants against landlords. *Security* benefits – such as village defense against counterrevolutionary military forces – can also broadly unite peasants. Insofar as revolutionaries can organize and lead peasants by providing such benefits, they can, in turn, profit from the willingness of peasants to act together in defense of the collective benefits. Then, on the basis of such willingness, the revolutionaries can ask for major sacrifices of resources and manpower from the peasantry – in order to sustain the extra-local party and army organizations that are indispensable to win national state power. Thus, Joel Migdal is undoubtedly right to analyze the process of institutionalization of a peasant-based revolutionary movement as an exchange between revolutionary politicians and peasants. But he could have suggested good reasons why this revolutionary exchange – much more than reformist or conservative exchanges – probably has to take place on the basis of collective benefits for the peasants.[17]

If the above points are true, then we can understand the kind of dilemma faced by organized revolutionaries if and when they attempt to operate in the countryside. The revolutionaries must discover or create among the peasantry the demand for collective benefits. They must be able to supply the relevant benefits with great sensitivity to the specific features of local political and social arrangements. All of this must be done without getting themselves and their initial supporters killed or driven away. And not until after such delicate and dangerous political work has been completed can the revolutionaries expect to benefit greatly from widespread peasant support.

It is hard to imagine the successful institutionalization of such social exchange between peasants and revolutionaries except in places and times unusually free from counterrevolutionary state repression. Marginal, inaccessible geographical areas are the most suitable places for the process to begin, but for it to spread and succeed, no doubt exogenous events must intervene to drastically weaken the existing state power. Just as such developments in the realm of the state must occur to create a revolutionary situation in the first pattern of peasant-based revolution, so must they occur in the second pattern to facilitate the institutionalization of peasant participation in the organized revolutionary movement. In both patterns of revolution, defeats in wars and international military interventions are the most likely ways for existing state power to be disrupted – opening the way either for autonomous peasant revolts, or for appeals by organized revolutionaries to peasant support in the countryside.

Our second question – what roles do political and military organizations play in peasant-based revolutions? – has brought us far from the immediate circumstances of the peasantry. State power, it turns out, plays a decisive role in limiting the possibilities for emergence and success of such revolutions. Moreover, organized (political and military) revolutionary movements play crucial roles in peasant-based revolutions, but in alternative ways. Either they consolidate revolutionary new regimes separately from, and in necessary tension with, the peasantry, or they directly mobilize peasant support to defeat counter-revolutionaries and consolidate the new regime. Peasant participation is a pivotal arbiter of revolutionary success in both patterns, yet – ironically – peasants are politically autonomous collective actors only in the pattern where developments in the realms of the state and organized national politics go on "above their heads." In the other pattern – Joel Migdal's pattern of "institutionalized" peasant revolution – organized revolutionary movements are the key collective actors, as they struggle politically to bridge the gap between peasants and the national state.

Having come this far from the peasantry itself, we must now in a sense step back still further – into the sphere of the world political economy. For the third – and last – organizing question directs our attention to the great emphasis placed by our authors on capitalist imperialism as a world-historical impetus to peasant-based revolutions.

DOES CAPITALIST IMPERIALISM CAUSE PEASANT-BASED REVOLUTION – AND, IF SO, HOW?

In *Social Origins of Dictatorship and Democracy,* Barrington Moore explained peasant revolts and revolutions by looking, first, at the structural vulnerability to peasant insurrections of different kinds of premodern agrarian sociopolitical orders. Then he investigated how, in "the process of modernization itself" (Moore, 1966: 459), different degrees and forms of agricultural commercialization could enhance or preclude possibilities for peasant revolts against landed upper classes. Like Moore, three out of four of the scholars under consideration here – Wolf, Migdal, and Paige – seek to generalize about the macro-structural and world-historical contexts that promote peasant-based revolutions.[18] Yet, whereas the relevant context for Moore consisted of variously structured agrarian states undergoing commercialization and industrialization in alternative possible ways, the macro-historical context for Wolf, Migdal, and Paige is envisaged in global rather than cross-national terms. In one way or another, each of these authors stresses *imperialistic Western capitalism* as the fundamental promoter of peasant revolutions. The – not insignificant – differences among them have to do with exactly how this world-historical force is conceived and the specific ways in which it influences or creates potentially revolutionary peasant forces.

For Eric Wolf (1969a) the "peasant rebellions of the twentieth century are no longer simple responses to local problems. . . . They are . . . parochial reactions to major social dislocations, set in motion by overwhelming societal changes" (Wolf, 1969a: 295). The agent of change is "a great overriding cultural phenomenon, the world-wide spread and diffusion of a particular cultural system, that of North Atlantic capitalism" (Wolf, 1969a: 276). Wolf sees the spread of North Atlantic capitalism primarily as the impingement of market economics upon precapitalist societies in which "before the advent of capitalism . . . social equilibrium depended in both the long and short run on a balance of transfers of peasant surpluses to the rulers and the provision of a minimal security to the cultivator" (Wolf, 1969a: 279). Intrusive capitalism has upset the prior balances: peasant populations have increased markedly, even as peasants have lost secure access to their lands and been transformed into "economic actors, independent of prior social commitments to kin and neighbors" (Wolf, 1969a: 279). Simultaneously, there has occurred "still another – and equally serious – repercussion . . . a crisis in the exercise of power" (Wolf, 1969a: 282). For the spreading market has created more distant and exploitative relationships between peasants and their traditional overlords, whether tribal chiefs, mandarins, or landed noblemen. And it has also created partial openings for new kinds of elites – entrepreneurs, credit merchants, political brokers, intellectuals, and professionals. Out of this disequilibrated transitional situation peasant revolutions have sometimes emerged. Specifically, they have happened when a political fusion has occurred between armed organizations of one marginal kind of new elite – the "new literati" of intellectuals and professionals – and "the dissatisfied peasants whom the market created, but for whom society made no adequate social provision" (Wolf, 1969a: 288–89). Thus peasant revolutions are for Eric Wolf one possible resolution of the profound societal disequilibria caused for preindustrial populations, elites and peasantries alike, by the world-wide expansion of North Atlantic capitalism.

Joel Migdal's (1974) vision of the forces at work to prompt potential revolutionary involvement by peasants in the Third World is not greatly different from Eric Wolf's – but there are two distinctive nuances in Migdal's approach. First, in contrast to Wolf's broad focus on society as a whole, Migdal looks more narrowly and in greater depth at peasant villages as such. Migdal's basic argument is that peasants in the twentieth-century Third World have been undergoing a disruptive economic transition from predominant "inward orientation" – marked by subsistence agriculture and strong communal and patronage controls – to greatly increased "outward orientation" – marked by the substantial involvement of individual peasants and households with extra-local "multiplier mechanisms: markets, cash, and wage labor" (Migdal, 1974: 87). According to Migdal, traditional peasant villages remained "inwardly oriented" in order to give their members assured, minimal security in the face of exploitative overlords and uncertain ecological conditions. When recurrent crises did strike, moreover, traditional peasants attempted to protect themselves through greater self-exploitation and reliance upon patrons or communal ties. Only an extraordinary crisis of unparalleled impact and continuity could push peasants into greater "outward orientation" in their economic behavior.

Like Wolf, Migdal sees the roots of this crisis in the worldwide expansion from the eighteenth century of the capitalist-industrial West. Yet – and here is the second distinctive feature in Migdal's argument – he especially highlights the *political mediation* of that expansion. Migdal speaks of "imperialism" rather than of "capitalism" or "markets" as the prime force promoting changes within and between nations. And he portrays disruptive changes – such as population growth following from public health programs, and increased market penetration due to tax impositions, transportation improvements and legalized land transfers – as resulting primarily from increases in state controls over formerly locally-autonomous peasant villages. "Imperialism," says Migdal, "caused a reorganization of societies' centers, enabling them to achieve new levels of efficiency in the transfer of wealth from the peripheries. Direct colonial rule or indirect imperial domination led to vast increases in the state's power through more effective administrative techniques. Bureaucracies were more complex and coherent and, as a result, were able to penetrate rural areas on a much broader spectrum than previously" (Migdal, 1974: 92). Because of the increasingly "outward" economic orientation that many peasants have been forced to adopt in response to the changes wrought by strengthened states, Third World peasants have found themselves at the mercy of extra-local economic conditions which leave them insecure or exploited within the national society and world economy. As a result, Migdal argues, they become potential supporters of political parties and movements, from conservative, to reformist, to revolutionary.

Predictably, Jeffery Paige (1975) understands the global forces promoting what he calls "agrarian" revolutions differently from Wolf and Migdal. What interests Paige is not the external impact of "North Atlantic capitalism" upon precapitalist agrarian societies, but the *new kinds* of economic enclaves – agricultural export zones – created within underdeveloped countries by world markets in agricultural commodities. Indeed, according to Paige, "the economy of the typical underdeveloped country can be described as an agricultural export sector and its indirect effects" (Paige, 1975: 2). In the newly formed commercial zones lie the seeds of contemporary agrarian revolutions. Without completely discounting the involvement of other social and political forces in recent revolutions, Paige maintains that the "relationship of the rural population to the new forms of class cleavage and class conflict introduced by the agricultural export economy is essential in understanding the origin of . . . agrarian unrest in the developing world" (Paige, 1975: 3). Class conflicts in export agriculture have come to the fore since World War II, because political conditions have been propitious: "The strength of colonial and imperial political controls long prevented the political expression of these conflicts, but with the decline of colonial power in the postwar era, the commercial export sectors of the underdeveloped world have become centers of revolutionary social movements" (Paige, 1975: 3).[19] In sum, whereas Wolf and Migdal see peasants in the contemporary Third World *reacting to encroaching world capitalism,* with their local revolts or attachments to national political movements sometimes producing revolutions as part of this reaction, Paige sees agrarian cultivators *reacting from within the capitalist world economy* to overthrow landed upper classes heretofore dependent upon colonial or imperial state coercion for their survival.

The differences between Wolf and Migdal, on the one side, and Paige on the other, may seem worthy of extended discussion and adjudication, but I propose to step quickly around them. For if the arguments of parts one and two of this essay are valid, then both camps may be saying partially correct things about the ways in which globally expanding capitalism (or imperialism) has helped to cause peasant-based revolutions. The historical record certainly seems to affirm that *both* peasants economically or politically threatened by newly penetrating capitalist forces, and agrarian cultivators involved in export-agricultural production have been – alternatively, or simultaneously – constituents of peasant-based revolutions. In Vietnam, for example, the revolution gained support from northern peasants resentful of French colonial controls, and also from southern peasants set in opposition to the great landlords who dominated the export-oriented rice economy. The Vietnamese Communists were able to sink roots in both groups, drawing from them resources to wage prolonged revolutionary war.

More interesting to me than the disagreements among Wolf, Migdal, and Paige are the shared features of the ways they think about the role of imperialist capitalism in promoting peasant-based revolutions. Despite their considerable differences, all three authors emphasize imperialism's *commercializing* influence upon agrarian societies and peasant life. Through this emphasis upon agrarian commercialization, the views of these primarily Third World-oriented authors end up meshing well with the more Old World-oriented analysis of Barrington Moore (1966). Capitalist commercialization either develops endogenously as Moore portrays it, or it is imposed from without as Wolf, Migdal, and Paige suggest. Commercialization promotes peasant-based revolution by creating new social strata prone to revolution (as Paige would have it). Or it arouses peasants to defensive revolts by intensifying exploitation and weakening traditional dominant strata (as Moore, Wolf, and Migdal would have it). Thus, commercialization – perhaps endogenously generated, perhaps induced by imperialist capitalism – is envisaged as promoting peasant-based revolutions, because of its effects on agrarian class relations and peasant communities.

But even if everyone seems in cozy agreement about the prime causal role (if not the exact forms and effects) of capitalist commercialization, there is still room to doubt whether such commercialization is a necessary cause – or even an essential concomitant – of peasant-based revolution. Take the Chinese Revolution, undoubtedly socially based in the peasantry. Although scholars disagree, many believe that Chinese agriculture was *not* on the whole any more commercialized in the first half of the twentieth century than it had been for centuries before (see Elvin, 1973; Perkins, 1969; Skinner 1964–65). Certainly the northern areas of China, where the Communists eventually developed their deepest ties to the peasantry, were not highly commercialized relative to other parts of China; nor had these areas experienced significant modernizing changes. The most important changes for the worse experienced by Chinese peasants between 1911 and 1949 were huge increases in taxation and violations of physical security. These woes were due to intense civil warfare followed by foreign military invasions by the Japanese. By addressing the issues of taxes and security, and by transforming long-standing local political and class relations between peasants and landlords, the Chinese Communists were able to mobilize peasant support for their revolutionary acquisition of state power. In all of this there is no indication that increased agrarian commercialization – whether endogenously generated or due to imperialist penetration – was the decisive cause of peasant involvement in the Chinese Revolution.

With the strong emphasis on capitalist imperialism as a promoter of increased agrarian commercialization, another aspect of imperialism has been relatively neglected. Expanding North Atlantic capitalism has, since its inception, had enormous impact upon inter-state relations and the politics of lagging countries. In the second section of this essay, we established that suspensions of state coercive power have been necessary to every successful peasant-based revolution, and that revolutionary political parties willing and able to mobilize the peasantry have been central to many such revolutions. Therefore, it obviously stands to reason that imperialism may have helped to promote peasant-based revolutions not simply because of its economic effects on peasants but also because of its effects on states and organized politics.

What sorts of effects on states and politics? Both the Chinese and the Vietnamese Revolutions point to relevant ones. In the Chinese case, defeats in wars and steady encroachments on Chinese sovereignty by Western capitalist nations and by Japan pushed the Manchu rulers into reforms that led to conflicts with the landed gentry. Out of these conflicts grew the Revolution of 1911 and the subsequent dissolution of the imperial state. In turn, foreign ideologies and models of party organization facilitated the emergence of revolutionary movements among educated urban Chinese. And finally, during World War II, military conflicts between the Chinese Guomindang government and the Japanese, and between the United States and Japan, opened the geopolitical space needed by the Communists to mobilize the peasants of North China for social revolution and military victory (see Skocpol, 1979: 67–80, 147–54, and ch. 7).

In Vietnam, French imperialism conquered and colonized the country. The direct effects on the peasantry were very great – mediated in the North especially by colonial tax exactions (as Joel Migdal's theory would emphasize) and mediated in the South especially by export-oriented agriculture (as Jeffery Paige's theory would emphasize). Yet the Vietnamese Revolution also grew out of the impact of colonialism upon the politics of indigenous middle-class Vietnamese who received modern educations yet were denied important elite posts in the French-dominated colonial state. Nationalist and revolutionary political movements were the predictable result. Still, the progress, even survival, of these movements depended upon a weakening of French power – and that came only with the inter-imperialist military rivalries of World War II. The Japanese captured colonial Vietnam and in 1945 displaced the Vichy French administrators, only themselves to face defeat soon thereafter at the hands of the United States and Britain. The disruptions – and ultimate vacuum – of state power during World War II gave the Vietnamese Communists an ideal opportunity to claim the nationalist mantle, to assert sovereignty on the heels of the departing Japanese, and finally to mobilize Vietnamese peasants (especially in the North) to resist France's attempt to reimpose colonial control (see McAlister, 1971: pts. 4–8; Dunn, 1972: ch. 5).

Thus, the *military and political reverberations* of imperialist expansion contributed crucially to the emergence and success of the Chinese and Vietnamese Revolutions. Without the breakdown of the imperial and colonial regimes, without the emergence of organized revolutionary parties, and without the openings created for them by inter-imperialist military rivalries, the peasants of China and Vietnam could not have been mobilized for revolution. And given the local agrarian structures of China and Vietnam, the peasants could not have become revolutionary in the absence of direct mobilization.

In *States and Social Revolutions* (1979), I analyzed the causes and outcomes of three revolutions – the French, Russian, and Chinese – also discussed by Barrington Moore in *Social Origins* (1966). My approach placed much greater emphasis than Moore's on the relationships among states, and on relationships between state organizations and social classes, including the peasantry. Capitalist development figured in my analysis more as a motor of inter-state competition, and as a propellant of changing relations between states and classes, than it did as an agent of commercialization and market penetration. Imperialism has been seen as promoting peasant-based revolutions primarily through the effects of agrarian commercialization in Third World countries. Yet the impacts of globally expanding capitalism on states and politics in the Third World may have been equally or more important – the touchstone case of Vietnam suggests as much. Perhaps, therefore, future analyses of the role of capitalist imperialism in causing and shaping peasant-based revolutions in the Third World could profit from taking the kind of state-centered approach used in *States and Social Revolutions.*

Capitalism's global expansion has, to be sure, encroached upon and remade traditional agrarian class relations. Yet that expansion has also been accompanied by colonization and decolonization, and by a continuation of the inter-state military rivalries that marked capitalism's European birthplace, even in feudal times. Peasant-based revolutions – in which peasant revolts or mobilization become pivotal in intertwined class and national-state transformations – have grown not only out of capitalist agrarian commercialization. Such revolutions have emerged more invariably out of occasionally favorable political situations shaped in large part by the inter-state dynamics of the modern world-capitalist era. For these dynamics have, at crucial conjunctures, weakened indigenous or colonial state controls over the peasantry. Moreover, they have often allowed, even impelled, revolutionary political movements to forge new relationships with the mass of the peasantry. Only in favorable political circumstances such as these, has the insurrectionary potential of peasants – whether traditionalist or commercializing, landed or landless – actually been able to propel revolutionary transformations.

CONCLUSION

"Before looking at the peasant," Barrington Moore wrote in *Social Origins,* "it is necessary to look at the whole society" (Moore, 1966: 457). His point is amplified by Michael Adas in the Introduction to *Prophets of Rebellion,* a recent comparative investigation of millenarian peasant-based protests against European colonialism: "When I first conceived this study," writes Adas, "I intended to focus specifically on peasant protest, but as I gathered evidence it became clear that elite groups played key roles in the genesis and development of these movements" (Adas, 1979: xxv). The burden of this review of recent scholarship on peasant-based revolution has been that, here as well, peasants are only part of the story. Too close a focus on peasants themselves, even on peasants within local agrarian class and community structures, cannot allow us to understand peasant-based revolutions.

A holistic frame of reference is indispensable, one that includes states, class structures, and transnational economic and military relations. Ironically, of the four students of peasants and revolutions whose works have been reviewed here, only Eric Wolf (1969a) – the one who wrote earliest and least theoretically – comes close to a suitably holistic analysis. Since Wolf – and since Barrington Moore's *Social Origins* (1966) – the tendency among scholars has been to look more narrowly (if also often more systematically) at peasants and agrarian economies, seeking broad theoretical generalizations about peasant politics from that level of analysis alone. Much of value has been learned about agrarian class relations and peasant communities. But an integrated explanation of peasant involvement in revolutions, from the eighteenth-century French Revolution to the anticolonial revolutions of the mid-twentieth century, has not yet been achieved.

No doubt such an explanation can only be developed in conjunction with explanations of other forms of peasant-based political protest (and its absence or failure) in various epochs of world history. Yet as we move forward, we will do well to keep in mind a basic truth: during all the centuries of peasant existence from ancient to modern times, the forms of revolt open to peasants, as well as the political results conceivably achievable by peasant protests, have been powerfully shaped by the stakes of political struggles, domestic and inter-societal, going on within the ranks of the dominant strata. Peasant revolutions are not at all an exception to this enduring truth. They are, indeed, its fullest and most modern expression.

NOTES

1. The discussion of Scott's views in this essay will be based exclusively on his 1977 essay on revolutions as such. His book (Scott 1976) analyzes only cases of peasant rebellions, and it is very cautious (cf. p. 194) in what it suggests about peasant-based revolutions. "Hegemony and the Peasantry," however, suggests that Scott is moving toward a general, culturally oriented theory of the peasantry as a social class with inherent revolutionary potential.

2. By talking about "Old World" versus "Third World" frames of references, I do not mean to say that there is no overlap between the historical cases of peasant-based revolutions analyzed by Moore as opposed to those discussed by Wolf, Migdal, Paige, and Scott. Actually there is considerable shared interest in Russia and – especially – China. What I mean to suggest is that Moore approaches his cases as historically established "agrarian bureaucracies," analyzable in the same terms as Western European agrarian states, whereas the others tend to treat their cases as countries which have not long before fallen under the sway of Western capitalist imperialism. For all four authors writing since Moore the Vietnamese Revolution is the touchstone case, whereas for Moore, Russia and China were the key cases of peasant-based revolution.

3. For reasons that will later become clear, Joel Migdal's reasoning on the issue of which peasants are most prone to revolution is tangential to this dispute over propertied versus propertyless peasants. For the time being, therefore, I shall leave Migdal aside.

4. Actually, Paige's notion that the simple fact of income from capital gives upper classes room to make reformist concessions to farmers or laborers is very dubious. Market conditions can exert severe constraints on possible concessions. Moreover, the line between reforms and structural changes is not always easy to maintain. Paige's own discussion of Malayan rubber plantations (1975: 50–58) illustrates the inadequacies of his basic theory.

5. There is no avoiding the conclusion that Paige (1975) contradicts the arguments of Wolf (1969a) and Scott (1977a). At first glance one might suppose that the contrasting theories were intended to apply to separate kinds of situations – that

is, Wolf and Scott primarily to traditional agrarian societies and Paige only to commercialized export zones. However, in practice, Paige applies his theoretical logic much more broadly. In his theoretical chapter, he often refers to agrarian class relations in non-export-oriented societies (or areas), and in his case history of Vietnam, he seeks to explain class relations and peasant politics in the nonexport areas of central and northern Vietnam as well as in the export-oriented zones of southern Vietnam.

6. On the social origins of the leaders of modern Vietnamese political movements see Wolf (1969a: 178–81). The cultural and intellectual roots of these movements are thoroughly explored in Woodside (1976).

7. On the enormous importance of nationalism in Vietnamese Communism see McAlister (1971) and Dunn (1972: ch. 5). Quite inappropriately, in my opinion, Paige tries to draw a firm distinction between communally-oriented nationalist revolutionary movements such as the U.P.A. of Angola and class-oriented socialist revolutionary movements such as Vietnamese Communism. But the Vietnamese Communists were effective precisely because they *combined* nationalism with class-based appeals to the peasantry! And, indeed, it is hard to see how any successful revolutionary movement in the Third World could avoid having strong nationalist overtones.

8. On these sects see McLane (1971) and Popkin (1979). Popkin (1979: 193–213) is especially good in explaining how the Cao Dai and Hoa Hao appealed to southern peasants and thereby made themselves formidable organizational competitors to the Communists.

9. See Paige's statistical analysis of "world patterns" in *Agrarian Revolution,* chapter 2. He indicates (1975: 94–96) that the presence of Communist or Trotskyist parties at protests in export agricultural zones was used as a key indicator of "revolutionary-socialist events."

10. Paige posits (1975: 32, 37) that only conservative (i.e., landlord-dominated) solidarity should occur when a landed upper class coexists with a landed peasantry.

11. See also the excellent discussion in Popkin (1979: 133–70).

12. On the leftist revolutionary movements in Portuguese Africa (Angola, Guinea, and Mozambique) see Davidson (1974). On peasants in the Cuban Revolution, see Wolf (1969a: ch. 6).

13. James Scott (1977a) suggests that revolutionary outcomes are likely to be better for the peasantry if their revolts are autonomous and spontaneous in relation to the revolutionary leadership. But a clear counter instance was the Russian Revolution where, in large part *because* of the extreme spontaneity and local autonomy of the peasant revolts, the peasants in the end faced the coercive extension of Bolshevik state power into the countryside. Chinese peasants, by contrast, benefitted after 1949 from the fact that the Chinese Communists had found it necessary to mobilize their direct political support in order to achieve national power in the first place (see Skocpol, 1979: chs. 6–7).

14. Popkin (1979) effectively underlines the insecurities and exploitation built into many traditional agrarian structures, and points out that peasants have good cause to attempt to "remake" these structures through revolts or participation in political movements.

15. On the organizing activities of the Communists in Vietnam see Popkin (1979: 213–42); Pike (1966); and Race (1972).

16. I have not seen systematic investigations of such questions, but useful speculations can be found here and there in Dunn (1972) and Chaliand (1977).

17. Popkin (1979: chs. 5–6) has some very insightful things to say about the collective mobilization of peasants.

18. In "Hegemony and the Peasantry" (1977a), Scott concentrates almost exclusively on

the peasantry itself, analyzing why it is a class capable of making revolutions. In his previous work on peasant rebellions (1976), Scott stressed the ways in which Western imperialism exploits or uproots traditional peasants, fundamentally undermining the security of their subsistence-oriented economic practices and moral customs. The will to revolt, according to Scott, grows out of this confrontation between peasant traditionalism and modernizing capitalist forces. Thus his views seem to closely parallel those of Wolf (1969a) and Migdal (1974).

19. Although Paige does not realize it, this comment about political conditions since World War II introduces explanatory variables into the picture that his ahistorical and apolitical theoretical model cannot handle. Moreover, the validity of Paige's statistical analysis (1975: ch. 2) of "world patterns" of agrarian politics between 1948 and 1970 is called into serious question once we realize that, during this time, decolonization was happening in Asia and Africa, but U.S. neocolonial hegemony over Latin America remained quite firm. Many of Paige's findings about revolutionary movements versus agrarian revolts may reflect not, as he argues, the inherent political potentials of migratory and sharecropper estates versus commercial haciendas. They may reflect instead the internationally conditioned differences between African and Asian politics versus Latin American politics during the post–World War II period.

REFERENCES

Adas, Michael. (1979). *Prophets of Rebellion: Millenarian Protest Movements Against the European Colonial Order*. Chapel Hill: University of North Carolina Press.

Chaliand, Gerard. (1977). *Revolution in the Third World: Myths and Prospects*. New York: Viking Press.

Davidson, Basil. (1974). "African Peasants and Revolution." *The Journal of Peasant Studies* 1: 269–90.

Dunn, John. (1972). *Modern Revolutions*. Cambridge: Cambridge University Press.

Elvin, Mark. (1973). *The Pattern of the Chinese Past*. Stanford: Stanford University Press.

McAlister, John T., Jr. (1971). *Vietnam: The Origins of Revolution*. Garden City, N.Y.: Doubleday Anchor.

McLane, John R. (1971). "Archaic Movements and Revolution in Southern Vietnam," in Norman Miller and Roderick Aya, eds., *National Liberation: Revolution in the Third World*. New York: Free Press.

Migdal, Joel S. (1974). *Peasants, Politics, and Revolution: Pressures Toward Political and Social Change in the Third World*. Princeton: Princeton University Press.

Moore, Barrington, Jr. (1966). *Social Origins of Dictatorship and Democracy*. Boston: Beacon Press.

Paige, Jeffery M. (1975). *Agrarian Revolution: Social Movements and Export Agriculture in the Underdeveloped World*. New York: Free Press.

Perkins, Dwight H. (1969). *Agricultural Development in China, 1368–1969*. Chicago: Aldine.

Pike, Douglas. (1966). *Viet Cong*. Cambridge: M.I.T. Press.

Popkin, Samuel L. (1979). *The Rational Peasant: The Political Economy of Rural Society in Vietnam*. Berkeley and Los Angeles: University of California Press.

Race, Jeffrey. (1972). *War Comes to Long An: Revolutionary Conflict in a Vietnamese Province*. Berkeley and Los Angeles: University of California Press.

Scott, James C. (1976). *The Moral Economy of the Peasant: Rebellion and Subsistence in Southeast Asia*. New Haven: Yale University Press.

————. (1977a). "Hegemony and the Peasantry." *Politics and Society* 7: 267–96.

————. (1977b). "Protest and Profanation: Agrarian Revolt and the Little Tradition." *Theory and Society* 4: 1–38, 211–246.

Skinner, G. William. (1964–65). "Marketing and Social Structure in Rural China." *Journal of Asian Studies* 24: 3–43, 195–228, 363–99.

Skocpol, Theda. (1979). *States and Social Revolutions: A Comparative Analysis of France, Russia, and China.* Cambridge and New York: Cambridge University Press.

Wolf, Eric. (1969). *Peasant Wars of the Twentieth Century.* New York: Harper & Row.

Woodside, Alexander B. (1976). *Community and Revolution in Modern Vietnam.* Boston: Houghton Mifflin.

10

Rentier state and Shi'a Islam in the Iranian Revolution

The recent overthrow of the Shah of Iran, the launching of the Iranian Revolution between 1977 and 1979, came as a sudden surprise to outside observers – from the American friends of the Shah, to journalists and political pundits, and to social scientists including those, like me, who are supposed to be "experts" on revolutions. All of us have watched the unfolding of current events with fascination and, perhaps, consternation. A few of us have also been inspired to probe the Iranian sociopolitical realities behind those events. For me, such probing was irresistible – above all because the Iranian Revolution struck me in some ways as quite anomalous. This revolution surely qualifies as a sort of "social revolution." Yet its unfolding – especially in the events leading to the Shah's overthrow – challenged expectations about revolutionary causation that I developed through comparative-historical research on the French, Russian, and Chinese Revolutions.[1]

"Social revolutions" as I define them are rapid, basic transformations of a country's state and class structures, and of its dominant ideology. Moreover, social revolutions are carried through, in part, by class-based upheavals from below. The Iranian Revolution seems to fit this conception. Under the old regime, the Shah ruled through an absolutist-monarchical military dictatorship, styling himself a cosmopolitan Persian King in the 2,500-year-old image of Cyrus the Great. Iran's dominant class, ostentatiously pro-Western in its cultural style, consisted of state bureaucrats, foreign capitalist investors, and domestic capitalists closely tied by patronage and regulation to the state machine. The Revolution itself involved revolts against this dominant class by urban workers, unemployed people, and old and new middle classes. Finally, the removal of the Shah was accompanied by the dispossession of many (especially politically

This article is an elaboration of remarks prepared for a plenary "Sorokin Lecture" at the Annual Meeting of the Southern Sociological Society in Louisville, Kentucky on 9 April 1981. A still earlier version of these ideas was presented to the 1980–81 Mellon Seminar of the Institute for Advanced Study on 17 February 1981. I am grateful to Daniel Bell for comments on the first draft of this article.

privileged) capitalists, by the removal of all top officials and the reorganization of the administrative, judicial, and coercive state apparatuses, and by attacks on the lifestyles and institutional supports of Westernized dominant groups in Iran. As in most contemporary Third World countries, it is hard to distinguish political and social revolution in any firm way, because the state and its incumbent elites are so central to the ownership and control of the economy. But the Iranian Revolution has been so obviously mass-based and so thoroughly transformative of basic sociocultural and socioeconomic relationships in Iran that it surely fits more closely the pattern of the great historical social revolutions than it does the rubric of simply a political revolution, where only governmental institutions are transformed.

My previous work on social revolutions – not only my in-depth study of the French, Russian, and Chinese cases, but also my more superficial investigations of contemporary Third World cases – led to certain conclusions about the causes of this class of events. Social revolutions, I have argued, are not simply products of rapid modernization that lead to widespread social discontent and disorientation. Many theorists have suggested that this sequence produces revolution.[2] But I have stressed, following Charles Tilly, that the mass, lower-class participants in revolution cannot turn discontent into effective political action without autonomous collective organization and resources to sustain their efforts.[3] Moreover, the repressive state organizations of the prerevolutionary regime have to be weakened *before* mass revolutionary action can succeed, or even emerge. Indeed, historically, mass rebellious action has not been able, in itself, to overcome state repression. Instead, military pressures from abroad, often accompanied by political splits between dominant classes and the state, have been necessary to undermine repression and open the way for social-revolutionary upheavals from below. In my view, social revolutions have not been caused by avowedly revolutionary movements in which an ideological leadership mobilizes mass support to overthrow an existing system in the name of a new alternative. Avowedly revolutionary leaderships have often been absent or politically marginal until after the collapse of prerevolutionary regimes. And popular groups, especially peasants, have contributed to revolutionary transformations by revolting for concrete ideals and goals separate from those espoused by the revolutionary leaderships that end up consolidating revolutions by building up new state organizations. In my book *States and Social Revolutions,* I was unremittingly critical of all theorists who have assumed that revolutions are "made" deliberately by revolutionary, mass-based social movements. Instead, I insisted on a structural perspective to get at the historically unfolding intersections of the efforts of differently situated and differently motivated groups – groups *not* operating even under the shared rubric of a revolutionary ideology. As I put it in the book, quoting the abolitionist Wendell Phillips: "Revolutions are not made. They come."

The initial stages of the Iranian Revolution obviously challenged my previously worked-out notions about the causes of social revolutions. Three apparent difficulties come immediately to mind. First, the Iranian Revolution does seem as if it might have been simply a product of excessively rapid modernization. Through the decade of the 1960s, and at an accelerating pace in the 1970s, Iranian society underwent land reform, massive migrations from countryside to cities and towns (above all to Teheran), unprecedentedly rapid industrialization, and the sudden expansion of modern primary, secondary, and university education. When the Revolution came, all sectors of Iranian society seemed discontented with the Shah and with their own situations. Perhaps, therefore, the Revolution *was* straightforwardly the product of societal disruption, social disorientation, and universal frustration with the pace of change.

Second, in a striking departure from the regularities of revolutionary history, the Shah's army and police – modern coercive organizations over 300,000 men strong – were rendered ineffective in the revolutionary process between 1977 and early 1979 *without* the occurrence of a military defeat in foreign war and without pressures from abroad serving to undermine the Shah's regime or to provoke contradictory conflicts between the regime and the dominant classes.[4] Not only was the Shah himself ultimately left unprotected by the incapacitation of his armed forces, but these forces themselves proved unable to replace the Shah with a military regime (or a military-supported regime) that could preserve the integrity of the existing state organizations. Instead, both the Shah and his armed forces alike eventually succumbed to a domestic, mass-based revolutionary movement.

Indeed, third, if ever there has been a revolution deliberately "made" by a mass-based social movement aiming to overthrow the old order, the Iranian Revolution against the Shah surely is it. By the end of 1978, all sectors of urban Iranian society were coalescing under the rubrics of Shi'a Islam and were following the direction of a senior Shi'a cleric, the Ayatollah Ruhollah Khomeini, in uncompromising opposition to the Shah and all who remained connected to him. An extraordinary series of mass urban demonstrations and strikes, ever growing in size and revolutionary fervor, even in the face of lethal military repression, pitted the unemployed, workers, artisans, merchants, students, and middle-ranking officials of Iran against the Shah's regime. What Western socialists have long dreamt of doing (without success except where war has intervened to help), the people of urban Iran did accomplish as they mobilized in an all-inclusive movement against a "corrupt," "imperialist" monarchy. Their revolution did not just come; it was deliberately and coherently made – specifically in its opening phase, the overthrow of the old regime.

There can be no question, therefore, about the sharp departure of the outbreak of the Iranian Revolution from the causal configurations that occurred in the outbreak of the French, Russian, and Chinese Revolutions. Fortunately, in *States and Social Revolutions* I explicitly denied the possibility of fruitfulness of a general causal theory of revolutions that would apply across all times and places. I am not caught in the embarrassing position of having to argue that the Iranian Revolution is "really just like the French, Russian and Chinese Revolutions." Nevertheless, I did suggest in the conclusion to my book that its basic framework of analysis should be applicable to other revolutions, even in different types of societies and different world-historical circumstances from the "classical" cases I studied. Indeed, the Iranian Revolution, too, must be understood from a macroscopic and historically grounded structural perspective, one that examines the interrelations of state, society, and organized politics in Iran, and situates Iran in changing international political and economic contexts. Only from this sort of perspective can we understand the vulnerabilities of the Shah's regime, the cross-nationally distinctive sociopolitical roots of the revolutionary movement that brought it down, and the remarkable struggles since early 1979 over the creation of new state organizations in revolutionary Iran. The Iranian Revolution *can* be interpreted in terms analytically consistent with the explanatory principles I used in *States and Social Revolutions* – this is what I shall briefly try to show. However, this remarkable revolution also forces me to deepen my understanding of the possible role of idea systems and cultural understandings in the shaping of political action – in ways that I shall indicate recurrently at appropriate points in this article.

THE VULNERABILITIES OF A RENTIER ABSOLUTIST STATE

Like the rulers of the Old Regimes in France, Russia, and China, the Shah of Iran was an "absolute monarch." And in an important sense, the Shah was much more powerful than absolute monarchs of old, for he had at his disposal a thoroughly modernized army and a ruthless, omnipresent secret police force. Yet the Shah's state was much less rooted, less embedded in society – especially rural society – than the "agrarian bureaucracies" of prerevolutionary France, Russia, and China.

Throughout the nineteenth century, Iran's monarchs were "Oriental despots" who, despite awesome trappings of personal authority, reigned only by manipulating divisions among armed tribes, regional landlord potentates, and self-governing urban corporate groups.[5] A modern Iranian state, with a nationally centralized army and administration, emerged only in the 1920s, after Reza Kahn, the colonel of a tiny professional military force, seized power in a coup d'état and expanded his army to pacify and unify the country. Shah Reza Pahlavi (as he crowned himself in 1925) constructed a kind of agrarian bureaucracy, a centralized state coexisting with landed aristocrats. During his reign Iran gained greater national unity and autonomy than ever before in modern times, yet still did not escape its destiny at the geopolitical interstices of great power rivalries. During World War II, Iran was occupied by Britain and the Soviet Union; Reza Shah, who had made the mistake of flirting with the Germans, was packed off into exile. After the war, Iran struggled for renewed national autonomy, first against the Soviets and then against the British and their oil interests. The upshot, after the failure of Muhammed Mossadegh's populist brand of nationalism, was American encouragement for a reassertion of royal power by Reza Shah's son, the (late) Shah Mohammed Reza Pahlavi. Helped by the US Central Intelligence Agency to defeat his domestic adversaries in 1953, the second Pahlavi Shah thereafter set his country on a course of cautious (though increasingly assertive) alliance with the newly hegemonic United States. Help from a far-away imperialist power was used to give Iran's state increased leverage in relation to the older, nearby imperial powers, Britain and Russia, and eventually to help it bid for regional military power in the Middle East.

Under the second Shah, the domestic underpinnings of the Iranian state also changed as the state became increasingly addicted to revenues from exports of oil and natural gas. Iran's government became a "rentier state," awash in petrodollars, and closely linked to the rhythms of the world capitalist economy.[6] Especially after the mid-1960s, this state did not need to wrest taxes from its own people, and the economic basis of its revenues was an industry oriented primarily to exports, and employing only a tiny percentage of the domestic labor force. The state's main relationships to Iranian society were mediated through its *expenditures* – on the military, on development projects, on modern construction, on consumption subsidies, and the like. Suspended above its own people, the Iranian state bought them off, rearranged their lives, and repressed any dissidents among them. The Shah did not rule through, or in alliance with, any independent social class. During the 1960s, he launched a "White Revolution" to buy out landlords, redistribute land to wealthier peasants, and extend bureaucratic state control into the villages. Poor planning left much of the agrarian economy impoverished, however, forcing millions of poorer peasants to migrate to the towns and cities. Urban Iran grew to become almost 50% of the population before the Revolution, and all urban strata relied heavily for privileges, employment, and services on burgeoning state expenditures.

As a wealthy rentier state, the prerevolutionary Iranian regime was politically unassailable in certain ways – and potentially vulnerable in others. Because of ecological and sociopolitical arrangements in the countryside, Iranian peasants lacked the capacity to revolt autonomously.[7] Yet even if they could have revolted, it would hardly have mattered; for landlords were not a mainstay of the Shah's regime and agriculture was becoming ever more marginal in the national economy. Industry, construction, and services were the foci of national economic expansion fueled by the regime's expenditures. In turn, these expenditures were closely linked to shifts in the price of oil and the international demand for it. When the OPEC cartel raised oil prices in the early 1970s, the Shah suddenly had huge revenues for crash programs in industrial and military modernization. Along with windfall profits, rising wages, and new employment opportunities, urban Iranians experienced escalating inflation and an influx of privileged foreign skilled workers and technicians. Then, in 1975–77, world demand for Iranian oil contracted, and many projects had to be cut and workers thrown out of employment. All urban strata together could blame the state for their troubles, and the Shah himself was universally understood to be the autocratic embodiment of state authority. Indeed, the Shah was no figurehead monarch, but rather a practicing patrimonial absolutist.[8] He played bureaucrats and military officers off against one another, never allowing stable coalitions or lines of responsible authority to develop. The Shah personally made all major decisions – about official appointments, about military procurement, about major state economic investments. Once the Iranian state came under revolutionary pressure in 1977–78, the Shah's absolutist role would become very consequential. Universal social resentment was focused upon his monarchical person, yet without him the state could not function. Military officers, for example, lacked the corporate solidarity to displace the Shah in a coup and save the state at his expense. And once the United States prodded the Shah to leave Iran in January 1979, top government officials found it hard to hold together in the face of the revolutionary onslaught. (Remarkably, a leading military general as well as SAVAK's second-in-command secretly defected to the Ayatollah Khomeini even before the end!)[9]

Still, all of the foregoing vulnerabilities of the prerevolutionary Iranian regime could well have had little significance. The Shah, after all, had both munificent wealth and ominous repressive power at his disposal. Whatever the ups and downs of oil prices and revenues, he should have been able to ride out waves of urban social discontent, just as many other (less well endowed) Third World rulers have been able to do. That he was unable to survive, that both he and his state succumbed to revolution, can be explained only by reference to the extraordinarily sustained efforts made by urban Iranians to wear down and undercut the Shah's regime. These efforts, in turn, were based in traditional centers of urban communal life and in networks of Islamic religious communication and leadership. A look at such supports for intense opposition to the Shah is now in order.

URBAN COMMUNITIES AS THE BASIS FOR POLITICAL RESISTANCE

In many social revolutions, the most politically significant popular revolts have been grounded in village communities, damaged by "modernizing" social change, but still intact as centers of autonomous, solidary opposition to dominant classes and the state. Peasant village communities were *not*, however, the basis for popular insurrections in the Iranian Revolution. Instead, opposition to the Shah was centered in urban communal enclaves where autonomous and solidary collective resistance was possible. Historically in Iran, the socioeconomic world of the bazaar was the center of urban life, and there were strong links between the merchants and artisans of the bazaar and the agricultural producers in the countryside. Of course, as the Pahlavi Shahs used state power to promote modern capitalist industrialization and new forms of urban life, the bazaars of Teheran and other cities and towns were bypassed and squeezed, both economically and spatially. Yet the dislocations of Iran's hectic modernization also channeled new people and resources into the bazaar: rural migrants sought employment and social services. Small artisanal-industrial enterprises, employing less than ten workers, expanded in tandem with large modern factories (so that, as of 1977, 72% of all workers were employed in units of ten employees or less). And bazaar merchants, from major wholesalers to tiny retail shopkeepers, continued to handle much of the burgeoning import trade by which urban Iranians, especially the nonwealthy, fed and clothed themselves.[10] Far from being disorganized agglomerations of isolated, disoriented people, Iran's traditional urban communities remained buzzing centers of economic activity and rich associational life. Islamic religious groups and occasions were especially important in tying merchants, artisans, and workers together. Mullahs trained to interpret Islamic law adjudicated commercial disputes and taxed the well-to-do to provide personalized welfare services for devout poorer followers. Both clerical preachers and devout laymen orchestrated a never-ending succession of prayer-meetings and ritual celebrations of key Islamic holy days.[11]

The bazaar also enjoyed ties to even those expanding modern sectors of Iranian society that seemed to be (and, in a sense, were) displacing its activities. Many Iranian university students, oriented to new careers in the bureaucracy or the professions, were children of bazaaris, and many wealthier bazaar merchants were involved in state-sponsored industrial projects. Indeed, the bazaar could conceivably have remained in loose alliance with the Shah's regime despite state-sponsored modernization. But by the mid-1970s, the Shah seemed determined to attack the traditional aspects of bazaar life. He attempted to bring self-regulating merchants' councils fully under state control, he tried to extend state involvement in wholesale and retail trade, and he launched an "anti-corruption" campaign against alleged profiteering in the bazaar. All of this coincided with the Shah's steady efforts to exclude the Islamic clergy, the ulama, from educational, legal, and welfare activities that historically had been theirs to perform. Thus, even as the bazaar remained a vital, solidary social world, somewhat autonomous from the centers of state power in Iran, the Shah attacked the leaders of this world and aroused their defensiveness and potential opposition.[12]

In the mass movements against the Shah during 1977 and 1978, the traditional urban communities of Iran were to play an indispensable role in mobilizing and sustaining the core of popular resistance. Modern industrial workers who struck depended on economic aid from the bazaar, and secular, professional middle-class opponents to the Shah depended on alliances with the clerical and lay leaders of the bazaar, who could mobilize mass followings through established economic and social networks. Those theorists who argue that rapid modernization alone produces revolution are wrong – even though the Shah's crash program did create widespread disruption and discontent. In fact, disruption and discontent *alone* do not give people the collective organizational capacities and the autonomous resources that they need to sustain resistance to political and economic powerholders. In Iran, it was crucial that the cities and towns were not merely disorganized receptacles of millions of fresh rural migrants with only state employments and disbursements to sustain them. Revolutionary potential inhered, instead, in the socially coherent and somewhat independent world of the bazaar, surviving damaged but intact into the 1970s, as a locus of politically autonomous social life for millions of urban Iranians. Still, we have not yet solved the mystery of why, even if it was collectively possible for them to launch demonstrations and sustain strikes, urban Iranians ended up actually doing so in such large, well-coordinated numbers. And we have not explained why, to a cross-nationally and historically very unusual degree, so many Iranians were willing to face death again and again in the recurrent mass demonstrations that finally wore down, demoralized, and paralyzed the army, the Shah, and his US supporters. To deal with these issues, we must address the historical and changing place of Shi'a Islamic religious organizations and belief in Iranian society and politics.

SHI'A ISLAM IN THE FORGING OF A REVOLUTIONARY MOVEMENT

Shi'a Islam is a major but nondominant branch of Islam, and Iran is the only nation-state where Shi'a rather than Sunni believers are in the majority. As a religious world-view, Shi'a Islam arguably has especially salient symbolic resources to justify resistance against unjust authority, and to legitimate religious leaders as competitors to the state. The founding myth is the story of Husayn's willing martydom in the just cause of resisting the usurper caliph, Yazid. And legitimate authority in the Shi'a community has long been shared between political and religious leaders, neither of whom can unambiguously claim to represent fully the will of the "Hidden Imam," a supreme leader who went into transhistorical occultation in the ninth century. The Shi'a "clergy,"[13] or ulama, are trained to interpret Islamic law for believers, and they can claim, as well or better than monarchs, to represent authentically the will of the Hidden Imam.

In the actual course of Iranian history, however, Shi'a Islam has been used at times (especially during the Savafid Dynasty) to justify the ulama's alliance with monarchs, and at other times to justify pious clerical withdrawal from the tainted secular world of politics.[14] Furthermore, the Husayn myth can lead among ordinary believers to submissive calls for Husayn's intercession to ensure individual salvation, rather than to collectively oriented acts of martyrdom in defiance to unjust authority.[15] In short, political developments are not logically deducible from Shi'a beliefs as such; rather Shi'a believers are inspired to varying political activities depending on the varying places of religious activities and outlooks in the changing life of Iranian society as a whole. By the nine-teenth century, under the weak Qajar Shahs in Iran, the Shi'a ulama had achieved independent financial means – as landowners and as collectors of a special religious tithe (half used to support the clergy and religious students, and half used for social welfare disbursed by leading clerics, or ayatollahs). The ulama also enjoyed strong followings in the populace, especially of the cities and towns. At times in the nineteenth century, when Shahs were deemed vacillating in the face of Western imperialist intrusions into Iranian society, leading members of the ulama actually mobilized huge Islamic "nationalist" protests against government policies.[16] Yet the clergy were not unified in any single, disciplined hierarchy, and they were tied in many complex ways to the Qajar establishment of landed aristocrats, tribal chiefs, and patrimonial officials. Some ulama might support modern reformist movements, but well into the twentieth century (indeed as late as 1953, when the Shah reasserted royal power with US help), other leading clergy provided strong active or tacit support for the Iranian monarchy as an institution. Not until *after* the second Pahlavi Shah definitively broke with the clergy did its political center of gravity shift toward firm political opposition and, finally, revolution.[17]

During the 1960s and 1970s, the late Shah used state power and programs of modernization to attack the Shi'a clergy.[18] Land reform from above in the 1960s dispossessed many individual clerics and also religious institutions, and served to cut the clergy's ties to the landed upper class. Educational, welfare, and legal reforms created modern, professional, state-employment competitors to the Shi'a clergy in all of their historically important social functions. Left intact by the Shah were a few traditional centers of Islamic religious education (like Qum), now bypassed by most students seeking higher education, as well as the ulama's social alliance with the people of the bazaars, who continued voluntarily to pay the religious taxes. Contemptuously, the Shah supposed that the old-fashioned, "turban-headed" clerics would silently fade from the scene as the inevitable course of modernization progressed. But, before this could happen, the still-numerous ulama of Iran, and their shrunken but still-significant lay and student followings, reacted by developing a politically aggressive and populist brand of Islamic traditionalism. Exiled to the traditional shrine center of Iraq in the 1960s, the Ayatollah Khomeini began to preach to students and pilgrims that the Shah was an agent of anti-Islamic foreign imperialism, and he called on the ulama to assert their right to lead "the Islamic community" in direct opposition to such unjust authority.[19] Khomeini's appeal and message gradually became predominant among students in Qum, and spread throughout (especially urban) Iran via the previously established networks linking mullahs and tithe-paying lay people to that city of religious learning.[20] All of this, in the mid-1970s, began to resonate with *widespread* Iranian disgust with the Shah and the policies of his regime – policies that did seem to be more closely attuned to military aggrandizement, ensuring oil supplies to the West, and following cues from the United States, than to the indigenous demands of the Iranian people.

Once protests against the Shah began, the networks and symbols of communication among Shi'a clerics, and between clerics and lay people (through mosques and religious occasions) became crucial to orchestrating and sustaining widespread popular resistance to the state.[21] The Husayn myth provided a framework for labeling and reacting against the Shah as the evil, tyrannical "Yazid of the present age." The Islamic annual calendar of collective rituals, the weekly public prayer meetings, and the prescriptions for public funeral processions to mourn the dead all provided widely understood forms in which to channel simultaneous mass political action. Significantly, too, Iranians could join together even beyond the ranks of the religiously devout, because Shi'a Islam and Khomeini's visibly uncompromising moral leadership provided a nationally indigenous way to express common opposition to an aloof monarch too closely identified with foreigners. Even secular Iranians could participate under these rubrics. And those Iranians who were devout – especially young men from bazaar families – could find inspiration in the Husayn myth for martyrdom in the face of repression. Thus, the huge mass demonstrations were often led by men wearing white shrouds to symbolize their readiness to risk death at the hands of the army. It *did* matter that the Iranian crowds were willing to face the army again and again – accepting casualties much more persistently than European crowds have historically done – until sections of the military rank-and-file began to hesitate or balk at shooting into the crowds. Over time, the crowds would therefore grow while the army became less and less active and reliable as an instrument of repression.

In sum, Shi'a Islam was both organizationally and culturally crucial to the making of the Iranian Revolution against the Shah. Radicalized clerics, loosely following the Ayatollah Khomeini, disseminated political ideas challenging the Shah. Then the networks, the social forms, and the central myths of Shi'a Islam helped to coordinate urban mass resistance and to give it the moral will to persist in the face of attempts at armed repression. All of this meant that a very "traditional" part of Iranian life – albeit a traditional part fitting in new ways into a steadily changing modern sociopolitical scene – provided crucial political resources for the forging of a very modern-looking revolutionary movement. Many social-scientific theorists of revolution have argued that revolutionary ideologies and organizations must convert and mobilize mass followings before a revolution is possible. Actually, this has rarely been the case in social revolutions of the past, which "were not made," but came unintentionally on all concerned. In Iran, uniquely, the revolution was "made" – but not, everyone will note, by any of the modern revolutionary parties on the Iranian scene: not by the Islamic guerillas or by the Marxist guerillas, or by the Communist ("Tudeh") Party, or by the secular-liberal National Front. Instead it was made through a set of cultural and organizational forms thoroughly socially embedded in the urban communal enclaves that became the centers of popular resistance to the Shah. Even when a revolution is to a significant degree "made," that is because a culture conducive to challenges to authority, as well as politically relevant networks of popular communication, are already historically woven into the fabric of social life. In and of themselves, the culture and networks of communication do not dictate mass revolutionary action. But if a historical conjuncture arises in which a vulnerable state faces oppositionally inclined social groups possessing solidarity, autonomy, and independent economic resources, then the sorts of moral symbols and forms of social communication offered by Shi'a Islam in Iran can sustain the self-conscious making of a revolution. No innovative revolutionary propaganda retailed to "the masses" overnight, in the midst of a societal crisis, can serve this purpose. But a world-view and a set of social practices long in place can sustain a deliberate revolutionary movement.

SINCE THE SHAH: THE STRUGGLE OVER A NEW IRANIAN STATE

Once the broad and heterogeneous revolutionary alliance arrayed around the Ayatollah Khomeini triumphed in Iran, many Western observers hoped that Western-oriented liberals would shape the new regime. The Shah's overthrow depended on the symbolic forms of Islam, but the revolution was in essence a struggle for Iranian liberal democracy – so the optimistic Western argument went.[22] Then, as the months of 1979 went by and the liberals of the National Front lost out thoroughly to clerical and lay proponents of an avowedly Islamic Republic, with strong powers for a supreme religious leader and for Islamic jurisprudents written into the new Constitution,[23] Western observers switched their hopes to modern-educated intellectuals who were trying to govern in uneasy alliance with the clergy-dominated Islamic Republican Party. Supposedly, the mullahs, ayatollahs, and other traditionally educated Iranians were "medieval," and not technically competent to run a modern polity. Especially after Iraq invaded Iran and the professional military leadership had to be reinvigorated, predictions of the imminent eclipse of the "theocrats" in Iran again flourished in the Western media.[24] Where liberal republicans had failed, technically trained modern officials – military officers and government bureaucrats – might succeed in displacing (or taming the powers of) the Islamic clerics. But no such developments occurred. Many observers in the West were thus truly confounded as the Shi'a clerics and their followers succeeded step by step, from 1979 into 1981, at consolidating their cultural and political hegemony as custodians of the Iranian Revolution.

But placed in historical perspective in comparison to the course of struggles in earlier social revolutions, the events since early 1979 in Iran do not seem so surprising.[25] In the classic social revolutions, liberals and democratic social-ists – people who wanted to limit or to decentralize state power – invariably lost out to political leaderships able and willing to mobilize and channel mass support for the creation of centrally controlled agencies of coercion and adminis-tration. New state organizations built up within social-revolutionary situations were more mass-incorporating than either prerevolutionary states or abortive liberal political arrangements, and these new state organizations became ideo-logically and organizationally more autonomous in relation to foreign powers and domestic social classes. The particular political leadership that created such state organizations – winning out in the process over other leaderships advocat-ing counterrevolutionary, liberal, or decentralist political solutions – were equipped with mass-mobilizing political capacities and with ideological world-views that gave them the self-assurance to use unlimited coercive means to establish vanguard control in the name of the whole revolutionary people. Thus, to understand which political leadership will win out in (at least the initial stages of) the consolidation of state power in a social-revolutionary situation, one must ask *not* which leaders are "most modern" by some Western or technical stan-dard, but which possess, or can easily develop within given historical circum-stances, the appropriate political resources. In Iran after the demise of the Shah and the partial disintegration of his state, it was precisely the radical-fundamentalist Shi'a clerics, following the Ayatollah Khomeini and organized by Ayatollah Mohammed Beheshti under the rubric of an Islamic Republican Party, who could develop the appropriate resources to triumph as revolutionary state-builders.

Some of the clerical leaders' resources were cultural. For example, "Imam" Khomeini's role as a continuing central focus for the revolutionary leadership resonated with the popular messianic yearning for the return of the Twelfth Imam, who long ago disappeared from human sight to await the coming of a perfect Islamic community as the telos of history.[26] Other ideational resources available to the entire revolutionary leadership were more specifically ideologi-cal, derived from the politically assertive interpretation of Islam and clerical leadership elaborated by Khomeini. In the fall of 1979, the Italian journalist Oriana Fallaci conducted a remarkable interview with Khomeini, during which she asked about the tensions between democracy and clerical authority embod-ied in the then soon-to-be-ratified Islamic Constitution:

Fallaci's question: In drafting the new constitution, the assembly of experts passed one article . . . by which the head of the country will have to be the supreme religious authority. That is you. And the supreme decisions will be made only by those who know the Koran well – that is, the clergy. Doesn't this mean that, according to the constitution, politics will continue to be determined by the priests [clergy] and no one else?

Khomeini's answer: This law, which the people will ratify, is in no way in contradiction with democracy. Since the people love the clergy, have faith in the clergy, want to be guided by the clergy, it is right that the supreme religious authority should oversee the work of the prime minister or of the president of the republic, to make sure that they don't make mistakes or go against the Koran.[27]

Thus Khomeini and his clerical associates thought of themselves as the true interpreters of Islam, automatically worthy of willing followership by all good officials and people in Iran. And Islam to them was an all-encompassing totality. As Khomeini put it to Fallaci, "the word Islam does not need adjectives such as democratic. Precisely because Islam is everything, it means everything. It is sad for us to add another word near the word Islam, which is perfect."[28] Dissidents, as they emerged in opposition to policies sanctioned by Khomeini, could simply be reclassified as "corrupt" and "evil," not part of the true Islamic nation. Clerical judges could then as easily condemn to prison or death members of such formerly anti-Shah groups as liberals or Kurds or Marxists as they could condemn the former officials of the Shah's regime itself.

Their location in the social structure, as well as the political legacies of the revolutionary movement against the Shah, afforded the Shi'a clergy even more decisive advantages in the struggles to mobilize and channel mass support for a new Iranian regime. Liberal groups and Leftist parties might enjoy support in the universities, among the middle strata, and among organized sectors of the industrial workforce, but the mullahs had unparalleled access to the majority of poorer Iranians – small merchants, artisans, workers, unemployed, and rural people – through the mosques, local Islamic courts, and informal local institutions for popular education and welfare. Under the Shah, more severe repression and surveillance had been directed against secular oppositionists, making it difficult for them openly to appeal to popular support. And during 1977–78, the central locales for revolutionary mobilization of the lower and middle classes had been the traditional urban *residential* communities where the Islamic clergy were established leaders.

Once the Shah's regime was destroyed, popular demonstrations led by the Shi'a clergy could continue to be fielded – now directed against "US imperialism," a powerful symbol for Iranians mindful of American interventions in the past, and against all domestic political forces led by non-Islamic or by secular elites. Within the localities, armed militias and local committees of surveillance were organized under clerical leadership. Leading clerics came to dominate the new Majlis (Parliament) after riding to power through an electoral system that in practice required the illiterate majority of Iranians to gain the mullahs' help in voting. Islamic legal education was expanded enormously after early 1979; meanwhile the universities were purged of "Western cultural influences" and then closed down pending basic curricular revisions. Islamic courts recaptured their long-eclipsed centrality in the nation's judicial system, and the judiciary claimed authority to review legislation and administrative actions. Possible competing centers of authority within the state – such as the military command, or the bureaucratic ministries and the Presidency under Abolhassan Bani-Sadr – were brought thoroughly under the control of the leaders of the courts, the

Majlis, and the Islamic Republican Party. Remarkably in the overall history of religion and the state in Shi'a Iran, the central phalanx of the clergy fused its authority and activities with the state itself. This was not a "return to tradition" in Iran, but rather a strikingly innovative contemporary departure, in which Khomeini and his associates took upon themselves a vanguard, state-building and state-controlling role analogous to that of the Jacobins in revolutionary France and the Communists in revolutionary Russia and China.

Would the Iranian theocrats fall from power before the end of the revolutionary interregnum, as did the Montagnard Jacobins in France, or would they manage to maintain vanguard control, as did the Communists of Russia and China? As of the time this article was completed, in the summer of 1981, it was certainly too early to tell. But already by then the Shi'a leaders of Iran had proved themselves more able to establish their Islamic Republic than the French Jacobins had their Republic of Virtue – and this despite the lack of military successes in the Iranian revolutionaries' wars with Iraq and with domestic regional rebels. Nor have the Iranian Shi'a leaders been very successful at managing, let alone expanding, national economic production in agriculture or industry. Why had not "objective" constraints and failures undermined clerical rule in Iran before mid-1981? And how might an enduring Islamic regime look if the clerical vanguard succeeds in retaining control after the unexpected death (in late June, 1981) of its crafty organizer, the Ayatollah Beheshti, and after the inevitably coming death or enfeeblement of Imam Khomeini?

Ironically enough, Iran's Islamic Republic has enjoyed surprisingly propitious international conditions for survival. Whereas the French revolutionaries in the mid-1790s faced multiple military invasions from an alliance of European enemies, revolutionary Iran has been directly at foreign war only with Iraq, a less populous state that has not been able to parlay early victories into continued military momentum. In a bogged down, inefficient defensive conflict, the Iranian military's awkward admixture of regular soldiers and revolutionary guards has been able to hold its own – and, after all, Shi'a culture justifies prolonged suffering even in a losing or inconclusive struggle against an evil foe! Meanwhile, Iran's superpower neighbor, the USSR, is reluctant to invade directly for fear of provoking the United States. The Iranians themselves continually excoriate US imperialism in their domestic propaganda, but sheer distance and the nearby Russian presence prevent *that* superpower from intervening militarily. Thus the Iranian Islamic Republic has been able symbolically to assert its revolutionary autonomy against Soviet and (especially) American imperialism, without fearing military repercussions from these major powers. And at the same time, it has been able to hang on doggedly in an inconclusive, limited conflict with neighboring Iraq.

Iran's international economic role has been just as helpful to the Islamic revolutionaries as her geopolitical position. Continued international sales of oil, albeit at a lower rate than before the Revolution and before the war with Iraq, have been the key to the fiscal survival of the fledgling Islamic Republic of Iran amidst an unvictorious war and domestic economic disorder. Indeed, one might wonder how Islamic clerics, whose world-view and skills have so little to offer to the productive development of the Iranian economy, could remain indefinitely in power in a contemporary nation-state. There may be a not-so-comforting answer to this question. In past social revolutions, new regimes have often recapitulated the ills of the old in newly mass-incorporating ways. Prerevolutionary Iran was, as we have seen, a rentier state, where revenues from exports of oil and natural gas were channeled by the state, not so much into truly productive economic investments, but instead into lavish purchases of modern armaments and into elite luxury consumption. An Iranian Islamic Republic could remain, for quite some time, another sort of rentier state: a populist, welfare-oriented rentier state, with the ulama passing out alms in return for moral conformity on a grander scale than ever before. Unemployment and underemployment could continue at high levels in a stagnant national economy. Like all regimes forged through social revolution, the Iranian Islamic Republic is puritanical in its official moral style. But rather than this entailing the triumph of a new work ethic to spur the development of Iran's agriculture and industry before the oil revenues run out, it can simply mean the enforcement of orthodox Islamic mores for families and residential communities, as the Shi'a clergy lead the masses of Iran toward the timeless utopia of the ideally just Islamic commonwealth.

Of course, events in Iran may outrun the Shi'a revolutionary leadership. The clerics may lose their political unity and the army or a secular political party may step in. Or regional revolts and foreign subversion may lead to the dismemberment of the country. But if the cleric-ruled Iranian regime does survive, it will only testify to a wonder that is possible in the world of the late twentieth century: when a historically distinctive politico-religious culture, the exigencies of social-revolutionary state-building, and the material windfalls of exported oil intersect, they can hand power to modern-day proponents of an Islamic Republic of Virtue. These Islamic Jacobins may well endure quite a bit longer than their eighteenth-century French predecessors. Nevertheless, they cannot last indefinitely. For when the oil runs out, or if international demand goes severely slack for a prolonged period, then the material basis for an unproductive revolutionary utopia will be gone. Iranian history will then reach a watershed perhaps even more momentous than the revolutionary events of the present time.

NOTES

1. See Theda Skocpol, *States and Social Revolutions: A Comparative Analysis of France, Russia, and China* (Cambridge University Press, 1979).
2. See, for examples: Chalmers Johnson, *Revolutionary Change* (Little Brown, 1966); Ted Robert Gurr, *Why Men Rebel* (Princeton University Press, 1970); Ivo K. and Rosalind L. Feierabend and Betty A. Nesvold, "Social Change and Political Vio-

lence: Cross-National Patterns," in Hugh Davis Graham and Ted Robert Gurr, eds., *Violence in America* (Signet Books, 1969); and Edward A. Tiryakian, "A Model of Societal Change and Its Lead Indicators," in Samuel Z. Klausner, ed., *The Study of Total Societies* (Doubleday, Anchor Books, 1967).

3. See Charles Tilly, *From Mobilization to Revolution* (Addison-Wesley, 1978).
4. Some American analysts, for example Michael Ledeen and William Lewis in *Debacle: The American Failure in Iran* (Knopf, 1981), have argued that President Jimmy Carter's human rights policies put pressure on the Shah to avoid domestic repression of those challenging his regime. However, as Barry Rubin points out in *Paved with Good Intentions: The American Experience and Iran* (Oxford University Press, 1980), Chapters 7–9, the Carter Administration directed its human rights effort primarily against practices in the Shah's prisons, and maintained public support for the Shah throughout the escalating troubles of 1977–78. The Carter Administration did not develop a timely, consistent plan for "saving" the Shah's regime, but it did encourage him to plan and act on his own with symbolic American backing. Perhaps the Shah expected and wanted more initiative from the United States, but the failure of that to materialize does not constitute "pressure" against his regime. By the 1970s, the Shah was far from being a US puppet in any realm of domestic or foreign policy.
5. See the excellent analysis in Ervand Abrahamian, "Oriental Despotism: The Case of Qajar Iran," *International Journal of Middle Eastern Studies* 5 (1974), 3–31.
6. For the concept of a "rentier state," I am indebted to Hossein Mahdavy, "The Patterns and Problems of Economic Development in Rentier States: The Case of Iran," in M. A. Cook, ed., *Studies in the Economic History of the Middle East* (Oxford University Press, 1970).
7. See Farhad Kazemi and Ervand Abrahamian, "The Nonrevolutionary Peasantry of Modern Iran," *Iranian Studies* 11 (1978), 259–303.
8. Arguably, a state whose revenues come from charges on an easily extractable, exported resource such as oil is *extremely* amenable to control by an individual autocrat and his or her immediate relatives and personal following. However, the divide-and-rule tactics of a patrimonial ruler are classic; they have been applied in varying ways in all historical types of states. In states with strong bureaucratic features, rulers who do not apply such tactics risk de facto or actual removal from power by solidary collectivities of civilian or military officials.
9. Rubin, 239–40.
10. For a good synthesis of information on rural-urban migration and the working class, see Fred Halliday, *Iran: Dictatorship and Development* (Penguin Books, 1979), Chapter 7.
11. See Gustav Thaiss, "The Bazaar as a Case-Study of Religion and Social Change," in Ehsam Yar-Shater, ed., *Iran Faces the Seventies* (Praeger, 1971).
12. A good account of the Shah's attack on the merchants appears in Paul Balta and Claudine Rulleau, *L'Iran Insurgé* (Paris: Sindbad, 1979), 167–172.
13. "Clergy" does not necessarily convey the right connotations, for the Shi'a ulama are not like Catholic priests. They do not administer sacraments, are not hierarchically organized, and do not intercede directly between believers and God. Rather, the ulama are like a cross between Protestant ministers, who interpret and preach on holy texts, and judges, who adjudicate disagreements in terms of legal norms.
14. See Said Amir Arjomand, "Religion, Political Action and Legitimate Domination in Shi'ite Iran: Fourteenth to Eighteenth Centuries A.D.," *Archives Europpennes de Sociologie* 20, 1 (1979), 59–109; and Shahrough Akhavi, *Religion and Politics in Contemporary Iran* (State University of New York Press, 1980), Chapters 1 and 2.
15. On this point, see Mary Hooglund, "Accommodation and Revolution: Symbiotic

Ideologies in Shi'ite Islam," paper presented in the panel on "Islamic Ideology" at the Annual Meeting of the American Anthropological Association in Washington, DC, 7 December 1980.

16. See Hamid Algar, *Religion and the State in Iran, 1785–1906: The Role of the Ulama in the Qajar Period* (University of California Press, 1969); and Nikki Keddie, *Religion and Rebellion in Iran: The Tobacco Protest of 1891–1892* (London: Frank Cass, 1966).

17. Said Arjomand, in an article on "Shi'ite Islam and Revolution in Iran" forthcoming in *Government and Opposition,* is particularly good at analyzing how the Shi'ite clergy became "disembedded" from the state and landowners as a result of Pahlavi policies. Without this, the clergy could not have turned into a radical, populist political leadership.

18. See Akhavi, Chapters 2 and 5; and Michael M. J. Fischer, *Iran: From Religious Dispute to Revolution* (Harvard University Press, 1980), Chapter 4.

19. Khomeini's *Islamic Government* presents what was originally a series of lectures to students and clerics. It is remarkable for its invocation and reinterpretation of Islamic texts in support of a politically assertive stance by the clergy, in opposition both to the Shah and to Westernized groups in Iran. See the translation by Joint Publications Research Service, Arlington, Virginia (Manor Books, 1979).

20. Ironically, Khomeini and his militant followers were eventually able to make use for their own political purposes of traditional Qum-centered networks of tithe-collection and communication consolidated by a politically quietist leading Ayatollah (*marja'-i taqlid*), Sayyid Aqa Husayn Burūjirdī, who was hegemonic in Shi'a religious affairs from about 1947 to his death in 1961. As Hamid Algar writes in "The Oppositional Role of the Ulama in Twentieth-Century Iran," in Nikki Keddie, ed., *Scholars, Saints, and Sufis* (University of California Press, 1972), 243–44, one of Burūjirdī's most important accomplishments "was his organization of the affairs of the *marja* [supreme religious authority] on a more efficient basis: bookkeeping was introduced to record the sums of money received and dispersed . . . [from religious tithes], and a register was established of local agents authorized to collect money and forward it to Qum. This network of communication, set up by Burūjirdī, . . . survived his death and serves to disseminate guidance in political as well as narrowly religious matters." In the 1960s and 1970s, when the Shah cut state subsidies to the Shi'a clergy, they were also able to use this (and other) tithe collecting systems to sustain themselves through contributions from merchants and other devout lay people.

21. See especially Fischer; and Arjomand. Both are good on the cultural and religious-organizational underpinnings of the revolutionary movement. Fischer emphasizes more than Arjomand the broad alliance of *disparate* forces that participated in the Shah's overthrow. It was not just an Islamic movement, still less a clergy-led effort to install theocratic rule. These features became more important *after* the Shah's overthrow, in the struggle to control the institutions that would replace the former regime.

22. See, for example, Michael M. J. Fischer, "Protest and Revolution in Iran," *Harvard International Review* (March 1979), 1–6. "It is to be hoped," wrote Fischer, "that the leadership of Ayatullah Khomeini . . . has helped midwife the bourgeois revolution twice begun before. . . . In the long run, the intelligentsia's democratic and open style – religious and secular – must succeed" (6).

23. A valuable translation into English of the Constitution of the Islamic Republic of Iran appeared in *The Middle East Journal* (Spring 1980), 181–204.

24. For example: Sharif Arani, "The Theocracy Unravels," *The New Republic,* 6 December 1980, 19–21.

The Iranian Revolution

257

25. Although the launching of the Iranian Revolution in the movement of 1977–79 against the Shah challenged the generalizations I put forward in *States and Social Revolutions* about the causes of the French, Russian, and Chinese Revolutions, the struggles for power in revolutionary Iran since early 1979 actually can be understood quite straightforwardly in terms of the frame of reference I offered in Part II of the book for analyzing revolutionary outcomes. See especially Chapter 4, "What Changed and How: A Focus on State-Building."

26. Khomeini did not have to assert the messianic identity directly, for "Imam" is an ambiguous term in Iranian Shi'a discourse. It can refer simply to a prayer leader or to a leading learned cleric; or it can refer to the historic twelve Imams after Mohammed, and to the long-awaited Messiah.

27. Reproduced in the *International Herald Tribune*, 15 October 1979, 5.

28. *Ibid.*

BIBLIOGRAPHY

The notes give citations for quotations and major points. This bibliography includes other works used as general background for the article.

Abrahamian, Ervand. "The Crowd in Iranian Politics, 1905–1953." *Past and Present* (December 1968), 184–210.

Amirsadeghi, Hossein. *Twentieth-Century Iran.* New York: Holmes and Meier, 1977.

Arjomand, Said Amir. "The Shi'ite Hierocracy and the State in Pre-Modern Iran: 1785–1890." *Archives Europeénes de Sociologie* 22, 1 (1981).

Bakhash, Shaul. *Iran: Monarchy, Bureaucracy, and Reform under the Qajars, 1858–1896.* London: Ithaca Press, 1978.

Fallaci, Oriana. "Interview with Mohammed Riza Pahlavi." In *Interview with History*, trans. by John Shepley. Boston: Houghton Mifflin, 1976, 262–87.

Graham, Robert. *Iran: The Illusion of Power.* New York: St. Martin's Press, 1979.

Keddie, Nikki R. "Class Structure and Political Power in Iran Since 1796." *Iranian Studies* 11 (1978), 305–330.

Keddie, Nikki R. "The Origins of the Religious-Radical Alliance in Iran." *Past and Present* (July 1966), 70–80.

Keddie, Nikki R. "The Roots of the Ulama's Power in Modern Iran." In N. R. Keddie, ed., *Scholars, Saints and Sufis: Muslim Religious Institutions Since 1500.* Berkeley and Los Angeles: University of California Press, 1972, 211–30.

Merip Reports: Middle East Research and Information Project. "Iran's Revolution: The Rural Dimension." No. 87 (May 1980).

Merip Reports: Middle East Research and Information Project. "Iran's Revolution: The First Year." No. 88 (June 1980).

Nobari, Ali-Reza. *Iran Erupts: News and Analysis of the Iranian National Movement.* Stanford, Ca.: Iran-America Documentation Group, 1978.

Pahlavi, Mohammed Reza. *Mission for My Country.* London: Hutchinson, 1961.

Saikal, Amin. *The Rise and Fall of the Shah.* Princeton, N.J.: Princeton University Press, 1980.

Sanghvi, Ramesh. *Aryamehr: The Shah of Iran: A Political Biography.* London: Macmillan, 1968.

Thaiss, Gustav. "Religious Symbolism and Social Change: The Drama of Husain." In Nikki R. Keddie, ed., *Scholars, Saints, and Sufis: Muslim Religious Institutions Since 1500.* Berkeley and Los Angeles: University of California Press, 1972, 349–60.

Vielle, Paul. "Les Paysans, la Petite Bourgeoisie Rurale, et l'État après la Réforme Agraire en Iran." *Annales: Economies, Sociétés, Civilisations* 27 (1972), 347–372.

Zabih, Sepehr. *Iran's Revolutionary Upheaval: An Interpretative Essay.* San Francisco: Alchemy Books, 1979.

Zonis, Marvin. *The Political Elite of Iran.* Princeton, N.J.: Princeton University Press, 1971.

11

Explaining revolutions in the contemporary Third World

JEFF GOODWIN AND THEDA SKOCPOL

Frontiers of research move with history, although often with a lag. Two decades ago, most comparative research on revolutions remained focused on the classical *great revolutions* of the West: those of England, France, and Russia. Occasionally, a bold scholar included non-European revolutions (particularly the Chinese and Mexican) in broader comparative studies.[1] It was not until the mid-1970s, however, that comparative scholars began to focus on the features distinctive to Third World social revolutions – the social and political upheavals in smaller, dependent states outside of Europe. At first, perhaps, scholars supposed that such social revolutions would happen only occasionally during decolonization such as those that played themselves out after World War II. Yet modern world history has continued to be punctuated by social revolutions, not only in post-colonial Southeast Asia, Algeria, and Portuguese Africa, but also in formally independent states such as Cuba, Ethiopia, Iran, and Nicaragua. As new social revolutions have continued to occur, scholars have been challenged to broaden their scope of comparative studies beyond the classical revolutions of Europe, and they have entertained models of causation applicable across many smaller non-Western nations in the twentieth-century world context.

In this article, we point to what we consider the most promising avenues for comparative analyses of contemporary Third World revolutions. In particular, we shall offer some working hypotheses about the distinctively *political* conditions that have encouraged revolutionary movements and transfers of power in some, but not all, Third World countries.

Two myths have long colored popular views about revolutions in the Third World: that destitution, professional revolutionaries, or perhaps both are sufficient to precipitate revolutions; and that local events in Third World countries are easily manipulated by imperialist Great Powers. Thus, in attempting to explain Third World insurgencies, many people point to the incredible poverty found in large parts of Latin America, Africa, and Asia – the sort of sheer misery that capitalist industrialization and redistributive welfare states have largely eliminated, contrary to Karl Marx's expectations, in the advanced capitalist countries. Others have emphasized the role that professional revolutionaries, often backed by foreign powers, have played in "subverting" Third World regimes with the "organizational weapon" of the disciplined revolutionary party. Indeed, many see the hand of Moscow (or Beijing, Havana, or Teheran) behind Third World insurgencies, *exploiting* the social problems of these societies for their own nefarious purposes. Still others see the prime foreign influences on Third World nations as emanating from capitalist powers, especially the United States. When revolutions do not occur in poor nations, it is often suggested, it is because the United States has artificially propped up local agents of capitalist imperialism.

These ideas, however, do not take us very far toward an explanation of just why and where revolutions have occurred in some countries of the contemporary Third World, but not in others. Very many Third World countries are poor, for example, but revolutions have occurred in only a few of them, and not necessarily in the poorest. Why did China and Vietnam have social revolutions, but not India or Indonesia? Why Cuba, one of the more developed Latin American countries when Castro seized power, but not Haiti or the Dominican Republic? Why Nicaragua, but not Honduras? One need merely raise these questions in order to realize that the "misery breeds revolt" hypothesis does not explain very much. Leon Trotsky once wrote that "the mere existence of privations is not enough to cause an insurrection; if it were, the masses would be always in revolt."[2] His point is still relevant for much of today's Third World.

Similarly, although professional revolutionaries have certainly helped to organize and lead many Third World insurgencies, revolutionary groups in many, perhaps most, countries remain small and relatively insignificant sects. The Third World may be the principal theatre of revolutionary conflict in this century, but much of it remains quiescent. And when political passions *have* flared in developing countries, they have more often taken the form of ethnic or subnationalist movements than revolutions. Would-be revolutionaries, Tilly has written, "are almost always with us in the form of millenarian cults, radical cells, or rejects from positions of power. The real question," he emphasizes, "is when such contenders proliferate and/or mobilize."[3] As Goldfrank argues, explanations of revolution that focus on human misery and professional revolutionaries "are not wholly illusory, but as theory they do not take us very far. Both widespread oppression and inflammatory agitation occur with far greater frequency than revolution, or even rebellion."[4]

The great capitalist powers, furthermore, obviously cannot prevent – or reverse – all Third World revolutions, as seen in the difficulties confronted by France in Vietnam and Algeria and by the United States in Vietnam, Cuba, Nicaragua, and Iran. Imperialist interests certainly exist, but they must operate through local regimes or through *private agents* whose activities are underwritten and strongly shaped by the local regimes. And particular types of regimes in the Third World do not always reliably produce the sort of antirevolutionary stability desired in Paris or Washington, D.C. – any more than local revolution-aries can always produce the changes desired by Moscow, Havana, or Teheran.

Recent academic analyses of Third World insurgencies have helped to dispel myths such as the ones we have just criticized, yet the academic analyses have not replaced the myths with completely adequate arguments. Much of the recent comparative and theoretical literature on Third World revolutions – including the important work of Wolf, Paige, Migdal, Scott, and Popkin – investigates the role of peasants in these upheavals.[5] This body of work examines the specific grievances and motivations for peasant rebellion or peasant support for avowedly revolutionary guerrilla movements, emphasizing that much more than poverty or the activities of professional revolutionaries alone is involved. These writings argue that certain sorts of peasants – not usually the poorest – are more willing or able to rebel than others.

To be sure, the scholars who have recently analyzed Third World revolutions as peasant-based conflicts have their disagreements. At least two important and ongoing debates have come out of this work: the Wolf-Paige debate about just what sort of peasants are revolutionary, and the Scott-Popkin debate on the relative weight of economic, organizational, and cultural determinants of peas-ant behavior, and on the nature of peasants' psychological motivations for rebelling. We do not propose to rehash these debates here, however, because we believe that they have overemphasized the situation of the peasantry alone. Although the debates about peasants and revolution have enriched our under-standing of agrarian socioeconomic relations and peasant political behavior, these debates have focused insufficient analytic attention on two other issues – themselves closely related – which can take us further toward an understanding of revolutionary movements and transfers of power in the contemporary Third World. The first issue is the formation of revolutionary coalitions that invariably extend well beyond peasants alone. The second issue is the relative vulnerability of different sorts of political regimes to the formation of broad revolutionary coalitions and, perhaps, to actual overthrow by revolutionary forces. Drawing from our own recent comparative studies, as well as from political analyses by other scholars, we can explore these matters and suggest a fruitful theoretical approach to explaining why revolutions have happened in some Third World countries but not in others.[6]

FROM PEASANTS TO REVOLUTIONARY COALITIONS

Although peasants have undoubtedly been as central to most Third World insurgencies as they were for the classical social revolutions,[7] the characteriza-tion of Third World revolutions as *peasant wars* or *agrarian revolutions* – a characterization that sometimes carries an implication of homogeneous peasant communities rebelling spontaneously – has shifted our attention away from the role of other actors in revolutionary dramas. Revolutionary outbreaks and seizures of power are often carried through by coalitions, alliances, or conjunctures of struggles that cut across divides between urban and rural areas and among different social classes and ethnic groupings. (Of course, such revolutionary coalitions tend to break apart or recompose in new ways if and when they actually seize state power, but this is a subject that lies beyond the scope of this article.)

With some notable exceptions, the literature that emphasizes the role of peasants in revolutions tends to ignore the role of professional revolutionary organizations, groups that tend to be disproportionately middle class in social composition.[8] This tendency is understandable in part as a reaction against the myth that revolutions are simply the work of small conspiratorial groups of subversives. But even if professional revolutionaries cannot simply *make* revolutions where they will, they have obviously played an important role in organizing, arming, and leading many revolutionary movements. This role, moreover, is often a necessary one. Indeed, except for those peasants who happen to live in relatively autonomous and solitary villages, as did the peasants of France, Russia, and central Mexico, rural cultivators simply do not have the organizational wherewithal to rebel in the absence of outside leaders. Professional revolutionaries, furthermore, have usually been successful precisely to the extent that they have been able to work with *various sorts* of rural folk. This is another point that tends to get lost in debates about just what sorts of peasants are most rebellious. The most successful revolutionary organizations – including those in Vietnam, Zimbabwe, and Nicaragua – have won the support not just of poor or middle peasants, but also of landless and migrant laborers, rural artisans, rich peasants, and even landlords.

What is more, as Gugler and Dix have recently emphasized, urban groups have also played important, even crucial, roles in a number of Third World revolutions.[9] Indeed, the 1978–1979 overthrow of the Shah of Iran was quintessentially an urban revolution. In Cuba and Nicaragua as well as in Iran, students, professionals, clerics, and even businesspeople, as well as workers and the urban poor, joined or supported broad-based coalitions against dictatorial regimes. Gugler and Dix suggest that the participation of such people may be essential to the success of revolutionaries in all of the more urbanized countries of the contemporary Third World.

How can professional revolutionaries put together broadly based coalitions? Not surprisingly, revolutionary coalitions tend to form around preexisting nationalist, populist, or religious discourses that legitimize resistance to tyranny and, just as important, are capable of aggregating a broad array of social classes and strata. Nationalism, in particular, has proven to be a more inclusive and powerful force for revolutionary mobilization than class struggle alone. Revolutionaries have fared best where they – and not conservative or reformist leaderships – have been able to harness nationalist sentiments. Ironically then, Marxist groups in the Third World have generally been most successful when they have deemphasized class struggle and stressed the goal of national liberation instead – or, at least, when they have attempted to mobilize different types of people through the selective use of both nationalist and class appeals.

Nevertheless, it should be emphasized that revolutionary movements are much more than simply ideological movements. As Popkin and Wickham-Crowley have recently argued, revolutionary movements have won broad popular support when they have been willing and able to deliver state-like collective goods to their constituents.[10] One such collective good is the establishment of "liberated areas" secure from attack by the incumbent regime, whose repressive actions could ensure popular acquiescence with otherwise unappealing armed revolutionaries able to provide little more than a modicum of protection. In addition, the collective goods provided by revolutionaries may also include public education, health services, law and order, and economic reforms such as tax and interest reductions, the elimination of corvée labor, and land reform. Popkin notes that revolutionaries have been particularly effective in winning popular support when they have initially focused on "local goals and goods with immediate payoffs" before attempting to mobilize the population for more difficult tasks – including, ultimately, the overthrow of the incumbent regime. In Vietnam, for example, peasants "in the late 1960s still laughed about the early attempts by young Trotskyites and Communists to organize them for a national revolution, for industrialization, or even for a world revolution! Only later, when peasants (and workers) were organized around smaller and more immediate goals, were larger organizational attempts successful."[11] During the 1960s, a number of Latin American revolutionary groups, which attempted to replicate the Cuban Revolution – including the Sandinistas of Nicaragua – failed to make headway, largely because they were too quick to engage incumbent regimes in armed struggle, well before they had solidified broad popular support through the provision of collective goods.[12]

In addition to collective goods, revolutionary organizations may also offer selective incentives to encourage participation in various sorts of activities, particularly dangerous ones like actual guerrilla warfare. Such incentives for actual or potential cadres and fighters, and their families, may include extra tax or rent reductions or an additional increment of land beyond that allocated to supporters in general. In any event, it is the ongoing provision of such collective and selective goods, not ideological conversion in the abstract, that has played the principal role in solidifying social support for guerrilla armies.

The argument we have just made does not, however, support Tilly's claim that the sudden withdrawal of expected government services drives people to revolt.[13] In many Third World countries, few government services have ever *been* provided to the bulk of the population. In fact, the evidence suggests that those governments that do not deliver collective goods to people, and then repress reformers who try to do something about the absence of such services, are the governments most likely to generate support for revolutionaries. This analysis, moreover, accords with what we are beginning to learn about *ruling* revolutionary parties. Walder has recently shown that such parties obtain popular support or compliance not simply through coercion or through impersonal ideological appeals to atomized individuals (as the "totalitarian" image would have it), but through patronage and the development of networks of loyal clients.[14] Revolutionary movements that have to build social support over a long period of time operate in a similar way. In terms of what they are actually doing (and not simply what they are saying), revolutionary movements can usefully be viewed as proto-state organizations, or what Wickham-Crowley calls "guerrilla governments."[15] The presence of revolutionary movements offering collective services in territory claimed by the official state implies a situation of "dual power," in Trotsky's classic phrase.

Revolutionaries are most effective in creating such situations of dual power when they are willing and able to organize precisely those social groupings that the incumbent regime has not incorporated into its own political system. Of course, those activists in the Third World who have been schooled in classical Marxist theory have often been content with organizing the urban working class, however small its ranks, and have sometimes eschewed a strategy of armed struggle altogether, even in the face of very repressive regimes. The factors that make revolutionary cadre organizations willing to appeal to broad coalitions, as well as the (undoubtedly somewhat different) factors that prompt them to choose armed struggle, are not sufficiently well understood. Still, even revolutionaries who have attempted to mobilize broad coalitions for armed struggle have been pushed to the margins of politics when and where the regimes they have sought to topple have in some way politically incorporated important social classes and strata that might otherwise have joined revolutionary coalitions. The breadth of revolutionary coalitions is determined, in short, not just by how many groups the cadres try to organize, but also by the political space the incumbent political regime makes *available* to revolutionaries because of the regime's structural characteristics and strategies of rule. Other things being equal, the narrower the regime, and the more repressive, the broader the coalition potentially available to be mobilized by revolutionaries.

This brings us to the second issue largely neglected in recent work on peasants and revolutions, namely, the relative vulnerability of different sorts of political regimes to revolutionary coalitions. Revolutionary movements, needless to say, do not form in a political vacuum. Indeed, political context is absolutely crucial in determining whether such movements will or will not prosper. Recent work on Third World revolutions has not convincingly demonstrated that any one class, class fraction, or class alliance is any more consistently revolutionary than the industrial proletariat was supposed to have been. Exactly who becomes revolutionary, and when, is a preeminently political question. Revolutions are ultimately "made" by revolutionaries, but not of their own free will – not within political contexts they themselves have chosen, to paraphrase Karl Marx, but within very specific sorts of political contexts that are not the same for all who would make revolutions.

WHICH REGIMES ARE VULNERABLE TO THE GROWTH OF REVOLUTIONARY COALITIONS?

Revolutionary movements, history suggests, typically coalesce in opposition to closed or exclusionary, as well as organizationally weak (or suddenly weakened), authoritarian regimes. By contrast, multiparty democracies or quasi-democracies, even those in very poor countries like India, Malaysia, the Dominican Republic, and Honduras, have not facilitated the growth of revolutionary coalitions. The ballot box may not always be "the coffin of class consciousness," to use Dawley's evocative phrase, but it has proven to be the coffin of revolutionary movements.[16] Thus far, in fact, avowedly socialist revolutions – which according to classical Marxism were supposed to follow after and build upon the achievements of bourgeois-democratic revolutions – have occurred only in countries that never established liberal-democratic political systems in the first place.

In addition to liberal democracies, so-called "inclusionary" authoritarian regimes – including fascist and state-socialist regimes, as well as the single-party corporatist regimes found in some nations of Africa and Asia – have so far been immune from revolutionary transformations. Although these regimes lack civil rights, they either sponsor mass political mobilization or regulate the official representation of, and bargaining among, various social groups, including working-class and other lower-strata groups. They impose controlled forms of political participation on key social groups, co-opting leaders and handing out certain benefits in the process; this tends to undercut possibilities for political action independent of the existing regime.

Many authoritarian regimes do not, however, bother to mobilize social groups into politics, even in controlled ways; they leave the prerogatives of the state and the benefits of politics entirely in the hands of rulers and narrow cliques. Such exclusionary authoritarian regimes are conducive to the formation of broad revolutionary coalitions for a number of related reasons. First, the economic grievances of groups excluded from the political system tend to be quickly politicized. As Lipset has argued:

The exclusion of workers from the fundamental political rights of citizenship effectively fuse[s] the struggle for political and economic equality and cast[s] that struggle in a radical mold. . . . Where the right to combine in the labor market [is] severely restricted, . . . the decision to act in politics is forced on trade unions. Whether they [like] it or not, unions [must become] political institutions; they [have] first to change the distribution of political power within the state before they [can] effectively exert power in the market.[17]

Lipset is writing about urban workers, and trade-union organizations in particular, but his analysis also holds for other lower-class groups and their organizational vehicles.

Closed authoritarian regimes also provide a highly visible focus of opposition and a common enemy for groups and classes that may be nursing very different sorts of economic and political grievances (including grievances about one another). Political legitimacy is usually very problematic for authoritarian rulers, especially when religious authorities distance themselves from, or even outright oppose, such regimes, after having previously accepted them. Similarly, the political legitimacy of authoritarian rulers has sometimes been undermined simultaneously in the eyes of many groups when the rulers have orchestrated blatantly fraudulent elections in an effort to justify their continuing power.

Most importantly, perhaps, exclusionary regimes tend to radicalize, or at least neutralize, moderate and reformist politicians, including those that choose to participate in pro forma elections. Such moderates might compete with revolutionaries for popular support, or else initiate a gradual transition to a more open or inclusionary political system, typically through alliances with the armed forces. But exclusionary regimes tend to attack and undermine exactly these moderate elements.

Finally, closed authoritarian regimes, without intending to do so, valorize the potential oppositional role of armed revolutionaries. Because such regimes are so closed, they readily turn to vicious repression when faced with demands for even the most moderate political or economic adjustments. Thus closed authoritarian regimes place a premium on the things armed revolutionaries are best prepared to do – namely, provide opponents of a regime with the means of self-defense, such as guns, clandestine networks, safehouses, and even liberated territory within which to survive and carry on oppositional politics.

Of course, given exclusionary conditions, the growth of revolutionary movements is made even easier when rebels can operate in peripheral areas that the authoritarian regimes they oppose are unable to control. This happens when authoritarian regimes have never fully penetrated certain areas (as in Central America and Lusophone Africa), when they lose control of areas due to war or invasion (as in Southeast Asia), or when they are unable to prevent neighboring countries from harboring revolutionaries. "[R]evolutionary warfare and its countering," Fairbairn has suggested, "is basically competition in government. The aim of the revolutionary guerrilla is to create a kind of administrative vacuum into which it can insert its own 'parallel hierarchies' or 'alternative government.'"[18] If a kind of administrative vacuum already exists on the exclusionary regime's territory, or if it suddenly emerges, then the task of the armed revolutionaries will be the easier.

On the other hand, authoritarian regimes that are militarily and organizationally strong and have secure borders generally do not provide sufficient leeway for armed revolutionaries to mobilize mass support, even though they too tend to radicalize their opponents. Like it or not, then, some of the most brutal and repugnant authoritarian regimes in the Third World, such as those found in Latin America's southern cone, in various East Asian and Middle Eastern countries, and especially in South Africa, are probably too powerful and ruthless to be toppled by armed struggle.

From the viewpoint of would-be revolutionaries, the ideal situation is to face an exclusionary and repressive authoritarian regime that lacks strong control of its entire territory or borders (or else suddenly loses such control). During World War II, parts of Nazi-occupied Europe fit this formula. More to the point for this analysis of the contemporary Third World, quite a few states in Southeast Asia, Central America, and Africa fall into this category: they are, simultaneously, politically exclusionary, repressive, and not fully in control of their nominal territories. Facing such regimes, revolutionaries can build broad coalitions among many groups fundamentally opposed to the existing political arrangements and authorities, because many groups in society need the coercive means and uncompromising political formulas that the revolutionary cadres have to offer.

WHICH REGIMES ARE VULNERABLE TO ACTUAL OVERTHROW?

Even regimes that confront formidable revolutionary movements, however, do not invariably fall to those forces. Indeed, when speaking of regime vulnerability, a distinction should be made between vulnerability to the *formation* of a mass-based revolutionary movement within the territory a regime claims to rule, and vulnerability to actual *overthrow* by that movement. We need to understand what makes for the second type of vulnerability as well as the first, without analytically collapsing the two.

Unfortunately, the existing theoretical literature on revolutions will not give us the answers we need. Johnson has argued that "flexible" political elites can avert revolutionary takeovers by bringing about "conservative change."[19] This view might seem to account for the failure of a number of revolutionary movements, yet Johnson remains vague, to say the least, about which sorts of political leaderships, operating in which kinds of regimes, can actually accomplish this conservative change. Meanwhile, Huntington is certainly right about the very specific need certain states have to incorporate newly mobilized groups into the political system, if those states are to stave off revolutions.[20] Like Johnson, however, Huntington does not sufficiently explore why some regimes can do this and not others. Huntington argues, for example, that the great revolutions of history have taken place either in highly centralized traditional monarchies (such as Bourbon France, tsarist Russia, and imperial Manchu China) or in narrowly based military dictatorships (such as pre-1911 Mexico, pre-1952 Bolivia, pre-1944 Guatemala, and pre-1959 Cuba),[21] or in colonial regimes (such as Vietnam and Algeria after World War II). Yet, historically, not all centralized monarchies proved susceptible to revolutionary overthrow. More important for our present purposes, not all twentieth-century military dictatorships or colonial regimes have been swept away by revolutions – not even all of those that have faced strong revolutionary movements.

In our view, two specific types of exclusionary and repressive authoritarian regimes are especially vulnerable to actual overthrow by revolutionary movements: neo-patrimonial or Sultanistic dictatorships identified with a foreign power and colonial regimes based on so-called direct rule by the colonizing country. These regimes are not only much more narrowly based than other political orders, including other forms of authoritarianism, but they are also more brittle and *unreformable*. They are usually unable to bring about conservative change or the political incorporation of newly mobilized groups that might weaken existing revolutionary movements.

The susceptibility of neo-patrimonial dictatorships to revolutionary takeovers

The vulnerability to revolutionary overthrow of neo-patrimonialism – and, in particular, of the extreme sort of neo-patrimonialism often called Sultanism – has been explored in recent work by Eisenstadt and Goldstone.[22] Sultanistic neo-patrimonial regimes are centered in the personal manipulation of individual dictatorial rulers, who allow no stable group prerogatives in the polity – not even collective prerogatives for military officers or upper social and economic classes. Examples of successful revolutions against such personalist dictatorships include the 1911 Mexican Revolution against the regime of Porfirio Diaz, the 1959 Cuban Revolution against the regime of Fulgencio Batista, the 1979 Nicaraguan Revolution against the regime of Anastazio Somoza, and the 1979 Iranian Revolution against the neo-patrimonial monarchy of the Pahlavi Shahs.

Sultanistic neo-patrimonial regimes are especially vulnerable to actual overthrow by revolutionary movements for several related reasons. First, compared to more impersonal and bureaucratic forms of authoritarian rule, personalist dictators are more likely to generate elite and middle-class opposition. Landlords, businesspeople, clerics, and professionals, for example, often come to resent the blatant corruption of such dictators and their inner circle; their tendency to monopolize significant sectors of the economy; their heavy-handed control of the flow of ideas and information in schools and in the press; their use of family connections to monopolize government positions, contracts, and other business and professional opportunities; and their penchant for granting special privileges to foreign capitalists and blindly serving the geopolitical interests of great powers in exchange for foreign aid.

Second, when elites and the middle class join the political opposition, foreign backing for personalist dictators is more likely to be withdrawn, even if those dictators were long supported as the best guarantors of stability. The United States, significantly, was ultimately unwilling to support old allies like Diaz, Batista, Somoza, or the Shah in the face of the broad, multiclass opposition movements to those dictators – even as the United States failed to find or create that elusive, democratic "third force" that could stave off revolution by providing an attractive alternative to both revolution and the status quo.

Finally, the armed forces of Sultanistic neo-patrimonial regimes tend to be especially corrupt and incompetent, in part because the dictator is more concerned with preventing his own personal overthrow by military coup than with establishing an effective fighting force. Coalitions between officers and civilians that might threaten the dictator are discouraged, and reform-minded officers are incessantly purged to prevent such coalitions from coming together through coups. Thus when personalist dictators finally decide to step down after the growth of broad oppositional movements and the withdrawal of foreign sponsorship, their armies, which have been bred and winnowed for sycophantic loyalty to the leader, tend to disintegrate, opening the way for guerrilla armies or irregular forces to seize power.

Despite these special vulnerabilities, however, even long-standing neo-patrimonial dictatorships are not invariably swept away by revolutionaries, and they may not even have to confront significant revolutionary movements.[23] As we suggested earlier, radical groups may simply eschew a strategy of armed struggle, even under very repressive conditions. In addition, the armed forces of neo-patrimonial dictatorship – their lack of professionalism notwithstanding – may still manage to control dissidence on their territory and police their borders, leaving little space for revolutionaries to mobilize. Elites and middle classes are not always driven into a coalition with revolutionaries, furthermore, especially if the dictator dispenses patronage according to more or less rational and impersonal criteria and does not repress the moderate opposition in too heavy-handed a fashion. Also, ethnic divisions among the populace may prove too durable and fractious for revolutionaries to bridge, even in the presence of a dictator despised by all. Eisenstadt, in fact, has argued that neo-patrimonial societies make things difficult for revolutionaries, because such societies tend to be characterized by ascriptive, especially ethnic and religious, forms of organization and by the circulation of the elite cliques.[24] Combinations of many of the conditions listed in this paragraph seem to explain why the dictatorship of Mobutu Sese Seko of Zaire has survived for so long, and may account for the recent displacement of Alfredo Stroessner of Paraguay by a rival elite faction.

If neo-patrimonial dictators grant civilian and military moderates some minimal breathing room, furthermore, the threat posed by an emerging (or even potential) revolutionary movement may help forge a civilian-military alliance capable of removing the dictator. This alliance may, in turn, broaden political participation before revolutionaries become sufficiently powerful to bid for power. Ferdinand Marcos of the Philippines and François Duvalier of Haiti were recently ousted in this manner, although the civilian component of the transition in Haiti has been relatively weak. And in the Philippines, it is too soon to tell whether the democratic opening engineered by Corazon Aquino and her followers will overcome tendencies toward reaction and revolution.

It bears emphasizing, too, that *all* of the counterrevolutionary tasks described above – territorial control, the co-optation or accommodation of elites and the middle class, the removal of an unpopular leader, and the transition to a more open political regime – are more easily accomplished by bureaucratic- (as opposed to neo-patrimonial) authoritarian regimes. Indeed, bureaucratic-authoritarian regimes give power and prerogatives to collectives – such as cohorts of military officers – who can bargain with, or even displace, one another without unraveling the regime. But Sultanistic neo-patrimonial regimes pit personal dictators against elites, and elites against one another, rendering political stability highly dependent on the unrelenting wiliness and vigilance of the individual ruler. Sooner or later, however, individual sultans falter or die; and sons, such as the second Iranian Shah or Haiti's "Baby Doc," often prove less strong-willed than their fathers.

The analysis in this section, we might note, raises questions about Tilly's argument that revolutionary movements are more likely to succeed when they can forge alliances with "polity members."[25] Coalitions between polity members and what Tilly calls "challenger groups" are often, if not always, antirevolutionary in their consequences. In fact, such coalitions may be formed precisely in order to prevent the further growth of movements led by radical political forces. Contrary to Tilly's hypothesis, social-revolutionary movements seem more likely to seize power when civilian-military coalitions are *unable* to form and initiate a political *opening* from above.

The vulnerability of directly ruled colonies

The connection between revolution and particular types of colonial rule has not been explored to the same extent as the connection between revolution and neo-patrimonialism. However, so-called direct colonial rule – which occurs when a colony is governed directly by metropolitan officials, and indigenous elites are not allowed to share power nor readied to accept sovereignty after colonialism ends – shares a number of similarities with personalist dictatorships. The resemblances to neo-patrimonialism render direct colonialism especially vulnerable to revolutionary overthrow. Examples of directly ruled colonies that gave way to broadly based revolutionary coalitions include the former French colonies of Vietnam and Algeria and Portugal's former African colonies, Guinea-Bissau, Angola, and Mozambique. Currently, moreover, direct colonial rule or its equivalent confronts broadly based nationalist movements of a more or less radical complexion in a number of territories: the Israeli-occupied West Bank and Gaza Strip; the Western Sahara, a former Spanish colony now occupied by

Morocco; Eritrea, a former Italian colony that was absorbed into Ethiopia; Namibia, a former German colony now occupied by South Africa; East Timor, a former Portuguese colony absorbed into Indonesia; and New Caledonia, a French colony in the South Pacific.

Direct colonial rule cannot easily give way to a stable, nonrevolutionary political system led by either military or civilian elements, for a number of interrelated reasons. Like neo-patrimonialism, direct colonial rule – authoritarian by definition and typically quite repressive – also radicalizes its political opponents. Direct colonialism undermines actual or potential moderate and reformist leaderships since, unlike indirect colonialism, it does not attempt to preserve a traditional indigenous elite or to create a new one so that formal political power may one day be "safely" transferred to the colony without jeopardizing the colonizer's economic interests. Direct colonial rule also tends to create more indigenous elite and middle-class opposition than indirect colonial rule. Important business and professional opportunities, as well as upper-level administrative positions, are reserved by and for the colonialists. That exclusion from such positions is based on an explicitly racial criterion, and not on education or ability more generally, can only heighten the alienation of indigenous upper-class and middle-class elements from the colonialists.

The colonial power, like a personalist dictator, also provides a common and highly visible focus of opposition for groups that may have very different reasons for seeking national independence. The armed forces in such colonies, moreover, are not likely to be a force for reform. Direct colonial armies are led by officers whose principal loyalties are to the colonial power and who have few if any connections to indigenous political groups with an interest in decolonization. To be sure, officers and soldiers within direct colonial armies may end up calling for a retreat from colonial wars (as happened in the Portuguese colonial situation at the bitter end). But the sudden withdrawal of colonial armies – like the flight of a dictator – may simply open the way for revolutionaries to seize power.

In addition, directly ruled colonies, like neo-patrimonial dictatorships identified with a foreign power, create contexts in which political symbols of nationalism and cultural self-assertion may be harnessed by revolutionaries in addition to the forces of class struggle. In both types of exclusionary authoritarian regimes, economically rooted grievances come to be directed at political rulers backed by foreign powers, as well as at foreign landlords and businesspeople; as a result, such grievances overlap with and may therefore be subsumed, at least in part, within more inclusive demands for *national liberation.* Of course, revolutionaries who confront such regimes typically struggle with balancing class and nationalist issues, but this is a blessed dilemma that their counterparts in indirectly ruled colonies or in independent authoritarian regimes less closely tied to a foreign power do not have the opportunity to confront.

Compared to direct colonialism, indirect colonial rule – as well as more impersonal and bureaucratic forms of authoritarianism in independent countries – tends to be both militarily stronger and more coherent as well as more capable of a transition to an independent and more inclusive political system, including parliamentary democracy. Indirect colonial rule, as noted above, purposely grooms a reliable elite to whom formal political power can be transferred without jeopardizing the economic interests of the colonizer. The armed forces in such colonies, moreover, recruit officers from the indigenous population who tend to have strong loyalties to the local society – as opposed to the colonizing power – or at least strong corporate loyalties, which set them apart from the colonialists. Such officers often become linked to broader forces in the local society that favor political reform and national independence. In contrast, officers in directly ruled colonies and neo-patrimonial regimes are chosen and promoted for their loyalty to the colonizing power or for their purely personal loyalty to the dictator and thus they either cannot or do not form ties to reformist political elites.

Given these considerations, it is not surprising that a number of indirectly ruled colonies *defeated* mass-based revolutionary movements during the 1940s and 1950s, through a combination of military might and transitions to independent or more open political systems. Examples of this phenomenon happened in Malaya, Kenya, and the Philippines. Less formidable rebellions, moreover, were also defeated or contained in India, Indonesia, and Burma. As these lists suggest, the British were particularly adept at avoiding revolutions in their colonies through the use of indirect rule. Significantly, the white settler community in what was then known as Southern Rhodesia unilaterally declared independence from Britain in 1965, precisely in order to avoid a similar process of decolonization. White rule, however, undercut the potential influence of black moderates in Zimbabwe and ensured that armed revolutionaries would dominate the nationalist cause.

More recent political transitions in the formally independent countries of El Salvador, Guatemala, and Peru – all countries where powerful leftist insurgencies are currently underway – have led to the political incorporation of centrist and even some leftist parties and organizations. The political opening in Peru was the most extensive, and its breadth was undoubtedly related to the fact that it was not a calculated response to insurgency, but occurred, coincidentally, just as the insurgency began in that country. Whether the political openings in any of these countries will be sufficiently extensive to thwart armed leftist insurgencies remains uncertain, however, particularly in El Salvador, where the armed forces are not especially professional nor the recent political opening especially broad. However, these openings did remove unpopular dictators and are likely to guarantee a continued flow of foreign aid, particularly from the United States. Analogous to the empowerment of indigenous elites in indirectly ruled colonies, these political openings in independent and more bureaucratic authoritarian regimes explain why guerrillas cannot easily come to power. In instances like these, prolonged and even stalemated military struggles can go on and on, while the proponents of reform, revolution, and reaction fight it out.

CONCLUSION

As summarized in Figure 11.1 and Table 11.1, our analysis suggests that revolutionaries in the contemporary Third World are most likely to succeed when civil society as a whole can be politically mobilized to oppose an autonomous and narrowly based direct colonial regime or a Sultanistic neo-patrimonial regime. In her recent comparative study of the Iranian and Nicaraguan revolutions, Farhi suggests that the "most important characteristic of the Iranian and Nicaraguan pre-revolutionary states was their almost total autonomy from internal classes."[26] This has been a characteristic, in fact, of virtually all Third World states that have been toppled by revolutions. In contrast, when radicals confront a state with significant social connections – even if the state is authoritarian and its ties are restricted to the middle and upper classes – then revolutionary coalition building becomes very difficult. Furthermore, if a state traditionally allied with economic elites can politically incorporate at least some popular sectors or organizations, then the prospects for revolutionary success become still more remote.

It follows from what we have argued that the Third World has been the

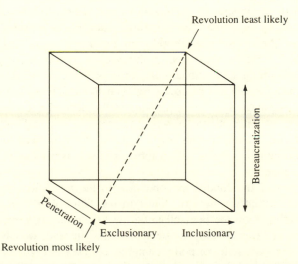

Figure 11.1. A graphic representation of states according to degrees of (1) *penetration* of national territory, (2) *incorporation* of socially mobilized groups, and (3) *bureaucratization* of the state administration and armed forces.

Table 11.1. *Some characteristics of exclusionary polities*

Patrimonial dictatorships and directly ruled colonies	Bureaucratic-authoritarian regimes and indirectly ruled colonies
Relative weak, corrupt, and disorganized civil administration and army	Stronger and more coherent civil administration and army
Political openings difficult: military reformism and civil-military pacts unlikely	Political openings easier: military reformism and civil-military pacts more likely
Basis for popular and elite opposition to ruler	Elite opposition much less likely
External support more likely to be withdrawn, especially as elite opposition develops	External support more likely to persist, especially following a political opening
Probability of state disintegration when dictator or colonial power departs or is removed	State disintegration less likely during political crises and transitions

principal site of social revolutions in this century, not simply because of the poverty or socioeconomic structures one finds there. The Third World is also where one finds most of the world's exclusionary and repressive political systems, based in administrative organizations and armies that do not fully penetrate civil society or control the territories they claim to rule. By contrast, democratic polities in the First World, and a combination of Communist party patronage and coercive repression in the Second World, have prevented the emergence of strong revolutionary movements (or else, as in Poland, have staved off outright seizures of power by such movements). The unraveling of Communist patronage systems in portions of the Second World may allow the future growth of oppositional movements there. These will often be ethnic separatist, however, rather than revolutionary; and it is hard to imagine that threatened Communist armies will crumble or retreat as patrimonial and colonial armies have done.

Our analysis of the conditions conducive to the formation of revolutionary coalitions and actual transfers of power in the Third World has shifted away from the emphases on the peasantry and the effects of commercial capitalism that characterized earlier comparative approaches. Instead, we have followed in the footsteps of such state- or polity-centered analyses of revolutions as Samuel Huntington's *Political Order in Changing Societies,* Charles Tilly's *From Mobilization to Revolution,* and Theda Skocpol's *States and Social Revolutions* – although the hypotheses offered here go beyond what any of these books had to offer.

We have suggested that the structures of states and armies, as well as the political relations between states and various sectors of society, provide the keys to explaining revolutions in the Third World. Revolutionary coalitions have formed and expanded in countries in which one finds not only poverty, imperialism, professional revolutionaries, and peasants of a certain sort, but also political exclusion and severe and indiscriminate (while not overwhelming) repression. In turn, revolutionary movements have actually succeeded in overthrowing those regimes that have been rendered brittle and unreformable by the structural features and strategies of rule characteristic of direct colonialism and Sultanistic neo-patrimonial dictatorship.

Revolutionary movements will undoubtedly continue to emerge in the Third World, where many states are not only exclusionary, but also fiscally, administratively, and militarily weak. And if the past is any guide, such movements will be especially likely to triumph where the political regimes they oppose remain narrow as well as repressive.

NOTES

1. For example: Samuel P. Huntington, *Political Order in Changing Societies* (New Haven, Conn.: Yale University Press, 1968); Barrington Moore, Jr., *Social Origins of Dictatorship and Democracy: Lord and Peasant in the Making of the Modern World* (Boston: Beacon Press, 1967); and Eric R. Wolf, *Peasant Wars of the Twentieth Century* (New York: Harper and Row, 1969).
2. Leon Trotsky, *The History of the Russian Revolution,* trans. Max Eastman (New York: Monad Press, 1961; originally 1932), p. 249.
3. Charles Tilly, *From Mobilization to Revolution* (Reading, Mass.: Addison-Wesley, 1978), p. 202.
4. Walter L. Goldfrank, "The Mexican Revolution," in *Revolutions: Theoretical, Comparative, and Historical Studies,* ed. Jack A. Goldstone (San Diego, Calif.: Harcourt Brace Jovanovich, 1986), p. 105. This article originally appeared in *Theory and Society* in 1979.
5. See: Wolf, *Peasant Wars;* Jeffery M. Paige, *Agrarian Revolution: Social Movements and Export Agriculture in the Underdeveloped World* (New York: Free Press, 1975); Joel Migdal, *Peasants, Politics, and Revolution* (Princeton, N.J.: Princeton University Press, 1974); James Scott, *The Moral Economy of the Peasant* (New Haven, Conn.: Yale University Press, 1976); James Scott, "Hegemony and the Peasantry," *Politics & Society* 7 (1977): 267–296; and Samuel L. Popkin, *The Rational Peasant* (Berkeley: University of California Press, 1979).
6. In addition to the works of other scholars cited below, we are drawing upon: Jeff Goodwin, "Revolutionary Movements in Central America: A Comparative Analysis," working paper No. 0007, *Working Paper Series, Center for Research on Politics and Social Organization* (Cambridge, Mass.: Department of Sociology, Harvard University, 1988); Jeff Goodwin, "Revolutionary Movements in Southeast Asia, 1940–1954: A Comparative Analysis," working paper No. 0008, *Working Paper Series, Center for Research on Politics and Social Organization* (Cambridge, Mass.: Department of Sociology, Harvard University, 1988); Jeff Goodwin, "States and Revolutions in the Third World: A Comparative Analysis" (Ph.D. diss., Harvard University, November 1988); Theda Skocpol, "What Makes Peasants Revolution-

ary?" *Comparative Politics* 14, no. 3 (April 1982): 351–375; and Theda Skocpol, "Rentier State and Shi'a Islam in the Iranian Revolution," *Theory and Society* 11, no. 3 (May 1982): 265–283.

7. On peasants in the classic social revolutions, see Theda Skocpol, *States and Social Revolutions: A Comparative Analysis of France, Russia, and China* (Cambridge, Eng.: Cambridge University Press, 1979), chapter 3.

8. Exceptions to this include Migdal, *Peasants, Politics, and Revolution;* and John Dunn, *Modern Revolutions* (Cambridge, Eng.: Cambridge University Press, 1972).

9. Robert H. Dix, "The Varieties of Revolution," *Comparative Politics* 15 (1983): 281–294; Robert H. Dix, "Why Revolutions Succeed and Fail," *Polity* 16 (1984): 423–446; and Josef Gugler, "The Urban Character of Contemporary Revolutions," *Studies in Comparative International Development* 27 (1982): 60–73.

10. Popkin, *Rational Peasant;* and Timothy P. Wickham-Crowley, "The Rise (and Sometimes Fall) of Guerrilla Governments in Latin America," *Sociological Forum* 2 (1987): 473–499.

11. Popkin, *Rational Peasant,* p. 262.

12. Richard Gott, *Guerrilla Movements in Latin America* (Garden City, N.Y.: Doubleday, 1971).

13. See Tilly, *From Mobilization to Revolution,* pp. 204–205.

14. See Andrew Walder, *Communist Neo-Traditionalism: Work and Authority in Chinese Industry* (Berkeley: University of California Press, 1986).

15. Wickham-Crowley, "Guerrilla Governments in Latin America."

16. Alan Dawley, *Class and Community: The Industrial Revolution in Lynn* (Cambridge, Mass.: Harvard University Press, 1976), p. 70.

17. Seymour Martin Lipset, "Radicalism or Reformism: The Sources of Working-class Politics," *American Political Science Review* 77 (1983): 7.

18. Geoffrey Fairbairn, *Revolutionary Guerrilla Warfare: The Countryside Version* (Harmondsworth, Eng.: Penguin Books, 1974), p. 139.

19. Chalmers Johnson, *Revolutionary Change,* 2d ed., rev. (Palo Alto, Calif.: Stanford University Press, 1982), pp. 95–109.

20. Huntington, *Political Order in Changing Societies,* especially chapter 5.

21. Ibid., p. 275. For Guatemala, Huntington seems to have in mind the short-lived democratic political transition of 1944 away from the dictatorship of General Jorge Ubico. Most analysts, however, ourselves included, do not consider this a social revolution or (in Huntington's terms) a "great revolution."

22. S. N. Eisenstadt, *Revolution and the Transformation of Societies* (New York: Free Press, 1978); and Jack A. Goldstone, "Revolutions and Superpowers," in *Superpowers and Revolutions,* ed. Jonathan P. Adelman (New York: Praeger, 1986). Of course, these scholars are elaborating ideas borrowed from the classic comparative political sociology of Max Weber.

23. In this and the following paragraphs, we have drawn insights especially from Richard Snyder, "A Comparative Analysis of the Vulnerability of Sultanistic Regimes to Revolution," unpublished Senior Honors Essay, Committee on Degrees in Social Studies, Harvard College, 1989. Snyder examines in depth the cases of Haiti, Paraguay, the Philippines, and Zaire.

24. Eisenstadt, *Revolution and the Transformation of Societies,* especially pp. 282–285.

25. Tilly, *From Mobilization to Revolution,* pp. 213–214.

26. Farideh Farhi, "State Disintegration and Urban-Based Revolutionary Crisis: A Comparative Analysis of Iran and Nicaragua," *Comparative Political Studies* 21 (1988): 231–256.

BIBLIOGRAPHY

Dawley, Alan, *Class and Community: The Industrial Revolution in Lynn.* Cambridge, Mass.: Harvard University Press, 1976.

Dix, Robert H., "The Varieties of Revolution," *Comparative Politics* 15 (1983): 281–294.

Dix, Robert H., "Why Revolutions Succeed and Fail," *Polity* 16 (1984): 423–446.

Dunn, John, *Modern Revolutions.* Cambridge, Eng.: Cambridge University Press, 1972.

Eisenstadt, S. N., *Revolution and the Transformation of Societies.* New York: Free Press 1978.

Fairbairn, Geoffrey, *Revolutionary Guerrilla Warfare: The Countryside Version.* Harmondsworth, Eng.: Penguin 1974.

Farhi, Farideh, "State Disintegration and Urban-Based Revolutionary Crisis: A Comparative Analysis of Iran and Nicaragua," *Comparative Political Studies* 21 (1988): 231–256.

Goldfrank, Walter L., "The Mexican Revolution" in *Revolutions: Theoretical, Comparative, and Historical Studies,* ed. Jack A. Goldstone. San Diego, Calif.: Harcourt Brace Jovanovich 1986, pp. 104–117.

Goldstone, Jack, "Revolutions and Superpowers" in *Superpowers and Revolutions,* ed. Jonathan R. Adelman. New York: Praeger 1986, pp. 38–48.

Goodwin, Jeff, "Revolutionary Movements in Central America: A Comparative Analysis," working paper No. 0007, *Working Paper Series, Center for Research on Politics and Social Organization.* Department of Sociology, Harvard University, Cambridge, Mass. 1988.

Goodwin, Jeff, "Revolutionary Movements in Southeast Asia, 1940–1954: A Comparative Analysis," working paper No. 0008, *Working Paper Series, Center for Research on Politics and Social Organization.* Department of Sociology, Harvard University, Cambridge, Mass., 1988.

Goodwin, Jeff, "States and Revolutions in the Third World: A Comparative Analysis," unpublished Ph.D. dissertation, Department of Sociology, Harvard University, Cambridge, Mass., 1988.

Gott, Richard, *Guerrilla Movements in Latin America.* Garden City, N.Y.: Doubleday 1971.

Gugler, Josef, "The Urban Character of Contemporary Revolutions," *Studies in Comparative International Development* 27 (1982): 60–73.

Huntington, Samuel P., *Political Order in Changing Societies.* New Haven, Conn.: Yale University Press 1968.

Johson, Chalmers, *Revolutionary Change,* 2d ed., rev. Palo Alto, Calif.: Stanford University Press 1982.

Lipset, Seymour Martin, "Radicalism or Reformism: The Sources of Working-class Politics," *American Political Science Review* 77 (1983): 1–18.

Migdal, Joel, *Peasants, Politics, and Revolution.* Princeton, N.J.: Princeton University Press 1974.

Moore, Barrington, Jr., *Social Origins of Dictatorship and Democracy: Lord and Peasant in the Making of the Modern World.* Boston: Beacon Press 1967.

Paige, Jeffery M., *Agrarian Revolution: Social Movements and Export Agriculture in the Underdeveloped World.* New York: Free Press 1975.

Popkin, Samuel, *The Rational Peasant.* Berkeley: University of California Press 1979.

Scott, James, *The Moral Economy of the Peasant.* New Haven, Conn.: Yale University Press 1976.

Scott, James, "Hegemony and the Peasantry," *Politics & Society* 7 (1977): 267–296.

Skocpol, Theda, *States and Social Revolutions: A Comparative Analysis of France, Russia, and China.* Cambridge, Eng.: Cambridge University Press 1979.

Skocpol, Theda, "Rentier State and Shi'a Islam in the Iranian Revolution," *Theory and Society* 11 (1982): 265–283.

Skocpol, Theda, "What Makes Peasants Revolutionary?" *Comparative Politics* 14 (1982): 351–375.

Snyder, Richard, "A Comparative Analysis of the Vulnerability of Sultanistic Regimes to Revolution," senior honors essay, Committee on Degrees in Social Studies, Harvard University, Cambridge, Mass. 1989.

Tilly, Charles, *From Mobilization to Revolution.* Reading, Mass.: Addison-Wesley 1978.

Trotsky, Leon, *The History of the Russian Revolution,* trans. Max Eastman. New York: Monad Press 1961.

Walder, Andrew, *Communist Neo-Traditionalism: Work and Authority in Chinese Industry.* Berkeley: University of California Press 1986.

Wickham-Crowley, Timothy P., "The Rise (and Sometimes Fall) of Guerrilla Governments in Latin America," *Sociological Forum* 2 (1987): 473–499.

Wolf, Eric R., *Peasant Wars of the Twentieth Century.* New York: Harper and Row 1969.

12

Social revolutions and mass military mobilization

"The changes in the state order which a revolution produces are no less important than the changes in the social order."[1] Franz Borkenau's insight, published in 1937, has become the central theme of more recent comparative studies. "A complete revolution," writes Samuel P. Huntington in *Political Order in Changing Societies,* "involves . . . the creation and institutionalization of a new political order," into which an "explosion" of popular participation in national affairs is channeled.[2] Similarly, in my *States and Social Revolutions: A Comparative Analysis of France, Russia, and China,* I argue that in "each New Regime, there was much greater popular incorporation into the state-run affairs of the nation. And the new state organizations forged during the Revolutions were more centralized and rationalized than those of the Old Regime."[3]

Huntington has developed his arguments about revolutionary accomplishments in critical dialogue with liberal-minded modernization theorists, while I have developed mine in critical dialogue with Marxian class analysts. Modernization theorists and Marxians both analyze revolutionary transformations primarily in relation to long-term socioeconomic change. These scholars also highlight the contributions of certain revolutions to liberalism or to democratic socialism – that is, to "democracy" understood *in opposition to* authoritarian state power.

The classical Marxist vision on revolutionary accomplishments was unblinkingly optimistic. According to this view, "bourgeois revolutions" clear away obstacles to capitalist economic development and lay the basis for historically progressive but socially limited forms of liberal democracy. "Proletarian revolu-

This essay is a revised version of a paper originally presented at the thematic panel, "Attacking the Leviathan: States and Social Conflicts," at the Annual Meeting of the American Political Science Association in Washington, DC, September 3, 1984. During the process of revision, I benefited from comments and criticisms by the members of the 1986–87 Harvard CFIA Seminar on International Institutions and Cooperation, and by the members of the 1986–87 Workshop on Politics and Social Organization in the Harvard Department of Sociology. The suggestions of Jeff Goodwin, Marta Gil, and John Hall were especially helpful.

tions," in turn, create the conditions for classless economies and for universal social and political democracy, accompanied by the progressive "withering away of the state." The first modern social revolution to be accomplished in the name of Marxism, the Russian Revolution of 1917, obviously belied this vision, however, for it established a communist dictatorship that ruled in the name of the proletariat while actually exploiting workers for purposes of crash industrialization, and imposing a brutal "internal colonialism" on the peasant majority.[4]

Reacting to the Stalinist denouement of the Russian Revolution, liberal-minded theorists operating within the broad framework of modernization theory have offered their own view of the accomplishments of revolutions. Theorists as disparate as S. N. Eisenstadt and Michael Walzer agree that the only salutary revolutions have been the mildest ones – the least violent and the least suddenly transformative of preexisting social and political relations.[5] In contrast to such supposedly liberal revolutions as the French and the English, the more severe and thoroughgoing revolutions boomeranged to produce totalitarian dictatorships – more penetrating authoritarian regimes – rather than democratization as these modernization theorists understand it.

Modernization theorists, moreover, tend to view the political aspects of the revolutions as inefficient and probably temporary aberrations in the course of socioeconomic development. An ideologically committed vanguard may rise to central-state power – and perhaps stay there – through the mobilization and manipulation of grass roots political organizations such as militias, workplace councils, or neighborhood surveillance committees. From the perspective of modernization theorists, however, this kind of revolutionary political mobilization – known either as "the terror" or as totalitarianism, depending on whether it is a phase or an institutionalized outcome in any given revolution – is both morally reprehensible and technically inefficient for dealing with the practical tasks that modern governments must face.

Converging on what might be called a realist perspective, analysts like Huntington and myself have reached different conclusions about the political accomplishments of revolutions. In the realist view, a special sort of democratization – understood not as an extension of political liberalism or the realization of democratic socialism, but as an enhancement of popular involvement in national political life – *accompanies* the revolutionary strengthening of centralized national states directed by authoritarian executives or political parties.

Briefly put, this happens because during revolutionary interregnums competition among elites for coercive and authoritative control spurs certain leadership groups to mobilize previously politically excluded popular forces by means of both material and ideological incentives. Popular participation is especially sought in the forging of organizations that can be used to subdue less "radical" contenders. New state organizations – armies, administrations, committees of surveillance, and so forth – are at once authoritarian and unprecedentedly mass-mobilizing. In some revolutions, especially those involving prolonged guerrilla wars, this process works itself out prior to the formal seizure of national-state power; in others, especially those in which inter-elite struggles are fought out in urban street battles, it tends to occur during and after that seizure. Either way, the logic of state-building through which social revolutions are successfully accomplished promotes both authoritarianism and popular mobilization.

In the realist view, moreover, the strengthened political and state orders that emerge from social-revolutionary transformations may perform some kinds of tasks very effectively – certainly more effectively than did the old regimes they displaced. But which tasks? Perhaps because we have argued with the modernization and Marxian theorists, Huntington and I tend to explore the accomplishments of revolutionary regimes in such areas as maintaining political order during the course of socioeconomic transformation, enforcing individual or collective property rights, and promoting state-led industrialization. Yet I would argue that the task which revolutionized regimes in the modern world have performed best is the mobilization of citizen support across class lines for protracted international warfare.

There is a straightforward reason why this should be true: the types of organizations formed and the political ties forged between revolutionary vanguards and supporters (in the course of defeating other elites and consolidating the new regime's state controls) can readily be converted to the tasks of mobilizing resources, including dedicated officers and soldiers, for international warfare. Guerrilla armies and their support systems are an obvious case in point. So are urban militias and committees of surveillance, which seem to have served as splendid agencies for military recruitment from the French Revolution to the Iranian. Moreover, if revolutionary leaders can find ways to link a war against foreigners to domestic power struggles, they may be able to tap into broad nationalist feelings – as well as exploit class and political divisions – in order to motivate supporters to fight and die on behalf of the new regime. Talented members of families that supported the old regime can often be recruited to the revolutionary-nationalist cause, along with enthusiasts from among those who had previously been excluded from national politics.

Whether we in the liberal-democratic West like to acknowledge it or not, the authoritarian regimes brought to power through revolutionary transformations – from the French Revolution of the late 18th century to the Iranian Revolution of the present – have been democratizing in the mass-mobilizing sense. The best evidence of this has been the enhanced ability of such revolutionized regimes to conduct humanly costly wars with a special fusion of popular zeal, meritocratic professionalism, and central coordination. Whatever the capacities of revolutionary regimes to cope with tasks of economic development (and the historical record suggests that those capacities are questionable), they seem to excel at motivating their populations to make supreme sacrifices for the nation in war.

That is no mean accomplishment in view of the fact that the prerevolutionary polities in question excluded most of the people from symbolic or practical participation in national politics.

In the remainder of this brief essay, I will illustrate the plausibility of these arguments by surveying two groups of social revolutions in modern world history. First, I will examine the classic social revolutions that transformed the imperial-monarchical states of Bourbon France, Romanov Russia, and Manchu China, probing their accomplishments in relation to the expectations of the liberal, Marxian, and realist perspectives just outlined. Then I will discuss a number of the nation-building social revolutions that have transformed postcolonial and neocolonial countries in the 20th century. I shall pay special attention to the ways in which the geopolitical contexts of particular revolutions have facilitated or discouraged the channeling of popular political participation into defensive and aggressive wars. Whether "communist" or not, I argue, revolutionary elites have been able to build the strongest states in those countries whose geopolitical circumstances allowed or required the emerging new regimes to become engaged in protracted and labor-intensive international warfare.

Can one make rigorous statements about the geopolitical circumstances that affect revolutions in progress, and that are in turn affected by them? Revolutionary outbreaks do seem to make wars more likely because domestic conflicts tend to spill over to involve foreign partners, and because revolutions create perceived threats and opportunities for other states. Beyond this, however, no glib generalizations are possible; for example, more sweeping revolutions do not automatically generate greater wars or stronger efforts at foreign intervention. As we are about to see, the geopolitical contexts of social revolutions in the modern world have varied greatly; so have the intersections of domestic state-building struggles with international threats or conflicts. At this point in the development of knowledge about these matters, the best way to proceed is through exploratory analyses and comparisons of a wide range of historical cases.

SOCIAL REVOLUTIONS AND WAR-MAKING IN FRANCE, RUSSIA, AND CHINA

The word "revolution" did not take on its modern connotation of a fundamental sociopolitical change accompanied by violent upheavals from below until the French Revolution of the late 18th century.[6] This etymological fact appropriately signals the reality that the French Revolution (unlike the English, Dutch, and American) was a *social* revolution, in which class-based revolts from below, especially peasant revolts against landlords, propelled sudden transformations in the class structure along with permanently centralizing changes in the structures of state power. In *States and Social Revolutions*, I group the French Revolution for comparative analysis with the Russian Revolution from

1917 to the 1930s and with the Chinese Revolution from 1911 to the 1960s. The French Revolution, I argue, was neither primarily "bourgeois" in the Marxist sense nor "liberal" in the modernization sense. Nor was the Russian Revolution "proletarian" in the Marxist sense. Rather, the French, Russian, and Chinese revolutions, despite important variations, displayed striking similarities of context, cause, process, and outcomes.

All three classic social revolutions occurred in large, previously independent, predominantly agrarian monarchical states that found themselves pressured militarily by economically more developed competitors on the international scene. Social revolutions were sufficiently caused when (a) the centralized, semibureaucratic administrative and military organizations of the old regimes disintegrated due to combinations of international pressures and disputes between monarchs and landed commercial upper classes, and (b) widespread peasant revolts took place against landlords. After more or less protracted struggles by political forces trying to consolidate new state organizations, all three revolutions resulted in more centralized and mass-mobilizing national states, more powerful in relation to all domestic social groups, and also more powerful than the prerevolutionary regimes had been in relation to foreign competitors. In particular, all three social revolutions markedly raised their nations' capacities to wage humanly costly wars.[7]

The differences in the outcomes and accomplishments of the French, Russian, and Chinese revolutions are not well explained by referring, as a Marxist analyst would do, to the greater role of bourgeois class forces in the French case or to the unique contributions of proletarian revolts to the urban struggles of 1917 in Russia. Nor can one explain the different outcomes, as the modernization theorists do, by suggesting that the milder, less violent, and less thoroughgoing the revolutionary conflicts and changes, and the briefer the rule of an ideological vanguard, the more efficient and liberal-democratic the revolutionary outcome. None of these revolutions had a liberal-democratic outcome, and none of them resulted in a socialist democracy. Instead, the differences in the essentially mass-mobilizing and authoritarian outcomes and accomplishments of the French, Russian, and Chinese revolutions are in large part attributable to the international geopolitical contexts in which the conflicts of these revolutions played themselves out. They are also attributable to the political relationships established, during and immediately after the revolutionary interregnums, between state-building leaderships and rebellious lower classes. One feature that these three social revolutions have in common is that all of them enhanced national capacities to wage humanly costly foreign wars.

The French Revolution has typically been characterized as a modernizing liberal-democratic revolution or as a bourgeois, capitalist revolution. In terms of economics, it is difficult if not impossible to show that the French Revolution was necessary for the "economic modernization" or "capitalist development" of France: the absolutist old regime had been facilitating commercialization and petty industry just as much as postrevolutionary regimes did.[8] Politically, more-over, analysts tend to forget that the end result of the French Revolution was not any form of liberalism, but Napoleon's nationalist dictatorship, which left the enduring legacy of a highly centralized and bureaucratic French state with a recurrent tendency to seek national glory through military exploits.

The political phases of the French Revolution from 1789 through 1800 cer-tainly included attempts to institutionalize civil liberties and electoral democ-racy, as well as the important legalization of undivided private property rights for peasants and bourgeois alike. Moreover, the fact that the French Revolution created a private-propertied society rather than a party-state that aspired to manage the national economy directly left open space for the eventual emer-gence of liberal-democratic political arrangements in France. At the time of the Revolution itself, however, democratization was more emphatically and enduringly furthered through "careers open to talent" in the military officer corps, through mass military conscription, and through the more efficient press-ing of the state's fiscal demands on all citizens.

From a European continental perspective, the most striking and consequential accomplishment of the French Revolution was its ability to launch highly mobile armies of motivated citizen-soldiers, coordinated with enhanced deployment of artillery forces. The Jacobins from 1792 to 1794 began the process of amal-gamating political commissioners and *sans-culotte* militias with the remnants of the royal standing armies.[9] Even though they did not find a way to stabilize their "Republic of Virtue," the Montagnard Jacobins fended off the most pressing domestic and international counterrevolutionary threats. Yet their fall was not the end of military mass-mobilization in France. Napoleon consolidated a con-servative bureaucratic regime and came to terms with private property holders (including the peasant smallholders) and with the Church (including the local priests so influential with the peasantry). Then he expanded the process of French military mobilization, deploying citizen armies of an unprecedented size and a capacity for rapid maneuver.[10] The enhanced popular political participa-tion and the messianic sense of French nationalism and democratic mission unleashed by the Revolution were thus directed outward. Before their eventual exhaustion in the unconquerable vastness of Russia, French citizen armies redrew the political map of modern Europe in irreversible ways and inspired the emergence of other European nationalisms in response.

Russia and China both experienced thoroughgoing social revolutionary trans-formations that resulted in the rule of communist-directed party-states. These social revolutions occurred under Leninist party leaderships in the modern industrial era, when the model of a state-managed economy was available; and both occurred in countries more hard-pressed geopolitically than late 18th-century France had been. The authoritarian and mass-mobilizing energies of the immediate postrevolutionary regimes, both in Soviet Russia and Communist

China, were mainly directed not to *imperial* military conquests as in France, but to the promotion of national economic development, which was deemed to be the key to national independence in a world dominated by major industrial powers. Even so, in due course both of the new regimes demonstrated greatly enhanced capacities (compared to the prerevolutionary era) for successfully waging international war.

From the modernization perspective, the Russian and the Chinese revolutions were tyrannical and antidemocratic: they were more violent and transformative than the French Revolution, and ideological vanguards stayed in power both in Russia and in China. (By contrast, the Montagnard perpetrators of the Terror fell from power in France.) The Soviet regime, however, through the Stalinist "revolution from above," became more coercive and inegalitarian than did the Chinese Communist regime after 1949. Modernization theory cannot explain the contrasts between the Russian and Chinese new regimes. The civil war interregnum of the Chinese Revolution, stretching from 1911 to 1949, was much more protracted than the brief Russian revolutionary civil war of 1917–1921; and in practice, the Soviet regime probably built directly upon more structures and policies from Russia's tsarist past than the Chinese Communist regime did on China's Confucian-imperial past. Nor do the contrasting revolutionary outcomes make sense from a Marxian perspective: the Russian Revolution was politically based on the urban industrial proletariat, and thus should have resulted in practices closer to socialist ideals than the peasant-based Chinese Revolution.

The somewhat less murderous and less authoritarian features of the Chinese Communist state after 1949 – at least from the point of view of local peasant communities – can be attributed to the guerrilla mode by which the Chinese Communist Party came to power. The party could not achieve national state power directly in the cities; instead, it found itself faced with the necessity of waging rural guerrilla warfare against both the Japanese invaders and its Kuomintang competitors for domestic political control. Nationalist appeals helped the Chinese communists in the early 1940s to attract educated middle-class citizens to their cause. Attention to the pressing material and self-defense needs of the peasantry in North China also allowed the communists to gain sufficient access to the villages to reorganize poor and middle-class peasants into associations that would support the Red Armies economically and militarily.[11]

After 1949, the Chinese communists were able, by building upon their preexisting political relations with much of the peasantry, to carry out agricultural collectivization with less brutality than the Bolsheviks.[12] Simultaneously, the relatively favorable geopolitical context of postrevolutionary China, situated in a world of nuclear superpower balance between the Soviet Union and the United States, allowed the Chinese communists to place less emphasis upon creating a heavy industrial capacity for mechanized military forces than they might otherwise have done. Their limited resources sufficed, however, to establish an independent Chinese nuclear capacity, symbol of major-power status in the post-World War II era.[13]

Communist China was able to pursue economic development policies that stressed light industries and rural development as well as some heavy industries. Meanwhile, the party could also infuse peasant-based, guerrilla-style military practices inherited from the revolutionary civil war into standing forces that could intervene effectively in the Korean War and make limited forays against India and Vietnam. As Jonathan Adelman has argued, performance of the People's Liberation Army in the Korean War battles of 1950–1951 was "simply outstanding" compared to the "disastrous" Kuomintang military performance against the Japanese in the 1930s and 1940s.[14] The Revolution, Adelman concludes, had "created a whole new Chinese army."[15]

By contrast, the Soviet regime consolidated under Stalin's auspices took a much more brutal stance toward the peasant majority. Essentially, it substituted an autocratic dictatorship for a mass-mobilizing revolutionary regime. The Bolsheviks originally claimed state power in 1917 through political and very limited military maneuverings in the cities and towns of Russia, and they initially abstained from efforts at nationalist military mobilization. Most of the Russian populace acquiesced in their rule simply because of the exhaustion brought by Imperial Russia's defeat in World War I. The Russian revolutionary civil war of 1917 to 1921 was won by the deployment of urban guards and conventionally structured standing armies. Peasants were involved only as reluctantly coerced conscripts.[16] The one major foreign adventure of the fledgling Bolshevik regime, the invasion of Poland in 1920, ended in military defeat. In fact, the new Russian regime was fortunate that World War I had defeated or exhausted its major foreign opponents. For new-born Soviet Russia did not conform to the pattern of most other social revolutions: its central authorities were not in a good position to channel mass political participation into international warfare. Instead, they turned toward deepening internal warfare – against the peasantry and among elites.

After 1921, the Bolshevik regime lacked organized political ties to the peasant villages, which had made their own autonomous local revolutions against landlords in 1917 and 1918. Stalin rose to power in the 1920s and 1930s by convincing many cadres in the Soviet party-state that Russian "socialism" would have to be built "in one country" that was isolated and threatened economically and militarily by Western industrial powers. The crash program of heavy industrialization was alleged to be necessary not only to build Marxian socialism, but also to prepare Russia for land-based military warfare. The peasantry became a domestic obstacle to Stalinist policies when it refused to provide economic surpluses at exploitative rates. Stalin's subsequent bureaucratic and terroristic drive to force peasant communities into centrally controlled agricultural collectives succeeded only at a terrible cost in human lives and agricultural productivity; the political reverberations in urban and official Russia helped to spur his purges of the Soviet elite in the 1930s. The Stalinist consolidation of the new regime was thus initially a product of conflicts between an urban-based party-state and the peasantry, played out in a geopolitically threatening environment – though *not* in an environment in which direct national mobilization for international war was either necessary or possible.[17]

It is significant that Stalinism evolved into a *popular* mass-mobilizing regime as a result of the travails of World War II.[18] When the invading Nazis conducted themselves with great brutality against the Slav populations they conquered, Stalinist Russia finally had to mobilize for a total international war. Despite the setbacks of the first few months, the Soviet Union met the military challenges of World War II much more effectively than tsarist Russia had met the exigencies of World War I.[19] The Soviet people and armed forces fought back with considerable efficiency and amazing zeal in the face of terrible casualties. For the first time since 1917, Soviet rulers were able to use Russian nationalism to bolster their leadership. Stalin did not hesitate to revive many symbols of Russian national identity from prerevolutionary times, and he also restored prerogatives of rank and expertise in the military.[20] It is therefore not surprising that, when World War II ended in victory for the U.S.S.R. and the Allies, the Soviet rulers' domestic legitimacy – as well as the country's global great-power status – had been enhanced significantly.

SOCIAL REVOLUTIONS IN DEPENDENT COUNTRIES: GEOPOLITICAL CONTEXTS AND THE POSSIBILITIES FOR MILITARIZATION

In the classic social revolutions of France, Russia, and China, long-established monarchical states were transformed into mass-mobilizing national regimes; most other social revolutions in the modern era, however, have occurred in smaller, dependent countries.[21] In some, such as Vietnam and the Portuguese colonies of Africa, which had been colonized by foreign imperial powers, social-revolutionary transformations were part of the process of national liberation from colonialism. In others, such as Cuba, Mexico, Iran, and Nicaragua, neopatrimonial dictatorships were caught in webs of great-power rivalries within the capitalist world economy and the global geopolitical system. Social revolutions in these countries have forged stronger states that are markedly more nationalist and mass-incorporating than the previous regimes and other countries in their respective regions. Still, the new regimes have remained minor powers on the world scene.

With the exception of the Iranian Revolution of 1977–1979, which was primarily carried out through urban demonstrations and strikes, all third-world social revolutions have depended on at least a modicum of peasant support for their success. In most instances, both peasants and city dwellers were mobilized for guerrilla warfare by nationalist revolutionary elites; only in the Mexican and Bolivian revolutions were peasant communities able to rebel on their own as did the French and Russian peasant communities.[22] Most third-world social revolutions have been played out as military struggles among leaderships contending to create or redefine the missions of national states. And these revolutions have happened in settings so penetrated by foreign influences – economic, military, and cultural – that social-revolutionary transformations have been as much about the definition of autonomous identities on the international scene as they have been about the forging of new political ties between indigenous revolutionaries and their mass constituents.

Consequently, the various international contexts in which third-world revolutions have occurred become crucial in conditioning the new regimes that have emerged from them. One basic aspect of the international situation is the relationship between a country undergoing revolution and the great powers, whatever they may be in a given phase of world history. Military, economic, and cultural aspects of such relations all need to be considered in our analysis. The regional context of each revolution also matters: What have been the possibilities for military conflicts with immediate neighbors? Have revolutionized third-world nations faced invasions by third-world neighbors, or have they been able to invade their neighbors without automatically involving great powers in the conflict? As I will illustrate in the remainder of this section, attention to international contexts can help us to explain at least as much about the structures and orientations of social-revolutionary new regimes in the third world as analyses of their class basis or propositions about the inherent logic of modernization and the violence and disruptiveness of various revolutions.

SOCIAL REVOLUTIONS IN THE SHADOW OF A GREAT POWER

A great power can use actual or threatened military intervention to prevent revolutionary transformations near its borders, as the Soviet Union has done in postwar Eastern Europe and as the United States used to do in Central America. Short of that, major political transformations of any kind that proceed in a great power's sphere of military dominance are invariably profoundly influenced by possibilities for rebellion or accommodation. Throughout the 20th century, social revolutions in Central and Latin America, if they happened at all, have been affected by the actions and inactions of the United States as the hegemonic power in the hemisphere. These revolutions have also been affected by the global power balances of their day. The cases of Mexico, Cuba, Bolivia, and the still-unfolding revolution in Nicaragua suggest a number of ways in which the great powers have influenced the shape of the new regimes that emerged from social-revolutionary interregnums.

In one sense, the most "benign" example of U.S. influence is demonstrated in relation to Mexico: the social revolution there was originally allowed to proceed, and was eventually consolidated into a regime that is a unique hybrid between a Western-style electoral democracy and a single-party authoritarian regime.[23] Still, we should note that unlike most other social-revolutionary regimes in the modern world, that of Mexico has never been able to engage in mass mobilization for international warfare. Nationalist self-assertion has been restricted to state-led economic development, particularly in periods such as the 1930s and 1940s, when the United States was distracted by larger domestic or world crises. Popular political participation has been managed by a corporatist, patronage-oriented party-state that preserves order in economically inefficient ways.

Originally, the anti-imperialist thrust of the Mexican Revolution was directed primarily against the European powers that were heavily involved in the economic and military affairs of the prerevolutionary regime of Porfirio Díaz; yet relations with the United States increasingly figured in successive phases of the revolution.[24] The Mexican Revolution could not have broken out at all in 1910–1911 had not the northern forces opposed to Porfirio Díaz been able to move back and forth across the U.S. border, counting on tacit American support in an era when the European great powers were the prime targets of Mexican nationalists. In addition, if the United States had been able and willing to launch sustained antirevolutionary interventions, the Revolution could not have continued after the defeats of Francisco Madero and General Victoriano Huerta made it potentially socially radical. Some scattered U.S. interventions were launched, but they were so minor that their only consequence was to provoke Mexican resentment. World War I and the presidency of Woodrow Wilson brought these American counterrevolutionary efforts to an end and gave the Mexicans space to begin the process of consolidating a new regime under populist and nationalist auspices. During the 1930s and World War II, U.S. abstention from unusual levels of meddling in Mexican affairs was again important in allowing Lazaro Cárdenas to complete construction of a populist, single-party "democracy" with sufficient nationalist clout to expropriate U.S. oil companies.[25]

Due to the basic geopolitical context, there was never any question of a new regime devoted to mass mobilization for military purposes at any point during the Mexican Revolution. Full-scale war with the United States would obviously have been fatal to any revolutionary leadership, and attempts to export revolution to the south would probably have provoked the ire of the northern colossus. Given some breathing space by the United States, Mexican revolutionary nationalists chose instead to ritualize mass mobilization into the subordinate incorporation of peasant communes and workers' unions into the ruling Institutional Revolutionary Party. They produced what is perhaps the most nonmartial nationalist regime ever to emerge from a social-revolutionary transformation in the modern world. They also produced a patronage-oriented party-state that has become steadily more economically inefficient over the years, requiring a constant flow of graft to buy off elite factions and to co-opt popular leaders.[26]

The other major social revolution right on America's doorstep, the Cuban Revolution of 1959, culminated in a new regime remarkably adept at mobilizing human resources for military adventures across the globe. The failure of the United States to prevent or overthrow Fidel Castro's triumph over the Batista dictatorship helped to account for this outcome. But the global superpower rivalry of the United States and the Soviet Union was also a crucial ingredient, for Soviet willingness to protect and bankroll the new regime gave Cuban "anti-imperialists" a leverage against the United States that would have been unimaginable to the earlier Mexican revolutionaries.

Once established in power, Castro could assert Cuban national autonomy against the overwhelming U.S. economic and cultural presence. Having done so, he could then protect his rule from U.S.-sponsored overthrow only by allying himself domestically with the Cuban Communist Party and internationally with the Soviet Union. Subsequently, Cuba has become economically and militarily so dependent on Moscow that it finds itself serving Soviet interests throughout the third world.[27] Cubans are trained and mobilized for foreign service both as military advisors and as educated civilian technicians, which is a way in which Castro can partially repay the Soviets. In addition, it is an opportunity for a small, dependent revolutionary nation to create enhanced mobility for trained citizens.[28] It also allows Cuba to exert considerable military and ideological influence on the world scene – an amazing feat for such a tiny country located only ninety miles from a hostile superpower.

The weakest and poorest southern neighbors of the United States to experience social revolutions have been Bolivia in 1952–1964 and Nicaragua since 1979. These two cases demonstrate opposite effects of U.S. determination to counter radical change in contexts where the Soviet Union could not or would not do as much as it did for Castro's Cuba.

In Bolivia, spontaneous popular revolts by peasant communities and tin miners initially expropriated major owners, both domestic and foreign, and threatened to create a nationalist new regime that was not under the influence of the United States.[29] After international tin prices collapsed, however, the new Bolivian authorities accepted international aid, including help from the United States, to rebuild a professional military apparatus. In due course, the refurbished military took over, establishing Bolivian governments which, while not attempting to reverse the peasant land expropriations of 1952, have followed both domestic-economic and foreign policies that are amenable to American interests. In essence, the United States used a combination of benign neglect and cleverly targeted foreign aid to deradicalize the Bolivian Revolution. A number of circumstances facilitated American containment policies. Bolivian revolutionaries in 1952 had no foreign wars to fight, and popular radicalism (led by Trotskyist cadres) remained focused on internal class struggles. What is more, Bolivian revolutionaries were not reacting to – or capitalizing upon – a bitter prior history of direct Yankee military interventions, which was the case in Cuba and Nicaragua.

In Nicaragua as in Cuba, U.S. authorities initially acquiesced in the overthrow of a corrupt and domestically weakened patrimonial dictator even though he had originally been installed under U.S. sponsorship. Then, again as in Cuba, a dialectic got underway between a revolutionary radicalization couched in anti-American rhetoric and increasing efforts by U.S. authorities to roll back or overthrow the revolution.[30] American counterrevolutionary efforts became more determined and sustained after Ronald Reagan was elected President in 1980. At first, they seemed to make some headway when economic shortages and domestic unrest in the face of an unpopular military draft tended to undercut the Sandinistas' legitimacy as leaders of a popular guerrilla movement against the Somoza regime. Because of domestic political constraints, however, the United States has been unable to invade Sandinista Nicaragua, having to rely instead on economic pressures and the financing of Nicaraguan counterrevolutionary fighters; but the latter have proved to be neither militarily efficient nor politically adept.

Predictably – in the light of the history of foreign efforts to subvert emerging revolutionary regimes in such ways – these U.S. measures have simply provided the Sandinistas with excuses for economic shortages. More importantly, the U.S. efforts have nourished sustained but not overwhelming counterrevolutionary military threats, which have actually helped the Sandinistas to consolidate a mass-mobilizing authoritarian regime through nationalist appeals and an unprecedented military buildup. In short, U.S. policies since 1980, declaredly aimed at "democratizing" Nicaragua, have had the opposite effect; they have undermined elements of pluralism in a postrevolutionary regime and enhanced the nationalist credentials of the more authoritarian Nicaraguan Leninists. Still, as of this writing in 1987, it remains possible that shifts in American policy may stop this process of militarization short of full-scale war in Central America.

MILITARIZED THIRD-WORLD REVOLUTIONS UNDER COMMUNISM AND ISLAM

Far removed from the areas of the New World that are close to the United States, the Vietnamese and Iranian revolutions are two instances in which great-power rivalries, along with geographical distance, have made it possible for revolutionary regimes to take a stand against "American imperialism" without being overthrown by U.S. military intervention. What is more, Vietnam and Iran in the mid-20th century, like France in the late 18th, are examples of the awesome power of social-revolutionary regimes to wage humanly costly wars and to transform regional political patterns and international balances of power. Both revolutions demonstrate this, even though one is a "communist" revolution and the other "Islamic" and thus militantly anticommunist.

Analysts of agrarian class struggles have stressed that the Vietnamese Revolution was grounded in peasant support in both the northern and southern parts of the country.[31] But attempts to explain the overall logic of this revolution in terms of the social conditions of either the northern or the southern peasantry have inevitably missed the other main ingredient in the revolution's success. From the French colonial period on, educated Vietnamese found the Communist Party of Vietnam and the various movements associated with it to be the most effective and persistent instruments of resistance to foreign domination – first by the French colonialists, then by the Japanese occupiers during World War II, then by the returning French, and finally by the United States. The Vietnamese communists were their country's most uncompromising nationalists; they were willing, when conditions required or allowed, to wage guerrilla warfare through peasant mobilization.[32] By contrast, foreign occupiers and their Vietnamese collaborators worked from the cities outward, especially in the south, which had been the center of French colonial control.

Geopolitically, the Vietnamese communists benefited from the distance the French and American forces had to traverse to confront them, from the availability of sanctuaries in Laos and Cambodia, and (after the partial victory in the north) from their ability to receive supplies through China from both China and the Soviet Union. Had the United States been able or willing to use nuclear weapons in the Southeast Asian theatre, or had the Soviet Union and China not temporarily cooperated to help the Vietnamese, it seems doubtful that the Vietnamese Revolution could have reunified the country, notwithstanding the extraordinary willingness of northern and many southern Vietnamese to die fighting the U.S. forces.

Since the defeat of the United States in southern Vietnam, the Hanoi regime has faced difficult economic conditions; it seems to tackle such problems with much less efficiency and zeal than it tackled the anti-imperialist wars from the 1940s to the 1970s. As the unquestionably dominant military power in its region, the Vietnamese state has invaded and occupied Cambodia and engaged in occasional battles with a now-hostile China. Vietnam continues to rely on Soviet help to counterbalance U.S. hostility and the armed power of China. But, what is perhaps more important now that Vietnam is indeed "the Prussia of Southeast Asia," the Vietnamese communists still find it possible to legitimate their leadership through never-ending mobilization of their people for national military efforts. The Chinese threat, Cambodian resistance, and American opposition to the normalization of Vietnam's gains have provided just the kind of internationally threatening context that the Vietnamese communists, after so many years of warfare, find most congenial to their domestic political style.

The militant Shi'a clerics of Iran, who seem to be so different from the Vietnamese communists, are another mass-mobilizing and state-building revolutionary elite that has been helped immensely by a facilitating geo-political context and protracted international warfare.[33] The Iranian Revolution is still in progress, and it is therefore too early to characterize its outcome in any definitive way. Nevertheless, the process of this remarkable upheaval has already dramatized the appropriateness of viewing contemporary social revolutions as promoting ideologically reconstructed national identities involving the sudden incorporation of formerly excluded popular groups into state-directed projects. Moreover, this revolution shows that mass mobilization for war, aggressive as well as defensive, is an especially congenial state-directed project for revolutionary leaders.

From both Marxian and modernization perspectives, the Iranian Revolution, especially the consolidation of state power by the Ayatollah Khomeini and the Islamic Republican Party since the overthrow of the Shah in 1979, has been a puzzle. Marxist analysts have been reluctant to call this a "social revolution" because class conflicts and transformations of economic property rights have not defined the main terms of struggle or the patterns of sociopolitical change. Modernization theorists, meanwhile, have been surprised at the capacity of the untrained and traditionist Islamic clerics to consolidate their rule; these theorists expected that, after a brief "terror," such noncommunist and ideologically fanatical leaders would give way to technically trained bureaucrats if not to liberal-democratic politicians.

In fact, from 1979 through 1982, the Islamic Republican Party in Iran systematically reconstructed state organizations to embody direct controls by Shi'a clerics. Step by step, all other leading political forces – liberal Westernizers, the Mujhahedeen, the Tudeh Party, and technocrats and professional military officers loyal to Abolhassan Bani-Sadr – were eliminated from what had once been the all-encompassing revolutionary alliance. The party did this by deploying and combining the classic ingredients for successful revolutionary state building.

For one thing, the Islamic Republican clerics shared a commitment to a political ideology that gave them unlimited warrant to rule exclusively in the name of all the Shi'a believers. Khomeini had developed a militant-traditionalist reading of Shi'a beliefs, calling on the clerics themselves to govern in place of secular Iranian rulers corrupted by Western cultural imperialism. The Islamic Republican Constitution for Iran officially enshrined such clerical supervision over all affairs of state; concrete political organizations, including the Islamic Republican Party that dominated the Majlis (parliament), also embodied this orientation.

Moreover, the Islamic Republican clerics and their devout nonclerical associates did not hesitate to organize, mobilize, and manipulate mass popular support, including the unemployed as well as workers and lower-middle-class people in Teheran and other cities. Islamic judges supervised neighborhood surveillance bodies; Islamic militants organized revolutionary guards for police and military duties; and consumer rations and welfare benefits for the needy were dispensed through neighborhood mosques. Iranians never before involved in national political life became directly energized through such organization; those with doubts were subjected to peer controls as well as to elite supervision. With these means of mass-based power at their disposal, the Islamic Republican

Party had little trouble eliminating liberal and leftist competitors from public political life.

Right after the Shah's overthrow, ideologically committed Islamic cadres, backed by mass organizations, reconstructed major public institutions in Iranian national life. Not only special committees of revolutionary justice, but also traditionally educated clerical judges took over the criminal and civil legal system, reorienting it to procedural and substantive norms in line with their understanding of the Koran. The next targets were Western-oriented cultural institutions, particularly schools and universities. These were first closed and then purged, turned into bastions of Islamic education and revolutionary propaganda. Civil state bureaucracies were similarly purged and transformed; and so, in due course, were the remnants of the Shah's military forces, particularly the army.

The kinds of transformations I have just summarized took place not automatically but through hard-fought political, bureaucratic, and street struggles that pitted other elites – alternative would-be consolidators of the Iranian Revolution – against the militant clerics and their supporters. As these struggles within Iran unfolded, the emerging clerical authoritarianism repeatedly benefited from international conditions and happenings that allowed them to deploy their ideological and organizational resources to maximum advantage.

Overall, the version of the Iranian Revolution that the clerics sought to institutionalize has been virulently anti-Western, and defined especially in opposition to "U.S. imperialism." Opposition to Soviet imperialism has also been a consistent theme. Fortunately for the clerics, the fiscal basis of the Iranian state after as well as before the revolution lies in the export of oil, for which an international market has continued to exist.[34] A geopolitical given is coterminous with this economic given: neither the Soviet Union nor the United States has been in a position to intervene militarily against the Iranian Revolution, in part because Iran lies between their two spheres of direct control. It is also fortunate for Iran's radical clerics that the United States has acted in ways that were symbolically provocative while not being materially or militarily powerful enough to control events in Iran. The admission of the deposed Shah to the United States, the subsequent seizure of the American embassy by pro-Khomeini youths, and the ensuing unsuccessful efforts of the U.S. authorities to free the American hostages, all created an excellent political matrix within Iran for the clerics to discredit as pro-American a whole series of their secular competitors for state power.

Then, in the autumn of 1980, the secularist-Islamic regime of Saddam Hussein in neighboring Iraq attacked revolutionary Iran; since the Iraqis perceived Khomeini's regime as weak and internally disorganized, they expected it to fall. What happened with the Jacobins in 18th-century revolutionary France then repeated itself in revolutionary Iran. At first, the foreign invaders made headway, for the remnants of the Shah's military, particularly the army, were indeed disorganized at the command level. But revolutionary Islamic guards poured out to the fronts, and the Iraqi offensives began to come up against fanatically dogged resistance. Islamic fundamentalists and Iranian secular nationalists pulled together, however grudgingly, to resist the common enemy.

Domestic Iranian power struggles have not stopped during the war with Iraq. During the final months of his attempt to survive within the Khomeini regime, President Bani-Sadr tried to use the newly essential regular army to build up secular-technocratic leverage against clerical rule. But he and his followers, along with many army officers, were defeated and removed. Thereafter, during 1981 and into 1982, despite setbacks in the war due to the initial lack of coordination between revolutionary guards and regular army forces, a new Islamic military loyal to the clerical regime was gradually synthesized for Iran.[35] It was able to combine regular strategic planning for battles with the use of such unconventional tactics as human waves of martyrs willing to clear Iraqi mine fields with their bodies. By early 1982, the Iranians had succeeded in driving the Iraqis out of their country; the latter have been on the defensive ever since, as the consolidated clerical regime in Iran has doggedly pursued the war in the name of its transnationalist ideological vision.

In the end, the Iranian Revolution will probably settle down into some sort of Islamic-nationalist authoritarianism that coexists, however uneasily, with its neighbors. The Iranian armies are unlikely to overrun the Middle East the way the French revolutionary armies temporarily overran much of continental Europe. Iran is still a third-world nation; on the global scene, it faces superpowers who can inhibit its wildest aspirations. Nevertheless, Iran's military accomplishments have already disproved the expectation of modernization theorists that a regime run by anti-Western Shi'a clerics would not be viable in the contemporary world. By consolidating and reconstructing state power through ideologically coordinated mass mobilization, and by directing popular zeal against a faraway superpower and channeling it into a war against a less populous neighboring state, the Islamic Republicans of Iran have proven once again that social revolutions are less about class struggles or "modernization" than about state building and the forging of newly assertive national identities in a modern world that remains culturally pluralistic even as it inexorably becomes economically more interdependent.

CONCLUSION

If, as Franz Borkenau argued, students of revolutions must attend to "changes in the state order," much remains to be understood about the kinds of political transformation that revolutions have accomplished and the activities to which their enhanced state capacities have been directed with varying degrees of success. In this essay, which is suggestive rather than conclusive, I have speculated that many social-revolutionary regimes have excelled at channeling enhanced popular participation into protracted international warfare. Because of the ways revolutionary leaders mobilize popular support in the course of struggles for state power, the emerging regimes can tackle mobilization for war better than any other task, including the promotion of national economic development. The full realization of this revolutionary potential for building strong states depends on threatening but not overwhelming geopolitical circumstances.

The full exploration of these notions will require more precise theorizing and more systematic comparative research, going well beyond the historical illustrations offered here. Yet further investigations of war-making as a proclivity of social-revolutionary regimes could hardly be more timely. The image of teen-age Iranians blowing themselves up on Iraqi land mines as a way to heaven should remind us that the passions of 16th- to 18th-century Europe have yet to play themselves out fully in the third world of the 20th century. These passions will not often embody themselves in social-revolutionary transformations, but when they do – and when geopolitical circumstances unleash international conflicts and do not proscribe the outbreak of war – we can expect aspirations for equality and dignity, both within nations and on the international stage, to flow again and again into military mass mobilization. Arguably, this is the mission that revolutionized regimes perform best. In the face of serious (but not overwhelming) foreign threats, they excel at motivating the formerly excluded to die for the glory of their national states.

NOTES

1. Borkenau, "State and Revolution in the Paris Commune, the Russian Revolution, and the Spanish Civil War," *Sociological Review* 29 (January 1937), 41–75, at 41.
2. Huntington, *Political Order in Changing Societies* (New Haven: Yale University Press, 1968), 266. Chapter 5 in its entirety is also relevant.
3. See Theda Skocpol, *States and Social Revolutions: A Comparative Analysis of France, Russia, and China* (New York and Cambridge: Cambridge University Press, 1979), 161.
4. This characterization comes from Alvin Gouldner, "Stalinism: A Study of Internal Colonialism," in *Political Power and Social Theory* (research annual edited by Maurice Zeitlin) 1 (1980) (Greenwich, CT: JAI Press), 209–59.
5. Eisenstadt, *Revolution and the Transformation of Societies* (New York: Free Press, 1978); Walzer, "A Theory of Revolution," *Marxist Perspectives*, No. 5 (Spring 1979), 30–44.
6. Karl Griewank, "The Emergence of the Concept of Revolution," in Bruce Mazlish, Arthur D. Kaledin, and David B. Ralston, eds., *Revolution: A Reader* (New York: Macmillan, 1971), 13–17.
7. Thorough elaboration and documentation of this conclusion appears in Jonathan R. Adelman, *Revolution, Armies, and War: A Political History* (Boulder, CO: Lynne Rienner Publishers, 1985), chaps. 3–11.
8. For fuller discussion and references, see Skocpol (fn. 3), 174–77.
9. S. F. Scott, "The Regeneration of the Line Army During the French Revolution," *Journal of Modern History* 42 (September 1970), 307–30.
10. Adelman (fn. 7), chap. 3; Theodore Ropp, *War in the Modern World*, rev. ed. (New

York: Collier Books, 1962), chap. 4; Alfred Vagts, *A History of Militarism*, rev. ed. (New York: Free Press, 1959), chap. 4; John Ellis, *Armies in Revolution* (New York: Oxford University Press, 1974), chap. 4.

11. Mark Selden, *The Yenan Way in Revolutionary China* (Cambridge: Harvard University Press, 1971); Ellis (fn. 10), chap. 4.

12. Thomas P. Bernstein, "Leadership and Mass Mobilisation in the Soviet and Chinese Collectivisation Campaigns of 1929–30 and 1955–56: A Comparison," *China Quarterly* 31 (July–September 1967), 1–47. Bernstein characterizes Chinese collectivization techniques as "persuasive" in contrast to the more "coercive" Soviet practices. Subsequent to collectivization, however, the Chinese "Great Leap Forward" did devolve into considerable coercion by cadres against peasants.

13. Franz Schurmann, *The Logic of World Power* (New York: Pantheon, 1974), part II.

14. Adelman (fn. 7), 139.

15. *Ibid.*, 144.

16. Ellis (fn. 10), chap. 5.

17. Background for this analysis of Stalin's "revolution from above" comes especially from Bernstein (fn. 12); Stephen F. Cohen, *Bukharin and the Bolshevik Revolution* (New York: Knopf, 1973); and Moshe Lewin, *Russian Peasants and Soviet Power*, trans. Irene Nove (Evanston: Northwestern University Press, 1968).

18. An insightful discussion of the different phases of nationalist mobilization in Russia and China appears in William G. Rosenberg and Marilyn Young, *Transforming Russia and China: Revolutionary Struggle in the Twentieth Century* (New York: Oxford University Press, 1982).

19. Adelman (fn. 7), chaps. 4–7.

20. Alf Edeen, "The Civil Service: Its Composition and Status," in Cyril E. Black, ed., *The Transformation of Russian Society* (Cambridge: Harvard University Press, 1960), 274–91; see esp. 286–87.

21. For useful overviews, see Eric R. Wolf, *Peasant Wars of the Twentieth Century* (New York: Harper & Row, 1969), chaps. 1, 4–6; John Dunn, *Modern Revolutions* (Cambridge: Cambridge University Press, 1972), chaps. 2, 4–8.

22. Alternative modes of peasant involvement in social revolutions are analyzed in Theda Skocpol, "What Makes Peasants Revolutionary?" *Comparative Politics* 14 (April 1982), 351–75.

23. Huntington (fn. 2), 315–24, discusses the postrevolutionary Mexican regime. See also Nora Hamilton, *The Limits of State Autonomy: Post-Revolutionary Mexico* (Princeton: Princeton University Press, 1982), and Roger D. Hansen, *The Politics of Mexican Development* (Baltimore: The Johns Hopkins University Press, 1971).

24. On the Mexican Revolution and its relations with foreign states, see Wolf (fn. 21), chap. 1; Dunn (fn. 21), chap. 2; Friedrich Katz, *The Secret War in Mexico: Europe, the United States, and the Mexican Revolution* (Chicago: University of Chicago Press, 1981); Walter Goldfrank, "World System, State Structure, and the Onset of the Mexican Revolution," *Politics and Society* 5 (No. 4, 1975), 417–39; and John Womack, Jr., *Zapata and the Mexican Revolution* (New York: Alfred A. Knopf, 1969).

25. Hamilton (fn. 23), chaps. 4–7.

26. Hansen (fn. 23); Susan Eckstein, *The Poverty of Revolution: The State and the Urban Poor in Mexico* (Princeton: Princeton University Press, 1977).

27. Kosmos Tsokhas, "The Political Economy of Cuban Dependence on the Soviet Union," *Theory and Society* 9 (March 1980), 319–62.

28. Susan Eckstein, "Structural and Ideological Bases of Cuba's Overseas Programs," *Politics and Society* 11 (No. 1, 1982), 95–121.

29. My account of the Bolivian case draws upon Huntington (fn. 2), 325–34; Robert J.

Alexander, *The Bolivian National Revolution* (New Brunswick, NJ: Rutgers University Press, 1958); Bert Useem, "The Bolivian Revolution and Workers' Control," *Politics and Society* 9 (No. 4, 1980), 447–69; and Jonathan Kelley and Lawrence Klein, *Revolution and the Rebirth of Inequality* (Berkeley and Los Angeles: University of California Press, 1981).

30. My account of Nicaragua draws upon Walter LaFeber, *Inevitable Revolutions: The United States in Central America* (New York: W. W. Norton, 1983); Shirley Christian, *Nicaragua: Revolution in the Family* (New York: Vintage Books, 1986), and Lawrence Shaefer, "Nicaraguan–United States Bilateral Relations: The Problems within Revolution and Reconstruction" (Senior honors thesis, University of Chicago, 1984).

31. See, for instance, Wolf (fn. 21), chap. 4. For a discussion of alternative perspectives on the Vietnamese peasantry, see Skocpol (fn. 22).

32. Dunn (fn. 21), chap. 5; Huynh Kim Khanh, *Vietnamese Communism, 1925–1945* (Ithaca, NY: Cornell University Press, 1982); John T. McAlister, Jr., *Vietnam: The Origins of Revolution* (New York: Knopf, 1969).

33. The following discussion draws on Theda Skocpol, "Rentier State and Shi'a Islam in the Iranian Revolution," *Theory and Society* 11 (No. 3, 1982), 265–84. It also relies heavily on R. K. Ramazani, *Revolutionary Iran: Challenge and Response in the Middle East* (Baltimore: The Johns Hopkins University Press, 1986), and Shaul Bakhash, *The Reign of the Ayatollahs: Iran and the Islamic Revolution* (New York: Basic Books, 1984).

34. Ramazani (fn. 33), chaps. 13–14; Shaul Bakhash, *The Politics of Oil and Revolution in Iran* (Washington, DC: Staff Paper, The Brookings Institution, 1982); and "Oil Revenue Lifts Iranian Economy," *The New York Times,* Friday, July 9, 1982, pp. D1, D4.

35. Ramazani (fn. 33), chap. 5; William F. Hickman, *Ravaged and Reborn: The Iranian Army, 1982* (Washington, DC: Staff Paper, The Brookings Institution, 1982).

CONCLUSION

Reflections on recent scholarship about social revolutions and how to study them

Comparative and historical scholarship about social revolutions has proliferated in recent years. This has happened, of course, primarily because events in the world have riveted the attention of scholars by throwing up new puzzles to be addressed. The Vietnamese Revolution dramatized issues of peasant mobilization by guerrillas for prolonged nationalist resistance against foreign powers. The Nicaraguan Revolution of 1979 and the agonies of El Salvador throughout the 1980s raised anew questions about the variable fortunes of repressive regimes and armed revolutionaries in Central America and beyond. The overthrow of the Shah of Iran in 1979 flew in the face of all previous theories of revolution and modernization (Keddie 1992). Urban demonstrators, rather than peasant revolts or a protracted guerrilla war, brought about the demise of the Pahlavi regime. And it was soon replaced, not by Western-style liberalism or Soviet-style communism, but by a dictatorship of militant Shi'a clerics determined to assert Islamic virtue in the face of "imperialist" influences.

By the end of the 1980s, moreover, previous patterns of revolution were in some ways turned on their heads, as the communist regimes of Eastern Europe met their sudden demise. Perhaps these revolutions would open doors to democracy, rather than leading toward new forms of political tyranny, as most revolutions had done in the past. This same possibility was also raised by the evolution of the Nicaraguan Revolution into a kind of (uneasy) constitutional political pluralism (see the discussion in Foran and Goodwin 1993). Remarkably, in Nicaragua the armed Sandinista revolutionaries initially consolidated a mass-mobilizing revolutionary regime and then acquiesced in the creation of a new constitutional system that guaranteed basic civil rights and competitive elections. In 1990, the Sandinistas lost an election and proved willing to reliquish key governmental offices to Violetta Chamorro and her parliamentary allies. (The Sandinistas remained in control of much of the military and public administration, however.) Although it is far from certain whether constitutionalism will prove stable in Nicaragua, such a peaceful turnover of executive authority was a first in the history of revolutionary state-building.[1]

Some very talented social scientists – including rising young stars such as Farideh Farhi, John Foran, Jack Goldstone, Jeff Goodwin, Tim McDaniel, Afsaneh Najmabadi, and Timothy Wickham-Crowley – have undertaken to make sense of the Vietnamese, Nicaraguan, Iranian, and other social revolutions of the middle to late twentieth century. Many such efforts, I am proud to say, have been influenced by key theoretical and methodological aspects of my 1979 book, *States and Social Revolutions.* In retrospect, it is now safe to say that this book was an agenda-setting book for social scientists who study and theorize about revolutions. *States and Social Revolutions* was agenda-setting *not* in the sense that subsequent students of revolutions have simply agreed with and "applied" its ideas. Rather, my work on revolutions has proved to be agenda-setting in richer and more interesting ways. Some researchers have creatively adapted and reworked the theoretical and methodological principles embodied in my 1979 book and subsequent articles in order to generate powerful comparative-historical analyses of the causes, processes, and outcomes of social revolutions other than the French, Russian, and Chinese cases. Other scholars have taken polemic issue with arguments in *States and Social Revolutions,* using a confrontation with it as an occasion to advocate fundamentally different theoretical and methodological approaches for macroscopic social science. Adapters and arguers alike have taken *States and Social Revolutions* as a touchstone for their efforts. This is the most that any work of scholarship can ever hope to achieve – to become the starting point, both basis and departure, for subsequent research and debates.

In the pages that follow, I shall offer a personal perspective on selected works and trends in the recent social scientific literature about revolutions and methods for studying them. Because my own research nowadays is *not* focused on revolutions (I now work on so-called welfare states, and especially on U.S. politics and public policymaking), I am not in a position to offer a comprehensive overview of all of the research and theorizing about revolutions that has occurred since 1979. People are certain to find important items missing from my discussion and list of references. What I offer instead of comprehensiveness is an opinionated discussion of some major books and articles, particularly those that have either built upon or taken sharp issue with my own arguments about social revolutions or about the methods that should be used to develop knowledge about them.

I begin by surveying what various scholars have recently found about the causes, processes, and outcomes of mid-twentieth-century social revolutions. What patterns have been established, and how well do they accord with the principles of analysis that I set forth in *States and Social Revolutions?* Has there been some degree of cumulation in what social scientists have learned about (especially the causes of) social revolutions?

Then I move on to argue with some major scholars – above all Michael Burawoy, Michael Hechter, and William Sewell, Jr. – who have recently criticized institutionalist comparative-historical scholarship on revolutions. These critics offer sharp – and mutually contradictory! – alternatives to the sort of comparative causal research about political and social-structural conditions for social revolutions that I and other scholars have done. Should macroscopic social scientists, in fact, heed these calls to abandon the use of comparative-historical methods to study states in relation to social structures? Should they instead turn toward Marxist theorical research as explained by Burawoy, or toward deductive rational choice modeling as pushed by Hechter, or toward interpretive narrative history as advocated by Sewell? I do not think so; but why not? What do I have to say in response to the earnest criticisms and sweeping programmatic declarations of Burawoy, Hechter, and Sewell?

At the end of this essay, I shall comment briefly on current challenges and new directions in the study of social revolutions. Although much has been accomplished by regime-centered comparative-historical analyses of the causes of social revolutions in modern world history, additional and different things remain to be done. Findings about social revolutions need to be theoretically integrated with findings in closely related kinds of studies. Further scholarship, both causal and interpretive, must be done to clarify the place of ideas, culture, and ideologies in the origins and course of social revolutions.

Now that we have some sense of the stops on the tour through the recent literature that we are about to take, let us board the bus and be off. I do not pretend to be an unbiased tour guide. I appreciate certain parts of the scenery much more than others, and will make no secret of my opinions. But I shall try to point out the major landmarks, and make the journey as informative and entertaining as possible.

EXPLAINING SOCIAL REVOLUTIONS: BEYOND FRANCE, RUSSIA, AND CHINA

In the conclusion to *States and Social Revolutions,* I called for further comparative-historical studies to illuminate the conditions under which recent social revolutions have occurred in types of regimes that were clearly different from the agrarian protobureaucratic monarchies, all of them old empires, that I studied for my 1979 book. I acknowledged that social revolutions of the mid-twentieth century have usually involved avowed revolutionary vanguards who mobilized social support and waged prolonged guerrilla struggles *prior to* victory over old regimes. All the same, I did *not* suggest a turn toward "voluntarist" analyses from the point of view of the leaders and theorists of such movements. Instead, I called for a further application of a structural perspective focusing on "*state organizations* and their relations both to international environments and to domestic classes and economic conditions" (Skocpol 1979: 291; emphasis in original).

Since the mid-1970s, in fact, social-scientific research on revolutions has become much more historical – that is, focused on processes over time – and much more based on in-depth comparisons of cases than it was in the 1960s and early 1970s, when grand theoretical schemas (e.g., Johnson 1966) or large-N statistical studies of "political violence" (e.g., Gurr 1970) tended to predominate. Along with general intellectual trends, both Jeffery Paige's 1975 book *Agrarian Revolution* and my 1979 book helped to spur this transition. We now have a great deal of excellent, analytically explicit historical and comparative-historical work, including careful general theorizing illustrated with comparative cases (e.g., Adelman 1985; Boswell 1989; Foran 1992; Goldstone, Gurr, and Moshiri 1991; Goodwin 1992; Gugler 1982; Higley and Pakulski 1992; Kim 1991; Roxborough 1989; Selbin 1993; Shugart 1989; and Walzer 1980); theoretically informed single-case studies (e.g., Arjomand 1986, 1988; Colburn 1986; Foran 1993a; Goldfrank 1979; Kelley and Klein 1981; Najmabadi 1987, 1993); theoretically informed juxtapositions of two cases (e.g., Farideh 1990; Foran and Goodwin 1993; Kim and Leach 1991; Liu 1988; McDaniel 1991; Midlarsky and Roberts 1985; Waterbury 1975); and full-scale macroanalytic comparisons of from several to many cases, juxtaposing actual and partial or failed instances of revolution (e.g., Dix 1984; Goldstone 1991; Goodwin 1988, and forthcoming; and Wickham-Crowley 1991, 1992) or counterrevolution (Farman-Farma 1990).

All of these studies have enriched understanding and debates about the causes, processes, and (occasionally) outcomes of social revolutions. Yet two of them, in my view, stand out above the rest.[2] One is by a former student of mine, Jeff Goodwin, while the other was researched and written by Timothy Wickham-Crowley, someone I never met or heard of until I had the privilege to read his nearly completed work. Both of the studies I am about to describe are splendid examples of *macroanalytic* comparative-historical social science (the reader can remind himself or herself of the basic types of comparative history by consulting the Skocpol–Somers essay reprinted as Chapter 3 of this volume). Both Jeff Goodwin (1988; forthcoming) and Timothy Wickham-Crowley (1992) define clear outcomes to be explained. Both attempt to sort out possible causal conditions and configurations of causal conditions, testing available theoretical hypotheses *and* generating new ones through comparisons across cases. Finally, and most important, both of these studies compare cases where actual social revolutions have occurred, to cases where revolutionary movements made only partial headway, and to cases where revolutionary movements might have flourished, but in fact did not. As we are about to see, what makes these two studies so extraordinarily informative about the conditions favoring or frustrating social revolutions in the twentieth-century Third World is precisely their nuanced and effective use of macrocausal comparative-historical research as a tool for theory testing and theory building.

Social revolutions in colonies and dictatorships

Goodwin's *State and Revolution in the Third World* focuses on left-wing, armed revolutionary vanguards that, during recent decades, sought to mobilize popular support in order to overthrow incumbent regimes and promote fundamental socioeconomic and political changes. In this study (1988; forthcoming), Goodwin considers only why such "guerrilla revolutionary" attempts succeeded or failed at challenging the regimes they opposed; he does not analyze what happens after revolutionary "victory," if any (but see Foran and Goodwin 1993 for an insightful recent move toward analyzing revolutionary outcomes as well). By focusing closely on the roots and course of guerrilla revolutionary challenges, Goodwin is able to explore a two-tiered "dependent variable." He asks why would-be guerrilla vanguards were able to develop broad sociopolitical coalitions of support in some times and places, but remained voices in the wilderness in other times and places. And he asks why, among movements that mobilized broad support, some actually took state power, while others were forcibly repressed or got no further than achieving a military stalement.

An extraordinary feature of Goodwin's research is that it covers in considerable depth eight countries in two different regions of the world and time periods. Within each region and period, Goodwin compares four cases that have many similarities of social structure, geoplitical situation, and world-historic ideological context; yet his four cases also show full variation on his outcomes of interest. The first set of cases Goodwin examines are countries of Southeast Asia, all previous Western colonies occupied by Japan during World War II, where armed revolutionary vanguards made varying degrees of headway between 1940 and 1954: in Indonesia, left-wing guerrillas did not succeed in building broad mass support (they lost out to nonradical nationalists); in Malaya and the Philippines such guerrillas did build mass movements during the war, but afterward they gradually lost support and could not take state power; and in Vietnam, the Communist guerrillas both built broad support and achieved state power in the North in 1954. Goodwin's second set of cases are sovereign Central American nations that faced guerrilla challenges of varying severity in the 1970s and 1980s: would-be guerrillas made surprisingly little headway in Honduras; they built considerable mass support without achieving victory in Guatemala and El Salvador; and they both built support and displaced a dictator in Nicaragua in 1979. After doing comparisons within each of these regions/ periods, Goodwin is also able to note analytical similarities across them. His is an unusually effective research design in comparative-historical social science.

Goodwin's basic conclusions can be straightforwardly stated (although the important nuances cannot be conveyed here). He uses careful comparisons – among his cases and, in general terms, to many other Third World countries as well – to show that neither sheer poverty nor peasant discontent, not merely modernization or class oppression, and certainly not the simple appearance of guerrillas or foreign aid to them, can explain the relative successes and failures of guerrilla revolutionary movements. There have been many, many attempts to launch such movements in the Third World, but only some have made headway – and those not in the poorest countries, or in countries with the most oppressed popular groups, or the regions or countries most socioeconomically transformed by market forces. In some detail, moreover, Goodwin shows that neither foreign sponsorship of revolutionaries (e.g., by Moscow or Beijing or Havana) nor imperialist support for challenged governments (e.g., by the United States) was sufficient to account for successes and failures, apart from domestic governmental conditions.

After setting aside these previous academic and practical theories, Goodwin looks to the structures of imperial and national state institutions, and to political connections between states and social groups in what he calls the "polity," to account for the varying fates of guerrilla revolutionary movements within his two regions and across his eight cases. Armed revolutionaries became truly mass-based challengers, Goodwin argues, only when they mobilized sustained support from more than peasants alone; they had to build nationalist support coalitions that include rural people, urban workers, middle-class people, and even (in some cases) upper-class acquiescers. This happened, according to Goodwin, only when armed revolutionaries were contending with repressive, politically exclusionary regimes that did not successfully "penetrate" all of the territories they nominally claimed to rule.

In Southeast Asia during World War II, the Japanese occupiers disrupted previous Western colonial controls and ruled ruthlessly in three out of the four countries Goodwin studied: Malaya, the Philippines, and Vietnam. The result was the growth of broadly supported communist guerrilla movements for "national liberation" – movements that were "on the ground" for Western colonial powers to contend with when they returned after the defeat of Japan in the war. In Central America during the 1970s and 1980s, broadly supported guerrilla movements grew up to challenge authoritarian regimes in Nicaragua, El Salvador, and Guatemala.

In contrast to repressive and exclusive regimes, Goodwin argues, "inclusionary" political regimes do not give much scope to the building of broad support for revolutionary movements. During their occupation of Indonesia in World War II, the Japanese sponsored a nationalist and populist native movement as a counterweight to the Dutch. That movement was able to crowd out would-be communist revolutionaries during and after the war. In Central America, moreover, Honduras has from time to time been a partially democratic regime, one that affords sufficient political space to reformist intellectuals, trade unionists, and church groups to make resort to support for armed Marxist guerrillas unattractive to them (in contrast to the situation in the other countries, where such would-be reformers were often forced by repression into making alliances with the armed revolutionaries).

Goodwin makes yet further distinctions among repressive, politically exclusionary regimes – to account for why mass-supported armed revolutionaries actually come to state power in some of them, but not others. In the first place, he argues that *directly ruled colonies,* where the imperial rulers directly staff important state offices with their own nationals and repress reform-minded indigenous elites, have been much more vulnerable to actual defeat and displacement by revolutionary guerrillas than have been *indirectly ruled colonies,* where the imperial power sponsors indigenous elites, to whom it can later gradually hand power without completely disrupting existing administrative-military institutions. After World War II, Japanese defeat led to the restoration of repressive, direct French colonial rule in Vietnam, a situation that allowed the Vietnamese Communists to continue to build support in the name of national liberation. But in Malaya and the Philippines, restored British and American imperial rulers governed in partnership with indigenous elites, to whom national sovereignty was eventually ceded. During and after the transition to independence, the governments of Malaya and the Philippines were able to use military force and limited reforms to crush or contain marginalized communist guerrillas.

As for the repressive regimes of Central America, they too varied in terms of state structures and state–society linkages, Goodwin argues. El Salvador and Guatemala have been corporate military regimes, run by collective groups of military officers with linkages (that vary over time, and by groups of officers) to middle- and (especially) upper-class groups. "Reformist" coups created partial openings at the top within these regimes, Goodwin argues, helping them to retain some domestic middle-class support and U.S. patronage when challenged by insurgent movements. These regimes have waged consistent, relatively effective military struggles against guerrillas and their lower-class supporters. By contrast, however, pre-1979 Nicaragua was a neopatrimonial "one-man" dictatorship. Anastasio Somoza Debayle ruled through a virtually private military force, the National Guard, and used state patronage in highly corrupt ways to favor his own family and friends. This form of authoritarian regime, Goodwin argues, politically excluded and tended to alienate most middle-class and even upper-class Nicaraguans, as well as peasants and workers. It also ended up losing U.S. support and foreign aid. Thus the Sandinista armed revolutionaries were able to build very broad political support and alliances, sufficient in the end to weaken Somoza's personal army and prompt him to flee the country. After that, as is typical when neopatrimonial regimes confront the departure of the dictator, a sudden vacuum of administrative, military, and political authority occurred – into which the Sandinistas and their allies could step.

Goodwin argues, in sum, that a range of authoritarian and politically exclusionary polities in the twentieth-century Third World have been susceptible to the growth of mass-based and guerrilla-led revolutionary challenges. But only directly ruled colonies and neopatrimonial dictatorships have been vulnerable to actual seizures of state power by the challenging revolutionary movements. He suggests that his basic conclusions are applicable well beyond the regions and periods he covered in detail, helping us to understand communist guerrilla successes and failures in the Balkans after World War II, and helping us to understand why French and Portuguese directly ruled colonies gave way to revolutionaries in Africa (Algeria, Mozambique, Angola, and Guinea-Bissau), while British indirectly ruled colonies passed more smoothly to noncommunist indigenous regimes (and even to democracy, in India and the West Indies). The insights about the special vulnerability of neopatrimonial dictatorships are also applicable to the case of Iran after the 1960s.

Guerrilla revolutionary movements in Latin America

Now let me turn to Timothy Wickham-Crowley's remarkable recent book, *Guerrillas and Revolution in Latin America* (1992). Wickham-Crowley exam- ines the emergence and development (or nondevelopment) of armed left-wing guerrilla movements, specifically movements that university students and com- munist party splinter groups tried to launch throughout Central and South America during and after the Cuban Revolution of 1956–59. Why did some of these cadre attempts at armed revolution make initial headway in building peasant support in (certain regions) of the countrysides of their respective nations, while other attempts – such as, most spectacularly, Che Guevara's effort in Bolivia in the 1960s – never got anywhere with the peasants (and often resulted in the death of the would-be revolutionary leaders)? What is more, in those cases where peasant support did enable guerrillas to build up military power sufficient to survive and truly challenge incumbent regimes, why in turn did only Castro's 26th of July Movement of the late 1950s in Cuba and the Sandinista Front of the late 1970s in Nicaragua make a transition to broad, cross-class, national efforts that actually succeeded in seizing state power?

Like Goodwin, but in a different way, Wickham-Crowley developed a very impressive comparative research design to gather systematic information about a range of possible conditions influencing the fortunes of guerrilla-led revolu- tionary efforts. His "universe" is Latin America, a world-region with certain overarching similarities of culture, social structure, and geopolitical location to the "south" of a meddling superpower, the United States. His time period starts in the later 1950s, allowing him to hold constant certain world-historical tendencies in left-wing intellectual culture. Within this universe, Wickham- Crowley compares the national and regional fortunes of leftist insurgencies in two temporal "waves" of attempted guerrilla warfare: For the period 1956 to 1970, he compares movements in Cuba, Venezuela, Guatemala, Colombia, Peru, and Bolivia; for the period after 1970, he compares movements in Nicaragua, El Salvador, Guatemala, and Colombia. Note that Wickham-Crowley has more "units of analysis" than if he had treated nations as unbreakable blocs; the same nation can be examined twice if movements or conditions change. Nor is this all. In the final chapter of his blockbuster book, Wickham-Crowley goes beyond these in-depth case analyses to look at twenty-eight cases altogether, using the Boolean algebraic methods of Charles Ragin (1987) to examine additional countries/periods in Central and Latin America for the presence or absence of the outcomes and key configurations of explanatory variables that he identified in his in-depth comparisons. Wickham-Crowley is thus able to validate a substantively fascinating and impressively complete theory of "winners, losers, and also-rans" among Latin American guerrilla revolutionary movements since the 1950s. This is an extraordinary accomplishment!

Without at all doing justice to the subtlety and complexity of Wickham-Crowley's findings (and especially not to his explorations of conditions underlying principal "causes" or of the *alternative configurations* of conditions that led to guerrilla movements' failures), we can summarize the five conditions he identified as, in combination, necessary to explain the revolutionary victories in Cuba 1959 and Nicaragua 1979.

First, of course, there had to be organized *attempts* at guerrilla struggle for avowedly revolutionary purposes. As I read his evidence, Wickham-Crowley cannot precisely explain why these attempts occurred exactly when and how they did. In any event, they were very widespread across Latin America after the symbolically galvanizing event of the victory of Fidel Castro and his associates in Cuba. Still, in addition to telling the historical story, Wickham-Crowley offers a sociologically nuanced account of who the guerrilla vanguards were – middle- and upper-class higher-educated youth. He analyzes the intellectual and institutional conditions that propelled certain such young people to go from certain universities and political parties into the countryside.

Once in the countryside, the guerrilla vanguards had to find geopolitical space and develop social support to survive and propel their movements forward. Second, therefore, Wickham-Crowley explores a variety of social-structural and historical conditions that encouraged popular groups – especially regionally specific groups of peasants – to support or refuse to support guerrilla leaderships. Here insights are taken – and synthesized – from many social scientists and historians who have tried to approach revolutions in the Third World almost solely from the point of view of rural social structures and peasant grievances. Wickham-Crowley's synthesis goes well beyond previous work, because he also looks at conditions affecting the creation of ties between guerrillas and rural communities. If his work in this second area can be faulted in any way, it may be for a bit too much socioeconomic determinism (following the lead of Paige 1975). As both Ian Roxborough (1989: 107) and Jeff Goodwin (1993) argue, there may be strictly territorial-geopolitical reasons why remote rural regions are safe for guerrillas; and there may be conditions of local politics that influence possibilities for rural popular mobilization more than economic structures or processes do. But these are quibbles. Overall, Wickham-Crowley convincingly shows that some peasant and rural support is necessary if initial guerrilla attempts are to survive and grow.

Wickham-Crowley's third condition for guerrilla success – the growth of guerrilla military strength – is arguably not independently important. It approaches tautology with that which is to be explained, and Wickham-Crowley in any event attributes such growing guerrilla strength to the presence of active peasant support (his second factor). At most, one can say that discussion of this issue allows Wickham-Crowley to explore and show in depth that foreign aid to either guerrillas or regimes is not decisive – of itself, net of the domestic social structures and governmental institutions on which Wickham-Crowley principally focuses – in determining the growth of guerrilla-led movements. Wickham-Crowley and Goodwin agree on this finding.

Like Goodwin, moreover, Wickham-Crowley emphatically underlines that even quite widespread peasant (and other lower-class) support for a guerrilla insurgency is not enough to topple a challenged regime; the cases of Guatemala and El Salvador dramatize this point loud and clear. The fourth and fifth conditions that Wickham-Crowley highlights are the ones he considers decisive for separating "winners" from partially successful "also rans": Regimes in Latin America since 1956 that were actually overturned by revolutionaries were personalist neopatrimonial dictatorships – Wickham-Crowley calls them "mafiacracies" – that, prior to their overthrow, lost previous backing and aid from the United States.

Clearly, for Wickham-Crowley as for Goodwin, the form of the regime and its links to society is the crucial factor, for it in turn influences both the dynamics of domestic political conflicts and coalitions, and the stance of U.S. foreign policymakers. According to Wickham-Crowley's historical accounts, peasant-rooted, militarily viable guerrilla movements had to achieve a breakthrough to broad, cross-class political support, building truly national alliances that include urban social groups, encompassing some middle- and upper-class people. The mafiacracies of Cuba under Batista and Nicaragua under Somoza made this possible, because urban upper- and middle-class people were alienated by the dictator's extreme corruption, favoritism, and arbitrariness, as well as by his repressiveness. Many reformers were driven into political alliances with guerrillas. What is more, personalistic dictatorships tend to weaken or undercut military professionalism, thus rendering regime armies less effective against the guerrillas. U.S. policymakers, in turn, tend to lose enthusiasm for former-client dictators as they themselves prove politically and militarily inept at home. At the end, both Batista in Cuba and Somoza in Nicaragua lost U.S. support. When the dictators departed the scene, the state organizations they had previously manipulated and corrupted collapsed, opening the door to the armed revolutionaries.

By contrast, as Wickham-Crowley shows, more bureaucratic or "collectivist" forms of authoritarian government in Latin America have often been able to maintain alliances with (at least sectors of) broader middle- and upper-class groups. Such regimes may or may not have retained U.S. patronage, but either way they have been able to wage prolonged and relatively effective military struggles against guerrillas, including guerrillas with considerable peasant support. Such collectivist-authoritarian regimes in Latin America have either defeated armed revolutionaries outright (as in Guatemala and Argentina) or else fought them to a military stalemate (as in El Salvador).

Explaining social revolutions: What we have learned

Between them, the Goodwin and Wickham-Crowley studies are responsible for much of the solid knowledge we in the social sciences now have about the causes of actual and failed social revolutions involving colonial or independent regimes challenged by armed guerrilla movements between the end of World War II and the present. Taking these studies (and other related ones) together with *States and Social Revolutions,* we have much coherent knowledge of the full range of regimes and social structures that have – and have not – been susceptible to social revolutions in the modern world.

Democracies, we know, even imperfect ones, have rarely been susceptible to either the expansion or the victory of revolutionary movements. Neither have forms of authoritarian government that include populist, mass-incorporating political parties. What is more, although all kinds of repressive and exclusive authoritarian regimes are potentially vulnerable to the growth (even sudden growth) of broad-based, cross-class organizations or alliances of revolutionary challengers, the fact is that such regimes can crush or fight off such challengers as long as their state organizations remain administratively and coercively coherent. Collective authoritarian ruling groups – such as monarchies, corps of military officers, imperial-colonial governments, South Africa's Afrikaner Nationalist party, or home-bred communist parties – can maintain repressive and exclusive forms of rule for a very long time. Such regimes may well inspire attempts at armed revolutionary organization, as well as considerable social sympathy for such attempts. But through ruthless repression they can also make it hard for either popular rebels or armed revolutionaries to make headway.

Of course, types of authoritarian and exclusive rule that are stable at some times and in some circumstances can change, opening the door to state breakdowns from above, and perhaps to revolts or social revolutions from below. We need more historical research on the processes that can, over time, lead collective authoritarian rulers to lose coherence, confidence, and – above all – coercive effectiveness. Yet we already know a great deal. In effect, my book *States and Social Revolutions* analyzed the institutional structures and historical processes that rendered *some* absolute monarchies of the "old world" vulnerable to the development of fundamental political quarrels between landed upper classes and monarchs. Such quarrels, in turn, could actually disorganize centralized and partially bureaucratic monarchies, bringing about the breakdown of armies, because landed classes and military officer corps were overlapping – not truly differentiated socially or organizationally – in the sorts of agrarian bureaucracies I studied, the places where the world's first social revolutions broke out.

From the recent research of Goodwin, Wickham-Crowley, and others, we know that the "patrimonialization" of an authoritarian state with a professional military can create the conditions for state breakdown – and also inspire the formation of broad revolutionary coalitions. Most such ascents to power of personalistic dictators have occurred within regimes that were previously military dictatorships. That is what happened prior to the Mexican Revolution of 1911 (see Goldfrank 1979), prior to the Cuban Revolution of 1959, and prior to the Nicaraguan and Iranian revolutions of 1979. What is more, one of the communist regimes of Eastern Europe that was relatively independent of Soviet backing – the Romanian regime – had also become a neopatrimonial dictatorship. Nicolae Ceausescu had in effect displaced collective Communist and professional military rule prior to the overthrow of the Romanian government in 1989 (Fisher 1990; and Goodwin 1992).

Interestingly enough, an understanding of neopatrimonialism can also improve upon the analysis I offered of the Chinese Revolution. In *States and Social Revolutions,* I was correct to situate the start of the Chinese revolutionary process with the overthrow of the imperial agrarian-bureaucratic monarchy in 1911; yet in retrospect I did not offer as much explanation as I might have of the dynamics of the Communist guerrilla struggles between 1927 and 1949. Chinese Communist guerrillas survived, and their political fortunes and nationalist credentials improved over time, not just because of local peasant mobilization and the geopolitical stresses of warlordism and the Japanese invasion during World War II. These were important, but also important was the type of competitor movement and regime the Chinese Communists faced: a Kuomintang movement/regime that, after the 1920s, was profoundly weakened by the rise to power of a personalistic, neopatrimonial dictator, Chiang Kai-shek. Chiang's corrupt and patronage-oriented techniques of rule on the Chinese mainland after 1927 *both* politically alienated many educated middle-class and elite Chinese (thus creating urban sympathizers and cadre recruits for Communist nationalism) and, at the same time, undercut military effectiveness against the Japanese invaders and the Communist Red armies. I recounted all of this in *States and Social Revolutions* (1979: chap. 7); but now that we have the work of Goodwin and Wickham-Crowley we can better understand the general interplay of guerrillas and neopatrimonial regimes that also figured in a phase of the Chinese revolutionary interregnum.

Collective authoritarian regimes have also lost power in other ways. World

War II certainly pulled the rug out from under Western colonial empires, furthering the fortunes of many nationalist movements, including avowedly revolutionary guerrilla movements. And the decision of Gorbachev's reformist Soviet regime to withdraw the Red Army' security shield from the Eastern European communist regimes unquestionably encouraged both demoralization from within and challenges from without to those (essentially imperially implanted) regimes. Finally, too, the examples of both the Soviet Union and South Africa show that even a previously self-confident and unassailable form of collective authoritarianism can suddenly begin to change from the top, and perhaps experience state breakdown or fundamental structural transformation, if a radical reformer – a Gorbachev or DeKlerk – rises to power from within, and then sets out to introduce changes that other elite groups, especially within the state itself, find unacceptable. I do not believe that either the former Soviet Union or South Africa has experienced a true social revolution. But they certainly are in the process of going through radical sociopolitical transformations, uneasily guided from above, whose end results are not fully predictable.

So far, I have summarized what we social scientists know about possibilities for social revolution in terms of whether, how, and why particular types of regime are vulnerable to administrative-military breakdown. That consideration has to remain basic, because social revolutions simply do not happen without such breakdowns. From the research on directly ruled colonies and neopatrimonial regimes, moreover, we know that some of the same sorts of regimes that are "brittle" as administrative-military organizations are also (unintentionally) susceptible to the growth of broad-based revolutionary challenges, bringing together elements of upper, middle, and lower classes in opposition to the colonial power or the personalistic dictator.

Yet we also know that the explanation of conditions for (and against) social revolutions cannot be purely state-centric. In *States and Social Revolutions* – and even more clearly in the essay "What Makes Peasants Revolutionary?" that is reprinted as Chapter 9 of this volume – I argued that *either* widespread revolts of local peasant communities *or* significant peasant support for guerrilla revolutionary challengers had been an essential contributory condition, along with administrative-military breakdown from above, in all modern social revolutions. Wickham-Crowley's (1992) research supports this argument, including the conclusion that the social and political conditions that further peasant-based resistance "from below" are somewhat independent of the conditions that further regime vulnerability (both military and political) "from above."

Still, Wickham-Crowley and I both agree that the recent Iranian Revolution was exceptional. In this instance there were no widespread local-peasant revolts in 1979, and no rural guerrilla movement had built up the military power to bring down the Shah's regime. A great deal of further research has underlined the conclusion I drew in my 1982 article about Iran (reprinted here as Chapter 10). There was a "functional substitute" for peasant revolts or guerrilla support in the Iranian Revolution, in the form of urban popular demonstrations that were widespread, sustained over time in the face of spotty repression, and loosely coordinated by an Islamic moralistic rhetoric critical of the Shah's dictatorship (Najmabadi 1987, 1993; Foran 1992). Without these urban demonstrations, the Shah's rule, though weakened by its neopatrimonial character and his own personal indecisiveness due to illness, would surely not have crumbled in 1978–80. These demonstrations were made socially and culturally possible by politicized networks centered within urban bazaars and mosques, cross-class communities that were socially and procedurally intertwined with one another, and that operated under the leadership of merchants and Islamic clerics who were both politically alienated and somewhat organizationally autonomous from the Shah's dictatorship (Keddie 1992:67–71). Analytically speaking, these Iranian urban communities had some of the same sorts of sociopolitical (and even popular-cultural) characteristics as peasant communities or rural guerrilla-run zones in other instances of social revolutions. All the same, they were different, and no analyst can get around the fundamental uniqueness of this urban-centered aspect of the Iranian Revolution.[3]

One other instance of social revolution may also have had a distinctive kind of resistant social community at the center of the processes that disorganized the old regime. I have in mind the Bolivian Revolution of 1952 (see Kelley and Klein 1981 and Roxborough 1989 for what little – not enough – I know about this case). Strictly speaking, according to Wickham-Crowley's typology of regimes in Latin America, the pre-1952 Bolivian government was a collective military dictatorship allied with upper-class oligarchs, landlords, and mineowners. This regime should have been able to put down the middle-class populist political challenge it experienced from the Movimento Nacionalista Revolucianario (MNR) party. Indeed, as I understand events, repression *is* what happened at first. The MNR won an election in 1951, but then was challenged by an oligarchically directed military coup in 1952. The predictable course of events changed, however, when Bolivian miners – centered in isolated, solidary, and politically radicalized communities (they were members of Trotskyist unions) – rose up in armed revolt and seized a train heading to the capital city, La Paz, carrying ammunition and reinforcements for the military.[4] As a result, the military was disorganized and defeated, and the MNR came back to governmental power with the support of the armed miners. Then peasant communities across certain regions of Bolivia rose up against landlords and deposed them for good, turning a political and military crisis into a full-blown social revolution, Certainly, the pattern of spontaneous, community-based peasant revolts in the Bolivian Revolution very much resembles what happened in France in 1789 and Russia in 1917. But processes of administrative-military breakdown of the preexisting state did *not* resemble what happened to the French, Russian, or Chinese monarchies. Nor was the pre-1952 Bolivian regime a directly ruled colony or a neopatrimonial dictatorship. I am inclined to think that in Bolivia

1952, as in Iran 1979, a special kind of resistant popular community helped to bring down the old regime. In Bolivia, however, the miners were armed, and they took on the military directly.

Causal analyses of the conditions for social revolutions certainly have to examine *configurations* of conditions (for the methodology involved here, see Ragin 1987 and Wickham-Crowley 1992: chap. 12).[5] Studies must allow for the possibility of special (although theoretically understandable) *substitutes* for otherwise regular patterns – alternative causal configurations, if you will. Despite the complexity of all of this, we in the social sciences now know a lot about the various historical paths and configurations that have led to conjunctures of administrative-military breakdown and popularly based radical revolts – abstractly stated, the combination that adds up to social revolution. This was the causal combination that I suggested in *States and Social Revolutions*.

In that work I also highlighted the contribution of world-historically specific transnational structures and processes to social-revolutionary transformations. Further research has, I think, helped to enrich and better specify our sense of the international factors that contribute to revolutionary processes. Recurrent wars and ongoing geopolitical competition were critical background processes that spurred fiscal crises and intraelite conflicts in early-modern agrarian-bureaucratic monarchies.[6] Particular wars as events have sometimes directly contributed to regime collapses. World War I directly brought down the Tsarist regime in Russia, 1917; and World War II furthered social revolutions again, but in a different way. Here, as Jeff Goodwin has shown, the issue was not the direct effects of geopolitical competition among great military powers; it was the indirect facilitation of nationalist movements guerrilla insurgencies brought about by military occupations and disruptions of colonial rule. For neopatrimonial regimes, however, geopolitical military competition and wars have not been important spurs to social revolution. Instead, as scholars such as Roxborough (1989) and Foran (1992) have explicated, dislocations in transnational markets have been contributors to the growth of revolutionary oppositions, and shifts in great-power patronage have contributed to the weakening of regimes challenged by domestic opponents. We may also need to talk (more than people have done so far) about transnational ideological influences on revolutionary cadres and rulers alike. These influences clearly shift over time, and may contribute in important ways to the sorts of revolutionary movements or regime transitions that occur in different eras.

For mid-twentieth-century social revolutions against neopatrimonial regimes, transnational geopolitical, economic, and cultural processes have all worked *indirectly* – that is, in conjunction with, and through, domestically centered social structures and political-military processes. As both Goodwin and Wickham-Crowley have demonstrated, despite what many would-be revolutionaries or counterrevolutionaries think or hope, social revolutions in the Third World are not fundamentally either caused or prevented from abroad. The organizational type of state, linkages of military to nonmilitary rulers, and the articulations of states with social structures and politically active social groups are what matter most fundamentally. International processes matter as they influence such structures and relationships "on the ground" in the countries themselves.

Back in 1978, as I wrote the final pages of *States and Social Revolutions*, I expected that the principal kinds of regimes and social revolutions that would be featured in further comparative-historical studies would be decolonizing regimes transformed (or not) by guerrilla-led "national liberation" struggles based socially in peasantries. After waves of decolonization had played themselves out in Africa, Latin America, and beyond, I did not expect that there would be many more social revolutions to study. I believed that social unrest from below, and attempts at armed insurrections by marginal elites, would normally be put down by threatened rulers of contemporary independent national states. I believed this because of presence within such states – whether democracies, or party-states, or authoritarian dictatorships embodying alliances between military officer corps and propertied upper classes – of technologically modern, professionalized military establishments. Such professionalized militaries nowadays have a stronger-than-ever coercive advantage over insurgents. More than that, I argued (see Skocpol 1979: 289–90), modern professional militaries are sufficiently institutionally differentiated from upper propertied classes that they are not likely to be organizationally disrupted by the sorts of political quarrels between rulers and upper-class groups that had helped to break apart the French military in 1787–89 and the Chinese military in 1911–16. As of 1978, I expected many military coups in independent Third World nations, but not the sorts of social revolutions that happened – right after my book was published! – in Iran and Nicaragua.

World events and scholarship have now moved forward into the 1990s, and we have learned much more about the social and political conditions that lead toward, or deflect, social revolutionary transfers of state power. It turns out that I was both right and wrong back in 1978–79. I was obviously mistaken not to foresee more social revolutions in certain kinds of sovereign Third World states. Social revolutions in the modern world have occurred in certain neopatrimonial dictatorships, as well as in certain agrarian bureaucratic monarchies and in certain kinds of imperial possessions during transitions from colonial rule. Yet even if I did not understand all the types of regimes that might be vulnerable to social revolutions, I was wise enough back in 1978–79 about some fundamentals of theoretical and research strategy. Social-scientific knowledge about the causes, processes, and outcomes of social revolutions has been furthered above all by investigators who have focused on state organizations and patterns of state–society relations. Even more clearly, our knowledge of the causes of social revolutions has been furthered by those who have used macrocausal

historical analysis to compare both revolutionary and nonrevolutionary developments in various regions of the contemporary world.

SHOULD WE ABANDON COMPARATIVE HISTORICAL ANALYSIS?

During the past couple of decades, macroscopic social scientists have actually
been getting somewhere by using comparative-historical methods of investigation to focus on states, social structures, politics, and social change (along the
lines called for in Evans, Rueschemeyer, and Skocpol 1985). They have been
developing and improving explanations for variations in important processes
and outcomes in the world. This has certainly been true, as I have just demonstrated, for the study of social revolutions. It has also been true for the study of
other important macrophenomena, including the formation of national states in
Europe and beyond (e.g., L. Anderson 1986; Downing 1992; Tilly 1975);
transitions to democracy (e.g., Luebbert 1991; Huntington 1991; Rueschemeyer, Stephens, and Stephens 1992); the development of Western welfare states
(e.g., Castles 1978, 1985; Esping-Andersen 1990; Flora and Heidenheimer
1981; Immergut 1992; Malloy 1979; Orloff 1993; Skocpol 1992); the emergence
or political effects of major idea-systems (e.g., Fulbrook 1983; Smith 1987;
Wuthnow 1989); and the role of national states in promoting economic development, regulation, or social redistribution (e.g., Echeverri-Gent 1993; Evans
forthcoming; Hall 1986; Kohli 1987; and Vogel 1986). Ironically, however, just
as macrocomparativists have been achieving deeper, broader, and (to some
degree) cumulated knowledge of such important matters, some prestigious po-
lemicists in the social sciences have started denouncing comparative historical
analysis. (On second thought, this is probably to be expected, because a tendency in scholarship is hardly worth denouncing until it attains results and influence!)

For the purposes of this discussion, three examples of such broadside attacks
on institutionalist comparative-historical analysis are of interest. These are written by ambitious major scholars who have alternative programs to offer. Each
of the critics we are about to meet focuses considerable attention on *States and
Social Revolutions*, arguing that it is grievously flawed methodologically and
theoretically – that it is therefore not a good basis or model for further scholarship in macroscopic social science. Then each person outlines a ready-made
methodological and theoretical program to substitute for the entire kind of
scholarship that my 1979 book exemplifies in his eyes. Thus, the sociologist
Michael Burawoy wants to get rid of comparative-historical analyses in favor of
a restoration of a classical Marxist theory applied by partisan actors within
particular historical conflicts. The rational-choice sociologist Michael Hechter
wants to replace all historical and comparative-historical macroscopic scholarship with general, formal theorizing about the microfoundations of social action.

And the culturally oriented social historian William Sewell, Jr., wants to get rid of *comparative* causal analysis in historical sociology, replacing it with narrations of events in particularized and holistically considered times and places.

Let us look at what each of these weighty figures has to say, and discover why each is just plain wrong to question the value and validity of comparative-historical analyses of social revolutions. While each of these critics may reasonably call for other styles of scholarship to develop alongside of, and in addition to, comparative-historical analyses, their calls to substitute entirely new theoretical and methodological programs – programs that, in any event, are mutually incompatible – should not be heeded by those who seek to understand the dynamics of states, social structures, and political processes in the modern world.

A revival of the Marxist theory of history?

We begin with a broadside against *States and Social Revolutions* that Michael Burawoy (1989a) published in the journal *Theory and Society* – and I cannot resist a personal digression at this point. When I first read a draft of Burawoy's "Two Methods in Search of Science: Skocpol versus Trotsky," I was much interested to learn *why* Burawoy was advocating Leon Trotsky's theory of "permanent revolution" as a replacement for my state-centered, comparative-causal analysis of the French, Russian, and Chinese revolutions. Burawoy lauds Trotsky for his unshakable commitment to the Marxist understanding of history, and for his ability to rework that theoretical tradition from within to predict the course of events in which he (Trotsky) was a committed revolutionary actor. Reading this left me with feelings of sad remembrance and wry amusement. Trotsky was undoubtedly a brilliant intellectual and revolutionary, but what can one say about the predictive powers of his variant of class-conflict theorizing about revolutions? After all, Trotsky was thoroughly outmaneuvered during the 1920s by that master bureaucrat and terrorist, Joseph Stalin. Trotsky did not really understand what was going on after 1921 in the Soviet state or countryside, and he falsely put his faith in theoretical predictions that "permanent" working-class revolution would soon spread into Germany (and the rest of Europe). He and his followers were forced out of the Soviet Union and the Communist International, and Trotsky himself ended up with an axe through his head, murdered by a Stalinist agent. It is conceivable that Trotsky might have done better as an actor in the Russian Revolution if he had believed in a more state-centered theory of revolutions, and had not so fetishized "the working class." But even if this is not true, Burawoy's celebration of Trotsky's predictive powers as a Marxist theorist seems bizarrely misplaced.

Burawoy's real beef with me is that I am not a Marxist committed to revolutionary advocacy and willing to *presume* the basic truth of a Marxist vision of history. In contrast to Skocpol, Trotsky is praised because, for him, refutation of Marxist theoretical predictions "does not lead to the rejection of the Marxist research program but to the construction of new theories on the same Marxist foundation" (Burawoy 1989a: 764). Burawoy must realize that this essentially ideological attack on my scholarship will not prove very effective with most social scientists, so he disguises it as a purely "methodological" critique of my use of comparative-historical causal analysis in *States and Social Revolutions*.[7] Burawoy's methodological indictment has several parts, to each of which I have a ready response.

Ignoring my own summary charts (Skocpol 1979: 155–57), Burawoy (1989a: 768) presents a table purporting to summarize my historical case comparisons and the elements of my findings about the impact of international pressures, state-dominant class relationships, and local agrarian sociopolitical structures on possibilities for social revolutions in agrarian-bureaucratic monarchies. Using his table, Burawoy claims that I did not establish the plausibility of my claim that *both* state breakdowns from above and conditions facilitating peasant revolts had to be present for a successful social revolution to occur. Burawoy says I have no contrast cases where only one of these elements was missing.

But Burawoy inaccurately and incompletely presents my cases and findings. In fact, I showed that the English Revolution *did* involve mild international pressures, a fiscal crisis, and a split between the landed class and the monarch; in my analysis, it was *only* the absence of local agrarian class and political structures conducive to widespread peasant revolts against landlords that kept the English Revolution from becoming a social as well as political revolution. More telling, Burawoy leaves out of his table altogether the analytically crucial comparison I make between Russia in 1905–6 and in 1917. No doubt, Burawoy forgets about this comparison because it is the one that deals a deathblow to the Marxist theory of proletarian revolution. As I carefully show in *States and Social Revolutions*, Russia in 1905–6 experienced massive working-class strikes, middle- and upper-class struggles against the monarchy, *and* widespread peasant revolts – all the ingredients for a "class struggle" explanation of revolution. In 1906, however, the Tsarist armies returned to European Russia intact after the (hasty) conclusion of a modest war in the Far East, whereas by 1917 the Tsarist armies were overwhelmed and disorganized by three years of losses during a total modern war with Germany, a struggle from which Russia could not easily exit. The comparison of Russia 1905–6 to Russia 1917 is as close to a "controlled comparison" as one can get in comparative history. It is ideal for showing that an administrative-military breakdown of the Tsarist state, occasioned by massive international pressure and military defeat, was a crucial cause of successful social revolution in Russia, a cause independent of (urban or rural) class conflict as such.

Yet Burawoy's complaints about my use of comparative-historical causal analysis are actually more metamethodological than substantive. He inaccurately claims that I proceed purely "inductively" in my comparative-historical analysis.

And he asserts that I present hypotheses that are not, and cannot be, tested against alternative theoretical arguments. Given that I explicitly argued in *States and Social Revolutions* that comparative-historical methods were insufficient without historical understanding and theoretical imagination (Skocpol 1979: 38–40); given that I outlined ideas about the state derived from Weberian and Hintzean comparative analysis (Skocpol 1979: 19–32), along with ideas about collective action taken from Charles Tilly and resource-mobilization theory (Skocpol 1979: 13–14); and given that I used historical comparisons throughout my 1979 book to consider the adequacy of competing arguments, I am mystified by these charges. It seems to me that it is Burawoy who does not want any competition or empirical challenges to his favorite theory.[8] Why, after all, doesn't Burawoy himself lay out Trotsky's competing theoretical predictions – for example, about revolutionary possibilities in Russia compared with Germany – and see how they fare empirically compared with mine? The reason is perhaps obvious: I offer an analysis that illuminates why successful revolution did *not* happen in Germany, whereas Trotsky merely declared that a proletarian revolution was "inevitable" there – and in many other countries where no social revolution ever occurred.

Burawoy also claims that I arbitrarily selected historical cases of social revolution and other societal political conflicts only from certain periods of world history, thus protecting my causal analysis from (presumed) "falsification" by later revolutions. He does not actually show which later revolutions would actually falsify my theory or – more to the point – be better accounted for by a Marxist theory.[9] And Burawoy is wrong to say that I restricted my first investigation of social revolutions by chronology alone. As I made very clear, I was analyzing possibilities for social revolutions in a *particular type of old regime*, the agrarian-bureaucratic monarchy, of which pre-1789 France, pre-1917 Russia, and pre-1911 China (as well as my contrast cases) were all instances. I also tried hard to juxtapose agrarian-bureaucratic monarchies in roughly comparable circumstances (e.g., France and England; Germany and Russia; China and Japan); and I made comparisons across time in single countries (especially Russia and Germany). *States and Social Revolutions* had a properly restricted scope defined in institutional terms; it was about conditions for (and against) social revolutions in agrarian-bureaucratic monarchies. I left it to others to analyze conditions furthering or precluding social revolutions in other types of states and social structures (such as colonies or Third World dictatorships). Interestingly, Burawoy suggested in his critique that the state-centered theoretical hypotheses I put forward in 1979 would not prove fruitful for further work on more recent social revolutions. Obviously, Burawoy was not familiar with the rich range of comparative-historical studies – virtually none of them Marxist-inspired – that have appeared since the late 1970s. Indeed, the references to his *Theory and Society* article omit all of them, while including lots of books and articles by Marxists and philosophers of science.

Burawoy, one must conclude, is profoundly hostile to truly empirically grounded scholarship on social revolutions – or on other topics relating to large-scale historical change – because he is determined to maintain his faith in Marxism as a *teleology* of history. In my view, such a faith is possible to maintain *only* if one avoids the use of empirically sensitive methods, including but not restricted to macroanalytic comparative history, to sort out theories and hypotheses in relation to systematically assembled evidence. I would not (and never have) claimed that comparative-historical analysis is an infallible research approach for this purpose (see my frank discussion of comparative history's limits in 1979: 38–40). There are no infallible research approaches! (For a thoughtful discussion of the strengths and limitations of many different approaches used in the social sciences, see Little 1991). I only claim that this approach is *better than the alternatives* that have actually been used in writings about revolutions by scholars or political practitioners.

All too many of these writings have consisted of ideological wishful thinking or historically illustrated (but not tested) theoretical speculation. Trotsky's works can be characterized this way (although, to be sure, they are still well worth reading). Yet Trotsky, after all, had a good excuse: He was principally a revolutionary, not a scholar. Despite Burawoy's enthusiasm, neither Trotsky nor any other ideologically committed Marxist can be held up as a model of how social scientists today should proceed – at least not if their goal is to understand why and where social revolutions have actually occurred (or not) in the modern world, and where they might (or might not) occur next. I do not shrink from claiming that my writings, and similar comparative-historical studies that have followed after them, have done much more to further *that* goal than the writings of Leon Trotsky.

A challenge from rational choice?

Michael Hechter, like Michael Burawoy, has grand theoretical ambitions, but they are substantively very different. Where Burawoy calls for Marxist-inspired research to be practiced by ideologically committed scholars, Michael Hechter proclaims the virtues of a purely "scientific" approach, which he defines as deductive theorizing on the basis of general models about the microfoundations of all human action. Hechter lays out his critique of all comparative-historical sociology – especially mine – in a 1991 *American Journal of Sociology* article coauthored with Edgar Kiser on "The Role of General Theory in Comparative-historical Sociology."

The article begins by raising the horrible specter of a sociological discipline being overtaken by misguided people who want to reduce it to a traditional "historians' methodology" typified by a search for "the accuracy and descriptive completeness of narratives about particular events" and thus plagued by "loose conceptualizations," "implicative," "conjunctural" arguments, and "sufficient" rather than "necessary" explanations (Kiser and Hechter 1991: 2). The discipline of sociology, Kiser and Hechter claim (in what is surely one of the most amusing parts of their article), was traditionally committed to "general theorizing" and thus was free of the "nonrigorous methodologies" typical of historians. But recently, alas, comparative historical sociologists such as Reinhard Bendix, Michael Mann, Charles Tilly, and (apparently, above all) Theda Skocpol have led a revolt against "theory in general" that threatens to destroy sociology as a scientific enterprise.

Kiser and Hechter realize, of course, that my book *States and Social Revolutions* had causal-analytical rather than descriptive purposes, and that it was primarily critical of explanations derived from Parsonsian structure-functionalist or Marxist theoretical premises. These were, after all, the sociological "general theories" available when I did my research in the 1970s. Kiser and Hechter – unlike Burawoy – do not want to advocate a return to either of those *previous* "general theories" applied to revolutions. Instead, they want to show that I was unable to develop any alternative as sound as the brand new General Theory that they have to offer (to me, and to all of sociology): rational-choice theory. Kiser and Hechter attempt to knock out *States and Social Revolutions* not by dealing with *any* of its substantive ideas or findings, but by showing that – in very general logical terms – that it does not live up to what they claim, in the abstract, any "adequate explanation must entail."

Some of Kiser and Hechter's charges are simply false or naive. As usual, I am accused of having done a "purely inductive" comparative-historical analysis of France, Russia, and China compared with several other cases. As I have already pointed out, this charge is false: I used ideas about types of state–society regimes to help me select my cases, and I used Hintzean, Weberian, and resource-mobilization ideas as sources of inspiration for causal hypotheses to explore empirically. Bizarrely, Kiser and Hechter declare (1991: 13) that, because in comparative-historical investigations the cases "must be independent, the inductive method cannot be used to study changes in one case over time." But this simply reifies the inevitably analytical definition of "cases." In *States and Social Revolutions,* I could and did make comparisons between Russia 1905 and Russia 1917, and between Prussia/Germany 1807 and Germany 1848, because my "cases" were not simply countries; they were *episodes* of societal-level sociopolitical conflict within the histories of certain kinds of regimes. Similarly, in his 1992 book, Timothy Wickham-Crowley breaks national histories into multiple "cases," defined according to time periods when guerrilla vanguards attempted to build revolutionary movements.

Kiser and Hechter also accuse me of having worked with a limited and unsystematically selected "sample" of cases in *States and Social Revolutions,* and consequently with having produced results that are not "general." Of course, I never claimed to have mechanically generalizable results; my claims were restricted to agrarian-bureaucratic monarchies. Research in macroscopic social science (including all that has ever been produced by Kiser or Hechter) virtually never uses simple "representative" samples. When such attempts have been made, as for example in aggregate cross-national studies of "political violence," they have been plagued by vaguely conceptualized dependent and independent variables and highly unreliable operationalizations. But the more interesting point here is Kiser and Hechter's profound misunderstanding of how cumulative knowledge is actually developed in *practice*, by real social scientists, rather than as theorized in the pages of philosophy of science textbooks. In real life, scholars build upon each other's work over time. Thus, the later research of Jeff Goodwin, Timothy Wickham-Crowley, and other comparative-historical analysts of social revolutions has extended and refined the hypotheses about social revolutions that I put forward in 1979. My book was the beginning of a series of comparative-historical studies that combined deductive hypothesis formulation and inductive discovery of empirical regularities. Kiser and Hechter cannot really imagine that I could have done more in *States and Social Revolutions* alone. Thus their indictment against me must rest on ignoring – as indeed they do – all subsequent comparative-historical scholarship about social revolutions. They refuse to acknowledge the fruitfulness and broad scope of the theoretical conversations and further comparative-historical research that I helped to inspire.

The indictment against me could, however, still lead to a conviction if Kiser and Hechter could show that I overlooked a powerful general theory on which I should have relied. (Or I could be reduced to the status of a prehistoric totem, if Kiser and Hechter could show that such a general theory now exists, so that all current students of social revolutions should turn to it.) Thus Kiser and Hechter's most heartfelt complaint is that I did not "theoretically" explicate the empirical regularities I presented in *States and Social Revolutions*. By this they mean that I did not present them as deductively "necessary" in terms of general "mechanisms" logically derived in a deductive manner from a "general theory."

Readers of the article in the *American Journal of Sociology* must have arrived with breathless anticipation at this point in Kiser and Hechter's polemic (which comes two-thirds of the way through the piece): Surely Kiser and Hechter were about to pull the rabbit out of the hat! They would end their article by naming the General Theory that Skocpol and other empirically grubby comparative-historical analysts should have used. They would tell us exactly how that General Theory can elegantly and deductively explain social revolutions!

To be sure, Kiser and Hechter declare rational-choice theory to be *the* solution. But then they simply drop the ball. They do not provide anything resembling a general, deductive explanation of social revolutions. Instead, they change the subject for the rest of their article, discussing very different literatures about "state autonomy" and public policymaking. Their last gesture prior to departing from the complexities of social revolutions is to refer readers to the articles of Michael Taylor about collective action by peasants during revolutions. Taylor is said to have used rational-choice theory to devise a deductive, general theory of "revolutionary collective action." Unfortunately, once the frustrated reader rushes to the library and obtains Taylor's articles (1988, 1989), he or she discovers that rational-choice theory has (as yet) offered nothing remotely resembling a general deductive theory of social revolutions.

Michael Taylor, to be fair, never makes any such claim. His two articles are lengthy, wide-ranging, and thoughtful commentaries on the *possibilities* for using certain variants of rational-choice reasoning to provide "microfoundations" for very delimited and selected *aspects* of comparative-historical structural explanations such as the one I developed in *States and Social Revolutions.* Unlike Kiser and Hechter and other overweening proponents of rational choice as a general theory allegedly capable of "subsuming" all others, Taylor aims to do no more than combine rational-choice and structural propositions to explain revolutions (see 1988: 95). In his discussion of *States and Social Revolutions* as such, Taylor takes entirely for granted the validity of my comparative-structural analysis of conditions for state breakdowns in the agrarian-bureaucratic monarchies I studied, and concentrates solely on providing a rational-choice gloss on what I reported about the rebellious actions of French, Russian, and Chinese peasantries. He offers creative speculations, grounded in instrumental versions of rational-choice theory, about the sorts of individual motivations that might have encouraged peasants in French and Russian villages to engage in collective actions that (under the separately determined national political conditions that prevailed in 1789 and 1917) contributed to social revolutions. (I call Taylor's arguments "speculations," because of course we do not know, and never will know, what was in the heads of rebellious French and Russian peasants. Perhaps conveniently, even when it would be possible to gather such data, rational-choice theorists rarely do. Their "individuals" are not real people!)

Taylor does not claim that the peasant collective actions he is discussing – which are described, just as I described them, as community-based solidary movements of peasants who shared normative and moral ideas – were any different at "revolutionary" or "rebellious" macropolitical moments in French and Russian history. This was exactly the point I made in 1979: that peasants are not deliberate "makers" of revolutions; under certain macropolitical conditions that emerge above their heads, their local rebellious actions can lead to revolutions.

Overall, Taylor does not question the validity of my comparative-historical analysis, or of my structural explanatory approach. He assumes its accuracy, and simply argues that it is "incomplete" because it fails to spell out the individual-level actions and motivations that connect one macrostate to another in processes of social revolutionary conflict and transformation. This may be a fair observation on his part, yet I had good reasons for not spelling out every microprocess at work in the hundreds of years' worth of events analyzed in my 1979 book. I would have become incredibly bogged down, and the "big picture," which gives the book its power, would have been lost. Significantly, it takes Michael Taylor two very lengthy articles just to provide a rational-choice gloss on material in one out of seven chapters of my 1979 book. When one is finished reading his articles, one does not have an explanation of revolution – or of any aspect of the French, Russian, and Chinese cases – that is any different from those I provided.

The reason for the lack of profound differences between Taylor's analysis and my own may be that the "structural" perspective I articulated back in 1979 was *not* an attack on rational-choice theory (which was not prominent in the social sciences during the 1970s). My "structuralism" was, instead, a critique of Marxist, structural-functionalist, and frustration-aggression theories that tried to describe and explain revolutions in terms of *reified collective actors* – such as "the proletariat," or "the bourgeoisie," or "the revolutionary movement," or authorities charged with "re-synchronizing the social system." As I see it, both historical-structuralists like myself and rational-choice theorists like Taylor are united in opposing such collectivist reifications. I was not kidding when I wrote in 1979 that revolutions *involve* the conflicting actions of concrete groups and individuals (see Skocpol 1979: 17–18). The point is to come up with strategies of analysis and explanation that make sense of the complexity of intersecting courses of situated individual and group actions.

Moreover, I simply assumed that the peasants and others whose actions I narrated were acting rationally. Indeed, in my analysis of the French and Russian peasant communities that Taylor discusses so extensively, I took for granted Mancur Olson's (1965) insights about small-group action; my contribution was to show that relatively simultaneous and widespread local revolts in France and Russia contributed to the overall set of processes that came together to produce social revolutions. No doubt, the reason that Taylor is so easily able to provide a rational-choice gloss on my discussion of peasant communities and revolts is that he and I were starting from much more similar metatheoretical assumptions than he supposes. I just didn't make such a big fuss about it.

The jury is still out on whether rational-choice theorists will be able to add theoretical value to existing explanations of social revolutions (and other macroscopic phenomena) – rather than merely translating existing comparative-historical analyses into their own tribal language. At this point, I am willing to give rational-choice theorists the benefit of the doubt. I presume that they will one day enrich our understanding, providing some genuinely new and complementary insights about microprocesses – much as (say) the microtheorist Dennis Chong (1991) has done in complementary relationship to the macroanalysis of the U.S. civil rights movement provided earlier by Doug McAdam (1982). Even so, rational-choice theorists have little cause for anything except humility at this point. Despite the bombastic proclamations of Kiser and Hechter (1991), they have yet to go beyond speculative glosses or virtually untestable formal models referring to *very partial aspects* of overall social revolutions.

Thus, James DeNardo (1985) models conceivable strategies for particular radical vanguards and factions, yet concludes with elaborate recommendations for further research that would be virtually impossible to carry out, and would not explain much about revolutions anyway. Students of rebellious popular activities in various times and places (for examples in addition to Taylor 1988, 1989, see Berejikian 1992; Dennis 1986; Lichbach 1994; Muller and Opp 1986; and Popkin 1979) enrich our understandings of collective action, but hardly challenge the finding that state breakdowns are equally important and separately determined causes of social revolutions – a point that has, by now, been well established, and given considerable empirical substance, by Skocpol (1979), Goldstone (1991), Wickham-Crowley (1992), and Goodwin (1988 and forthcoming), and other comparative-historical analysts. Of course there are actors, with interests and ideas, who take part in bringing about "state breakdowns." And no doubt they act rationally. Rational-choice theorists may, in due course, illuminate the "microfoundations" of state breakdowns. But they will not be "subsuming" the work we comparative-historical analysts have already done. They will be standing on our shoulders.

A return to narrative history?

If Michael Hechter is worried about alleged historicist directions in the work of macroanalytical comparativists such as Theda Skocpol, he should meet someone who is a much more pressing threat to his theoretically deductivist, scientistic vision of sociology: William Sewell, Jr. I would like to be a fly on the wall while the two of them have a long talk about what is wrong with my scholarship – for they see very different things, and mostly opposite faults, in it.

In addition to discussing *States and Social Revolutions* in the article reprinted as Chapter 7 of this volume, Sewell has recently developed a lengthy methodological critique of the book in an essay entitled "Three Temporalities: Toward an Eventful Sociology." This bold piece aims to do no less than reorient all of historical sociology – an enterprise that Sewell, a newcomer recently arrived from French history, believes has been insufficiently "radically" developed. Scholars such as Immanuel Wallerstein, Charles Tilly, and Theda Skocpol have, in Sewell's view, made undesirable compromises with "positivist," "mainstream sociology." Books such as Wallerstein's *The Modern World-System* (1974), Tilly's *The Vendée* (1967), and Skocpol's *States and Social Revolutions* need to be "rehabilitated," as Sewell (forthcoming) puts it in an amazingly condescending formulation. By this he means that these works must be purged of any traces of teleology (a sin that Sewell attributes to Wallerstein and Tilly) and of comparative causal analysis (a sin he attributes to me). Sewell wants to see all of historical social science reoriented into narrative storytelling about "events" conceived as sudden turning points in the otherwise inexorable and unbreakable flow of History. Sewell admits (forthcoming) that the ideas he proposes are "close to the implicit intellectual baggage of most academic historians." (Michael Hechter, here is the target you were trying to get in your sights!)

I shall concentrate here on Sewell's confrontation with *States and Social Revolutions*. This is justified not only because this confrontation takes up the largest part of Sewell's essay, but also because Sewell's inability to find a consistent vantage point in relation to my book splendidly reveals the internal contradictions of his entire attempt to deconstruct and radically reorient historical social science.[10] In the course of some fifteen pages, Sewell offers three different, mutually contradictory commentaries on my 1979 book. First, he argues that *States and Social Revolutions* is inherently flawed as a comparative-historical analysis of the causes of social revolutions. Then he says that such flaws do not much matter, because all comparative-historical analysis is logically impossible, anyway. Finally, Sewell reverses ground, announces that my book is brilliant and compelling despite my worthless methodology, and tries to "rehabilitate" *States and Social Revolutions* as an example of the "eventful" historical sociology he advocates. Let's work our way through this, and see where we end up.

We need not tarry long with Sewell's first line of attack, because he simply mischaracterizes the arguments and methodology of *States and Social Revolutions*. When I first read Sewell's essay, I was mystified to see him make one false claim after another about arguments of my 1979 book. Had Sewell carefully read (or reread) *States and Social Revolutions?* Then I looked at his references and saw the answer: Sewell relies on Michael Burawoy's (1989a) summary of and commentary about the book. Thus Sewell's presentations of "Skocpol's" causal arguments, of "her" substantive case discussions, and of the structure of "her" case comparisons come straight from Michael Burawoy's inaccurate summary chart (1989: 768). Sewell's historical critiques are really commentaries on Burawoy, not on Skocpol. Consequently, the things Sewell has to say about the variables I use in my argument about the causes of social revolutions; about the features of the English case; about the absence of a critical contrast between a political and a social revolution; and about "my" treatment of the Chinese case – all are based on mistaken characterizations originating in Burawoy's rendition of what is said in my book.[11]

Similar problems arise from Sewell's mistaken claim, also following Burawoy, that I used "purely inductive" methods. Both Sewell and Burawoy strain to set me up as a mechanical "straw man," claiming that I presented comparative-historical analysis as an atheoretical technical "panacea" for macrosociologists. In fact, I explicitly started *States and Social Revolutions* with theoretical discussions, especially about the states and classes and types of state–society regimes. And I clearly presented comparative-historical analysis as a way of moving back and forth between theoretical hypotheses and historical cases. This approach, I declared, is "no substitute for theory" (1979: 39), yet it is useful as an "aid in the development of . . . explanations of revolutions" (1979: 35), because it

serves as "a valuable check, or anchor, for theoretical speculations" (1979: 39).
Comparative historical analysis can function in this way, I argued, because it

encourages one to spell out the actual causal arguments suggested by grand theoretical
perspectives, and to combine diverse arguments if necessary in order to remain faithful
to the ultimate objective – which is, of course, the actual illumination of causal regularities across sets of historical cases. Whatever the source(s) of theoretical inspiration,
comparative history succeeds only if it convincingly fulfills this goal. And when it *is*
successfully employed, comparative historical analysis is an ideal strategy for mediating
between theory and history. Provided that it is not mechanically applied, it can prompt
both theoretical extensions and reformulations, on the one hand, and new ways of
looking at historical cases, on the other. (Skocpol 1979: 39–40)

In all likelihood, Sewell was willing to take the shortcut of using Burawoy to
characterize (and attack) my substantive comparative-historical arguments in
States and Social Revolutions, because he does not really care about those
arguments. (Indeed, at no point during his entire essay does Sewell ever indicate
any concern about the accuracy of *any* empirical claims or theoretical arguments; he focuses only on their form.) Sewell wants to use me as an example of
the inherent, inescapable "logical deficiencies" that must plague (what he calls)
the application of "experimental" methods to history. In order to do any comparative-historical study, Sewell argues (forthcoming), a scholar must "fracture the
congealed block of historical time into artificially interchangeable units." (This
exactly echoes Burawoy's complaint [1989a: 769–70] about "freezing history,"
but at least Burawoy used more felicitous language.) Like Burawoy, Sewell
asserts that in my 1979 study I "assumed" my historical cases of revolutions to
be absolutely identical and interchangeable, while ignoring world-historical
sequences of, and connections across, the French, Russian, and Chinese revolutions. In general, Sewell argues, valid comparative-historical analysis is virtually impossible, because cases are virtually never both independent and equivalent. He suggests that the historian Marc Bloch may have been correct to suggest
that only neighboring countries should be compared. But even then, Sewell
says, mutual influences will probably make valid causal analysis logically impossible.

Sewell falsely charges that I ignored world-historical connections across my
revolutions, and the distinctive features of the individual cases. As readers of
States and Social Revolutions can readily see for themselves, I explicitly and
repeatedly discussed these matters (in the introductory chapter, and in the
substantive chapters). I never "assumed" that my cases were absolutely equivalent. Rather I argued on substantive, empirical grounds that – as agrarian-
bureaucratic monarchies – they were *sufficiently similar in relevant respects* to
be compared for the purpose of my investigation of the causes of social revolutions in such regimes. I also explicitly discussed the world-historical embed-
dedness of my cases, and explored the meaning of the connections that existed
across time, such as the ideas and retrospective understandings that linked

French Jacobins, Russian Bolsheviks, and Chinese Maoists. I argued on substantive, not logical, grounds that such world-historical linkages as undoubtedly were present did not gainsay the validity of my causal account of the origins of these social revolutions. Even so, I referred to these influences – as well as to many other unique features of each country and its context – in discussing similarities and uniquenesses in revolutionary processes and outcomes.

Sewell seems to imagine that given historical times and places are either inherently comparable, or inherently incomparable. But it all depends on the questions an investigator is asking in a given study. And there is no reason why an investigator has to make mechanical decisions even within one study. Cases can be treated as comparable for some investigative purposes, while their uniquenesses, or interconnections, can be acknowledged for other investigative purposes. That is the great advantage of in-depth comparative studies of a manageable number of cases.

As for Sewell's "logical" broadsides against all comparative methods in the social sciences, their naiveté is truly breathtaking. Consider, first, Sewell's accusation that comparativists must "fracture" history. Well, yes, for given, delimited analytical purposes we must. But all scholars (indeed all people, just by talking) do this all the time. How could anyone possibly deal all at once, all the time, with what Sewell grotesquely calls "the congealed block of historical time"? The very use of the term "French Revolution" (which Sewell uses constantly in his own scholarly work) is a "fracturing" (or to use Burawoy's phrase, a "freezing") of history. The use of the term implies that certain events in French history can be grouped together, and that there are comparable happenings across times and places called "revolutions."

More than that, Sewell himself brings all kinds of implicit theoretical assumptions into his use of the label "revolution." For example, he claims (forthcoming) that my grouping together of the French, Russian, and Chinese revolutions was inappropriate because "new classes and class relations arose over time," which probably changed "the conditions necessary and sufficient for revolutions." This is not a "purely logical" critique at all. What Sewell is doing here is smuggling the entire Marxist historical teleology and theory of revolutionary causation into his dismissal of my comparative study, even as he ignores the careful substantive justifications I gave for my selection and grouping of cases (see Skocpol 1979: 40–42).

Then there is the matter of Sewell's terrible confusion about what he labels "experimental methodology." In a blatantly inappropriate use of a term that already has a clear meaning in the social sciences, Sewell labels my comparative analysis in *States and Social Revolutions* "experimental." But in truth experimental techniques of causal inference are used only in fields like medicine and psychology, where investigators can manipulate situations and subjects, setting up tightly controlled "tests" of what difference it makes to introduce, or withhold, particular "treatments." No macroscopic social scientist (including me!)

claims to use experimental methods; and there are (in literatures that Sewell does not cite and apparently does not know about) extensive discussions of the important logical and substantive differences among experimental, statistical, and comparative approaches to causal analysis. There have also been exciting recent advances – for example, by Ragin (1987) – in the explication of the special features of case-based, configurational methods for discovering similar (and alternative) causal paths in history. Implicitly I used such macrocomparative methods in 1979; and Wickham-Crowley has since used them very explicitly and successfully to analyze the historical roots of social revolutions in Latin America. Sewell, however, seems blithely unaware of both Ragin's and Wickham-Crowley's scholarship. He is willing to dismiss the comparative-historical causal tradition in historical sociology without ever really coming to terms with it.

But, wait! The story isn't over yet. Having spent page after page building to the conclusion that *States and Social Revolutions* is a substantively flawed and (onto)logically impossible comparative analysis, Sewell suddenly shifts gears. Just as the reader expects him to drop Skocpol and go on to tell us about his own, completely distinct program for comparison-free historical sociology, Sewell suddenly gets cold feet. *States and Social Revolutions* is reprieved from execution at the very last minute. The book is not so guilty, after all. The prison doors are thrown open, and – pardoned by Governor Sewell – it emerges as a "powerful and convincing" "analysis of social revolutions," an "inspired compromise" between historical and sociological approaches to revolutions.

Amazingly, Sewell is even suddenly willing (for a couple of pages) to sanction comparisons of the French, Russian, and Chinese revolutions – comparisons that only a few pages before were declared logically impermissible because they committed the sins of "fracturing" history and juxtaposing non-neighboring countries. Now Sewell especially praises the insights Skocpol got from using a "rough causal logic" to compare France, not just with Russia, but especially with the more distant China. "I believe," Sewell declares (forthcoming) "that serious comparative thinking played a crucial role in developing her incipient theory of revolutionary process." "What persuades Skocpol's reader . . . is the fact that all three revolutions can be narrated convincingly in terms of the operation of analogous causal processes."

How in the world can Sewell square this praise for the comparative analysis of *States and Social Revolutions* with his prior "methodological" bashing of it? In one sense, he becomes hopelessly bollixed. Skocpol's comparisons were appropriate, Sewell says, in the "context of discovery" of regularities in history – they are no good, however, when she tries to use them in the "context of justification," to question other theories of revolution or validate her own causal hypotheses. But, prior to this point in the essay, Sewell has criticized and dismissed my allegedly "purely inductive" application of an "experimental method" of causal inference. He cannot have it both ways. He cannot now decide that my comparisons are only worthwhile when used to induce causal analogies. (The problem here, again, is that Sewell has tried to piggyback on Burawoy. It makes sense for Burawoy to criticize my "inductivism," because he champions a preconceived Marxism that cannot stand confrontation with actual patterns of history. But Sewell is too much of a historian to believe that I should have ignored the patterns I saw in history.)

Sewell soon drops this mess about inductivism, and gets on with his main purpose: to appropriate only those aspects of his reading of my book that fit his program for a narrative-based "eventful" historical sociology. What was really nice about *States and Social Revolutions*, according to Sewell, was that the bulk of its pages were spent on *narratives* about the conflicts and outcomes of the French, Russian, and Chinese revolutions. He praises my "narrative strategy" of presenting "the conjunctural, unfolding interactions of originally separately determined processes" (this was my own way of putting it; see Skocpol 1979: 320). This strategy, according to Sewell (forthcoming), is

distinct not only from the usual strategy of sociologists, but from the usual strategy of historians as well. Sociological analyses of revolutions tend to emphasize the primacy of some single cause of revolutions, systematically subordinating other causes to the chosen explanatory factor; historical analyses typically attempt to recount the course of a revolution in some semblance of its original complexity . . . [allowing] crucial causal processes . . . to get lost in a muddle of narrative detail. . . . Skocpol's strategy is an inspired compromise. It appropriates the power of the sociological strategy, but applies it to not one but several distinct causal processes. Yet by emphasizing "conjunctural, unfolding interactions," it also appropriates the historical strategy's concern with events, sequence, and contingency. Quite apart from considerations of comparative experimental induction [readers should note that comparative "induction" has now become bad again!], Skocpol has elaborated in *States and Social Revolutions* an extremely effective strategy for what might be dubbed multiple causal narrative . . . a kind of incipient theory of how events, by straining or rearranging structures, open the door to further transformative events.

With readers by now hopelessly confused about whether he really likes, or does not like, the comparative analysis in *States and Social Revolutions*, Sewell at last – blessedly – gives up the struggle and declares victory for himself. "Rehabilitated" and selected aspects of Skocpol are said to have unconsciously exemplified "eventful sociology": Only the narrative parts of the 1979 book really count. The comparative aspects of that book – and certainly its aim to develop tightly focused comparative causal analyses – are declared to be a "misplaced obsession" that obscures a "highly original contribution to eventful sociology" (Sewell, forthcoming).

Well, what is "eventful sociology"? As best I can tell from Sewell's brief and extremely abstract statements (in forthcoming), it is a sociology based on certain general ontological assumptions about social structures and historical happenings. Social structures, according to Sewell, normally have a "path dependent" quality – by which he seems to mean simply that they persist. But temporality is "heterogeneous." "Events" can occur, "defined as that relatively rare subclass of happenings that significantly transform structures" (Sewell, forthcoming). "History displays both stubborn durabilities and sudden breaks," Sewell breathlessly declares. If we assume the above is true, Sewell seems to believe that it follows with some sort of inherent necessity that historical sociologists should concentrate on "elaborating the event as a theoretical category" (forthcoming) and on writing narratives that reveal continuities and eventful shifts in particular times and places. Implicitly, at least, Sewell shows an overwhelming preference for historical narratives of one time and place at a time.

Now I, of course, should be grateful that Sewell is willing to let at least parts of my work into the blessed circle of this supposedly "radical" "eventful sociology." But his description of history as a "congealed block" that displays either "stubborn durabilities" or "sudden breaks" strikes me as utterly banal – and nothing other than the unreflective baggage of very old-fashioned historiography. To advise people to write "narratives" is really to advise nothing. For narratives can be structured in many, many ways. It takes powerful investigative (and justificatory) methods, as well as a rich array of ever-refined theoretical ideas, to figure out what "structures" and "conjunctures" count, and which happenings are transformative as opposed to merely humdrum. Historical social scientists, moreover, should not drop the ball of trying to figure out such matters *across* diverse times and places. For traditional historians shy away from such comparative-historical studies, even though certain phenomena – such as social revolutions – are inescapably conceptualized in comparative ways.

I ask myself: What if a graduate student trying to develop a Ph.D. thesis came into my office and I advised him or her to think and write in terms of Sewell's "eventful" program. Would I want to read the resulting rough thesis drafts? (No, I would put them in the mail to Bill Sewell at the University of Chicago.) I also ask myself: What if, back in the 1970s, my intellectual mentor in graduate school had been the Sewell of the early 1990s, giving out this narrative-oriented sort of metatheoretical and methodological advice, rather than the Barrington Moore, Jr., who wrote that great macroanalytic comparative historical study, *Social Origins of Dictatorship and Democracy* (1966). Would I ever have undertaken the lengthy research, the complex comparative studies, that led to the writing of *States and Social Revolutions?* Not a chance. I probably would never have gotten beyond telling stories about one national history. At best, I would have become hopelessly bogged down in looking for nonexistent surface similarities in sequences of happenings in two or three times and places. And I certainly never would have gotten around to making comparisons between histories of social revolutions, and histories of roughly similar sets of events that were not actual social revolutions.

The trouble with Sewell's program for historical sociology is simple to state: He will kill the enterprise if he succeeds in purging it of analytical comparisons and turning it into narrative "storytelling." The fact is that good narratives flow from astute comparative causal analyses (as Stinchcombe 1978 has also argued). Powerful and convincing narratives of historical processes – at least narratives of those continuities and changes that are relevant to macroscopic social science – cannot be devised at all without the use of systematic comparative analyses to sort out causal hypotheses and discover new causal analogies. Without tough-minded, analytical comparisons – necessarily cutting through the webs of history for the duration of a given investigation – we can never get straight which structures matter, or which processes count. Indeed, we would not be able to identify one of Sewell's transformative "events," even if it were staring us in the face.

When I was preparing to write the narrative chapters (and parts of chapters) of *States and Social Revolutions,* I did not just read narratives that historians had written, or muddle around in sequences of happenings. I explicitly relied on my comparative-causal analyses to guide my explorations and presentations of processes and events. I was excited to discover that, by tracing the interplay of my macrocausal factors – referring to relations between states and dominant classes and to agrarian sociopolitical structures – I could make more and more sense of the detailed processes of each revolution. I could also understand well why some nations experienced social revolutions and others did not. Sewell is correct to say that I should have devoted more space in 1979 to discussing the methodological connections between the comparative-structural and the conjunctural-narrative aspects of the investigations and presentations that went into *States and Social Revolutions.* (A very similar point was made years ago by Peter Manicas 1981, in one of the best reviews originally written about my book.) At the same time, however, Sewell is dead wrong to suggest that the narrative achievements of *States and Social Revolutions* exist – or could have been arrived at – apart from the macrocausal comparative analysis.

Sewell is similarly wrong to claim for his "eventful sociology" Mark Traugott's (1985) fine analytical-comparative study, *Armies of the Poor: Determinants of Working-Class Participation in the Parisian Insurrection of June 1848* (see the discussion in Sewell, forthcoming). Sewell seems to like this book because it presents a compelling narration of the events of France in 1848, more convincing than Karl Marx's classic account. Fine, I agree. But Traugott did not arrive at this narration by starting out with Sewell's banal program for historical sociology. Traugott arrived at the narration only *after* spending many years working, rather "obsessively," at a rigorous comparative causal analysis. Traugott broke open the "congealed block" of French history in 1848. He "froze" groups and organizations, taking them (temporarily) out of historical context. Then he explored existing theoretical hypotheses about their different activities in 1848. When those failed to be borne out, Traugott discovered new causally relevant analogies, and theorized them in innovative terms.[12] Only *after* all of this (inductive and deductive) macrocausal analysis was done could Traugott reassemble his findings in "narrative" form.

Traugott's book, like mine – and like many other recent studies of macrohistorical phenomena that Sewell simply ignores – proves that historical sociology thrives not despite, but because of, rigorous comparative-causal analysis. In my opinion, it would be too bad indeed if Sewell's advice were to distract even one bright young scholar from doing comparative-historical research devoted to sorting out the causes of important, analogous processes and outcomes in history. The moral of the story is that one cannot arrive at powerful narratives simply by setting out to tell stories.

LOOKING FORWARD: FRONTIERS FOR FURTHER RESEARCH

So vigorously have I defended *States and Social Revolutions* and other kindred macroscopic comparative studies, that readers may have concluded that I see – and foresee – no fruitful new departures in the study of revolutions. That is not the case. There are important new kinds of tasks that need to be done. In some instances, scholars are already taking up the new challenges.

In the first place, now that patterns and causal configurations have been quite well documented about social revolutions in several types of regimes in the modern world, there are possibilities for establishing explicit theoretical linkages between findings about social revolutions and findings about other sorts of sociopolitical processes. For example, scholars such as Adas (1979, 1981) and Barkey (1991) have established findings about peasant revolts in relation to various kinds of states, social structures, and world-historical circumstances; and it might be possible to integrate their findings with findings about peasant revolts and mobilization during social revolutions. In addition, there are rich literatures in comparative politics and political sociology on patterns and causes of various sorts of "regime transitions" – either from authoritarian to democratic polities, or from one kind of authoritarianism to another (e.g., Downing 1992; Huntington 1991; Luebbert 1991; Rueschemeyer, Stephens, and Stephens 1992; Snyder 1992). These literatures call out for better analytical integration with recent comparative-historical findings about the causes and outcomes of social revolutions. Finally, much useful work has been done by students of social movements in contemporary democracies, and the theoretical ideas some of them have developed about "resource mobilization" (e.g., Jenkins 1983) and "political opportunity structures" (e.g., Kitschelt 1986) can probably be extended and adapted to encompass the causal patterns that have been established by comparative-historical analysts of social revolutions and other macroscopic political conflicts.

Indeed, as this final example suggests, the kinds of theoretical work I have in mind here will not be purely deductive or oriented to microfoundations. It will, instead, be comparatively grounded theorizing about state institutions in relation to social structures and political processes. The aim will be to understand – in as general terms as possible – how various state–society configurations make sense of patterns of protest and conflicts, and better sense of regime continuities or breakdowns, and changes toward democracy or authoritarianisms. Much as the scholarship of Barrington Moore (1966) and Samuel P. Huntington (1968) once did, we need use more recent comparative-historical findings than theirs to reintegrate the study of social revolutions into broader comparative theories of social conflict and political change across historical time and throughout the world.

At the same time that some scholars pursue further macropolitical studies, and seek to link findings across literatures in this area, other scholars are bringing new questions and methods to the study of social revolutions as such (see Foran 1993b and Goodwin 1993 for insightful discussions of emerging research trends). Particular social revolutions can be investigated from new vantage points that promise to provide more in-depth, culturally interpretive, and narratively rich insights about their *processes* than broad, structurally oriented comparisons usually have offered (many comparative analyses lack the narrative component that I included in *States and Social Revolutions*). In-depth, processually oriented studies – which are typically single-case explorations, or juxtapositions of two historical cases – are already being pursued, particularly to probe the role of ideas, ideology, and culture in social revolutions. Thus in her juxtaposition of Nicaragua and Iran, Farideh Farhi (1990) pays considerable attention to ideological mobilizations that bring together diversely situated political actors by fusing elements from different cultural discourses. In his juxtaposition of Pahlavi Iran and late Tsarist Russia, Tim McDaniel (1991) reveals much about the cultural and ideational aspects of the overall processes of "autocratic modernization" and state–society breakdown that he explores for these two countries. In his long-term historical investigation of Iran, John Foran (1993a) asks about the roots and dynamics of "political cultures of resistance" as well as about changes in political and socioeconomic organization within and beyond Iran. And John Foran and Jeff Goodwin (1993) carefully trace the contributions of vanguard ideologies, in conjunction with political and socioeconomic conditions, in shaping the emerging postrevolutionary regimes of Iran and Nicaragua.

From the research already being done, it seems likely that the organizationally embedded and actor-centered strategy for cultural analysis that I suggested in my 1981–82 debate with William Sewell, Jr., is proving fruitful. Farhi, McDaniel, Foran, and Goodwin all look at cultural idioms and political ideologies in carefully situated and differentiated ways. They do not report finding perfectly integrated "cultural systems," or moments when one full-blown cultural or ideological framework is overthrown for another. They all talk about the outlooks and arguments of concretely situated groups and organizations. They analyze changes and recombinations of ideas over time before and during revolutions.

Enriching as such recent, culturally sensitive studies of social revolutions have been, they leave many analytical and explanatory issues as yet unresolved – while suggesting more and less fruitful directions in which scholars can go seeking better answers. At this point, I think, we can be sure that cultures and ideologies are *not* – in any self-contained sense – the simple "master" causal keys to old regime breakdowns or revolutionary processes or outcomes. We can also sense that Jack Goldstone's hastily defined "residualist" approach to culture in revolutions is not the way to proceed. In his 1991 book (see chap. 5), Goldstone introduced cultural differences across civilizations (in the style of Eisenstadt 1978) as a last-minute variable to explain the outcomes, but not the roots, of state breakdowns in early modern European and Asian states. Thus causes of state breakdowns were to be accounted for in noncultural terms, while culture suddenly was to become the master key to outcomes of state crises. More recently (see the conclusion to Goldstone, Gurr, and Moshiri 1991), Goldstone has added "legitimation crisis" to his explanation of conditions for revolutionary outbreaks, yet again has done so in a residualist fashion, turning to this formulation only when lists of "material" causes prove insufficient. In my view, none of these Goldstonian ways of handling culture and ideology are adequate. From an institutionalist perspective, we should be looking for the cultural and ideological dimensions of *all* institutions, organizations, social groups, and political conflicts, so that we can integrate those dimensions into all aspects of our explanations and accounts of both the roots and outcomes of social revolutions.

Will the integration of better understandings of culture and ideology into historical and institutional analyses of revolutions lead toward the conclusion (which John Foran 1992 and 1993b has already articulated) that "political cultures of resistance" are one of the necessary causal conditions for social revolutions? Perhaps. But those who take this point of view will need to go beyond offering mere descriptive presentations of mélanges of ideas articulated by various popular groups or revolutionary leaderships. It may well be that moral critiques of prerevolutionary authorities and social structures are to be found during the emergence of all revolutionary crises. Yet the varying ways in which these critiques develop – the cultural themes, the groups involved – are almost surely variable, and perhaps unique to each revolution. The emergence of "political cultures of resistance" in each revolution may be something best understood as an intervening causal process. This process would still be important to trace – and it would take interpretively rich historical studies to trace the crystallization of cultures of resistance in each revolution. We may, as Samuel Beer (1963) once wrote, need "imaginative reenactment" as well as causal explanation. But such research would not necessarily change the basic picture of the causes of social revolutions that has already been developed by scholars who have focused primarily on states in relation to social structures and international circumstances.

By now, as I have tried to show in this essay, the types of regimes and societies susceptible to social revolution are already well understood. About revolutionary outcomes, we know less, but still quite a bit. We understand the analytically relevant features of revolutionary conflicts and domestic and international circumstances that constrain revolutionary state-builders. Certainly, such conflicts and circumstances do not prevent revolutionary state-builders from acting on their ideological beliefs (see Foran and Goodwin 1993 on this point). Yet the conflicts and circumstances do prompt reinterpretations of state-builders' ideologies over time, and lead actions based on ideological purposes to result in different outcomes than the ones intended.

Students of social revolutions need to do much more to analyze the shifting configurations of factors that influence unfolding revolutionary conflicts and outcomes. The ideologies of politically active groups are certain to be among the causal factors that matter for explaining similar and varying revolutionary transformations. But ideology will not matter in isolation, or in an overriding way. The exigencies of political and social struggles about the shape of the state will surely remain at the center of studies of revolutionary outcomes – just as they have remained consistently at the center of the most fruitful recent research on the causes of social revolutions in the modern world.

NOTES

1. Foran and Goodwin (1993: 212) assert that the "Nicaraguan case . . . challenges Skocpol's argument that the exigencies of revolutionary state-building prevent the emergence of liberal-democratic post-revolutionary regimes." But as of this writing (in the summer of 1993), this conclusion is certainly premature. Nicaraguan democracy is very fragile – not yet truly institutionalized – and the threats come directly from the social conflicts and military organizations (the revolutionary army and the remnants of "Contra" counterrevolutionary military forces) that were central to the political struggles and state-building of the 1979 revolution and its aftermath. I would be happy to have my generalizations about revolutionary outcomes disproved (or, more precisely, weakened) by a stable democratic evolution in Nicaragua. But only time will tell whether this happens.
2. To be sure, Jack Goldstone's *Revolution and Rebellion in the Early Modern World* (1991) is also a very important study. Yet it is primarily about the contribution of demographic pressures to "state breakdowns" in the early modern Europe and Asia, rather than about the causes of social revolutions as such.
3. I thus disagree with Foran (1993b) that our general explanations of social revolutions should be recast with Iran as the "prototype" case. I also disagree with Farhi's (1990) decision to group Iran and Nicaragua together as examples of a distinct type of "urban-based" revolution. Unlike Iran (but like most other mid-twentieth-century social revolutions), Nicaragua had a guerrilla revolutionary movement with partial roots in the countryside. Indeed, all social revolutions except the Iranian have involved *both* urban and rural conflicts (during the fall of the old regime as well as after). Thus attempts to designate some social revolutions as "rural," and others as "urban" (see also Gugler 1982) strike me as misguided.
4. Here is one, isolated case of social revolution that might, in part, conform to the Trotskyist Marxist theoretical expectations held so dear by Michael Burawoy. (See

my subsequent discussion of his call for a return to a purely Marxist research program on revolutions.)

5. The methodological prescriptions and practices of Ragin (1987) and Wickham-Crowley (1992) can be usefully contrasted to the misguided suggestions by Geddes (1990) that comparative politics should proceed through mechanical applications of random sampling and single variable–testing techniques from inductive statistics. Given that Geddes offers her own substantive recommendations for how to extend the reasoning of Skocpol (1979) to Latin American cases, one can readily see the largely meaningless results she sketches, in contrast to the patterns that Wickham-Crowley was able to establish through his use of case comparisons and (subsequently) Ragin's Boolean techniques.

Another scholar who recommends the purely mechanical extension of inductive-statistical techniques to macroscopic comparative studies is Lieberson (1991). His argument is entirely constructed around an example – a probabilistic study of the causes of drunk-driving accidents – that is laughably inappropriate for thinking about the phenomena studied by comparative and historical researchers. Lieberson never deals with the substantive content of the problems or questions addressed in comparative and historical research; and he never deals with the actual methodological or substantive arguments of any of the books, articles, or research traditions that he dismisses.

6. Goldstone (1991) apparently argues against this proposition. Quite inaccurately, he suggests that I treated *war* as such as a cause of social revolutions in agrarian bureaucracies. But except for my analysis of Russia in 1917 (which Goldstone does not question), this is not true (a more accurate summary of my position appears in Goldstone 1980: 440–45). I argued that all the agrarian bureaucratic monarchies I studied were subject to varying degrees of international competitive pressure. That was a background condition that spurred monarchs to attempt to mobilize resources for the state (not necessarily, at any given moment, for a war as such). In turn, monarchs and dominant class groups entered into fierce political struggles over such attempts. I used *institutional variations* among agrarian-bureaucratic monarchies to explain the forms and consequences of such struggles, which in certain cases led to administrative-military breakdowns, one of the conditions for social revolution.

Goldstone (1991) seems to be trying to substitute demographic pressures for interstate competition as an underlying factor contributing to early modern state breakdowns; indeed, Goldstone wants to make demographic pressure a single master variable. But demographic pressures are not *invariably* associated with state breakdowns; they work through institutional configurations, just as I argued geopolitical pressures do. In any event, it is perfectly possible to accept much of what Goldstone has to say empirically about the impact of demographic trends on rulers and societies, without rejecting the encouragement that international competition and pressures gave to rulers' efforts to raise resources for their state organizations. Eighteenth-century France, for example, may well have been a relatively wealthy and powerful country facing strong demographic pressures. It was also an agrarian-bureaucratic monarchy with great-power ambitions often frustrated in wars with England, as well as a state with inefficient tax-collection mechanisms and institutions that encouraged dominant-class resistance to monarchical efforts at reform from above. I explained all of this (in Skocpol 1979: chap. 2) and showed how these international geopolitical and domestic institutional conditions together facilitated a top-down political crisis and administrative-military breakdown in 1787–89. Although this is not the place to go into all the details, I do not believe that anything Goldstone shows (in 1991: chap. 3) is incompatible with the arguments I offered in 1979. Collins (1993) makes this same point.

7. Burawoy claims (1989a: 760) that Trotsky and Skocpol have the same substantive theory of revolutions, so that the differences between them are entirely "methodological." This, of course, is absolute nonsense. Trotsky was committed to using class relations and conflicts to explain revolutions, and I use a Weberian, state-centered approach. The fact that both of us may *mention* the same range of variables is no indication at all that we theorize their interrelationships in the same ways.

8. Burawoy makes no secret of his own dogmatic Marxism. He has written (Burawoy 1989b: 80) that "the skepticism of the scientist is ineffective without passionate commitment not just to the scientific enterprise but also to a given theoretical framework. A certain dogmatism is necessary to discipline and channel the readiness to abandon one set of beliefs for another. Without dogmatism there is only chaos."

9. Without the explicit Marxist theoretical trappings, many of Burawoy's "methodological" critiques, including this one, also appear in Nichols (1986). Apart from what I have to say here, I have also replied to her in Skocpol (1986).

10. Sewell's less lengthy confrontations with Tilly (1967) and Wallerstein (1974) have a dated air about them. Sewell is correct to claim that Wallerstein's 1974 book suffered from blatant teleological functionalism. But this point has been made many times before (see, e.g., my 1977 essay reprinted as Chapter 2 in this book); and many historical sociologists subsequently working on world-system issues have tried to avoid Wallerstein's teleological faults. As for Tilly, Sewell inexplicably concentrates his fire on a nearly thirty-year-old book, Tilly's revised doctoral dissertation (1967), while ignoring all of Tilly's most recent – and less teleological – methodological and substantive writings about capitalism and state formation (cf. Tilly 1984). By this approach, Sewell himself should be dismissed (or declared in need of "rehabilitation"?), because his early major book, *Work and Revolution in France* (1980) was profoundly teleological – in the full-blown Hegelian sense of that tendency.

11. Thus: Sewell uses Burawoy's summary chart to argue that I said three factors were "necessary for social revolutions," when in fact I argued that two sets of institutional conditions (which I specified much more precisely, and differently, than Burawoy presented them) were, taken together, sufficient to explain successful social revolutions (as opposed to failures or other kinds of political upheavals). Sewell also follows Burawoy in claiming that the English Revolution of the seventeenth century grew out of a fiscal crisis with no military aspects; but, as I argued, the English king was trying to raise new revenues, in part, to pay for military forces to deal with rebels in Ireland and Scotland, and to fend off ever-present military threats from France (which might meddle in the rebellious areas). Sewell then follows Burawoy in claiming that my comparison between England and France does not distinguish conditions for political versus social revolution, when in fact it does. Finally, Sewell also follows Burawoy in ignoring the theoretically equivalent alternative causal paths that I built into my argument in *States and Social Revolutions*. The most amusing consequence of this is that Sewell spends a lengthy paragraph explaining that the Chinese Revolution is an "exception" to my argument about autonomous peasant revolts in France 1789 and Russia 1917. Sewell doesn't seem to notice that I presented exactly the same argument about the distinctive Chinese circumstances and revolutionary processes as he does! That must be because Sewell did not work directly from chapters 3 and 7 in *States and Social Revolutions* – or from my summary charts on pages 155–57 and 282–83. Instead, he relied on Burawoy's mistaken and tendentious summary of my book.

12. I happen to know quite a bit about the investigative and intellectual processes by which Traugott did the work that led to *Armies of the Poor*. As Traugott himself explains in his preface, early in the project he submitted an article empirically

exploring class-based hypotheses about the events of 1848 to the *American Journal of Sociology*. This article reported mostly "negative" findings about existing theories. Having already done research for my dissertation on revolutions, I was asked to be a reader of Traugott's article for the journal. I noticed patterns in his data that made sense in terms of what I had learned from my historical cases, and from reading the classic analytical comparative study by Katherine Chorley, *Armies and the Art of Revolution* (1943) – a book that, in turn, had been suggested to me by my teacher, Barrington Moore, Jr. I sent suggestions to Traugott via the journal review process. He ended up using rigorous comparisons to explore the new "organizational" hypotheses in great detail, in preparation for writing the book that Sewell likes so much. I submit that this history is a story of alternative-hypothesis testing, and of the fruitfulness across generations of scholars of comparative-historical causal analysis at its best. It is certainly not a story about a scholar who set out to write a narrative history focused on "events."

REFERENCES

Adas, Michael. 1979. *Prophets of Rebellion: Millenarian Protest Movements Against the European Colonial Order*. Chapel Hill: University of North Carolina Press.

Adas, Michael. 1981. "From Avoidance to Confrontation: Peasant Protest in Pre-Colonial and Colonial Southeast Asia." *Comparative Studies in Society and History* 23: 217–47.

Adelman, Jonathan R. 1985. *Revolution, Armies, and War: A Political History*. Boulder, CO: Lynne Rienner.

Anderson, Lisa. 1986. *The State and Social Transformation in Tunisia and Libya, 1830–1980*. Princeton, NJ: Princeton University Press.

Arjomand, Sair Amir. 1986. "Iran's Islamic Revolution in Comparative Perspective." *World Politics* 38(3): 383–414.

Arjomand, Said Amir. 1988. *The Turban for the Crown: The Islamic Revolution in Iran*. New York: Oxford University Press.

Barkey, Karen. 1991. "The State and Peasant Unrest in Early 17th-Century France and the Ottoman Empire." *American Sociological Review* 56(6): 699–715.

Beer, Samuel H. 1963. "Causal Explanation and Imaginative Re-Enactment." *History and Theory* 3: 6–29.

Berejikian, Jeffrey. 1992. "Revolutionary Collective Action and the Agent-Structure Problem." *American Political Science Review* 86(3): 647–57.

Boswell, Terry. 1989. *Revolutions in the World-System*. New York: Greenwood Press.

Burawoy, Michael. 1989a. "Two Methods in Search of Science: Skocpol versus Trotsky." *Theory and Society* 18: 759–805.

Burawoy, Michael. 1989b. "The Limits of Wright's Analytical Marxism and an Alternative." Pp. 78–99 in *The Debate on Classes*, edited by Erik Olin Wright et al. London and New York: Verso.

Castles, Francis G. 1978. *The Social Democratic Image of Society*. London: Routledge and Kegan Paul.

Castles, Francis G. 1985. *Working Class and Welfare: Reflections on the Political Development of the Welfare State in Australia and New Zealand, 1890–1980*. London: Allen and Unwin.

Chong, Dennis. 1991. *Collective Action and the Civil Rights Movement*. Chicago: University of Chicago Press.

Chorley, Katherine. 1943. *Armies and the Art of Revolution*. London: Faber and Faber. Reprint. Boston: Beacon Press, 1973.

Colburn, Forrest D. 1986. *Post-Revolutionary Nicaragua: State, Class, and the Dilemmas of Agrarian Policy.* Berkeley CA: University of California Press.

Collins, Randall. 1993. "Maturation of the State-Centered Theory of Revolution and Ideology." *Sociological Theory* 11(1): 117–28.

DeNardo, James. 1985. *Power in Numbers: The Political Strategy of Protest and Rebellion.* Princeton, NJ: Princeton University Press.

Dennis, John Michael. 1986. "Explaining Social and Peasant Revolution in Central America: An Application of Skocpol to Nicaragua and Honduras." Unpublished M.A. thesis, Department of Political Science, University of Texas at Austin.

Dix, Robert H. 1984. "Why Revolutions Succeed and Fail." *Polity* 16(3): 423–46.

Downing, Brian M. 1992. *The Military Revolution and Political Change: Origins of Democracy and Autocracy in Early Modern Europe.* Princeton, NJ: Princeton University Press.

Echeverri-Gent, John. 1993. *The State and the Poor: Public Policy and Political Development in India and the United States.* Berkeley: University of California Press.

Eisenstadt, S. N. 1978. *Revolution and the Transformation of Societies: A Comparative Study of Civilizations.* New York: Free Press.

Esping-Andersen, Gösta. 1990. *The Three Worlds of Welfare Capitalism.* Princeton, NJ: Princeton University Press.

Evans, Peter B. Forthcoming. *Predators and Midwives: An Analysis of States and Industrial Transformation.* Princeton: Princeton University Press.

Evans, Peter B., Dietrich Rueschemeyer, and Theda Skocpol, ed. 1985. *Bringing the State Back In.* Cambridge: Cambridge University Press.

Farhi, Farideh. 1990. *States and Urban-Based Revolutions: Iran and Nicaragua.* University of Illinois Press.

Farman-Farma, Amir A. 1990. "A Comparative Study of Counter-Revolutionary Mass Movements During the French, Mexican, and Russian Revolutions with Contemporary Application." Unpublished Ph.D. dissertation, Faculty of Politics, Oxford University.

Fisher, Mary Ellen. 1990. "Totalitarianism, Authoritarianism, and Revolution: The Sultanistic Tendencies of Nicolae Ceausecu in Romania." Paper presented at the Workshop on Sultanistic Regimes, Center for International Affairs, Harvard University, November 2–3.

Flora, Peter, and Arnold J. Heidenheimer, ed. 1981. *The Development of Welfare States in Europe and North America.* New Brunswick, NJ: Transaction Books.

Foran, John. 1992. "A Theory of Third World Social Revolutions: Iran, Nicaragua, and El Salvador Compared." *Critical Sociology* 19(2): 3–27.

Foran, John. 1993a. *Fragile Resistance: Social Transformation in Iran from 1500 to the Revolution.* Boulder: Westview Press.

Foran, John. 1993b. "Theories of Revolution Revisited: Toward a Fourth Generation?" *Sociological Theory* 11(1): 1–20.

Foran, John, and Jeff Goodwin. 1993. "Revolutionary Outcomes in Iran and Nicaragua: Coalition Fragmentation, War, and the Limits of Social Transformation." *Theory and Society* 22: 209–47.

Fulbrook, Mary. 1983. *Piety and Politics: Religion and the Rise of Absolutism in England, Wurttemberg, and Prussia.* Cambridge: Cambridge University Press.

Geddes, Barbara. 1990. "How the Cases You Choose Affect the Answers You Get: Selection Bias in Comparative Politics." *Political Analysis* 2: 131–50.

Goldfrank, Walter L. 1979. "Theories of Revolution and Revolution Without Theory: The Case of Mexico." *Theory and Society* 7: 135–65.

Goldstone, Jack A. 1991. *Revolution and Rebellion in the Early Modern World.* Berkeley: University of California Press.

Goldstone, Jack A., Ted Robert Gurr, and Farrokh Moshiri, ed. 1991. *Revolutions of the Late Twentieth Century.* Boulder, CO: Westview Press.

Goodwin, Jeffrey Roger. 1988. "States and Revolutions in the Third World: A Comparative Analysis." Unpublished Ph.D. dissertation, Department of Sociology, Harvard University.

Goodwin, Jeff. 1992. "Owners, Rulers, and Rebels: Revolution in the Second and Third Worlds." Paper presented at the Twelfth Annual Albany Conference, "Making History from Above and Below," sponsored by the Department of Sociology, State University of New York at Albany, Albany, New York, April 24–25.

Goodwin, Jeff. 1993. "Conceptual Reification in the Comparative Study of Revolutions." Paper presented at the Annual Meeting of the American Political Science Association, Washington DC, August.

Goodwin, Jeff. Forthcoming. *State and Revolution in the Third World: A Comparative Analysis.* Berkeley: University of California Press.

Gugler, Josef. 1982. "The Urban Character of Contemporary Revolutions." *Studies in Comparative International Development* 27: 60–73.

Gurr, Ted Robert. 1970. *Why Men Rebel.* Princeton, NJ: Princeton University Press.

Hall, Peter. 1986. *The Politics of State Intervention in Britain and France.* New York: Oxford University Press.

Higley, John, and Jan Pakulski. 1992. "Revolution and Elite Transformation in Eastern Europe." *Australian Journal of Political Science* 27: 104–19.

Huntington, Samuel P. 1991. *The Third Wave: Democratization in the Late Twentieth Century.* Norman: University of Oklahoma Press.

Immergut, Ellen M. 1992. *Health Politics: Interests and Institutions in Western Europe.* Cambridge: Cambridge University Press.

Jenkins, J. Craig. 1983. "Resource Mobilization Theory and the Study of Social Movements." *Annual Review of Sociology* 9 (1983): 527–53.

Johnson, Chalmers. 1966. *Revolutionary Change.* Boston: Little, Brown.

Keddie, Nikki. 1992. "Can Revolutions Be Predicted; Can Their Causes Be Understood?" *Contention: Debates in Society, Culture, and Science* 2 (Winter): 59–82.

Kelley, Jonathan, and Herbert S. Klein. 1981. *Revolution and the Rebirth of Inequality: A Theory Applied to the National Revolution in Bolivia.* Berkeley: University of California Press.

Kim, Quee-Young, ed. 1991. *Revolutions in the Third World.* Leiden: E. J. Brill.

Kim, Quee-Young, and Jennifer M. Leach. 1991. "From Military to Social Revolution: A Comparative Analysis of Ethiopia and the Sudan." Pp. 113–28 in *Revolutions in the Third World,* edited by Quee-Young Kim. Leiden: E. J. Brill.

Kiser, Edgar, and Michael Hechter. 1991. "The Role of General Theory in Comparative-historical Sociology." *American Journal of Sociology* 97(1): 1–30.

Kitschelt, Herbert P. 1986. "Political Opportunity Structures and Political Protest: Anti-Nuclear Movements in Four Democracies." *British Journal of Political Science* 16: 57–85.

Kohli, Atul. 1987. *The State and Poverty in India: The Politics of Reform.* Cambridge: Cambridge University Press.

Lichbach, Mark I. 1994. "What Makes Rational Peasants Revolutionary? Dilemma, Paradox and Irony in Peasant Collective Action." *World Politics* 46 (2).

Lieberson, Stanley. 1991. "Small Ns and Big Conclusions: An Examination of the Reasoning in Comparative Studies Based on a Small Number of Cases." *Social Forces* 70(2): 307–20.

Little, Daniel. 1991. *Varieties of Social Explanation.* Boulder, CO: Westview Press.

Liu, Michael Tien-lung. 1988. "States and Urban Revolutions: Explaining the Revolutionary Outcomes in Iran and Poland." *Theory and Society* 17: 179–209.

Luebbert, Gregory M. 1991. *Liberalism, Fascism, or Social Democracy: Social Classes and the Political Origins of Regimes in Interwar Europe.* New York: Oxford University Press.

Malloy, James M. 1979. *The Politics of Social Security in Brazil.* Pittsburgh: University of Pittsburgh Press.

Manicas, Peter T. 1981. Review of *States and Social Revolutions. History and Theory* 20 (May): 204–18.

McAdam, Doug. 1982. *Political Process and the Development of Black Insurgency, 1930–1970.* Chicago: University of Chicago Press.

McDaniel, Tim. 1991. *Autocracy, Modernization, and Revolution in Russia and Iran.* Princeton, NJ: Princeton University Press.

Midlarsky, Manus I., and Kenneth Roberts. 1985. "Class, State, and Revolution in Central America: Nicaragua and El Salvador Compared." *Journal of Conflict Resolution* 29(2): 163–93.

Moore, Barrington, Jr. 1966. *Social Origins of Dictatorship and Democracy: Lord and Peasant in the Making of the Modern World.* Boston: Beacon Press.

Muller, Edward N., and Karl-Dieter Opp. 1986. "Rational Choice and Rebellious Collective Action." *American Political Science Review* 80(2): 471–87.

Najmabadi, Afsaneh. 1987. "Iran's Turn to Islam: From Modernism to a Moral Order." *Middle East Journal* 41: 202–17.

Najmabadi, Afsaneh. 1993. "States, Politics, and the Radical Contingency of Revolutions: Reflections on Iran's Islamic Revolution." *Research in Political Sociology* 6: 197–215.

Nichols, Elizabeth. 1986. "Skocpol on Revolution: Comparative Analysis vs. Historical Conjuncture." *Comparative Social Research* 9: 163–86.

Olson, Mancur. 1965. *The Logic of Collective Action.* Cambridge, MA: Harvard University Press.

Orloff, Ann Shola. 1993. *The Politics of Pensions: A Comparative Analysis of Britain, Canada, and the United States, 1880–1940.* Madison: University of Wisconsin Press.

Paige, Jeffery M. 1975. *Agrarian Revolution: Social Movements and Export Agriculture in the Underdeveloped World.* New York: Free Press.

Popkin, Samuel. 1979. *The Rational Peasant: The Political Economy of Rural Society in Vietnam.* Berkeley: University of California Press.

Ragin, Charles C. 1987. *The Comparative Method: Moving Beyond Qualitative and Quantitative Strategies.* Berkeley: University of California Press.

Roxborough, Ian. 1989. "Theories of Revolution: The Evidence from Latin America." *L.S.E. Quarterly* 3(2): 99–121.

Rueschemeyer, Dietrich, Evelyne Huber Stephens, and John D. Stephens. 1992. *Capitalist Development and Democracy.* Chicago: University of Chicago Press.

Selbin, Eric. 1993. *Modern Latin American Revolutions.* Boulder: Westview Press.

Sewell, William H., Jr. 1980. *Work and Revolution in France: The Language of Labor from the Old Regime to 1848.* Cambridge: Cambridge University Press.

Sewell, William H., Jr. Forthcoming. "Three Temporalities: Toward an Eventful Sociology." In *The Historic Turn in the Human Sciences,* edited by Terrence J. McDonald. Ann Arbor: University of Michigan Press.

Shugart, Matthew Soberg. 1989. "Patterns of Revolution." *Theory and Society* 18: 249–71.

Skocpol, Theda. 1979. *States and Social Revolutions: A Comparative Analysis of France, Russia, and China.* Cambridge: Cambridge University Press.

Skocpol, Theda. 1986. "Analyzing Causal Configurations in History: A Rejoinder to Nichols." *Comparative Social Research* 9: 187–94.

Skocpol, Theda. 1992. *Protecting Soldiers and Mothers: The Political Origins of Social Policy in the United States*. Cambridge, MA: Belknap Press of Harvard University Press.

Smith, Tony. 1987. *Thinking Like a Communist: State and Legitimacy in the Soviet Union, China, and Cuba*. New York: Norton.

Snyder, Richard. 1992. "Explaining Transitions from Neopatrimonial Dictatorships." *Comparative Politics* 24(4): 379–99.

Stinchcombe, Arthur. 1978. *Theoretical Methods in Social History*. New York: Academic Press.

Taylor, Michael, ed. 1988. *Rationality and Revolution*. Cambridge: Cambridge University Press.

Taylor, Michael. 1989. "Structure, Culture and Action in the Explanation of Social Change." *Politics and Society* 17(2): 115–62.

Tilly, Charles. 1967. *The Vendée: A Sociological Analysis of the Counterrevolution of 1793*. New York: Wiley.

Tilly, Charles, ed. 1975. *The Formation of National States in Western Europe*. Princeton, NJ: Princeton University Press.

Tilly, Charles. 1984. *Big Structures, Large Processes, Huge Comparisons*. New York: Russell Sage Foundation.

Traugott, Mark. 1985. *Armies of the Poor: Determinants of Working-Class Participation in the Parisian Insurrection of June 1848*. Princeton, NJ: Princeton University Press.

Vogel, David. 1986. *National Styles of Regulation: Environmental Policy in Great Britain and the United States*. Ithaca, NY: Cornell University Press.

Wallerstein, Immanuel. 1974. *The Modern World-System: Capitalist Agriculture and the Origins of the European World-Economy in the Sixteenth Century*. New York: Academic Press.

Walzer, Michael. 1980. "A Theory of Revolution." Pp. 201–23 (chap. 13) of *Radical Principles*. New York: Basic Books.

Waterbury, Ronald. 1975. "Non-revolutionary Peasants: Oaxaca Compared to Morelos in the Mexican Revolution." *Comparative Studies in Society and History* 17(4): 410–42.

Wickham-Crowley, Timothy P. 1991. *Exploring Revolution: Essays on Latin American Insurgency and Revolutionary Theory*. Armonk, NY: M. E. Sharpe.

Wickham-Crowley, Timothy P. 1992. *Guerrillas and Revolution in Latin America: A Comparative Study of Insurgents and Regimes Since 1956*. Princeton, NJ: Princeton University Press.

Wuthnow, Robert. 1989. *Communities of Discourse: Ideology and Social Structure in the Reformation, the Enlightenment, and European Socialism*. Cambridge, MA: Harvard University Press.

Index

absolute monarchy(ies)/absolutism, 37, 39, 63–5, 66, 85, 156, 176, 181, 311–12; in France, 175–6, 178, 179, 180; in Iran, 240, 243–5
Adam, Heribert, 106
Adas, Michael, 235, 334
Adelman, Jonathan R., 286, 304
administrative-military breakdowns, 5, 138–46, 148, 150, 156, 160, 311–12, 313, 314, 315, 319; *see also* state breakdowns
Africa, 74, 259, 265, 267, 308, 316; Portuguese colonies, 287
aggregate-psychological theories of revolution, 99, 100–4, 111
agrarian bureaucracy(ies), 5, 13, 31, 159–60, 236n2, 243, 312; bourgeois impulse and, 32–3; defined, 136; foreign pressures on, 138–46; peasant insurrections in, 146–53, 154; revolution in, 135–8; as statist societies, 156
agrarian-bureaucratic monarchies, 7, 15, 283, 303, 315, 316, 322, 328; possibilities for social revolution in, 319, 320; state breakdowns in, 324
"Agrarian Class Structure and Economic Development in Pre-Industrial Europe" (Brenner), 78, 81–82
Agrarian Revolution (Paige), 12, 73–5, 87, 214, 218–20, 222, 304
agrarian revolutions, 216–19, 220, 226, 227, 231–2, 261–2
agrarian societies/states: bureaucratization of, 38–44; characteristics of, 140–1; modernization of, 27–32; revolution in, 5, 113, 115, 121, 122, 129; revolutions from below in, 124; transformation of, into industrial nations, 25–49
Algeria, 214, 259, 268, 270, 308
Althusser, Louis, 172
Anderson, Lisa, 317
Anderson, Perry, 10, 65, 83–4, 85, 87
Angola, 74, 123, 214, 270, 308
Aquino, Corazon, 270

Arab caliphate, 74
Arab Moslem states, 74
Arendt, Hannah, 113
Arjomand, Sair Amir, 304
Armies and the Art of Revolution (Chorley), 144
Armies of the Poor (Traugott), 333–4
Asia, 74, 214, 259, 265
Asian Communists, 227
Attaturk, 13
authoritarian regimes/authoritarianism, 265–8, 270, 271, 272–3, 281, 294, 295, 307–8, 311–13
Avrich, Paul H., 108
Aztecs, 74

Babylon, 74
Balkans, 308
Bani-Sadr, Abolhassan, 252, 293, 295
Barkey, Karen, 334
Batista, Fulgencio, 19, 268, 269, 290, 310
Beer, Samuel, 336
Beheshti, Ayatollah Mohammed, 251, 253
Bendix, Reinhard, 9, 10, 12, 55, 72, 75, 76–7, 78, 87, 88, 322
Benson, Lee, 50n10
Berejikian, Jeffrey, 326
Billings, Dwight B., 8
Bismarck, Otto von, 36
Bismarck's Unification, 40, 41, 43
Bloch, Marc, 72, 89, 92n3, 328
Blum, Jerome, 62, 69n2
Bolivia, 16, 267, 288, 290, 308–11
Bolivian Revolution, 288, 314–15
Bolshevik Revolution, 195
Bolsheviks, 9, 147, 155, 200, 286, 329
Bonaparte, Louis, 36
Borkenau, Franz, 279, 295
Boswell, Terry, 304
Bourbon regime, 122, 140, 141–2, 144, 154–5, 267